INCLUDES EXPLOSIVE NEW MATERIAL

Paul Burrell—butler to Diana, Princess of Wales, and the man she called "my rock"—presents the untold story behind one of the most sensational chapters in the history of the House of Windsor.

The story of shocking secrets, absolute power, and unlikely alliances. The story behind previously unseen letters and photos and first-person insights. The story that will rewrite history and stand alone as the archive of Princess Diana's time as a Royal. The story of a faithful subject and his moving tribute to the Queen and Princess he served.

"THE YEAR'S STANDOUT MEMOIR. Whatever you think of the former butler . . . you cannot fault the energy of his storytelling. . . . Besides the screaming headlines which launched this page-turner, there are a thousand subtler jewels. . . . Many will dismiss it as froth, but with such devil in the detail *A Royal Duty* may come to be recognized as an historical document in its own right."
—*The Times* (London)

"I DEFY YOU NOT TO FIND IT GRIPPING. Burrell's account of belowstairs life at Buckingham Palace is JAW-DROPPING . . . UNPUTDOWNABLE."
—*The Daily Telegraph* (London)

"PAINTS AN INTIMATE PICTURE of Diana's troubled marriage, her fights with Prince Charles over his relationship with Camilla Parker Bowles, and her own lovers. . . . BURRELL . . . THROWS IN A FEW SHOCKERS."
—*The Atlanta Journal-Constitution*

continued . . .

A
ROYAL DUTY

PAUL BURRELL

A SIGNET BOOK

Photos not credited are furnished courtesy of the author:

Front cover photo of Diana, Princess of Wales © Patrick Demarchelier
Insert 1: page 4, above: Shelley/Carraro/Rex; page 7, above:
Nils Jorgensen/Rex; page 7, below: Nils Jorgensen/Rex;
Insert 3: page 2, above: Tim Rooke/Rex; page 3, above:
Today/NI Syndication; page 3, below: Kelvin Bruce; page 4,
above: Mirrorpix; page 4, below: Rex,; page 5, above: Mirrorpix;
page 6, above: Mirrorpix; page 6, below left: PA Photos; page 6,
below right: PA Photos; page 7, above: Robin Nunn; page 7,
below: PA Photos; page 8: PA Photos

SIGNET
Published by New American Library, a division of
Penguin Group (USA) Inc., 375 Hudson Street,
New York, New York 10014, U.S.A.
Penguin Books Ltd, 80 Strand, London WC2R 0RL, England
Penguin Books Australia Ltd, 250 Camberwell Road,
Camberwell, Victoria 3124, Australia
Penguin Books Canada Ltd, 10 Alcorn Avenue, Toronto, Ontario, Canada M4V 3B2
Penguin Books (NZ), cnr Airborne and Rosedale Roads,
Albany, Auckland 1310, New Zealand

Penguin Books Ltd, Registered Offices:
80 Strand, London WC2R 0RL, England

Published by Signet, an imprint of New American Library, a division of Penguin
Group (USA) Inc. This is an authorized reprint of a hardcover edition published
by G. P. Putnam's Sons. For information address G. P. Putnam's Sons, a division
of Penguin Group (USA) Inc., 375 Hudson Street, New York, NY 10014.

First Signet Printing, June 2004
10 9 8 7 6 5 4 3 2 1

CONTENTS

VI CONTENTS

> *To my wife, the children, and the princess—*
> *you will always be with me*

ACKNOWLEDGMENTS

Thank you. "They are two small words which mean so much, and people don't say them often enough these days," the princess always used to say.

I doubt there was a more prolific writer of thank-you letters than the Boss. She must have sat for hours at her desk in the sitting room at Kensington Palace, penning endless notes with her fountain pen, taking time to sit down and thank someone for their help, kindness, generosity, hospitality, advice, or friendship.

If there was one thing I encouraged her to do, it was to put down her thoughts on paper. If there was one thing she encouraged in me, it was the never-to-be-forgotten importance of writing a thank-you letter, something her father, the late Earl Spencer, had instilled in her as a child.

This is my written thank-you to the team who have supported me in the compiling of *A Royal Duty,* my own tribute to the life and work of the princess.

So, thank you:

First and foremost, to my wife, Maria, and my sons, Alexander and Nicholas. We have all shared a traumatic time, and your constant love, support, and understanding continue to make me the proudest husband and father, supported by relatives on both sides of our family.

To my dear friend Steve Dennis, for working your magic and being with me every step of the way on this literary journey, and for sharing with me the passion to enshrine the memory of the princess.

To my agent Ali Gunn, for your invaluable advice, never-ending encouragement, and laughter along the way. I am forever indebted to you.

The production of *A Royal Duty* has illustrated to me the mammoth effort required to make books such as this possible, and I believe I have had the best team in the industry: a huge thank-you to my publisher, Tom Weldon, for your vision and judgment, and for believing in me and this book in the first place; and to everyone else on the team at Penguin in London and New York, especially my editor, Hazel Orme, for your expert eye; Genevieve Pegg, Sophie Brewer, and Kate Brunt for your tireless efforts and patience behind the scenes; and American publishers Carole Baron and Jennifer Hershey, who have been awesome.

To the people of Naas in the Republic of Ireland, especially Mary Eiliffe, Laura and Kevin, and everyone else at the Townhouse Hotel for making Steve and me feel at home, and for keeping us sane over these past few months.

To my brilliant legal team, who fought the injustice of my trial at the Old Bailey: Lord Carlile, QC, Ray Herman, solicitor Andrew Shaw, and their able assistants Lesley and Shona. Words fail me for how much you believed in me during that nightmare time.

To the close friends of the princess: you all know who you are, and I will never forget your unstinting support in being prepared to take the witness stand in my defense. I know we stand as one in defending the memory of a remarkable woman, whose warmth and friendship touched us all.

What you are reading is a legacy that certain people wanted to destroy from a man they tried to silence.

Paul Burrell
October 2003

PREFACE

THE PRINCESS DIED AT 4 A.M. in a hospital in Paris on Sunday, August 31, 1997. The last time I saw her, she was waving goodbye from the back of her BMW, being driven away from Kensington Palace on Friday, August 15.

The previous day, we had been to Waterstone's bookstore in Kensington High Street. We drove because time was tight, and because we didn't fancy walking back with what she called her "heavy reading matter": half a dozen books on spirituality, psychology, and healing. Then we headed back to the palace so she could finish her packing with assistance from her dresser, Angela Benjamin. As we turned in to the palace drive, she was in a relaxed mood. "I'm looking forward to a quiet holiday, good company and lots of light reading!"

Her friend Rosa Monckton had hired a yacht with a crew of four to sail her and the princess around the Greek islands on a six-day Aegean holiday. When she returned, the princess was due to go on holiday with another female friend, Lana Marks, for five days in Italy, staying at the Four Seasons Hotel in Milan.

She had not intended to spend that final week of August with Dodi al-Fayed. Reservations had been made and flights booked for her to be with Lana. That holiday was canceled at the last minute because Lana's father died suddenly, which left the princess at loose ends until the boys returned to Kensington Palace on August 31. She accepted Dodi's substitute offer to spend time with him on his yacht, the *Jonikal,* cruising around the French Riviera and Sardinia.

Before she flew out to join Dodi, she would be back at the palace for one day, on August 21, but I wouldn't be there because I had deliberately booked my family holiday to Naas, in the Republic of Ireland, to coincide with the princess's. As she finished packing on August 15 to head off to the airport, I was sharing that happy pre-vacation feeling as I waited with Rosa inside KP. "We must do something about this one. He's not right for her, you know that. Will you do what you can?" I asked her. I knew that the princess would listen to Rosa and I sensed that Rosa shared my concern because "this was Dodi." Rosa nodded and smiled. She understood.

The princess had been fussing around in the sitting room, tidying her desk, putting the wastepaper bin out in the landing to be emptied, checking her shoulder bag. As the two friends came down the stairs to leave, she stopped halfway down and went through her cross-checking routine, thinking aloud: "Passport, phone, Walkman . . ."

I was leaning on the wooden banister, looking up at her in her simple Versace shift dress. "Do you know?" I said. "I've never seen you looking as good. You look perfect. You don't need the sunshine—look at your tan already!" And she skipped down the stairs, smiling.

We went through into the inner hallway. "Hang on to that a minute." She thrust her shoulder bag into my hands and disappeared into the ladies' room. Within minutes, she was ready to go. She stepped out into the sunshine and into the rear passenger seat of the BMW as the chauffeur started the engine. I fastened her seat belt.

"If you have a chance to ring me, you will, won't you?" she asked me.

"Of course," I said, having arranged that week for her

mobile telephone to be allocated a new number that only a handful of people would know.

"Have a nice time, Paul."

I walked back to the doorstep, and the princess waved. I watched the BMW turn left and out of sight. She was heading for Heathrow and an airplane to Athens.

THE BURRELLS JOINED my wife's side of the family, the Cosgroves, on a four-day holiday in an Irish town named Naas. We visited Kilkenny Castle and then the village where the BBC series *Ballykissangel* was filmed, visiting the famous Fitzgerald's pub. I was under strict orders from Maria to forget about work and the princess. "This is family time," she said.

The only problem was that I had promised the princess I would call. Four days of no contact would be noticed by the Boss, so I found myself making excuses to go for long walks.

The princess was on the deck with Rosa when I rang. She told me how sunny and hot it was. I told her how wet and miserable the Republic of Ireland was. She had finished a book on spirituality and was tackling a new one already, she said. I hung up, promising to speak to her again when I was back at my vacation home in Farndon, Cheshire, and she was on the *Jonikal* with Dodi. I told Maria that the long walk had done me a power of good.

On August 21, she made a short return to Kensington Palace, then dashed off to Stansted Airport for a flight to Nice to meet up with Dodi. While she had been away, the decoration of the sitting room had been finished and she saw the reupholstered sofas and the new sky blue curtains.

The completion of the new decor was ironic because, after flipping through the real estate brochures for American properties without much success, the chance had arisen to purchase a clifftop property in California: the home of British actress Julie Andrews. The princess was seriously considering buying a holiday home where she could spend up to six months of the year, while she kept KP as her London base.

A move to America had been in the cards since the spring. In August, between holidays, she had spread out the brochure and said, "America is where my destiny lies, and if I decide to do this, Paul, I would like you, Maria and the boys to join me."

As we knelt on the sitting-room floor, she pointed at the Julie Andrews property, featured on several color pages and floor plans. "This is the main reception area. This is where William's room will be, and Harry's. And that annex is where you will live with Maria and the boys. This can be a new life. Isn't it exciting? It is a land where anyone can achieve," she said.

I had longed to live in America but it all seemed too sudden. "I think you should slow down. Even I'm finding it impossible to keep up with you," I said, trying not to burst the bubble.

That afternoon the princess peppered me with questions. "Well, if we don't live there, what about Cape Cod? It's nearer to London. We can travel the world, Paul, and seek out all those people who need help."

We sat there imagining the American lifestyle: the jogs along the beach, the constant sunshine, the sense of freedom. And then there was one more thing. Something she had always talked about. The one thing she had always wanted at Kensington Palace but felt was not possible. "And we can get a dog," she said. The thought of America made her so happy. "I always said we would end up living in America, didn't I?" she said, conveniently forgetting Australia, which had been her first idea.

The princess was making decisions. Many things were discussed, secrets that I cannot mention here. Secrets that will go away with me. Surprises would be coming, and the prospect of all that excited her.

AFTER THE HOLIDAY in Ireland, I spoke to the princess nearly every day, though I never rang her from home. When we spoke, she was either lying on the deck of the *Jonikal* or relaxing out of the sun in her cabin.

From the first call, I knew she was getting restless in that environment. "It's roasting on the deck, it's like a fridge downstairs. I'm crawling the walls here!" she said.

Dodi had given her a silver photo frame, inscribed with a poem. She read it to me.

"That's a bit deep and meaningful, isn't it?" I jested.

"No!" She laughed. "It's sweet and romantic."

He had also given her a necklace and a pair of earrings. "He's got it bad, hasn't he?" She giggled.

I could see what was happening. The Boss had enjoyed the frisson of a new liaison, the excitement of the chase, the flattery of an attentive man who had fallen head over heels. But the novelty was wearing a bit thin. She knew that Dodi had fallen in love; he had told her so over dinner. But she hadn't reciprocated. It was too early, she said.

"So what did you tell him?" I asked curiously.

"I told him, 'Thank you for the compliment,' " she said.

In the mythology that has been peddled since the princess's death, there have been two ludicrous claims: that she and Dodi were going to get married, and that she was pregnant. The monstrous suggestion of pregnancy is not true.

As for marriage, which seems to have been a story that emerged from Dodi's friends, he might well have told them that he was planning to pop the question, but the princess was in no mood to accept. Happy she might have been. Hasty she was not.

In another call from the boat, she speculated about whether the next gift would be a ring. She was excited at the prospect but becoming increasingly worried about what it all meant. "What do I do, Paul, if it's a ring? I want another marriage like I want a bad rash," she said.

"It's easy. You accept it graciously and slip it on to the ring finger of your right hand. Don't put it on the wrong finger if you don't want to send the wrong signals!" I warned lightheartedly.

Ring finger. Right hand. We kept saying it.

"That means it will become a friendship ring," I said.

"What a clever idea. I will. I will," she said.

We never had another conversation about a ring, or whether one was actually produced.

There was another nagging doubt in the princess's mind about Dodi. "He keeps going into the bathroom and locking the door behind him. He keeps sniffing, blaming the air-conditioning system, and it disturbs me. Maybe I can help him, Paul." Then the conversation switched to how much she was looking forward to spending time with William and Harry. She couldn't count the days fast enough, and wanted to cut short her time with Dodi and return to London two days early. She had considered rearranging her flight, but Dodi persuaded her to stay.

"I'm just ready to come home now," she said. "I need to go to the gym."

"You've had enough of all that pampered luxury, then?" I asked.

There was a sigh. I did what I often did and tried to second-guess what she was thinking. "Don't tell me. You're feeling trapped on the boat and he's controlling your every move?"

"Right again. I need to come home."

SHE TOLD ME about the last-minute diversion to Paris on Friday, August 29. She spoke to me from the deck of the *Jonikal.* It was one of the last six phone calls she made in the final twenty-four hours of her life, as recorded in the call register of her mobile telephone.

I was on the telephone, sprawled on the sitting-room floor at my brother-in-law Peter Cosgrove's house in Farndon, two doors down from our first house, bought that spring as a holiday home. The family—Maria, the boys, Peter, his wife, Sue, and their daughters, Clare and Louise—had all given me privacy, but were growing impatient in the kitchen because I'd been on the telephone to the princess for around forty minutes.

In that call, the timetable for her arrival had changed. Originally, she'd been due back to London direct from the Mediterranean, arriving on Saturday, August 30, ahead of the boys' arrival on the Sunday. But Dodi had told her he needed to go to Paris for "business reasons." She seemed reluctant to go, but, again, Dodi had persuaded her.

"We've got to go to Paris, but I promise I will be back on Sunday," she said. "Now, I bet you can't guess where I am."

I tried at Sardinia.

"No. Monaco. And I bet you can't guess where I'm going tonight."

I guessed at a fine restaurant. "No. I'm going to visit the grave of Princess Grace. It will be a special moment."

It would be the first time she had returned to the grave since she attended the funeral in 1982. "I'm going to lay some flowers and say a few words," she added.

Then, her mind was back on land. She was thinking ahead and making plans, giving me instructions: remember to book Mr. Quelch at Burberry (the boys' tailor) for the following Monday. The Armani fitting for September 4. She asked what was in her schedule, and I told her lunch with Shirley Conran, and an appointment with aromatherapist Sue Beechey. Otherwise, she had plenty of free time with William and Harry.

As that marathon call neared its end, the princess told me: "I'm looking forward to catching up with friends, and I can't wait to see the boys. There's a lot we have to talk about, so don't be late! I'll tell you everything else when I see you."

In the background, an impatient family was calling me from the kitchen.

"Paul?" the princess asked. "I want you to promise me something."

"Of course," I added.

"Promise me you'll be there," she said in a chirpy voice, and I laughed at her worrying about me being late or not being there on the front doorstep when she arrived.

"Say it!" she demanded humorously. "I want to hear you say those words!"

I started to laugh. "Okay, okay, if it makes you feel happier, I promise I'll be there."

The princess laughed. Behind the kitchen door, the family guffawed. The poignancy of those final words only hit me later but has stayed with me ever since. I will carry on that responsibility of being there for her—even when others object.

"Good!" said the princess. "I'll see you when I get back."

It was the last time I spoke to her.

ONE

⚜

GROWING UP

THE LATE-NIGHT double-decker bus crawled sluggishly up the hilly back roads of the mining communities of Derbyshire, England. Sarah Kirk had enjoyed her night out and several half-glasses of mild at the Elm Tree pub three miles away.

Saturday nights were a chance to catch up with Dolly, her eldest daughter of eight children, a respite from caring for her sick husband, William, a miner, confined to bed with lungs congested with coal dust from a lifetime spent underground. As the bus slowed, Sarah gathered her gloves, pulled them on and stood up. Home. Almost. She stepped out onto the pavement, and began to walk alongside the bus, her breath like cigarette smoke in the raw November air. Her final breaths. Blinded by the back of the bus to her left side, she didn't see the motorcycle that struck and tossed her into the air. It was shortly after 11:15 P.M.

Sarah Kirk was the grandma I never got to meet. She died on the pavement at the top of the cobbled street that would become my childhood playground.

* * *

Had Grandma Kirk not died, my parents would not have married so soon—according to Dad, anyway. Circumstances shoehorned him into wedlock and fatherhood. Grandma's passing elevated Mum to the woman of the house at No. 57 Chapel Road, where she nursed Grandad, sharing the duty with her elder sister, Auntie Pearl, who lived down the street.

"What shall I do? Have a twenty-first birthday party or get married? We can't afford to do both," Mum said to the man who would become my father. They'd met in 1952—the year that Queen Elizabeth ascended the throne—but then Dad joined the RAF. They'd been dating since he returned.

In the weeks of mourning after the road accident, it seemed romance had died too. It was as if Dad had been given a choice of what to eat for dinner—or tea, as we called it in the north of England. Meat and potato pie or stew and dumplings?

Dad's reply was nonchalant. "Well, s'pose we'd better get married, then."

Four months after Grandma was killed, Beryl Kirk and Graham Burrell tied the knot on March 25, 1957.

June 6, 1958, was not a remarkable day for most people, but it was for my parents. On a beautiful sunny summer's evening, I was born in Scarsdale Maternity Hospital, Chesterfield. Mum and Dad had anticipated the arrival of a daughter and had already chosen her name, Pamela Jane. It was the midwife who broke the news on my delivery. "Well, Mrs. Burrell, it's not a Pamela," she said, "it's a boy!" So I became Paul.

I had arrived into the world, born on the Queen Elizabeth II ward.

Six months after I arrived at No. 57 Chapel Road, Grandad Kirk moved in with Auntie Pearl. She had recently been widowed, and took on the burden of caring for Grandad because Mum found it increasingly difficult to care for both of us. Within two years, Mum was pregnant again. She and my father still both shared the dream of having a daughter.

Elsewhere in the country, in a world vastly different from ours, another family was desperate for a child. At Park House, on the Sandringham estate in Norfolk, the Spencers had already produced two daughters, Jane and Sarah. A son, John, had also been born but died within a few hours. It was deemed a must that the next should be a boy, an heir to the then-Viscount Althorp.

In 1961, the hopes of both sets of parents were dashed. My brother, Anthony William, was born on March 30. Mum didn't make it to the hospital this time, so he was delivered in the front room by next-door neighbor Annie Tunnicliffe. She and Dad were still proud to have a healthy second son. But there was bitter disappointment at Sandringham: an heir was not produced. Instead a third daughter was born four months later on July 1, named Diana Frances. I was three years old.

Aside from my grandad's funeral four months before Anthony's birth, my only other vivid childhood recollection is of bathtime in the back room. A tin bath was dragged in from the washhouse and filled with tepid water in front of a roaring coal fire. As I soaked, Mum held a towel in front of the fire to warm it. The house was constantly cold. Bathtime wasn't so good if Mum was in a hurry, though. She'd stand me in the deep white ceramic sink in the corner of the back room, scrubbing me clean with what felt like a scouring pad as I held on to the single cold-water tap, its vertical lead piping rattling in its brackets on the wall.

Shortly after Grandad's funeral, we'd moved five doors down to No. 47. Chapel Road was cobbled, with black wrought-iron lanterns. Both of our homes were on the bottom row of the L-shaped street and faced west with rear yards backing onto open fields that sloped down to the east and the perimeter of the mines. There were shops in Chapel Road: Hartshorn's haberdashery, where Mum, a knitter, bought her wool; "Auntie Hilda's," with its tin signs on the outside wall advertising Bovril, Cadbury, and Oxo above a green-striped awning; and Fletcher's betting shop, where Dad never went. At the bottom of the road, just round the corner, was my favorite shop, Monty White's ice-cream parlor, where dollops of freshly made dairy ice cream were troweled on to cones in exchange for a three-penny bit. I haven't tasted ice cream like it since. Opposite our new home was Eldred's Bakery. I woke each morning to the smell of freshly baked bread, and, on Good Friday, cinnamon-spiced hot cross buns. It was the best of scents, but was soon chased away by the waft of sulfur and tar from the mine.

We moved into No. 47 using a fleet of wheelbarrows. Mum said it was the most desirable of properties: it had a bathroom. The rent went up, but the extra financial burden was worth the luxury of being able to go to the loo indoors. There was no such thing as fitted carpets: we had wall-to-wall linoleum, scattered with homemade rag rugs. With no central heating, my bedroom was so cold that, each morning, I woke to find condensation frozen on the inside of the windows. A black-and-white television sat on the sideboard. Dad ingeniously rigged up a frying pan with wire as an antenna and strung it to the wall. Miraculously, it caught the signal, even if the picture was hazy and rolled. Later in childhood, we sat around as a family and watched *Sunday Night at the London Palladium*, with the country's best-paid entertainer, Danny La Rue, often top of the bill. One day, in my life with the princess, he would become a good and true friend to my family.

Money was always tight. We only ever had fresh fruit when someone was ill. A bout of yellow jaundice at the age of eight brought me the exotic tastes of oranges, grapes, and bananas for the first time. Folks with a fruit bowl on their sideboard were considered posh. Fresh flowers in a vase were unheard of unless someone had died. I grew up thinking flowers were associated with death, and fruit with sick people.

*   *   *

M Y YOUNGEST BROTHER, Graham, named after Dad, was not planned, and when Mum found she was pregnant, the name Pamela Jane was lined up once again, with a much more poignant hope. Mum and Dad knew their third child was due in November 1965, and Mum prayed the birth to fall on the the ninth anniversary of Grandma Kirk's death.

When November arrived, Mum's water broke on the fourth. Age seven, I bawled to see her in pain and carried into an ambulance. Before the doors closed, I heard her say: "Please, Jesus, not on this day." I feared she thought she was going to die. Of course she just wanted to hang on for a few more hours, and, indeed, her labor dragged on well into the next day. Eventually Graham was heaved into the world with forceps and suction at 11 P.M. on November 5—fifteen minutes before the exact anniversary.

I HAD AN ORDINARY happy childhood in a community where toil provided a wage for people who were the salt of the earth, and whose values revolved around the family unit. Dad worked as a coal-delivery driver. He was strong-willed and a strict disciplinarian, very smart, and his hair was slicked back with that Brylcreem sheen. I remember him pressing his trousers into knife-sharp creases down the leg, a habit from his days in the RAF. He taught me how to press trousers expertly—my first lesson in valeting, I suppose.

A S A CHILD, I attended Grassmoor Junior School, with its huge paned windows, high ceilings, and echoing corridors lined with white ceramic tiles. It was situated off the main village road and faced an expanse of green, which was home to the cricket club. Pupils sat in rows at slanted wooden desks and scrawled with a nibbed wooden pen, dipped into an inkwell. It was "real writing," and my duty each morning as "inkwell monitor" was to fill the tiny porcelain pots with fresh supplies of Quink. Later in life,

I'd watch the princess write letters at Kensington Palace, and it would remind me of those days. She always used a gold-nibbed fountain pen, but instead of filling its cartridge she dipped the nib into a bottle of Quink. She wrote all her correspondence—personal letters, thank-you notes, and memos—in that way.

Mr. Thomas, who taught me all subjects, stood before the class. In his deep, booming voice, hardly softened by a Welsh twang, he said: "Write an essay on what you want to do when you leave school." In utter silence, the little heads of thirty children bent down. Most boys mapped out a future that followed in their father's footsteps to coal mining, but even at ten, I was sure that I wasn't going to do that mining. It seemed a punishing future of coal dust, damp, and darkness. Too much like hard work. "When I Grow Up I Want To Be A Vicar" was the title of my essay. Then Mr. Thomas would eventually lobby for me to gain a place at William Rhodes Secondary School for Boys, Chesterfield, a better education than the local school that most miners' kids attended. Mum and Dad were delighted that a pattern had been broken.

William Rhodes was an all-boys school where masters wore black gowns. It was a strict regime ruled by the cane. Headmaster Mr. Crooks, who always wore a mortarboard and put the fear of God into me, administered it frequently. He was a stickler for manners and pristine appearance. At Rhodes, there was an emphasis on competitive sports, but English language and literature were my forte.

History was another of my strong points. I collected trading cards of the greatest sailing ships, flags of the world, and kings and queens of England and Scotland. It kick-started my fascination with royalty and heritage, going back to the Norman Conquest of 1066. When other boys played after school, I stayed in and completed my homework, then remained at the desk in my bedroom and read book after book about kings and queens. I went on to pass English literature O level with an essay on Richard III, a man much maligned, misunderstood, and wrongly portrayed as hunchbacked, twisted and wicked. In truth, he was courageous and passionate in his reign, which lasted just two years. It should have taught me that members of the Royal Family who don't fit the mold can be cruelly judged by history.

WHEN I WAS nearly twelve we went to London as a family for the first time. We walked down the Mall, and the imposing, blanched stone frontage of Buckingham Palace came into sight. Mum and Dad wanted "to go and see where the Queen lives."

"I wonder if she's in, lads?" mused Dad.

Anthony and I were mesmerized by the awesome building before us. We stood with our faces between the black railings on the front gates, hands gripping a rail on either side as we watched the Changing of the Guard. It was the most incredible scene I had witnessed as a child, a world away from the life we lived. I still don't know why, but I looked up and said: "One day I want to work there, Mum." Perhaps it was my fascination with history and kings and queens. It was the same sort of thoughtless, dreamy remark that children make—they want to be a pilot if they see a plane flying over or, when Neil Armstrong became the first man to walk on the moon, an astronaut.

Dad ruffled my hair affectionately. "Sure you do, me duck."

AT AGE SIXTEEN, I applied to High Peak Catering College in Buxton, Derbyshire, and, in September 1974, I took up residence in an attic room in digs in the town. I pursued a two-year course in hotel management and catering. In that time, I learned everything from cooking the perfect meal to making up the neatest bed, and became a housekeeper, bookkeeper, and chef rolled into one. My claim to fame was a British catering award for sculpting Chesterfield's famous crooked spire entirely out of margarine.

In my second year, I drew up a list of places where my skills could be best utilized, including cruise ships and hotels. High on the list was Cunard, which operated the *QE2*, and then Buckingham Palace, which needed an army of staff, just like any five-star hotel. That summer I dispatched letters offering my services.

The first response came from Travco Hotels, offering a job at the three-star Lincombe Hall Hotel, Torquay. This meant leaving college early to begin work in June 1976 as assistant manager in time for the summer season, which would take me away from home for months. It was a job, but it was not ideal—I longed for more replies. I accepted, but asked Mum to open all mail addressed to me at home. That summer, I had an interview with Cunard in Southampton, and another at Buckingham Palace. I went home from Torquay and we drove, with brother Graham, to the capital.

I entered Buckingham Palace via a side entrance, wearing a dark suit. I was in awe of the place, walking down those same red-carpeted corridors into a history I had only read about after school. I felt like a serf entering a world where my face and class would never be accepted.

When I reached the first-floor office of Mr. Michael Timms, the Master of the Household's assistant, Mum's reassuring voice spoke in my mind: "Just be yourself and you'll be fine." It wasn't the best advice she had ever given me because I walked in for that interview, sat down without being asked and failed to call the prospective boss "sir."

"Do you always sit down before you are asked?" said Mr. Timms, in an officious, pompous manner. "Do you not respect your seniors?"

WITHIN TWO WEEKS, a follow-up letter had informed me I had been rejected "on this occasion," but all details would be kept on file. There was no word from Cunard. Both dream jobs seemed out of reach.

Torquay was where a shy, quiet boy grew into a more

outgoing, confident, assertive member of management with status. I was promoted to assistant manager to the group's flagship hotel, the Wessex in Bournemouth, that October. Unfortunately, Bournemouth was totally different. I hated every minute of my time there, living in a shoebox room. Homesickness crept in, and Mum and Dad were so worried that they drove down to visit me. Mum was horrified and said there was not enough space to swing a cat.

LIFE CHANGED on a cold November morning at No. 47 Chapel Road. Dad had left for work, and Anthony, then fifteen, was on a milk round. Mum, preparing breakfast in the back room for the still dozing Graham, heard the letterbox rattle. She dried her hands on a tea towel, walked into the front room, and picked up the mail from the floor. There were two letters addressed to Mr. Paul Burrell.

She didn't recognize the *C* logo on the first cream envelope, but on the rear it said "Cunard, Southampton." The second letter bore the black frank mark of Buckingham Palace, and on the reverse was the Queen's red-embossed coat-of-arms. They had arrived with a gas bill.

Mum tucked both letters into the pouch at the front of her apron, where they remained untouched for half an hour as she busied herself in the kitchen. Graham came downstairs to get dressed in front of the fire. Mum told him: "There's two letters for our Paul. One from Cunard. One from Buckingham Palace." She sat down and took a knife from the kitchen table. She slit open the royal envelope carefully. It was from Mr. Michael Timms, offering me a position of under-butler in the silver pantry. Apparently, I'd impressed him just a little more than I thought. The other letter was from Cunard's personnel department and offered the post of steward aboard the *QE2*. Mum stared at both letters. She knew in her heart that I would have jumped at the chance of a life at sea, and thought long and hard about what to do next.

Then she snapped into life. "He'll chuff off on that boat

and we'll never see him again," she told Graham, and tossed the Cunard letter, in its envelope, on the fire. Graham and she watched my potential career at sea go up in smoke. "As long as I live, Graham, you must never tell him what I've just done," she said. Then she propped the letter from Buckingham Palace in the center of the mantelpiece, before hurrying across the road to Eldred's Bakery to use the telephone.

I was in the storeroom at the Wessex when I was called to the phone.

"Paul. You've had a letter from Buckingham Palace offering you a job."

TWO

BUCKINGHAM PALACE

ONE OF MY FAVORITE memories of the life that would unfold for me at the palace didn't occur until a couple of years later.

I COULD NOT BELIEVE the regal sight before me.

The Queen, who was in deep concentration in her sitting room at Buckingham Palace, looked up and caught me staring, smiling. She stopped what she was doing. "Why are you smiling, Paul?" she inquired, a hint of amusement in her voice.

"If you could only see what I can see, Your Majesty."

We both grinned broadly. It was late at night, not long before bedtime, and there she sat, in a smart silk dress in her chair at the desk near the window. She was wearing the Imperial State Crown. And her pink mule slippers.

I had caught her by surprise when I entered the room to say good night after completing a final duty: ensuring that the nine corgis were comfortable in their beds farther down the plush red-carpeted corridor. The Queen, wearing her half-moon, rimless spectacles, sat at her desk, where a flexible table lamp's lowered arm cast bright light onto the papers she was working on. In the half-light, a thousand facets flashed back from the crown. I had often seen the Queen in her slippers, but never matched with the most glorious and priceless of the Crown Jewels. However, it was the eve of the State Opening of Parliament, and the Queen, as she does every year, simply needed to get used to the weight of the crown, the equivalent of two one-pound bags of sugar, on her head.

As she smiled at me, I asked, "Will there be anything else, Your Majesty?"

"No, thank you, Paul." She lowered her head to carry on with her paperwork.

I bowed. "Good night, Your Majesty."

IT HAD ALL BEGUN two years earlier, on December 20, 1976, when I moved from the claustrophobia of the Wessex, Bournemouth, to the vastness of Buckingham Palace, London. I'd trembled as I walked into the palace on that first day, wearing my best dark suit, and carrying a small suitcase. After being shown my room, I was fitted for uniforms.

It was like a costume party. Staring back at me was a reflection from the past, a stranger dressed in royal livery as if he was about to serve King George III, not Queen Elizabeth II. I wore a navy blue velvet riding cap; a white starched ruff frilled out round the neck over a collarless shirt; a black embroidered waistcoat with gold-threaded stripes and a plain silk back, fastened tight at the front with gold buttons embossed with the royal crest; red coarse-velvet breeches tied below the knee with gold buttons and a tassel; pink silk stockings and black patent leather buckled pumps. At my left side hung a sword and scabbard. I slipped on the white cotton gloves.

For a few minutes, I felt silly, then a huge sense of pride came over me as I pulled on the final piece to complete the full state livery: a scarlet tailcoat with thick gold trim running down the buttoned front and gold hoops around each arm. It was a uniform that had been handed down over at least two hundred years. Repaired, stitched, and musty, but with a magnificence that hadn't faded over time. Only one thing had changed: the insignia stitched to the upper arm of the left sleeve bore the initials "EiiR" encircled by the royal garter, *"Honi soit qui mal y pense"*—which means "Shame on him who thinks evil of it"—topped with the embroidered Imperial State Crown.

I tried on those clothes in the livery room in the palace basement, where it took all day to fit me out with the essential uniforms. All had been owned and worn by others before me. At Buckingham Palace, just as in Grassmoor, secondhand garments were commonplace. Even the shirts, trousers, and suits of the boy Prince Andrew were altered and passed down to Prince Edward.

Deputy sergeant footman Martin Bubb handed me five different uniforms. In addition to the full livery—for state occasions inside and outside the palace—there were four more. The scarlet, a tailcoat with top hat for semi-state occasions and Royal Ascot; the epaulet, a double-breasted, neck-high tailcoat only worn aboard the royal yacht *Britannia;* the tropical, a white, safari-like jacket worn in hot climates; and the everyday livery, a black tailcoat worn with white shirt, black tie, and scarlet waistcoat. I was also handed a red felt coachman's cape, boxes of shirts, and hangers with extra pairs of trousers.

The palace was empty, save for a skeleton household staff. The court had moved to Windsor Castle for the holiday and its newest recruit was ready to commence royal duty. In terms of being dressed, at least.

M Y FIRST-EVER TASK was assigned on Christmas Eve after I had been shuttled by train to Windsor. I was standing on the octagonal-shaped first floor in a stone tower on the northeast corner of the castle, overlooking the East Terrace, with its panoramic views of the gardens and the golf course. The monogrammed demitasse coffee cups rattled and clinked on a large silver salver as my clammy hands shook with nerves. My stomach churned. I fretted about making a mistake and felt painfully self-conscious in the uniform. I was about to enter the formidable presence of the entire Royal Family for the first time, down a corridor, in the cavernous state dining room where the Windsors were having dinner by candlelight. For two hours, I had watched an endless stream of uniformed footmen, under-butlers, pages, and wine waiters come and go up and down that corridor. It was a human conveyor-belt, stacked with plates, silverware, glasses, and dishes of food. Everything about the Royal Family, even private meal-times, is planned, scripted, and orchestrated to perfection. Behind the door, the backstage line-up got into position. Liveried footmen stood stiff-backed, holding dishes of food in an orderly queue. First the meat. Then potatoes. Vegetables. Salad. A voice always prompted the gastronomic procession to begin. "Meat . . . go." Thirty seconds pass.

"Potatoes and gravy . . . go." Thirty seconds pass.

"Vegetables . . . go."

"Salad . . . go."

It was some time before I was trusted to handle meat or potatoes. Empty china cups were the sum total of my early responsibilities.

Then I realized coffee was about to be served, and my big moment had arrived. Through the half-open door, with the tray weighing heavy in my arms, I caught a glimpse of the room's grandeur. Laughter and loud after-dinner conversation spilled through to me. Mr. Dickman, the palace steward in charge of the slick operation, sensed my nerves. "Don't worry, there's nothing to be concerned about," he said. "Just go into the dining room, stand in the corner, and the footman will come to you to replenish the tray. All you have to do is stand there. The footman will serve the coffee," Mr. Dickman explained.

The smile I returned must not have been very convincing. "They won't eat you!" said my new boss. He gave me a gentle push on the back. "Off you go, then, there's a good lad."

* * *

As LEAD FEET dragged me into that room, I remembered Mr. Dickman's instructions. "Don't stare or look at anyone in the eye. The Royal Family does not like to be watched when eating." I looked down, my eyes fixed on the shaking china cups.

Carefully. Ever so carefully. All I needed to do was walk ten yards to the corner of the room.

Got there. Looked up. In front of me was the biggest table I had ever seen: an oval of polished mahogany, about twenty feet long, with a central line of candelabra interspersed with extravagant floral arrangements. Crimson velvet curtains with gold tassels were drawn across the huge Gothic windows. Queen Victoria's colossal portrait stared down on her ancestors from above the Victorian stone fireplace.

Despite myself, I scanned the table for the Queen among the thirty members of her family, all in evening dress. The Queen Mother came into view; she was sitting in the middle, in the largest, gilded, thronelike chair, engrossed in an animated conversation with her favorite grandson, Prince Charles. The Queen was on his other side, in a much smaller chair like everyone else, opposite Prince Philip, the Duke of Edinburgh, listening intently to a conversation.

I noted the Queen's natural smile, and how small she looked in real life. I remember thinking, if Mum could only see me. If only the whole village of Grassmoor could have seen me.

Jewels glinted in the candlelight. The footman worked quickly and efficiently in serving the table, and I was glad to be doing nothing more than impersonating a statue holding a tray. I could see the young Princes Andrew and Edward, Princess Anne and her husband of two years, Captain Mark Phillips. Princess Margaret was dominating the conversation, with her high-pitched, shrill voice. The conversation was all so loud, I thought.

I looked away before I could be caught staring. My

salver was suddenly empty, and I walked slowly out of the room, unnoticed.

"See? Wasn't that bad, lad," said a smiling Mr. Dickman, on the other side of the doors.

In Grassmoor, New Year's, our family's tradition was to bring a lump of coal through the door. It was believed to bring good luck all year round. I would spend *this* New Year's at Sandringham House, the Edwardian country mansion on the 20,000-acre estate in Norfolk, one of the Queen's two privately owned residences. As the youngest footman, it was my awesome responsibility to welcome the New Year on behalf of the Royal Family. I stood inside the front doorway, awaiting my cue. Through the glass-paneled windows, as I shook with cold and nerves, I saw the champagne being served by the other footmen. The Windsors were all gathered, and the countdown to midnight had begun. On the stroke of 1977, the door was opened and I strode in to do my duty: I had to weave my way through the drawing room toward the fireplace, pick up a log from the pile, and throw it onto the burning embers. As the new log sizzled, a round of applause broke out. And as a reward for performing that tradition, I had the privilege to be the first member of staff to approach my new employer with the appropriate greeting.

"Happy New Year, Your Majesty." I beamed.

I SHOULD NEVER have become a footman so soon. After all, the letter that Mum had opened had offered the post of under-butler—someone who works in the china and glass pantry, working elbow-deep in soap suds, scrubbing plates and cups until they squeak clean in the wooden sinks. But a last-minute vacancy had arisen in the footmen's room, so I joined their number, under the stewardship of sergeant footman John Floyd, ranked number fourteen out of fourteen with a salary of £1,200. The top two slots of the Queen's personal footmen seemed light-years away.

Staff living quarters were of standard hotel room size,

sparsely decorated. Each one had a corner sink, single bed, desk, chest of drawers, wardrobe, and green carpet. They were gloomy, with high-set windows that let in little daylight, but Mum was at least heartened when I told her that there was enough room to swing a cat.

My room was on the all-male "Pages' Lobby," which hides behind that series of narrow windows on the Buckingham Palace east-facing frontage; the top-floor windows situated just beneath the pediment. I was not senior enough to have a room looking down on the Victoria Monument and the Mall, so my room was on the other side of the corridor, overlooking the inner quadrangle, the red-graveled courtyard encompassed by all sides of the palace. I often stood on the radiator to look down on the stone-pillared glass veranda of the Grand Entrance where everyone arrived, from heads of state to garden party guests. Adjacent to that was the black double-fronted "King's Door," used by those having a private audience with Her Majesty, such as the Prime Minister, arriving for the weekly Tuesday evening briefing.

There was an overwhelming amount of information about palace life to absorb. There was a maze of underground corridors, and a labyrinth of interconnecting rooms and hallways linking more than six hundred rooms. Buckingham Palace is like a foreign village on the mainland—its people speak the same language but live in a different world. It has its own police station and a twenty-four-hour fire brigade, a post office, doctor's surgery, laundry, a chapel and chaplain, electricians, carpenters, gilders, and plumbers. It also has its own bar.

A bewildering collection of job titles from the eighteenth century covers a multitude of household jobs: Master of the Household and Palace Steward; Page of the Presence, Page of the Backstairs, Page of the Chambers; Mistress of the Robes (who has to be a duchess), Woman of the Bedchamber, and ladies-in-waiting; Yeoman of the Silver Pantry, Yeoman of Glass and China, and equerries-in-waiting. Not to mention the Keeper of the Privy Purse and the Gentleman Usher to the Sword of State.

Buckingham Palace is run by an organization called the Royal Household, headed by the Lord Chamberlain. Beneath him is a family tree of six offices: Private Secretary's Office, Privy Purse and Treasurer's Office, Lord Chamberlain's Office, Master of the Household's Department, Royal Mews Department, and the Royal Collection Department. Staff like me worked for the Master of the Household, whose department was then split into three groups: H-branch for housekeeping, F-branch for food, and G-branch for general. Footmen worked in G-branch, reporting to Palace Steward Cyril Dickman.

Then there were procedures: the rules, protocols, and traditions. For the first year, I carried a pocket notebook to jot down the names and titles of colleagues and superiors, log the shortcuts to different places, draw minidiagrams of how to set a dining table. Even a tray had a layout plan: cup and saucer with handle and spoon pointing toward five o'clock; plates and saucers turned so the royal crests were at twelve o'clock; salt on right, mustard on left with the pepper behind; sugar bowl and tongs with cubed white sugar, never granulated; toast always served in a silver toast rack and never on a plate; no more than three balls of butter in the dish. And never forget the linen napkin.

Even the staff bathroom threw me. It had several narrow cubicles with chrome showerheads. I had never seen a shower before, and needed to ask how it was operated.

In the corridors, with the silk-papered walls, housemaids were not allowed to use vacuum cleaners before 9 A.M. to avoid disturbing the Royal Family. Instead, stiff yard brushes were used to sweep the deep red shag pile upright. Staff must never walk down the middle of the carpet because it was considered presumptuous: freshly brushed carpet was fit only for royal feet. Staff had to walk along its foot-wide border instead.

The art of being a good servant, I learned, was to perform as many of my duties as possible without being seen—ideally, servants should be invisible. At its most extreme, this requirement led a scurrying army of maids or footmen to hide until the coast was clear. At Sandringham

House, maids would dart into a walk-in cupboard under the stairs so as not to be seen when the Queen was coming down into the main hall. If a member of the Royal Family was approaching down a corridor and it was too late to disappear, the protocol was to stop walking, stand to attention, turn with back against the wall, and bow as they passed, without saying a word.

This game of "hide without seek" led to many bizarre situations as staff lurked behind a closed door of a back passageway leading to a bedroom, ear pressed to the door to listen for a quiet that signaled it was safe to proceed. From a shadowy recess, staff watched a drawing room until the last guest had left, then cleared empty glasses, stoked the fire, plumped the cushions, and brushed up the carpet.

When it came to snobbery, I found there were more noses stuck in the air in the Royal Household than in the Royal Family. There was a pecking order in everything, down to something as simple as staff mealtimes. It was a class system straight from the decks of the *Titanic,* encouraged by the hierarchical household masters whom the Princess of Wales would later refer to as "the men in gray suits."

The most junior members of staff—from under-butlers to footmen, chefs to maids, porters to postmen, grooms to chauffeurs—all sat at white-clothed tables with a buffet menu and beakers of cold water. The dining hall was in a ground-floor room with plastic seats and linoleum floors, rather like a workplace cafeteria. The atmosphere was loud, raucous, and down-to-earth.

The Stewards' Dining Room was on the first floor, with upholstered chairs and carpets. The mood was more businesslike. It was reserved for staff who had served fifteen years or more, or who had been decorated for loyalty— pages, Pages of the Presence, Pages of the Backstairs, Yeomen of the Pantries, sergeant footmen, the Queen's dressers, her chauffeur—and presided over by the Palace Steward. One notable treat was that they had a selection of bread, a varied cheeseboard and crackers.

Next door, another rung up the ladder, was the Officials'

Dining Room, reserved for personal secretaries and assistants, clerks, press officers, typists, and administrative personnel.

Then came the far grander Lady Barrington's Room, with its high ceilings and a central chandelier. Here, small talk and serious conversation occupied the assistants to the Master of the Household, the Chief Housekeeper, and the Paymaster. So senior were these staff that they were allowed a pre-meal sherry or whisky and wine with their meal.

Finally, beside the Bow Room, was the grandest room of them all, reserved for the crème de la crème of the household. Royal Collection portraits hung on the walls above the Chippendale and Sheraton sideboards. Food was served on fine china plates, eaten with silver cutlery, and wine from the royal cellars was poured into crystal glasses. This splendor was the sole preserve of ladies-in-waiting, senior Women of the Bedchamber, the Mistress of the Robes, private secretaries, press secretaries, the Keeper of the Privy Purse, the Queen's chaplain, equerries-in-waiting, and the Lord Chamberlain. It had a prim, stiff atmosphere akin to a private members' club. Oddly, it was four times larger than Her Majesty's dining room, and more grandly decorated.

The higher echelons of the dining system became a training ground for green footmen such as me. Before being entrusted with the responsibility of waiting at a royal table, I had to learn and polish my craft in the presence of the Lord Chamberlain, which was nerve-racking in those early days. I had to become expert at how to set the perfect dinner table—placing knives and forks one centimeter from the table's edge, and ensuring that every setting mirrored the next with faultless uniformity. Or how to fold a napkin into the symbolic shape of the Prince of Wales's feathers. Or how to ensure that vintage wine and champagne never filled a glass more than halfway up.

* * *

FOR THREE MONTHS, I shadowed a senior footman and learned quickly the intricacies of duty: from ensuring that the Queen's dinner was carried from the kitchen to her dining room hot and on time, to spit-and-polishing the boots of an equerry. It was important to be inconspicuous in this shadowing role, but I also needed to be ultra-observant. Away from the dining room, another of my roles was as a gentleman's valet.

Standing in complete darkness in the corner of one bedroom where a visitor was sound asleep, my mentor, Martin Bubb, showed off the skills required. The art was to be hush-quiet, swift, and have night vision.

Alarm clocks are not provided in royal palaces and castles. The footman or valet—or maid—enters a room on the stroke of a designated time to call his master or mistress. Treading deftly in the dark, Martin placed a small wooden "calling tray" of freshly brewed tea and a glass of orange juice with one digestive biscuit on a chair at arm's length from the bed. If that didn't have any effect, then the subsequent task usually did. Martin picked his way across the carpet and drew the curtains to flood the room with daylight.

As the gentleman stirred, Martin picked up from the floor discarded clothes from the previous night, put them on a wooden hanger, and placed it outside the door, along with the shoes, which needed polishing, and the socks and underwear for washing. For the day ahead, he chose fresh clothes and laid them out in a precise way: pressed and folded trousers flat across a chair seat with a pocket corner turned back so they could be easily picked up; a fresh folded shirt, placed at a vertical angle on the trousers, every button open and cuff links inserted; a clean pair of undershorts on top; shoes with laces undone beside an easy chair; socks on top. Martin then approached the dressing table and opened the top drawer to select some ties (a valet must always leave a choice). He left out a clean, pressed, and folded handkerchief.

Then he beckoned me to follow him into the adjoining bathroom. On closing the door, he explained the "bathroom procedure." He turned on the taps and ran a lukewarm bath, laid a mat on the floor, and pulled toward it a bathroom chair. "This is how you lay out a towel," said Martin. He draped it lengthways over the chair so that when the gentleman sat down he could pull it around him and stand up as if he was wearing a robe.

At that, Martin's job was done and we both left the bedroom.

This was exactly the same procedure adopted by dressers and valets not only for guests but for all senior members of the Royal Family.

The first time I valeted alone, it was to a rather elderly gentleman. I panicked when I couldn't find his discarded clothes on the floor, and wondered where on earth he had left them. Then his arm stretched out from under the duvet. He was still fully clothed.

Later I learned that the Prince of Wales had meticulous needs that his valets, from the late Steph Barry to Michael Fawcett, had to observe. A silver key, bearing his feathers, was attached to the end of a toothpaste tube like a sardine-tin key and turned to squeeze enough to fit on the brush. His cotton pajamas had to be ironed each morning.

To the outsider, the level of subservience may seem odd but the monarchy could not function without the huge machine that is the Royal Household. Every cog, from an under-butler to the Lord Chamberlain, turns at every minute of every day to ensure the smooth running of royal lives and duties.

The Queen is on friendly terms with most staff, and the relationship between employer and employee is one of mutual respect, with the formality of duty mixed with informality on staff occasions.

On a day when the Queen had engagements, a lift door opened and, as if by magic, the Queen appeared on the ground floor, sending ladies-in-waiting crumpling into curtsies and private secretaries and equerries into respectful nods. It was all extremely formal and subdued. On the party's return, though, the Queen often hovered near the lift and wanted to engage in conversation. Perhaps she'd relate an amusing incident or eccentric gesture from her day. Her Majesty would smile, chat, then thank her staff for an enjoyable day. As she turned to go back into the lift, the formality kicked back in, and the curtsies and bows would be more heartfelt.

From the moment I began working at the palace, I had—and still have—enormous respect for Her Majesty. She is a remarkable, kind, Christian lady, but it would be a little while before I got to know and understand her better. I was the footman who earned the nickname "Buttons." Martin Bubb and fellow footman Alastair Wanless christened me as such because I was assigned to the livery room to polish and stitch gold-embossed buttons onto dozens of uniforms. It was a tedious task that filled hours of my time during my three-month probation period.

As Britain prepared to celebrate the Queen's Silver Jubilee, palace staff had never worked so hard, with receptions and banquets held almost every week. For that momentous year, I remained of junior status and had no major role to play. From the vantage point of my room, I watched, that June, as the gilded Coronation coach, built for King George III, carried the Queen away from the quadrangle courtyard in state procession through the streets of London to St. Paul's Cathedral. Fellow footmen walked alongside the carriage in full state livery, surrounded by the Yeomen of the Guard (commonly called the Beefeaters) and the Household Cavalry. In the distance, I heard the thronging crowds cheering in proud patriotism.

It was only the second time that the Queen had ever ridden inside that impressive but not very comfortable carriage, the first occasion being her Coronation in 1953. On her return, I heard her remark at a cocktail reception: "I had forgotten how uncomfortable that ride could be."

Silver Jubilee medals with white ribbons were awarded

to everyone in the palace who had served a year on June 2, 1977. I was the only footman not to receive one, because I had only served six months. I could only wonder how many years I would have to languish as the fourteenth footman. As it turned out, I didn't have long to wait.

WORD SWEPT THROUGH Windsor Castle about "an accident" in one of the staff bedrooms, but the evidence pointed elsewhere. A half-consumed bottle of gin stood on the bedside table beside an opened container of pills. A man who had been suffering from depression lay unconscious in bed. There was the strange sight of an ambulance at the Augusta Tower Door on the south side of the castle. It arrived with no lights or sirens so as not to create a fuss. The ambulance men went to a second-floor room. The Queen's personal footman—one of the two who shadowed the monarch wherever she was in the world—was stretchered away, critically ill after a suicide attempt. It was April 1978. The footman in question survived but never returned to duty and retired on grounds of ill health. Around the same time, Ernest Bennett, the Queen's page (more senior in rank than a footman), retired after an impeccable service that dated back to the end of the Second World War. Those two events brought about a restructuring of the Queen's immediate household in which I gained an unlikely promotion.

Amid the relaxed repartee of the footmen's room at the palace, speculation was rife about who would be elevated to the privileged position of Queen's personal footman. My colleague Paul Whybrew was the first to be promoted, and one other was required. Unbeknownst to me, the Queen had been conducting a subtle reconnoiter of the footmen at luncheon and cocktail parties, observing from the corner of her eye their attention to detail, their manners, appearance, and overall performance.

Days later, I was summoned to the office of the sergeant footman, John Floyd. "Would you like the opportunity to become the Queen's footman?" he said.

There was only one answer, of course. Within the space of sixteen months, I'd gotten what was considered to be a dream job. Any position so close to the Queen is considered a special privilege. The key people around her are not the officials who share her administrative and state duties and diaries but her dressers, pages, and footmen who share her most intimate, private world. In fact, it was not unheard of for a private secretary to "test the water" with a footman to gauge the Queen's mood or reaction to a certain event before having an audience with her. Members of the household did valuable homework by gleaning snippets of information from her personal staff. My word began to carry some weight.

Having two Pauls as footmen made life easier for the Queen, because whenever she called the name, one of us would always appear—but it did nothing for our confusion. So, for the sake of clarity, Her Majesty dreamed up nicknames: I became "Small Paul," at five foot nine, and he became "Tall Paul," at six foot two.

It helped the Queen, if not Princess Margaret. On the telephone, height was of no use to tell us apart: "Which one is it? Small Paul or Tall Paul?" she would say, in her unmistakable articulate drawl that was far more grandiloquent than that of her sister.

It pained me to have to reply, "It's Small Paul, Your Royal Highness."

For a decade, the entire Royal Family called us by those names.

There was one considerable perk to becoming the Queen's footman. I moved across the corridor of the Pages' Lobby and into a front room with a magnificent view down the Mall. Mine was the fourth window from the end on the left, beneath the pediment.

EVERY MORNING, at 7 A.M., my day began by walking nine corgis: Brush, Jolly, Shadow, Myth, Smokey, Piper, Fable, Sparky, and Chipper, the only male in the pack. After their walk, they were allowed into the Queen's bedroom. The dogs—and a cup of tea—were her 8 A.M. wake-up call.

By 9 A.M., it was time for a second walk, and the Queen opened her bedroom door. I'd be waiting to lasso each head as it came out. Nine corgis on nine leads had some pulling power, and it was at Sandringham House that I discovered their true force.

Corgis are determined little creatures, and each dog wanted to be first to exit the front door. One morning, there had been a sprinkling of snow, and the steps, like the drive, were notoriously slippery in winter. As I turned to shut the doors with one hand, nine leads yanked me the other way. I fell, banged my head on the steps, and was knocked unconscious, the corgis scurrying off into the snow. The next thing I knew I was waking up with the faces of the Queen and Princess Anne above me. "Paul, are you all right?" said the Queen.

I had been lying there for around ten minutes when they found me, and helped me to my feet. I felt a huge lump on my head and had wrenched a muscle in my back; the pain was excruciating. The Queen called Sandringham GP Dr. Ford, and instructed me to take bed rest for the remainder of the day.

Thankfully, someone had rounded up the corgis.

FEEDING THEM was less trouble. The Queen liked to feed her cherished pets personally whenever she could. I chatted most naturally with Her Majesty at dog-feeding time, my one-on-one time with the Queen, and we had some good conversations over the years.

I got used to the sight of the Queen, with a silver spoon and fork, taking great delight in dishing out portions of dog food mixed with fresh rabbit and dry biscuit, and topped with gravy. Sometimes, as a special treat, leftovers of pheasant from the previous evening's dinner were added. It was my duty to place nine yellow plastic bowls on individual mats as she called their names one by one. At these times, the Queen was at her most jolly, talkative, and relaxed. She would recount stories from her day, injecting humor into them, and it was not unknown for me to share with her a hearty laugh.

She often began with: "Do you know? The most extraordinary thing happened . . ." Or if she had met an old friend, she would say: "Do you know who I saw yesterday?" Or if there had been a comical incident: "The funniest thing happened . . ." Even better was when one of her horses had been first past the post: "Did you know that one of my horses won at . . . ?"

It was during one of our many dog-feeding conversations that the Queen told me a remarkable story about another monarch, King Charles I. She took me back in time to his execution on January 30, 1649, when Oliver Cromwell rode into London on a wave of anti-royalism. "Do you know? The most extraordinary thing happened the other day. I received a letter from someone whose ancestor had been in the crowd when King Charles I was executed," the Queen started. She relayed the story of the monarch's final moments outside the Banqueting Hall in Whitehall, before he was beheaded. As Her Majesty mixed the dog food, she continued, "As they chopped off his head, a piece of his collarbone splintered into the crowd and it was picked up by their ancestor. It has passed down through generations of their family ever since. I have been sent that piece of bone."

I was ignoring the corgis at my feet by that stage. "What are you going to do with it, Your Majesty?"

"There is only one thing to do, Paul," she said, "and that is to return it to its rightful owner. I asked for it to be placed inside the coffin of King Charles I." She went on to explain that when the coffin was opened, they had seen that the King's severed head had been sewn back onto his neck. "And, do you know, because of the airtight coffin, his beard was still intact—totally preserved," said a rather astonished Queen to an even more astonished footman.

"Can you imagine it, Your Majesty—staring at the face of history?" I said. She chortled at the thought.

* * *

THE QUEEN'S SENSE of humor is carried by a skill for mimicry. Her forte was regional accents; she had a fondness for the vernacular of the East End, Ireland, Yorkshire, Merseyside, and Australia. She impersonated these with affection because she admired the characters, her people, whom she met on royal tours. Many prim and proper ladies-in-waiting and private secretaries have been reduced to fits of laughter by the monarch.

I shall never forget the Royal Ascot race meeting when, as I rode behind Her Majesty in scarlet livery in an open landau, a Cockney voice from the cheering crowd bellowed: "Gi' us a wave, Liz."

Such a natural, spontaneous greeting made the royal party smile, but Prince Charles, opposite his mother, had not heard what the man had said. "What did he say, Mummy?" he asked.

With a perfect East End accent, the Queen replied: "He said, 'Gi' us a wave, Liz.'" Charles and his father laughed as the Queen continued to wave.

If only more people could hear the Queen's natural laughter or see her smile more often. Behind the pomp and pageantry, the tradition and protocol, and the sense of duty she puts above all else, there is a warm, natural woman with a lighter side. A glimpse would melt the austere, severe, cold caricature the country has built up. The Queen is one of the easiest people to converse with, and is not at all grand or pompous. We would chat about her observations of the gardens, the wildlife, and fellow household staff. She is fascinated by people and would talk about those she had met, and those she was looking forward to meeting. Her Majesty is like a gracious country lady who just happens to be the monarch.

SHE IS ALSO THE most caring dog owner you could meet. When a corgi had a coughing spasm, she got down on her hands and knees to prise open its jaws while I squirted Her Majesty's recommended dose of cough mixture down its throat with a syringe. The corgis though, however cute they appeared, could fight. Once at Windsor, when the Queen was out to dinner, I had watched *Dallas* on BBC1 and was about to take them for a final walk. As I put on my coat, they raced down the corridor to the door, and all hell broke loose. Jolly, Princes Andrew and Edward's corgi, was being attacked like a fox snared by hounds. The smallest and weakest, she was being literally savaged by the others. As I turned the corner, the poor little thing's stomach had been torn open and there was blood and mess everywhere. Christopher Bray, the Queen's page, had heard the growling, yelping commotion, and, together, we managed the mayhem by snatching each dog from the mêlée and locking it behind a separate closed door.

In the process, we were both bitten and nipped, but I was shaking: I was convinced little Jolly was going to die. Not only that, the Queen would be furious.

The vet was called for the corgi and the doctor to treat Christopher's and my bites. It was nothing a tetanus jab and bandage couldn't mend, but Jolly was taken away and underwent emergency surgery. She survived, but only after twenty stitches to her abdomen.

When the Queen returned from dinner, I broke the news of the incident with some trepidation. It was then that I first discovered Her Majesty's tolerance. She was aghast but understanding. She went into her dressing room and came back with two homeopathic painkillers for me to take. "Here, Paul, this will help the healing process," she said.

Unbeknownst to me at the time, the dogs fought regularly. When they snapped and snarled at feeding time, the Queen shouted at them: "Oh, do shut up!" They would fall silent; for even the dogs obeyed the Queen.

While feeding the corgis, conversations often revolved around the subjects most important to the Queen: horses, dogs, Prince Philip, and her children. It was the joke among staff that such topics came in that order of importance. That is a little unfair. It is just that she is perhaps *more pas-*

sionate about horses and dogs. Wherever the Queen went, the dogs followed. The noise of scampering paws and panting breath became an early radar signal that Her Majesty was close at hand. The Duke of Edinburgh, for one, needed no reminding of their omnipresence. As the Queen sat working, the corgis slept as doorstops at the several entrances into the sitting room. They nearly always blocked his path, and he had to nudge the door open. In his husky voice, he once said: "Bloody dogs! Why do you have to have so many?"

"But, darling, they're so collectible," she replied.

FEEDING THEM was easy. Walking them was a chore, especially at Balmoral Castle in Scotland, where the climate could be so rainy. Her Majesty was adept at dropping the hint that it was time for a walk when the weather was foul. "Outies," she'd call, and I'd have no choice. Oh, God, I thought, because a walk had to be at least forty-five minutes. "Come on, Chipper, Piper, Smokey . . ." I attached nine red leads and trudged outside into the driving rain. In the bleak Scottish hills, I soon found shelter from a downpour in dense woodland near the river Dee, a short walk from the castle. I'd let the corgis run about there while giving the impression I had walked miles and miles. Each dog's collar had a round disk that was inscribed "HM The Queen" in case any got lost, which was the worst possible prospect. I shall never forget the day I came back with only eight drenched dogs. After forty-five minutes outside, I traipsed back, tired and wet.

"Oh, there's only eight," the Queen said with alarm. Shadow was missing.

Horror must have registered on my face, but the Queen just looked at me.

"Don't worry, Your Majesty, I'll go back out and find her." Still sheets of rain. Half an hour later, I found Shadow by the River Dee and I could breathe again.

Chipper became my firm favorite, and the Queen sensed the affinity between us. After I had been in service for a year she allowed him to sleep in my room, but only at Balmoral, Sandringham, and Windsor. At Buckingham Palace, my living quarters were deemed too far away, on the top floor. Everywhere else, though, Chipper slept at my feet at the bottom of a single bed until he died nine years later.

ROUTINE GOVERNS the monarch's life. The Queen's dresser entered the bedroom at 8 A.M. with the "calling tray" and a china pot of Earl Grey tea. The corgis rushed in and greeted her as the curtains were drawn back.

The royal milkman delivered his crate from Windsor long before anyone was awake. A herd of Jersey cows in Windsor Great Park provides the Royal Family with a daily fresh supply of milk in wide-necked bottles stamped in blue "EiiR Royal Dairy, Windsor," and sealed with a green-and-gold top. Cream arrives in waxed cartons emblazoned with a similar cipher.

At 9 A.M., Her Majesty walked through her sitting room and into her dining room, carrying her old-fashioned Roberts radio tuned permanently to BBC Radio 2. Minutes earlier, I had set a small dining table with a frugal breakfast: one slice of granary toast, a smear of butter, and a thin layer of dark, chunky marmalade. The room was used for family meals, but the Queen often ate here alone. The round table, big enough to seat four, was in the center of the room. The sunlight cast a silhouette of the large paneled window onto the huge rug that covered the floor. Gold-framed landscape paintings from the Royal Collection hung on walls, decorated with paneled blue silk.

It became a familiar sight to watch the Queen standing at the sideboard, waiting for the electric kettle to boil so that she could brew herself some tea in a silver teapot. She sat down and scanned the British newspapers, laid out in required order in a neat, flat file that showed each masthead: from the bottom, *The Times*, the *Daily Telegraph*, the *Daily Express*, the *Daily Mail*, and the *Daily Mirror*, with the full front of a folded *Sporting Life* horseracing paper on top. Her favorite magazines were *Harpers & Queen*,

Tatler, and *Horse and Hound.* She never read the *Sun* or the *Daily Star,* but was always informed of every royal story, thanks to a detailed summary compiled each morning by the press office and laid out next to the newspapers.

The *Daily Telegraph* was folded so that the crosswords faced out. The Queen always *had* to complete both puzzles. She sometimes fell weeks behind, but the daily crosswords were saved in an ever-growing pile and traveled with her to be tackled wherever she was in the world.

The first newspaper she always picked up was the *Sporting Life* to scan the day's race meetings and read the form. Her small pocket racing diary was constantly updated by her racing manager, with the dates, meetings, and types of race her horses would be competing in. On those days, when the Queen's colors were on any race card, she was even more eager to read the form and size up the rest of the field. If the Queen ever had an escape from duties of state, it was her passion for horses. She was fascinated with the "Sport of Kings," from horses to trainers, jockeys to stable hands, winners and losers.

If you ever need to engage in small talk with the Queen, the subject of horses is a surefire winner. But be sure to know your subject: her knowledge is expert and vast, from the winners of classic races to the structure of handicaps or weights, to the intricacies of breeding. I never dared take on such expertise. But I did occasionally hint that I'd love a tip from the top when one of her favorite horses ran.

"I see that High Clere is running today, Your Majesty. Does it stand a chance?" I said one day. "It depends, Paul," she replied, then launched into a scientific explanation of weights, rivals, class, and going, leaving me none the wiser. So, a royal tip never came my way but, loyal to the end, I would always back the Queen's horses at Royal Ascot and Epsom for the Derby, the one classic flat race that continues to elude her stable.

AT 10 A.M., the day's business began. The Queen sat at her desk in the sitting room, near the large window, with an old-fashioned switchboard-style speaker system in front of her. She pressed the thick, square button marked "Private Secretary" and said, ever so jolly, "Would you come up, please?"

"Of course, ma'am." Seconds later, the private secretary—Sir Martin Charteris, in those days—walked briskly along the corridor, carrying a small square basket of letters. With a gentle tap on the door, he entered and, for around an hour, stood beside the seated monarch to sort the queries, engagements and dilemmas of the country and Commonwealth. (Private secretaries—or anyone else, for that matter—never sit during an audience with the Queen unless invited to do so.)

The Queen is used to a day working alone at her desk or eating in her own company. There was no speakerphone to summon a footman or page when she needed one. Instead, she pressed a bell and a red disk dropped into a small round window of a wooden box on the wall in the pantry opposite her apartment. Each window was labeled SITTING ROOM, BEDROOM, DINING ROOM, AUDIENCE ROOM, DRAWING ROOM, and so on, and soon someone would be at her side.

The hours between eleven o'clock and one were allocated for private audiences at the palace or prelunch engagements. It was also when government ministers, privy councillors, or high commissioners were presented to the Queen in the splendor of the Bow Room or the eighteenth-century room to mark their appointment to office in a ceremony dictated by ancient tradition, called "kissing hands." Each appointee would kneel and, with his right hand, take her extended right hand—fingers slightly closed—and brush it with the lightest of kisses.

Throughout all these engagements, the Queen remained standing, sometimes for two hours at a time. It was little wonder that on her return to her sitting room she would ask: "Is the drinks tray ready, Paul?"

I had anticipated her request, since she often made herself a large glass of her favorite preluncheon tipple, gin and Dubonnet, in equal half measures, with two lumps of ice and a slice of lemon. Lunch was always at one o'clock and lasted approximately an hour.

* * *

IF THERE WAS no engagement, the corgis and the Queen went on afternoon walks in the gardens for up to two hours. As she donned headscarf and overcoat, she often turned to me and said: "Would you mind recording the race?," an instruction to set the video recorder for a televised meeting at Epsom or Ascot, York or Goodwood. If a race meeting was not televised, a special broadcasting live link—the same audio service fed into betting shops nationwide—was boomed into Buckingham Palace. She listened intently to a specific race for the name of one of her horses. Footman and pages learned never to interrupt the Queen during a race. It would have been the height of rudeness. For those three minutes, anything and everything could wait.

Wherever she was in the world, tea was served on the stroke of five o'clock. Whether she was in a Saudi Arabian royal palace, aboard the royal yacht *Britannia* or at Buckingham Palace, I ensured there was Earl Grey tea with a spot of milk, a sandwich with the crusts removed, and something sweet. Hot fruit scones, baked daily by pastry chef Robert Pine, were hardly ever eaten by the royals. The Queen always broke them up and fed them, piece by piece, to the corgis, treats for which they would beg, roll over, or spin round on the spot.

Tea finished, the drinks tray reappeared, but never before six, and the Queen enjoyed a gin and tonic. An official early-evening function, a cocktail party or dinner engagement, might complete a royal day. If a hectic schedule allowed, the Queen and the Duke of Edinburgh could relax together and enjoy dinner with the corgis spread out around the room. It was served at 8:15 P.M. at every royal residence—unless the Queen Mother was a guest.

For the Queen Mother was always late. Always. Strict timetables overran and dinner could be 8:30 P.M. or even 9 P.M. And she always arrived like an innocent. "Oh, am I late? Are you waiting for me?" she would say.

Clocks even stopped for her when gathering for church. Once, at Sandringham, the men had already set off and the Queen was waiting, with a lady-in-waiting, as I stood by the doors as usual. The service should have begun at 11 A.M. As the clock ticked on, an exasperated Queen stretched on her black gloves, finger by finger, and said: "Is Queen Elizabeth coming or are we waiting for nothing?"

On the stroke of eleven, a shuffling sound was heard coming down the corridor and the Queen Mother arrived with the customary large hat strewn with feathers. "Oh, am I late? Have you been waiting long?"

Thankfully, the Queen's routine normally went like clockwork. At Buckingham Palace, after being alone for dinner, the television was switched on in either the dining room or the sitting room. I'd stand just inside the doorway—and linger to provide a few extra moments of company as the Queen watched a murder mystery or the BBC *Nine O'Clock News*.

Once, when I was standing idly in the pantry, I heard a royal commotion. A whoop of delight came from the sitting room, backed up by a chorus of barking corgis. The page, Christopher Bray, and I looked at each other, bemused. We both dashed to the door, opened it and were beckoned in by the Queen. "Come quick—come quick," she said excitedly. She was on her feet, beaming with delight. "How wonderful," she said. Torvill and Dean had just won the gold medal at the Sarajevo Olympic Games with their ice-dance performance to Ravel's *Boléro*.

After dinner before each working day was over, I had two remaining duties to fulfill. I placed two glasses on a tray with a bottle of still Malvern water for the Queen, and a bottle of Glenfiddich whisky and a small bottle of Double Diamond beer for the Duke of Edinburgh. Then I took the corgis for their last walk. On my return, I led them to their room on the Queen's corridor. Her Majesty sometimes joined me for this bedtime ritual. Sometimes in full evening dress, perhaps, with a diamond necklace and earrings, she got down on her hands and knees, determined to make sure each was comfortable in its own basket or beanbag. "Make sure the window is open for them. Good night, Paul." For me, another day was over.

The Queen, though, had one more task. Before she

turned out the light, she religiously filled in her personal diary—always in pencil. One day, it would serve as a historical record, just like the diaries of Queen Victoria, for the Royal Collection. The Queen, even at bedtime, was bound by a sense of duty.

IN MAY 1978, a new girl joined the household as a seamstress. Her duties were to darn the socks of Prince Philip, make alterations to suits and shirts, patch bedsheets, and wash the corgis' towels. For a time, I didn't take much notice of her. She was diligent and, if first impressions mattered, easygoing, bright, and cheery. She didn't like me.

I think becoming the Queen's footman so quickly went to my head. The teenage boy from the northern pit village was now sharing chats with the monarch, trusted to make her life work. Such success broadened my horizons. I realized that anything was possible, and had a new confidence that made me walk those royal corridors as if I were ten feet tall. Even my northern accent was being chipped away and wrapped up in the grandness of palace language. I could never forget my roots or values, but perhaps, in those early days, I became too big for my boots. Certainly, the new recruit thought so. The daughter of staunch Catholic parents from Liverpool, she had arrived in London from the small village of Holt in North Wales.

It seemed that my mistake had been to march into the linen room with the corgis' dirty linen and drop it at her feet with the grand announcement: "Towels!"

She didn't need to express her disdain; the look on her face said it all. She told friends I was nothing but a "two-pence-ha'penny toff." Her name was Maria Cosgrove. My future wife.

By 1979, Maria had been promoted to senior housemaid and was given responsibility for the Belgian Suite, a self-contained suite of rooms overlooking the gardens. It was the most important suite in the palace, because it always accommodated visiting heads of state.

Maria's promotion coincided with my first state carriage

drive, as Queen's footman, in the spring. Dressed in full state livery, wearing the blue velvet riding cap, I perched on the back of the 1902 gilded state landau with its huge brass lanterns in procession from Victoria Station to the palace, via Whitehall and the Mall. The traditional duty of a footman is to protect all who ride in that carriage with his sword, but just being so close to Her Majesty and riding out with her for the first time in front of cheering crowds brought an internal euphoria.

I was on the left side directly behind the Queen, who wore a pink hat. Next to her was President Nicolae Ceauşescu of Romania, who slept in the Belgian Suite—with a gun under his pillow. Riding alongside me, on one of the horses from the Blues and Royals Household Cavalry Division that flanked the landau, was someone the Queen knew well: Lieutenant Colonel Andrew Parker Bowles, married to Camilla for the previous six years.

A TINY GATHERING OF footmen huddled around the drinks tray in the saloon drawing room at Sandringham House. Beside the grand piano and beneath the wooden balustrade of the minstrels' gallery, the footmen and housemaids had been busy: new logs were stacked beside the eight-foot-high baronial stone fireplace, with its lion and unicorn fenders; empty crystal glasses had been collected from the vast room's side tables; the carpet had been swept, cushions plumped, and the card table folded away after canasta and bridge. The Royal Family had retired to their rooms to change for dinner.

The footmen thought the coast was clear and decided to sneak a sly shot of gin. After all, no one would know how much had been consumed by the guests. As one footman tilted his head to knock back that quick drink, his eyes spotted a familiar face watching from a small internal window above. It was the Queen.

The footman almost choked. The Queen didn't report this serious breach of the rules, although her look said it all. It illustrated her acceptance of her staff's arduous duty and isolation from the outside world. The tolerance of the Queen was legendary.

Once when I was with the Queen, feeding the corgis in a narrow, ground-floor passageway at Sandringham, a door leading from staff accommodation to the main house burst open. Out spilled a senior member of staff, clearly drunk, who staggered and bounced off the wall opposite. Weaving through a minefield of corgis, he saw the Queen—watching him with fork and spoon in hand—slurred something unintelligible, and went on his way. I was convinced she would be furious and sack that long-serving individual for such behavior.

The Queen simply raised her eyebrows, said nothing, and went on feeding the corgis. The man got away with it. Unlike me. At Sandringham, I once removed a glass of gin and tonic from the Queen's sitting room, wrongly believing she had finished with it and gone to change for dinner.

Maria and the Queen's dresser, Elizabeth Andrew, were hiding in a cupboard under the stairs, out of sight as required, waiting for Her Majesty to go down for dinner so that they could tidy her room when they heard the Queen's consternation: "The beast—the beast. He's taken my brand-new drink!" and she went after me down the corridor.

PERHAPS THE QUEEN'S tolerance would not have been so great had she known the full truth of backstairs antics. Gin was also the favorite of many household staff, and also the most accessible. Footmen became expert at siphoning off gin every day from crystal decanters and pouring sneaky supplies into chrome kettles. No passing member of the household could suspect a footman walking down a corridor with a tea kettle. Pages were perhaps more cunning. Empty tonic-water bottles were filled with gin and concealed on the inside back of their tailcoats, which had pouched pockets sewn into the lining.

These supplies were used to keep afloat the giddy drinking parties in the corridors of the living quarters. Household staff worked hard and played hard, and spontaneous social occasions were many—lunchtimes and evenings. If the Queen didn't know about the secret gin stocks, she definitely knew a party scene existed, which she no doubt tolerated because of the release it gave loyal staff.

For parties, the below-stairs corridors would be festooned with bunting. No one kept their door shut. Music would fill the floors, and we danced to Donna Summer, Barry White, and Abba. We had to steer clear of the housekeeper, Victoria Martin, who had a schoolmistress attitude to discipline. "Boys are not allowed on the female wing!" she bellowed to me one afternoon. All I had done was take a shortcut from the nursery corridor to the Pages' Lobby via Finch's Lobby. She was fiercely protective of her girls and loathed the idea of housemaids and dressers straying onto the corridors of pages and footmen, or vice versa.

She patrolled those floors regularly. A royal standard of cleanliness was applied to servants' quarters for the women, and Miss Martin was a former naval officer. Maids were often heard to mutter, "Miss Martin has gone berserk again." The party scene had to be cleverly planned to coincide with the housekeeper's absence, a trip away, a vacation, or when she was tucked up in bed.

The staff who traveled to Sandringham or Balmoral found more liberal housekeepers in charge. This led to daily soirées, at which everyone broke free of the straitjacket of duty and let down their hair. Perhaps it was no wonder, in the Scottish Highlands of Aberdeenshire at least, that staff labeled it "Immoral Balmoral."

FOR THE QUEEN'S annual summer vacation, the court moves from Buckingham Palace to Balmoral Castle every year from the beginning of August to the beginning of October. In those days, the House of Windsor always traveled north aboard the royal yacht *Britannia* from Portsmouth on the weeklong Western Isles Cruise, which skirted the west coast of Britain through the Irish Sea and the scattering of Scottish islets before heading east en route to Aberdeen.

Cabin No. 44 on the lowest deck was mine from 1979 to 1986. It had a sliding metal door, one porthole, single bunk, writing bureau, and stainless-steel sink. It was unnerving to know that only a sheet of metal, held together by rivets, was between me and the sea. Directly beneath were the ship's propellers, which, come nighttime, sent me to sleep with a rapid, pulsing, mechanical whirl. On rough passages, the view from the porthole was like a washing machine on full spin.

Everything forward (for'ard) of the main mast was Royal Navy accommodation, with 250 officers and "yachties." Everything at the rear (aft) was the royal household, approximately thirty-strong and headed by the Queen.

Being at sea meant leaving behind one crucial duty—walking the corgis. They always flew to Aberdeen aboard an Andover of the Queen's Flight. Duty focused on looking after Her Majesty on the rear veranda deck, which comprised a glass-fronted sun lounge leading onto an open deck with a view of the ship's wake melting into the distance. A naval frigate always followed within sight.

Every day for breakfast at nine and tea at five I set up a card table for the Queen and Prince Philip. They joined everyone else in the dining room on the main deck for lunch at one and dinner at eight-fifteen. Crested china was used every day—the *same* collection from the royal yacht *Victoria and Albert*.

Negotiating the ship's passages, while loaded with the Queen's wooden tray, was an art in itself. It had to be turned lengthways to fit the narrow gangways and steep ladderlike metal steps. On many occasions, one roll of the ship toppled the tray and smashed cups, saucers, and plates. Serving meals in rough seas, as the ship rolled in a heavy swell, was quite an ordeal. I learned to stand with feet wide and knees bent for balance, and the Queen found it amusing not only to see members of the household turn green, but also the clownlike waitering of her footman.

On calmer days, in early evening, *Britannia* dropped anchor in a shallow bay. Motor launches ferried the royal party ashore for barbecues on deserted beaches with meat already prepared by the chef. Naval officers manned the open fire as the royals sat on rocks and rugs. This left household staff to relax aboard and hold drinks receptions or quizzes between separate messes, with questions broadcast by the wireless operator over the Tannoy.

O NE HIGHLIGHT for the Queen, as *Britannia* sailed off the Scottish coast of Caithness, was to pass the home of her mother. The Castle of Mey was perched on the edge of a cliff. Household staff appeared on deck and we waved napkins, tablecloths, or sheets as officers set off flares and sounded the deep blaring of the ship's whistle. By way of reply, the Queen Mother's staff hung linen from the turrets and leaded windows and set off fireworks from the rooftop. It was an impressive hello and goodbye. The Queen, armed with binoculars, stood on her deck and scanned for a sight of the Queen Mother, who, from land, also scanned for a sight of her daughter. When they spotted each other, they waved excitedly. The next time they met was a few days later, at Balmoral, when the Queen Mother would stay at the castle for two weeks before moving to her residence on the estate, Birkhall.

In preparation for the Balmoral vacation, and while *Britannia* was crawling up the coast, the Army had been transporting tons of luggage, in hundreds of trunks, from Buckingham Palace. The Queen packs up house and home, and temporarily deserts palace life. Huge white dust sheets are spread throughout her entire apartments, smothering her desk, sofas, chairs, dining table, and sideboards. Staff pack entire traveling wardrobes on casters, trunks of hats, china, silverware, crystal, framed photographs, boxes of books, television sets, video recorders, radios, spirits and fine wines. A single black dress and hat are included in case there should be a death. One leather trunk is packed with at least twenty tartan rugs, and another contains a prized collection of kilts.

Her majesty wore a kilt every day at Balmoral, as did the Queen Mother, Princess Margaret, and Princess Anne. The Queen wore the red Royal Stewart tartan or the green Hunting Stewart, but her favorite was the gray Balmoral tartan, which can only be worn by members of the Royal Family. Princes Philip, Charles, Andrew, and Edward even wore kilts as evening wear, with a black tie, but the ladies always changed from their day kilts into evening dress.

Skipping, interlinking arms, and weaving across the wooden-floored ballroom, waves of dancing tartan washed and swirled together at the Gillies Ball, the highlight of the Balmoral social season, when the ladies wore tartan sashes pinned with diamond brooches. It was one party scene of which Miss Victoria Martin approved, where the family, the household and estate staff mingled and danced together, Queen, Duke, princes, princesses, footmen, housemaids, gillies, and gardeners. A contingent of the Scottish Guard, the Black Watch, with its uniform of blue-and-green tartan kilts, would stand in the minstrels' gallery and fill the room with the strains of the bagpipes and bellowing accordions. Rhythmic clapping and whoops of delight would rise from the floor below.

It was in 1979 that I danced with the Queen—if not quite alone, on a packed floor filled with 150 people. In the interchanging sea of partners, the footman came up against the monarch in a dance called "The Gay Gordons." My linked line of three servants came face-to-face with another line of three with Her Majesty on one end. The two threesomes joined to form a circle of six and my hand linked with the Queen's. All I can remember is trying not to squeeze too hard with my sweaty palm.

The Queen's Pipe Major announced each dance, and, whenever there was a family dinner, he played his bagpipes around the table. But he had a more traditional duty each morning, in a custom started by Queen Victoria and continued by successive monarchs ever since. On the stroke of 9 A.M. each morning, at wherever the Queen is in official residence, he plays the bagpipes and marches alone beneath her bedroom window for ten minutes, a ritual to signal the beginning of the day. The tradition took on an extra charm as the sound of the bagpipes drifted down the glens around the 50,000 acres of Balmoral.

It is a magical castle, built by Prince Albert in 1853 for Queen Victoria so that she could escape the pressures of public life and relax with her family. Balmoral, more than any other residence, still retains that feel of a warm, family home where procedures are not so tight, life is more informal, and the Queen is in top form. As it was for her great-great-grandmother Victoria, the isolation of Balmoral is the perfect haven for the Queen, who, as a countrywoman, loves nothing more than walking through the Scottish glens. If Buckingham Palace is her office, Windsor Castle is her favorite weekend retreat. Sandringham House is perfect for shooting parties, but in an ideal world Balmoral would be her home.

Time seems to have stood still at the turreted castle, with ivy creeping round its gray stone walls. The *VRI*—the imperial ciphers of Queen Victoria—still adorns the flocked wallpaper that lines the magnificent hallways, and a green Hunting Stewart tartan carpet disappears down the gloomy corridors. Love of the country life and outdoor pursuits is seen throughout the castle in the fishing rods, waders, and landing nets that hang in the wood-paneled hallway where a grandfather clock stands on the black-and-white-checkered marble floor; stags' heads stare down from almost every wall in every corridor, hunting trophies from the past stalking expeditions of previous monarchs; beneath them, Landseer paintings depict more stags standing in misty glens and spaniels bounding through the heather and peat.

It was a self-sufficient lifestyle. Salmon caught in the River Dee and deer shot on the hills provided the first and main course at dinner. Fruit—blueberries, raspberries, and loganberries—picked fresh from the kitchen garden was served for dessert. Dinner never cost much at Balmoral, and the Queen was economical with the running costs of a private residence where she paid the bills and abhorred waste. Scraps from the dinner table fed the corgis. She walked around the castle switching off lights in unoccupied rooms to save energy. In the mornings, she only turned the electric heater on low in her dressing room.

Her Majesty seemed hardened to the cold and drafts. She regularly slept with the windows open to the elements. In mid-October, it was not unusual for dressers to find snow and frost, which come early to the Highlands, on the carpet beneath the windowsill. The corgis often huddled around that one electric heater.

My living quarters were equally chilly. So much so that a royal castle in October almost reminded me of my childhood home in Grassmoor, with its cold linoleum floors and ice on the inside of the windows.

In childhood days, I scratched my name on the icy windows. In a tradition at Balmoral, honeymooning royal brides, who stayed in the Royal Visitors' Suite, scratched their names into the windowpane with the diamond of their engagement ring.

By the end of 1979, the media was speculating on who might be the next royal bride. The search was already on for a suitable Princess of Wales.

THREE

⚜

A Princess in Love

"**A** RE YOU LOST?" I asked the bewildered-looking houseguest. "Can I help you?"

"Yes. I *am* sorry. Could you please show me the way back to my room?" the young lady replied. She stood in the dim ground-floor corridor of Balmoral Castle on a Saturday morning in September 1980, where she'd interrupted my brisk walk toward the staircase to the Queen's corridor. She was scanning the typed cards in brass nameplates on each guest-room door. I recognized her from the previous night, when I had taken her suitcase to her room on the first floor. Getting lost was easy—each corridor mirrored the next, with virtually identical wooden doors and green tartan carpets.

The castle was quiet. Prince Charles was with the Duke of Edinburgh, Princes Andrew and Edward on stag-stalking expeditions. The Queen Mother and Princess Margaret rarely surfaced before midday. The Queen was in her sitting room.

The young lady could not have been more apologetic on the short walk up the staircase. She smiled awkwardly and said, "I *am* so sorry about this. It's difficult to find your way around a strange house the first time."

As we approached her room, I offered reassurance. "Don't worry. It's normal. If you need anything else, don't hesitate to ask. The staff here are a friendly bunch."

She thanked me, stepped into her room with its single bed, and closed the door. The nameplate read: "Lady Diana Spencer." A few feet farther down the corridor was the next room: "HRH The Prince of Wales." On a previous visit in August, Lady Diana had stayed with her sister Jane, who was married to Sir Robert Fellowes, the Queen's assistant private secretary, at their grace-and-favour cottage, more than a mile away. So it was her second visit to the Balmoral estate, but her first stay at the castle, and she was being entertained as a guest of Prince Charles, with a collection of his other friends.

PAULINE HILLIER, the housemaid assigned to Lady Diana, entered the ground-floor utility room holding, at head height, a simple long black evening dress on its hanger. I stood, drinking a mug of coffee. "This is my lady's dress. She's only got the one and she's here for three nights. What is she going to do?" she said, concerned for Lady Diana Spencer, the nursery-school assistant from London.

Most visiting ladies brought with them more than one evening dress, and there were anxious looks downstairs about whether she would be socially embarrassed. She was only nineteen, a mere teenager in a royal social circle full of men and ladies in their thirties and forties.

There was enough for a first-time guest to fret about without having to worry about their wardrobe. Staying at the castle could be an experience fraught with anxiety for any newcomer. One needed to know how to properly address members of the Royal Family; what time to appear for drinks; and how to make socially acceptable dinner-table conversation in order to be warmly accepted into the fold. As it turned out, glorious warm evenings saved her from a fashion faux pas. The dress had to be worn only once to dinner, because on the two other evenings barbecues were held.

In the eyes of the household, Lady Diana was just another guest, a Sloane-type escort for the then thirty-two-year-old Prince Charles. She was quiet, and blushed easily, but there was nothing extraordinary about her. If the staff noted anything, it was that she was pretty, polite, devoid of pomposity—and her wardrobe was inadequate for a lady on the arm of the heir to the throne.

NOT LONG AFTER, ladies-in-waiting had reviewed the scant wardrobe of the woman known universally as "Lady Di" more carefully. It was why they ordered an off-the-rack outfit from a London store: a bright blue skirt and collarless jacket with a white, high-necked blouse and matching blue shoes. The princess-to-be did not have anything regarded as suitable for a special occasion. Something smart and businesslike was considered de rigueur for February 24, 1981, when the public announcement would be made at Buckingham Palace of her engagement to Prince Charles.

Before the announcement, downstairs had been abuzz with gossip, just as the media was hysterical with speculation. Word in the footmen's room, pantries, and kitchens since before Christmas was: "Lady Di is the one." Lady Amanda Knatchbull had been a previous favorite. She was the granddaughter of Lord Mountbatten—Prince Philip's uncle who had been murdered by an IRA bomb. But the smart money on Lady Amanda was blown away the moment Crown jeweler David Thomas visited the palace the week before the engagement.

He was spotted with a small attaché case, and the official word was that it contained signet rings for Prince Andrew to choose from as a gift for his twenty-first birthday on February 19. Few in the household believed this because, for such an accepted tradition, the operation was far too cloak-and-dagger, and the gossip moved up a gear.

David Thomas, responsible for the upkeep of the Crown

Jewels in the Jewel House at the Tower of London, had in fact brought ladies' rings. He had strict instructions not to include rubies or emeralds. A selection of diamonds and sapphires was set on a tray for—oddly—the Queen's perusal. Once the monarch had made her choice, the Prince of Wales gave his approval. Lady Diana was third in line to offer her opinion. The bride-to-be accepted the selection that had effectively been made for her, because she did not want to appear rude and ungrateful. As she later told me: "I would never have chosen something quite so gaudy. If I had the chance again, it would be more elegant and simple."

On the day the secret emerged, no one downstairs had an inkling of what was to be announced. The morning had started normally when I served the Queen breakfast at 9 A.M. Then she suddenly changed the strict timetable. "We will have tea at four o'clock," she told me, bringing forward her schedule by an hour. "There will be four of us—His Royal Highness [the Duke of Edinburgh], the Prince of Wales, and Lady Diana Spencer." She had to tell me this because I needed to know how many places to set for either ladies or gentlemen: ladies have small teacups; gentlemen have large breakfast cups. I knew the engagement was imminent: the timetable had been changed at short notice, and it was the first time Lady Diana had taken tea with the Queen.

Thus, I was among the first in Britain to know, and I was filled with excitement. After laying the table, I deliberately hung around in the Queen's corridor to catch a glimpse of the happy couple. Prince Charles and Lady Diana were smiling as they walked past me, hand in hand.

John Taylor, the Queen's page, went inside the dining room with a plate of hot scones. I couldn't resist peeking at the gathering through the gap at the door's hinge. Lady Diana sat, in her new blue outfit, with her prospective in-laws, bolt upright. She looked frightened to death. Afterward, clearing the table, I noticed she hadn't touched a scone or drunk her tea. I would learn later that she only drank coffee.

But it was no wonder she was a nervous wreck: tea with the Queen was followed by a loving public parade before the world's media in a carefully managed announcement. The prince and his fiancée had to walk out of the Bow Room, the central room at the rear on the ground floor, down the sweeping stone steps onto the lawn, where a bank of TV cameras, boom microphones, reporters, and photographers had congregated.

I had ten minutes to spare and had prepared to watch that moment of history from a first-floor audience room, but I hadn't reckoned on the Queen foiling my plan. "Paul, could you take the dogs out round the back of the lake? It will cause the least bother," she instructed me.

The corgis had probably never been leashed so quickly or walked so fast, because I was determined not to miss out. With nine corgis in tow, I dashed round to the far side of the lake just in time to see the prince and Lady Diana walk down those steps.

From that vantage point, I witnessed history in miniature: I really needed binoculars to see the two figures parading down the lawn, then standing for interviews before a constant flickering of silent flashbulbs.

"HAVE YOU SEEN HER? She's down there all by herself," said Mark Simpson late one night. He had made a discreet check on Lady Diana Spencer, who had moved into Buckingham Palace post-engagement. Mark couldn't help feeling sorry for the new lady in residence. "Let's go out and get her something from McDonald's," he suggested, a man on a mercy mission.

Lady Diana Spencer was alone in her room. Prince Charles was away on a month-long tour of Australia. His fiancée, used to living in a London flat shared with girl-friends, found herself in her own company for hours on end now. Mark was my next-door neighbor on the Pages' Lobby. He was also the household footman assigned to the Royal Nursery corridor, where Princes Andrew and Edward had kept rooms since childhood, and where their brother's fiancée had been allocated a bedroom, bathroom and an adjoining kitchen and utility area. She had moved to the palace for the five months prior to the wedding in July. Prince Charles's vast bachelor apartment was on the same floor but far from the nursery corridor.

Mark was tired after a full day on duty, but he couldn't bear to see Lady Diana so isolated. "We could have a little picnic and brighten up her day. Come on, let's go to McDonald's," Mark insisted. I was nervous. What if the Queen found out? What if Lady Diana told Prince Charles? What would happen if the Master of the Household saw us? It was not part of our remit to provide company and spontaneous treats for the future Princess of Wales. She was living in royal rooms, and it was not our place to be there, let alone to entertain her.

I urged caution: "I'm not sure, Mark. What happens if we're caught? Our heads will be on the block."

"C'mon, Paul, she'll be grateful for the company." Mark grabbed his coat and headed for the door. His conviction won me over and, against my better judgment, we walked to Victoria Street and picked up three Big Macs. We returned through the side entrance; staff always went out for fast food, so there was nothing out of the ordinary as we headed up to the Pages' Lobby. But I was too frightened to join Mark on his mission. "You go, Mark," I said, and he did. Soon, he came back to fetch me, after checking that the coast was clear. "C'mon, then," he said.

Like naughty schoolchildren, we crossed the corridor. Out of uniform. A warning from training days raced through my mind: "*Never* be seen in royal corridors in your civvies." What I was doing was virtual sacrilege and downright foolish but I was intrigued by Lady Diana, who had seemed so friendly on first meeting, and I trusted Mark. I walked directly behind him. Onto the red carpet. We passed the day nursery, Prince Edward's door, Prince Andrew's door. And then we arrived at a slightly ajar door, which opened into Lady Diana's little kitchen area.

And there she was, already devouring her Big Mac. She giggled a lot and was so friendly and down-to-earth. She kept repeating how thoughtful Mark had been and how grateful she was to have such an unexpected interlude. If I hadn't been so worried about being there, perhaps I would have appreciated her charm more, but this was much worse than the prospect of being caught on the female wing in the staff living quarters. After about ten minutes we left, and I have never been so pleased to leave a royal room.

"You see? She's one of us," he said, as we hurried back along the corridor.

I never took such a risk again at the palace, even if Mark did. He became a regular after-hours companion and, in time, the inevitable happened. He was caught—in the bedroom of the princess, on the edge of her bed—by a staggered Prince Charles. Mark returned to the Pages' Lobby, absolutely mortified. Lady Diana had been dressed in her nightie, and it didn't look good—not that there was anything going on. It was regarded as bad form but, thankfully, he didn't get into too much trouble.

Shortly afterward, he received a copy of a press photograph of the royal bride-to-be. It was signed in black marker pen: "To Mark, with love from Diana." I suspect it was the first autographed picture she ever issued.

Lady Diana had a lonely time in those months leading up to the wedding. She dared not go out because of the intense media spotlight. A wrong turn down a corridor could lead to a cocktail party or an official reception. A closed door might open onto a private meeting. It is not a comfortable or easy place for any newcomer. In staff quarters, at least there was a camaraderie, banter, and a mini-community, which made life more bearable, but Lady Diana did not have the same support network to depend on. She would sit up late, writing letters to her friends. Also, when the prince was away, she plucked up the courage to build up communication with the Queen. Once a week, the phone rang on the Queen's corridor. "Will the Queen be dining alone today?" she asked, in a quiet, almost timid voice.

If there was no engagement planned, one of us would

ask the Queen, "Lady Diana was inquiring whether Your Majesty would be alone for dinner tonight?"

"Oh, do ask her to join me," the Queen would say. "Dinner will be at eight-fifteen." Not once did she refuse. But Lady Diana was uncomfortable that to communicate with her future mother-in-law, she had to go through pages or footmen. She made the effort once a week but preferred a quick dinner in her room, where she could curl up and relax.

She had a genuine affection for the Queen. I remember her appearing regularly on the corridor with wet hair, having been for a swim. "Is the Queen alone?" she would say. Then she tapped on the door and entered the sitting room, bright and breezy: "Good morning, Your Majesty."

It always brought a smile to the Queen's face, because Lady Diana was so cheerful. Once married, she would no longer need to call the Queen "Your Majesty." She received instructions instead to call her "Mama" and Prince Philip "Pa" in private.

The Queen was always accommodating, even if she rarely went out of her way to ensure that her prospective daughter-in-law was settled. Adaptability and strength of character are perceived as part of duty, and the Queen herself had had to learn the harsh protocols and isolation of palace life during her childhood. It was assumed that, as Lady Diana came from the nobility and was no stranger to large households, she would cope with the transition. It is ironic that the Queen left her to her own devices out of faith in her: she had adopted the trusting attitude that "if she needs me, she knows where I am." The monarch had belief in her—even if the future Princess of Wales did not share it.

For Diana, leaving behind her old life—the flat in London, and the children at the kindergarten—was upsetting. When she returned one day to see the children, all the youngsters she adored kept tugging on her sleeves and asking, "Where have you been?" and "When are you coming back?" She found the whole experience a "traumatic nightmare" and left close to tears.

It wasn't any easier when she returned to her old flat at No. 60 Colherne Court, where she had lived with female flatmates, to remove her most precious possessions. She was alone with her thoughts in a flat full of memories as she polished and vacuumed. As she closed the door behind her, she felt the urge to cry, she said.

But, deep down, she was excited, too, and knew she had to be strong. To tackle the boredom she kept busy. She focused on the wedding as David and Elizabeth Emmanuel, the designers charged with creating her dress, made regular visits to her room for consultations and fittings. On each occasion, the waist had to be nipped in because she was on a diet in anticipation of the big day.

She had ballet and tap lessons in the Throne Room, dancing in a leotard. There, on a stepped dais at one end of the room, two broad-backed thrones sat beneath a gold-tasseled dark crimson canopy, which draped in a loose *W* shape from an ornate gold pelmet. Every wall was papered in light crimson silk, which incorporated a subtle but darker diamond pattern outline.

The upholstered ceremonial chairs, with gilded arms and legs, were side by side, their crimson backs embroidered with gold thread—one marked "EiiR," the other bearing the letter *P*. The Queen's throne was an inch higher than that of the Duke of Edinburgh, as tradition dictates for the monarch. The enormity of Lady Diana's privileged position could not have been lost on her.

LADY DIANA WAS ALSO a keen swimmer and, like Princess Margaret, used the blue-and-white-tiled swimming pool with its springboard and diving board most mornings. The only access to the pool was via a corridor off the Belgian Suite, where each day she would cross the path of housemaid Maria Cosgrove. Pleasantries turned into brief conversations, which then became lengthy woman-to-woman chats about palace life. Neither woman was ever lost for words. Maria had no airs, and Lady Diana found in her a warm and approachable ally, just as she had in Mark Simpson.

With the staff, Lady Diana found friendship. She blended into downstairs life far better than she ever did upstairs, and perhaps that had something to do with the fact that the Spencers knew the life of service as well as that of nobility. Lady Diana's grandmother Ruth, Lady Fermoy, was a close friend of the Queen Mother. In the hive of activity downstairs, the future princess found banter and good company.

Where she had gingerly trodden along the red carpets of the upstairs corridors, wondering about every potential wrong turn, she explored the tiled floors of downstairs life freely. She often sat with Yeoman of the Silver Pantry Victor Fletcher, a no-nonsense Yorkshireman who always held one arm of his black-rimmed glasses in the corner of his mouth as if it were a pipe. He knew all about duty and devotion, and provided his insights to his fascinated listener, who afforded him respect and called him Mr. Fletcher. She also visited the royal pastry kitchen and specialist chef Robert Pine, a tall, handsome man with thick black hair and mustache, whose sharp, dry wit, delivered with a Devon accent, always made her giggle. His treat was dollops of homemade ice cream or spoonfuls of bread-and-butter pudding. She wandered into the coffee room and sat with head maid Ann Gardner, whose neat, precise dress belied a sense of fun that produced a plethora of party anecdotes, entertaining Lady Diana as she consumed bowls of cereal.

She popped into the linen room to chat with girls toiling over the laundry, or went to the kitchen and spent time with chef Mervyn Wycherley. A stocky, muscular man keen on bodybuilding, he was honest about everything and made her laugh. She liked his gentle nature, hidden behind a loud and larger-than-life character. He soon established himself as one of her favorites. Evelyn Dagley, a housemaid on the nursery corridor, was also a true ally. Along with Mark Simpson's, hers was one of the first friendly faces Lady Diana encountered. Evelyn—shy, diligent, and passionate about her work—made sure Lady Diana's room was as comfortable as possible and assumed responsibility for her ever-expanding wardrobe.

Lady Diana made many friends downstairs, even Cyril Dickman, the Palace Steward—the boss—who might have been aloof, but was easygoing and approachable. He was a natural father figure and the font of all knowledge royal, and a walking instruction manual on tradition, etiquette, and protocol. Diana never forgot his kindness and the time he gave her in those early days. In future years at Balmoral, she sought out Mr. Dickman, renowned for his dancing, for a fox-trot or waltz at the Gillies Ball.

So at ease was she that Lady Diana began to roam upstairs corridors to find staff in the middle of their duties to share a chat or lend a sympathetic ear. It was at odds with normal protocol, and some staff preferred such familiarity kept downstairs, even if they didn't say anything. Despite having allies in the engine room of royal life, Lady Diana did not win universal approval. Among the servants, there were certain sticklers for tradition. It was a strongly held opinion in certain quarters that she should "know her place and remain upstairs." One woman, who had been in the household for forty years, could not believe the audacity when Lady Diana opened cupboards and helped herself to biscuits. It was the height of bad manners, said the indignant woman.

A chef even confronted her when she walked into his kitchen. "You shouldn't be down here in the kitchen," he told her pointedly. Lady Diana, so used to friendliness downstairs, turned on her heels and ran upstairs.

The majority of staff, however—especially the junior members—embraced Lady Diana and turned a blind eye to the so-called breach of protocol. They called her "a breath of fresh air from upstairs."

What few probably realized at the time was that she was also on a scouting mission, checking out and selecting a potential team to run the Prince and Princess of Wales's two new homes: the country retreat of Highgrove, Gloucestershire, and an apartment at Kensington Palace, London. Prince Charles had bought Highgrove, a three-story Georgian country house and estate, in 1980—the year before he became engaged. Its location in the Cotswolds was con-

venient for many things. It was about eight miles from Gatcombe Park and his sister Princess Anne. Close to the
Beaufort Hunt and a short drive from Bolehyde Manor,
the home of Lieutenant Colonel Andrew Parker Bowles
and his wife, Camilla.

THE PRINCESS OF WALES was grinning from ear to
ear and in full flight, bounding with the grace of a ballet dancer down the red carpet, cream silk slippers in one
hand, her twenty-five-foot bridal train rolled around the
other arm. She was being herself on a wedding day suffocated by pomp and pageantry, unrestricted for one small
moment by protocol. It was minutes after the world had
seen her kiss her prince on the balcony of Buckingham
Palace on July 29, 1981. The bride had taken me by surprise. I stood alone in scarlet livery, leaning casually
against a side wall in the Queen's corridor, wondering
when Her Majesty would return to her apartment. That
would be the signal that the bridal party was drifting back
from the Centre Room, which leads to the balcony, for the
wedding breakfast.

The new princess, surrounded by billowing ivory silk and
her veil streaming behind her, thought she had the run of
the carpet. One side of the corridor was made up of rows
of floor-to-ceiling French windows overlooking the quadrangle. She danced through the broad shafts of light on the
carpet, and the sun glinted off the Spencer family tiara. She
was full of confidence, brimming with life. She seemed so
happy and radiant. I knew it was an image to be remembered for the rest of my life, but I felt conspicuous and
didn't want to be caught staring at her in case I embarrassed her. I backed into the Queen's apartment and shut
the door.

It had been in that sitting room that I had witnessed
Lady Diana Spencer transformed into the Princess of
Wales, along with 750 million other television viewers. I
had sat cross-legged on the carpet in front of the
monarch's television set, surrounded by her corgis. Watch-

ing the royal television was technically not allowed, but, on that day at least, I knew the Queen wouldn't mind. Like the rest of the nation, this Queen's footman was mesmerized by the images of the day: the mass crowds; Lady Diana waving with her father, Earl Spencer, in the Glass Coach en route to St. Paul's Cathedral; her wedding train swamping the red-carpeted aisle; the Prince and Princess of Wales emerging on the steps. My duty was to stay behind to prepare for the wedding breakfast in the Ball Supper Room, next to the Picture Gallery, and the television was useful for monitoring progress, although I spent half the time looking for the Queen's other footman, Paul Whybrew, who had been lucky enough to ride behind Her Majesty and the Duke of Edinburgh in an open landau in the state procession.

As the newlyweds swept into the quadrangle, I remained glued to the television. On the screen I watched the Prince and Princess of Wales walk out onto the balcony—but in the room, I could of course hear the rapturous cheers of the crowd massed outside. I bolted upstairs to my top-floor room, which overlooked the Victoria memorial and the Mall, and knelt at the low, oblong window. As thousands of people from the outside took a picture of the golden couple, I took one from inside of the people, then rushed back downstairs. It was the same crowd that had kept me awake on the eve of the wedding, singing "God Bless the Prince of Wales" and "God Save the Queen," as a party atmosphere gripped the country. It had been a weeklong crescendo of hype.

TWO DAYS BEFORE the wedding, a reception, dinner and ball for almost a thousand guests had been held at Buckingham Palace, bringing together the crowned heads of Europe, ambassadors, high commissioners, archbishops and bishops, government ministers and prime ministers, past and present, using every palace reception room. I was assigned to the Throne Room, and, along with a senior page, looked after a round table of ten guests, which included the Prince of Wales, the then Lady Diana, and Princess Grace of Monaco, escorted by her son, Prince Albert. I have never seen such a beauty as Princess Grace, the legendary actress the world knew as Grace Kelly, who was married to Prince Rainier of Monaco. That evening she even outshone the bride-to-be, and her tiara was every bit as magnificent as the Queen's.

Lady Diana was captivated. The two ladies struck up an immediate rapport and were locked in conversation before the dancing began. In Princess Grace, Lady Diana had found a role model and inspirational figure: an outsider like her, who had married into royalty; a film star used to the media glare; a woman in a royal marriage where love was infected by duty. She asked Princess Grace for advice. "You will be just fine," said the former actress. "It gets worse, but you learn to cope."

AT THE WEDDING BREAKFAST, my greatest challenge was to avoid stepping on the princess's dress, which seemed to spill everywhere. I served the top table, which included the bride and groom, both sets of parents, bridesmaids, pages, and Princes Andrew and Edward.

Ceremony and protocol had returned, calming Princess Diana's spontaneous exuberance. The princess was quiet as she nibbled at the food. She would tell me, many years later: "My stomach was in knots. I was shattered." Despite her nerves, though, she felt a bright future lay ahead. All she ever longed for was a happy marriage with Prince Charles. The princess didn't just love him: she adored him.

IN LATER LIFE, the princess had one wish: that a more informed account would portray her true love for Prince Charles. She felt the public had been given a misleading impression of their relationship. Book after book and article after article have distorted history by virtually erasing the happiness and true love that existed in the early period of their marriage. It can be argued that the princess was partly responsible for some of that distortion when she col-laborated with journalist Andrew Morton for the publica-tion in June 1992 of his book, *Diana: Her True Story,* which was revised after her death. In it, he claimed it was the nearest anyone would get to reading the autobiography of the princess. That could never be true. For if, one day, the princess had chosen to pen her memoirs, she would have erased the false image of eternal misery that was said to have begun on day one of her marriage.

Had her true opinions been taken down in later life, with the benefit of hindsight, and not in 1992, when she made an emotional cry for help, the world would have had a different picture of the foundations of the marriage. True love, for that was what it was on both sides, survived a difficult adjustment in the early years and, far from rejecting the princess, Prince Charles did his best to understand his wife and be patient with the mood swings brought on by the eating disorder bu-limia, which she later admitted to suffering. Indeed, the love the princess had for her husband never fully disappeared. When irreconcilable differences set in after 1985, a rift be-came a gulf. Bitterness led to an exchange of invective be-tween two people who didn't understand each other's needs, but there was no "War of the Waleses." Wars require hatred, and there was no hatred between them—if there was a war, it was fought above their heads between their divided camps, offices, and overprotective advisers.

What must be understood is that the princess, through friends, cooperated with Andrew Morton at a time when her marriage was falling apart, when she was emotionally confused, when she was grieving for her beloved father, the Earl Spencer, and when Prince Charles's friends were tak-ing stands against her and she felt under attack. As she ex-plained in later life: "It was as if everyone around me had six pairs of eyes instead of one, staring and judging me all the time." She was angry, bitter, and cooperated with Mor-ton at the most vulnerable time.

The book's publication had the desired effect. She no longer felt alone, because now the British people knew the truth, and understood why there had been no more royal children. "Everyone understood me better. The book was a release for both Charles and I because we didn't have to pretend anymore, even if he was furious with me," she said.

But it was a classic case of acting with haste and repenting at leisure. After the book's publication, hindsight taught her that her desperation to be heard had given a misleading impression of Prince Charles, and the book had painted over the good times. In giving an angry snapshot, she had made a mistake, she later acknowledged.

For that reason, the 1992 account should not be allowed, as Morton claims in good faith, to stand as the testimony she would have given in 1997. She wanted to say more. I hope that my account, with the assistance of correspondence from one of Diana's lifelong friends, will enable the untold truths to balance the picture.

O N THEIR HONEYMOON, the Prince and Princess of Wales sailed the Mediterranean aboard the royal yacht *Britannia,* and the princess felt blissfully happy, not—as other accounts inform us—rejected by the man she affectionately called "hubby." As she wrote to a very close friend from the yacht:

> *I couldn't be happier and would never of* [sic] *believed how content or wonderful I feel.*
> *The cruise on Britannia was extremely spoiling and we spent most of the time giggling. . . . Marriage suits me enormously and I just adore having someone to look after and spoil. It's the best thing that has ever happened to me—besides being the luckiest lady in the world.*

On the yacht, they watched endless reruns of the video of their wedding, the first time they had had a chance to see it. Man and wife were reduced to fits of giggles over the princess's slip-up at the altar when, in repeating her vows, she muddled the order of Prince Charles's names. So happy were they that as they sat holding each other and watching the ceremony, they both cried.

As the princess wrote to that friend:

> *We practically blub every time we watch a video of the wedding, and I can just imagine in ten years time, one of the minor Wales's [sic] saying "Why did you call Daddy 'Philip'?" Oh well, something to look forward to.*

Unlike other brides, the princess was not going to return to her old job, the one at a London kindergarten. A massive adjustment that few of us could comprehend was thrust upon her. With the onset of bulimia, her emotions, and consequently her moods, were up and down. It strikes me as odd that people should have been surprised, in the light of all the upheavals she faced. The truth is that had it not been for Prince Charles, the princess would never have coped. She knew that. He understood the adjustment she was having to make, and, for someone who was supposed to have been distant and perplexed by her moods, he did a good job at lifting her spirits. As the princess wrote: "I overcame those depressions all due to Charles with his patience and kindness. I couldn't get over how tired and miserable I got, which was grossly unfair to him."

From the yacht, the royal couple headed to Balmoral. Estate workers were so delighted to welcome them that they produced a two-seated open cart, strewn with masses of purple heather. They climbed aboard, laughing at the absurdity of being pulled manually up the slight incline to the castle door by gillies, gardeners, and grooms. The princess arrived with one hundred sixty mangoes, a gift from President Sadat of Egypt, who had been a guest aboard the yacht.

In the romantic setting of Balmoral Castle, Prince Charles read to her and she did tapestry. They walked hand in hand into the glens, and she looked forward to barbecues in the warm summer evenings at the log cabin on the estate. She even managed to read a whole book in one day for the first time in her life. What also delighted her was a surprise visit from her former flatmate, Carolyn Pride, later Bartholomew, who came to stay at the castle as a guest of Prince Andrew. The princess was overjoyed that, in both Andrew and Carolyn, she had people of her own age to chat and relax with.

It may be true that, at this time, the princess discovered that Charles was wearing a pair of cuff links: two Cs linked together, a gift from Camilla. She confronted him, but that was not going to mar her happiness, and she responded in the only way she knew how, by getting even. It is no coincidence that on Highgrove and Kensington Palace writing paper, the lower curve of the letter C was linked into a D beneath the logo of a crown. The princess believed that it symbolized a peaceful marriage that would last forever.

I T WAS TEA TIME at Balmoral and the princess, wearing her waterproofs, tweeds, and "plus fours," appeared in the hallway with blood on her face. I did a double take as she passed.

She had spent the day hunting with Prince Charles and others, and came back wearing what looked like war paint. She had undergone a royal initiation ceremony for debutante hunters after claiming her first kill. As she stood in the glen, the stag's belly was slit open and its blood smeared onto her cheeks. She had been officially "blooded." The dead stag was slung across a pony and sent down to the castle with a soldier. Its head was removed, the antlers set aside, and the carcass hung in the game larder—alongside rows of snipe, pheasant, and grouse—to be cooked for the royal table.

The princess loved her time in the Scottish Highlands but, unlike the Windsors, didn't share a passion for blood sports. When she went hunting, she did so to please the prince. She knew and accepted that hunting—with shooting and fishing—was an integral part of life at Balmoral, and important to him. Others have suggested she sulked through the honeymoon and never made an effort, but whatever was on the agenda, she did her best to fit in.

Even two years into the marriage, she liked to be there for her husband. She wrote to a female friend in 1983: "I believe in making an effort, so am on my way to watch polo . . . for the second day running. I would much rather be asleep but it seems to bring C a lot of happiness. I'm sure it's to show off on his part!" In turn, the prince made concessions. He knew the princess preferred London to the countryside and made a deliberate shift in his routine. The princess had to pinch herself when, on some Sunday mornings, she found herself waking up at Kensington Palace with her husband, and not at Highgrove. There were elements of give-and-take on both sides.

Prince Charles was never happier than when he was hunting at Balmoral. After a hearty Scottish breakfast, including porridge, kippers, and kedgeree, all-male shooting and stalking parties loaded dogs, guns, and ammunition into Land Rovers and headed for the day to a preassigned destination in the glens. Each participant collected a waterproof satchel from the Tower Door at the side of the castle, which always contained a meat-filled bap, cold lamb chops, fruit, and a greaseproof paper parcel containing slices of plum pudding. There was also a flask of sloe gin or whisky.

After one fishing expedition, the prince stood in the hall and shouted for assistance: "Can someone come and help me?" I heard him from the Pages' Vestibule and went to investigate. He was standing with two giant salmon at his feet on the marble floor. "Could you please take them to Chef? I think we'll have them for dinner," he said. I bent down to pick them up but their slippery scales made them awkward to handle. Prince Charles watched me juggling pathetically with them. "Oh, come here!" he said impatiently. "Don't mess around. Look." He took one of my hands, and pushed my fingers deep into its gills. I thought I was going to pass out. "Now take them to the kitchen," said Prince Charles, and I carried them to Chef, holding them at arm's length.

* * *

AFTER BREAKFAST, the Queen rode out on the estate on a horse that had traveled from Windsor. She returned to meet the rest of the ladies, who surfaced around midday, in the drawing room. The Duke of Edinburgh had already arranged a rendezvous point with his wife, and the ladies, including the Queen Mother and Princess Margaret, ladies-in-waiting and other female house guests, drove out with a picnic lunch. Princess Anne was already there, having gone out with the otherwise all-male party earlier.

Stalking parties rarely returned to the castle until late afternoon. One poor man returned hungry for dinner only to be sent back out onto the moors after admitting he had wounded an animal, but had not killed it. The Queen was appalled. As a countrywoman, she hunted but could not abide suffering and, once shot, it was imperative animals were put out of their misery. "You must go back out, find it, and kill it," she insisted.

The man didn't return in time for dinner.

As I stood with the Queen surveying the table plan, which needed to be hastily rearranged, she muttered: "It's very inconvenient to be a gentleman short for dinner." With the admonished individual still out in the cold, she added: "We will just have to invite the officer of the guard to take his place."

So the table plan was restored to its traditional symmetry of man, woman, man, woman. The Queen was always the perfect host, determined that every guest should have an enjoyable time. She ensured all guests never sat next to the same person twice during any one stay. It would infuriate the princess because she wanted to sit next to Prince Charles all the time, but the rotation system put them farther and farther apart.

THE QUEEN ALSO AVOIDS having thirteen guests around one table; she said that a group of thirteen was reserved for Christ and his disciples.

Her Majesty, head of the Church of England and Defender of the Faith, is deeply religious: she attends morning worship every Sunday wherever she is in the world. She only spends one Sunday a year at Buckingham Palace—Remembrance Sunday. At other times, she worships at Windsor, Sandringham, and Balmoral. Even aboard the royal yacht *Britannia,* the dining-room table was removed and replaced with rows of chairs. The admiral, as captain of the ship, led the service and everyone stood to sing the "Seafarers' Anthem," for those in peril on the seas.

At church on land, the Queen always placed a £5 note in the collection box. Earlier, her dresser would have folded it tight, quarter-size, then pressed it flat with an iron. Then the Queen could drop it into the box with only her head visible on the front of the note.

On Good Friday, the Queen broke from routine and received Holy Communion from the Dean of Windsor in her private chapel at Windsor Castle, a short walk away from her apartment down the green-carpeted Grand Corridor. Each Easter, the most holy day in the Christian calendar, a sprig of Glastonbury thorn, symbolic of the crown of thorns that Christ wore on the cross, was placed on Her Majesty's writing table at the castle, sent by the Dean of Glastonbury Cathedral. The Queen always received an Easter egg from Charbonnel et Walker in Bond Street, which traveled the world with her until every last crumb had been eaten. I have known a royal Easter egg to last up to six months. The egg always arrived with her favorite sweets: a box of Bendicks Bittermints and Elizabeth Shaw peppermint creams.

THE STEADFAST, loyal figure of the Duke of Edinburgh stands beside the Queen through everything. The couple are happiest when alone in private after the day's duties have been performed. They have separate sitting rooms, studies, and audience rooms to allow them independence, but one master bedroom connects their suites. In eleven years of serving the Queen, dipping in and out of her private world, I never once heard a raised voice between husband and wife. Prince Philip might grumble and be tactless at times in public, but he is a dutiful, caring husband. It is a strange union of the formal and informal. Most of all, it is a true partnership.

When Princess Elizabeth, then twenty-one, wed her distant Greek-born cousin, then twenty-six, on November 20, 1947, they made a vow as man and wife. Six years later, at her Coronation, the naval officer further reinforced that pledge by swearing an oath of allegiance before God to serve the monarch, his wife. Within four years of his marriage to the Queen, he gave up the naval profession he adored to adapt to royal life. In his own marriage, Prince Philip observes protocol, and walks one step behind the monarch in public. But, in regard to family matters, the husband leads the wife: behind closed doors at the House of Windsor, Prince Philip is boss. From deciding whether to have picnics or barbecues—"Ask His Royal Highness, I don't know," the Queen would say—to keeping an eye on the privy-purse strings, he is the forthright master of the house in the eyes of staff.

The other side to the Duke was not as endearing. He had a legendary temper, which reduced some young valets and pages to tears. He had an awesome presence, which demanded respect, and an expectation of high standards, which was unremitting. He had a trained eye for what had *not* been done. When someone was found wanting, his volcanic temper erupted and his deep voice became a frightening bellow. Doors slammed and the entire floor seemed to reverberate with his furious parting shots: "You are all bloody idiots" or "It's all a load of bollocks." As a former naval officer, he expected his male staff to be able to handle it, but with his housemaids he was always kind and considerate.

THE NEWLYWED PRINCE and Princess of Wales returned from their honeymoon to Buckingham Palace with the Queen and Prince Philip, as decorators prepared the marital homes of Highgrove and apartments No. 8 and

No. 9 at Kensington Palace under the supervision of South
African interior designer Dudley Poplak.

During the early days of her marriage, the princess focused on creating domestic bliss. Most weekends, she
visited Highgrove to check on the progress of redecora-
tion. She also went into recruitment mode for household
staff, tapping into the downstairs friendships cultivated
at the palace. She soon encountered the prickly politics
of personnel issues when, in a message passed via protection officer Graham Smith, she encouraged Maria
Cosgrove to apply for the post of her dresser. In February 1981, Maria had been promoted as housemaid to the
Duke of Edinburgh. She was eager to join the princess
until Lady Susan Hussey, the Queen's lady-in-waiting,
learned of the approach. Maria was given no choice; she
was told she could not leave the service of Prince Philip.
So the princess recruited two other allies from downstairs for Kensington Palace—nursery-floor housemaid
Evelyn Dagley, as dresser, and Mervyn Wycherley as
chef.

In those early days, the prince and princess were known
for living a quiet life. There were nights out to the opera
and ballet, or social evenings with a circle of Prince
Charles's friends, but they were not party animals or wild
entertainers. The princess did not yet have the confidence
she became renowned for, or the assertiveness some staff
would one day fear. She was still timid in a royal environment, but she recognized how lucky she was to be in such
a position. It wasn't until the day one member of staff provided a short, sharp shock that she realized she had not
found favor with everyone.

The princess had been having a discussion with a member of the household about staff timetables, and, it seems,
a few choice words were exchanged about who was and
was not pulling their weight. The member of staff stood
opposite the princess, who was blushing as she tried to
take command. He felt he knew better than the nursery-
assistant-turned-princess, his new boss. He began to rant
and rave. As she stood against the wall, he leaned in and

put his hands at either side of the princess's head, palms on the wall. "If you weren't so fucking boring, then we would be doing more," he said. Within a few weeks, that member of staff had parted company with the prince and princess.

NOTHING HIT the Princess of Wales harder after a year of marriage than the death of Princess Grace of Monaco in a car crash on September 13, 1982. Princess Grace, with her daughter Princess Stephanie, was heading through the Alpes-Maritimes from Roc Agel, the Grimaldi family's Balmoral equivalent, on the way back to Monaco. Less than two miles into that journey, the Rover failed to negotiate a hairpin bend, flew off a mountain ridge, and careered one hundred feet down the hillside. Princess Stephanie survived, but her mother died in the Princess Grace Hospital. There would be much speculation about the condition of the car's brakes.

The Princess of Wales was at Balmoral when the Royal Family received the news. She dropped everything and attended the funeral of her friend without Prince Charles. It was her first solo foreign trip as a representative of the Royal Family.

The princess never forgot the lady she referred to simply as Grace. She often talked about her elegance and style, and remembered her death as a tragic loss to the world. She had a white, off-the-shoulder chiffon cocktail dress that she called "my Grace Kelly dress" because it was "so beautiful and elegant."

FOUR

THE QUEEN AND I

IF THE PRINCESS WAS pinching herself over the magnificently surreal world in which she found herself, then so was a certain footman. Often I sat in the seat beneath the low, oblong window of my bedroom, looking out over London from Buckingham Palace, thinking back to the cobbled streets of Chapel Road, wondering what would have happened had life kept me at the Wessex Hotel.

I felt incredibly fortunate, working in the shadow of the Queen. And from that top window, the view enhanced the disbelief: looking out across the Victoria Monument and down the width of the Mall, funneling into Admiralty Arch, the expanse of St. James's Park, littered with blue-and-white deck chairs in the summer, Big Ben towering on the horizon. If Mum was a huge influence on me in childhood, it was the Queen who influenced the man I became. Her Majesty set an example with her innate fairness, tolerance, serene calm, love of people, and that abiding, self-sacrificing sense of duty.

Where Mum spent her days putting the people of Chapel Road first, the Queen put first her duty to her country and its people. And there I was, a small cog aiding the running of her life. Many times, I wished Mum could have seen me, but my job was mainly carried out behind closed doors. Staff rarely get credit for running a household like a nonstop performance of choreographed theater, but a smile or a nod from Her Majesty was enough for us to feel a sense of huge job satisfaction.

Mum had had a telephone installed at Chapel Road so that we could keep in touch. "I can't believe you're actually talking to me from inside Buckingham Palace!" She was so excited for me. She would sit in the back room of our house, clutching the phone, chain-smoking, enraptured by the routine of my day. Just telling her about serving tea to the Queen brought gasps of excitement.

Providing a glimpse of this life to my family was a huge thrill. How many sons get the chance to invite their mums to meet the Queen? In my first year as Her Majesty's personal footman, I couldn't wait for the Christmas Ball when, every other year, relatives of the staff might be invited. "Mum, I want you to do me the honor of attending the Christmas Ball with me—and the Queen," I said. There was a northern shriek loud enough to bring the miners rushing out from the pit face. But then she sighed. "Oh, I'd love to, but I don't think I can, Paul. I'd embarrass you."

"Mum, don't be daft. Everyone else's mums will be there. You'll fit in with the rest of them, and I'll be there with you," I said.

She broke the family bank that week to buy herself a simple, long blue evening dress, with a chain belt, which she wore with a knitted shawl. She told the whole village that she was going to meet the Queen at a ball, and no one knew anyone who had ever met the Queen. Certainly no one had from the Top Rank bingo hall in Chesterfield.

At the ball, Mum was in awe of her surroundings, let alone the royals. She couldn't believe she was mingling in the same social environment as the monarch, the Duke of Edinburgh, Prince Charles, and Princess Anne. "I feel like Cinderella," she said, "and you are my Prince Charming!" We had linked arms, and walked in together.

When the Queen introduced herself to the staff relatives, I wondered if Mum was going to hold it together. "I could do with a fag now!" she said. I held her shaking hand tightly.

"Hello, Paul," said Her Majesty, approaching us.

Did you hear that, Mum? I thought. She called me Paul. I desperately willed Mum to note that informality, but I think she was dazzled by the diamond necklace in front of her.

But you can always rely on Her Majesty to break the ice, and she engaged Mum in a conversation about miners and Derbyshire. Mum smiled a lot. Afterward, she said she couldn't take her eyes off the Queen's neck. She had never seen real diamonds before, let alone so many. "She is everything I expected a Queen to be," said Mum, and that was her introduction to my life. Over the years, she would meet my employer a couple more times at the palace, and once at Balmoral when we accidentally met the Queen walking the corgis on the hillside.

Mum's etiquette was slightly better than my auntie Pearl's, when I invited her to another festive ball. Dressed to the nines, she stood rigid and wide-eyed as the Queen prepared to meet and greet the relatives.

Auntie Pearl waited for the Queen to start the conversation.

"I hear the weather in Derbyshire has been dreadful lately?" inquired the Queen, well briefed as ever.

Auntie Pearl was momentarily dumbstruck. Then she said the first thing that entered her head. "Yes, 'orrible, Your Majesty, really 'orrible," and overdid a dramatic curtsy.

Afterward, she was mortified that she had dropped her *h*s in front of the Queen. I laughed, and reassured her that the monarch loved regional accents.

Relatives and outsiders were not the only ones struck with terror at meeting the Queen. Even people who worked at Buckingham Palace were nervous at the prospect of an introduction to her, which happened every Christmas. On the final day of residence before the court switched to Windsor Castle, as it did in those days, the Queen's last duty of the year was to meet and greet every member of household staff, which numbered about three hundred. For two hours, she stood to receive each staff member individually, from the most junior to the most senior, to wish them a happy Christmas. It was always "Happy Christmas," *never* "Merry Christmas," to avoid connotations of drunkenness. But perhaps drink would have made the experience more bearable for many. Coffee-room maids and washing-up ladies or under-butlers and basement porters could be reduced to quivering wrecks at the mere prospect of approaching a monarch whom they never came into contact with in their downstairs world.

The Queen insisted on this protocol to recognize the work of the staff who made her life run smoothly. Once, when she was asked how many servants she had, she replied: "Actually, I have none. I have many members of staff, but no servants."

Even the staff introduction was classically orchestrated. The household stopped work and filed into a queue that snaked up and down the backstairs corridors into the Marble Hall on the ground floor, through the breakfast room, into the 1844 Room, and to the door of the Bow Room. The line formed in order of seniority. There were scarlet-waistcoated footmen, pages with dark-blue tailcoats and their distinctive velvet collars, chefs in crisp whites and toques, and maids in traditional black with white aprons. Out of fourteen footmen, Paul Whybrew went first, me second. We always thought it was peculiar because we saw the Queen every day, but still had to go through a ritual of being announced and presented. Later that afternoon, we would be back upstairs, helping to pack her rooms for the move to Windsor.

The Queen and the Duke of Edinburgh stood at one end of the Bow Room, and the staff would stand in the doorway at the opposite end until the palace steward called their name. It had the air of an investiture but, instead of a medal, staff received a small present that they had previously selected from a catalog. Ladies who washed dishes had to swap their rubber gloves for a pair of white cotton ones because all women had to wear gloves when presented to the Queen. Interestingly, the monarch—who always wore gloves for official engagements—received her staff with bare hands.

A ROYAL CHRISTMAS is magical and exhausting. Its yuletide spirit often came alive at Windsor Castle when children from the estate, including a choir from St. George's Chapel, walked up the hill en masse, holding lanterns, and congregated in the quadrangle to sing carols outside. The Queen stood alone on the carpeted steps on the corner of the Sovereign's Entrance, drinking mulled wine, absorbing the atmosphere. She could relax in the knowledge that she didn't have to wrap her own presents.

The monarch's gift production line began in early December. Store owner Peter Knight brought around two thousand items—toys, games, china, gadgets, home furnishings, and kitchenware—and set up a giant stall in one of the audience rooms. Each night after dinner, Her Majesty shopped alone, selected an item, wrote a loved one's name on a note, and placed it outside the room to be taken away and wrapped. Paul Whybrew and I chose the wrapping paper and ribbon, and competed to see who could wrap the most. There were approximately a hundred presents each year, and it was always a keenly fought contest. One night, when I was surrounded by paper and ribbon, the Queen popped into the room. I was burning the midnight oil. "It's about time you went to bed, Paul. You've done plenty." It took about three weeks to wrap those gifts, and sometimes there didn't seem to be enough hours in the day.

The Queen did not have decorations put up until she arrived at Windsor Castle. Buckingham Palace was devoid of festive decoration apart from a solitary sixteen-foot tree, chopped down on the Windsor estate, in the center of the Marble Hall. At Windsor our meticulously wrapped presents were torn open after tea at five o'clock on Christmas Eve, as tradition dictated, in the first-floor Crimson Drawing Room, where Sir Gerald Kelly's huge 1937 Coronation portraits of King George VI and the Queen Mother filled the walls on either side of the marble fireplace. Another giant Christmas tree stood in a bay window in the center of the room, and a fifty-foot-long trestle table was set up down one side. The table was sectioned off with red ribbon, allocated for an individual's stack of presents, with the Queen and the Duke of Edinburgh at one end, the ladies-in-waiting and equerries at the other. As staff, we were always outside the room, but the shrieks of delight, the barking of excitable corgis, and an atmosphere of conviviality signified that the Windsors' Christmas had begun. Downstairs, in the dungeonlike cellars that insulated sound, the staff, who had worked till midnight most days, would unwind with discos and parties.

On Christmas Day around the Commonwealth, nations tune in to watch the Queen's televised broadcast. (In those days, it was prerecorded in mid-December.) Windsor Castle was no exception. By three o'clock that afternoon, all members of the Royal Family met in the paneled Oak Room and gathered around the television set. Some sat on sofas and chairs, many stood. Toward the back, the Queen stood silently. By the time the broadcast was finished, she had disappeared into the gardens to walk the corgis. The Queen isn't one for soaking up attention.

STATE VISITS BROUGHT a special buzz, breaking up the household routine as much as Christmas. The visit of Ronald Reagan to Windsor Castle remains a fond memory.

A week before the president's visit, a fleet of black armored vehicles drove into the quadrangle to "sweep" the buildings ahead of what would be the first time a U.S. president had stayed officially at the castle. The Queen smiled as she watched the dramatic entrance of the security cavalcade. The Queen was having none of it. Her message to them was conveyed by a member of the household. "This is my castle, and if the security is good enough for me, then it is good enough for the president."

When President Reagan arrived by helicopter on June 7, 1982, a Page of the Presence and I were assigned to look after him and his wife, Nancy, in the 240 Suite, which takes up the entire first floor of Lancaster Tower, with its impressive views down the straight mile of the Long Walk. Even then Nancy was the driving force behind the man. The president didn't need valeting because she never left his side, and his clothes arrived immaculately packed and pressed. All we had to do was be at his disposal.

On the first night there was an intimate, candlelit dinner. Wearing scarlet livery, I was circulating with a tray of predinner drinks in the Green Drawing Room. As I waited alongside the president and his wife, I became aware of Ronald Reagan's shyness: he hesitated in going over to speak to the Queen. "Go on. Go over and talk with Queen Elizabeth," Nancy Reagan urged her husband, so he did.

I thought it was rather nice that even American presidents need cajoling to approach Her Majesty. Mum and Auntie Pearl were not alone.

STATE VISITS ARE the Chapel Road equivalent of bringing out your best china when a wealthier friend comes to visit. It all comes out: silver-gilt candelabra, and salt and pepper cruets so large that two people must carry them, the gold cutlery from the King George III era. The horseshoe table in the Ballroom at Buckingham Palace can seat 160 guests, many more than at Windsor, with its single 120-foot-long, 10-foot-wide table. So wide was the polished table that under-butlers had to tie dusters round their feet, climb on top, and walk down the middle to position the candelabra and flower displays. Each place setting was measured and set with a ruler, and chairs were neatly set into regimental lines before the Master of the Household inspected it.

Banquets were a slick operation designed to impress visiting heads of state, and choreographed to perfection with a traffic-light system operated by the Palace Steward, who sat like a lighting technician at a console with a full view of the room. Backstage, in the service areas, everyone watched the colored bulbs light up in a vertical sequence: amber for "Get Ready," green for "Go." On green, a calm procession of pages and footmen walked into the room in synchronization from different corners, belying the mad rush in the background, preparing for the arrival of the next course.

As a child, I was always told never to start eating a meal until everyone had been served. In royal circles, as soon as the Queen has been served, she starts, regardless of the fact that others are being served. It is deemed rude not to eat food while it is hot. In Queen Victoria's court, once she had finished eating, her plate was taken away with everyone else's, regardless of whether they had finished. These days, plates are not removed until everyone has put down their knife and fork.

If the traffic-light system is a more modern feature of backstairs life, then the permitted spying is not: the Grille remains a feature from a bygone age. It is an ornate latticed screen that covers a back wall in the palace Ballroom. From behind the partition, staff stand and watch the spectacle of a banquet, dozens of eyes from a downstairs world spying discreetly, with permission, on the great and the good in their finest attire.

ON ONE OCCASION. I wished there had been a protocol procedure for the ground to open up and swallow me. When the Queen is a visiting head of state to foreign countries, the need for perfection is just as great. It was my first overseas tour with the Queen, on her first visit to the Gulf States, in 1979. On the morning of departure, there was a customary champagne bon voyage for the staff, held by the monarch's most trusted aide, dresser Margaret MacDonald. She sat bolt upright in a wing-backed chair. She was a diminutive but immaculate figure with horn-rimmed spectacles, perfectly coiffured hair, bespoke silk

dresses made by the Queen's designer Sir Norman Hart-
nell, and three rows of pearls and a brooch, gifts from the
Queen. She was every inch a royal lady, and was affectionately known *only* to the monarch and Princess Margaret as
"Bobo"—she had been their nursery maid. To household
staff, she was "the eyes and ears of the throne," and no one
crossed her.

She had double-checked every detail before departure,
ensuring that every dress, hat and piece of jewelry was
packed. I'd had to polish and buff all of Her Majesty's
brown leather luggage, including the engraved plates, then
tie to each trunk and hatbox a yellow label—knotted and
hung at the same length—which read: "The Queen." Miss
MacDonald also ensured that my polishing skills on the
Queen's footwear were up to her high standards. Her demands were great, but she never forgot her humble downstairs roots; after arriving from Scotland, she had cried
herself to sleep because she missed her family so much.

Before we departed for the Gulf, she held court with anecdotes of previous tours. Perhaps we were too enthralled,
or perhaps the champagne went to our heads, but the carefully orchestrated organization on my début tour with Her
Majesty came unstuck. In a motorcade halfway to
Heathrow, the Queen's assistant dresser Peggy Hoath
turned to her colleague May Prentice and said, in complete
horror: "We've forgotten the Queen's outfit!"

I was in the front seat and have never swiveled round so
fast. The women's faces were ashen. We all knew the
Queen was due to embark on a Concorde within thirty
minutes. On that cold February morning, she was wearing
a heavy coat and woolen dress. The one still hanging in the
dressers' workroom at Buckingham Palace was an
Arabian-style, full-length silk design, which she intended
to change into before arrival in Kuwait. The chauffeur, who
shared our panic, flagged down a police motorbike out-
rider. Another car from the palace was sent out in pursuit,
carrying the dress under a second police escort.

The Queen was held up a little longer than usual in the
Hounslow Suite at Heathrow, and the Concorde missed its

scheduled takeoff slot. The Queen, as tolerant as ever, chuckled over the desperate measures taken to retrieve her dress. She was smiling when she was escorted to the aircraft steps by the Lord Chamberlain, who, by tradition, is the last person to whom the Queen says goodbye on departure, and the first she greets on arrival back home.

It was the Queen's first time on a Concorde, my first flight overseas after childhood holidays in Skegness, Scarborough, and Newquay. I sat next to the Duke of Edinburgh's valet, Barry Lovell, as we soared into the air and reached "the purple corridor"—the Queen's exclusive airspace where no other aircraft is allowed to fly. We flew in British Airways TriStars on long flights, and their first-class sections were refitted to the Queen's specifications: new carpets, a dining table, sofas, chairs, and beds. The economy section became a first-class service for the staff, who reclined across the rows of empty seats.

On land, having been met by the Emir of Kuwait, the Queen entertained a succession of Arab rulers aboard *Britannia,* and the royal yacht became a treasure ship as each ruler tried to outdo the previous guest with more and more lavish gifts: Persian rugs, sapphire and diamond jewelry, gold camels on lapis-lazuli bases, and a gold water pitcher in the shape of a falcon. In later years, staff were given generous gifts by the host in thanks for their hard work. On a tour to Jordan with the Queen, I was handed a gold Omega watch with the King's crest on its face, medals for service such as the Order of the Lion from Malawi, and a silver decoration from the King of Sweden.

This was also the first time that I boarded the floating palace of *Britannia,* in a foreign port. It was a magnificent sight to see her fully dressed with five standards fluttering from different masts, and a string of flags strewn from fore to aft. No matter how many times I stepped into her interior splendor, I had to keep reminding myself she was a yacht and not a country house. We set sail in glorious sunshine into Bahrain, having been allowed to sunbathe on the funnel deck.

The Queen was at her most relaxed when *Britannia*

ruled the waves, but that regal calm slipped as she walked down the steep gangway to go ashore for dinner. It was the only time I ever saw her lose her composure. Dressed in a turquoise silk evening dress, and wearing the diamond tiara, she skidded on the red carpet and slid the full length of the gangway in her slippery new evening shoes. I was already on land, standing by the car, and could only watch. How she kept her feet, I will never know. As she slid down, she gripped the handrails for dear life, shouting, "Help! Help!" By the time she got to the bottom, her white gloves were filthy, ruined by the polish on the handrails. In the car to dinner, she replaced them with the spare pair she always carries in her handbag.

WHEN IT CAME TO remaining on one's feet, the Queen was clearly more skilled than I. First, there had been the corgi incident at Sandringham. Later, on a trip to Kentucky, disaster struck. It was the second time the Queen discovered me flat on my back and had to ask: "Are you all right, Paul?"

The Queen's interest in horse breeding had taken us to a stud farm to see her brood mares and yearlings stabled with owner and breeder Will Farrish—who became American ambassador to London—at a beautiful farm with redwood barns and white fencing, on the outskirts of Lexington. I had been having back pains ever since my fall at Sandringham, and needed regular treatment for a slipped disk. After the flight to Kentucky, a sharp pain returned, and over the next six days, it worsened considerably.

On the last evening, with the Queen at dinner, I was walking gingerly down the main stairs that led to the dining room. A sharp pain shot down my left leg, I lost my footing and tumbled down twelve steps. As I lay there, I realized I felt no sensation below the waist. The Queen and the rest of the twelve-strong dinner party had dashed into the hallway. It seemed that everyone was staring down at me, not knowing what to do. Someone dialed 911, and the Farrishes' doctor, Ben Roache.

The Queen's dresser, Peggy Hoath, knelt at my side. "Peggy, I can't feel anything below my waist," I told her.

No one dared move me until the paramedics arrived; then I was braced and strapped to a stretcher, and the ambulance took me away with a police escort. At the Lucille Markey Parker Cancer Center in Lexington, the local general hospital, they spoke about emergency surgery. The hospital had already set aside a royal suite for an emergency, in line with a procedure observed wherever the Queen visits, but this was the first time a crippled royal servant had slept in the Queen's bed. My admission was afforded the same level of discretion. At the nurses' station, on the whiteboard detailing each patient, there was a margin but my name wasn't given. Instead, there was a crown, a foot, and the male symbol as picture code for "Queen's footman."

The diagnosis was that a disk had ruptured in my lower spine and wrapped itself round the sciatic nerve, leading to the loss of sensation below the waist. As I lay on a gurney, looking up at the lights, Lord Porchester, the Queen's racing manager, loomed over me. "The Queen has not taken this decision lightly . . ." He went on to explain that time didn't allow them to fly me home: "You are in the best possible hands, and the Queen will take care of everything for you," he said.

Later a doctor told me: "The center of a disk is like a shrimp, and it has curled its way around your sciatic nerve, which is being pinched, causing the temporary paralysis. We have to release the pressure and remove the ruptured disk. If we don't act now, you may never walk again." At midnight, the decision was made to operate.

The first face I saw after coming round was that of Nurse Doris Gallagher. Her words sounded far better than I felt. She said the operation had been successful and the loss of feeling would be temporary. "You will make a full recovery," she said. Still half drugged, surrounded by flowers and fruit sent by the dinner-party guests whose meal I had ruined, I watched a television set perched high in the corner of the room and tilted down. It showed a live broadcast of the Queen's plane taking off from Lexington airport; for they'd had to go ahead with their scheduled return home without me.

Within three days, I was moving around the ward, my home for two weeks, using a walker. I shuffled to the next room to see who my neighbor was. "Hi, I'm Ron Wright and this is my wife, Julie," said the cheery American who greeted me. Julie was feeding mashed potatoes on a spoon to their eighteen-year-old daughter Beth, propped up in bed, surrounded by tubes and machines. Days earlier, Beth had had a tumor removed from her brainstem. Suddenly my pain didn't matter anymore. Julie finished feeding her. "Beth has never heard an English accent before. Would you mind spending time with her?" her dad asked me.

For the rest of my stay I talked to Beth. Her mum said she was listening because her eyes were moving. When it was time for me to go home, I said goodbye, though I kept in touch with Ron Wright and his parents, Claude and Shirley, who read my letters to Beth. Three and a half years later, she died.

The Queen had kept her promise to look after me. I never saw a bill for those medical expenses and she flew me home in style in a new BAe 146 jet. It had not yet entered royal service and still needed to clock up more flying time before Her Majesty could climb aboard. I became a guinea pig, and the jet, refitted with beds in the royal compartment, was flown out to Kentucky for one convalescing footman. I was the first passenger to fly aboard the Queen's Flight BAe 146—even before the Queen herself.

I TRAVELED THE WORLD with the Queen—I went to China, Australia, New Zealand, the Caribbean, Europe, Algeria, Morocco. But a special trip was just a few miles away from Windsor Castle to Royal Ascot every year. It was the Queen's favorite date in the calendar.

In June 1982, the household staff were more interested in having friendly bets on whether the first child of the Prince and Princess of Wales would coincide with the four-day race festival, and whether it would be a boy or a girl. But a royal labor didn't take place, so the Queen's mind was on the race card. She never has a flutter because she doesn't carry money (except at church), but that doesn't stand in the way of her enjoyment. She gets her excitement from trying to pick winners for fun.

For me, the most amazing experience was being part of the fifteen-minute open-carriage ride from Home Park, down the country lanes, into the course via the Golden Gates and down the famous Straight Mile in a procession that has taken place since 1825. Sitting bolt upright on the back of the Queen's carriage, wearing scarlet livery and top hat, a footman must look straight ahead and remain expressionless, but his ears prick as the distant roar of the grandstand crowds grows louder by each furlong pole, and the band of the Blues and Royals strikes up.

Nor is Her Majesty distracted. No sooner have the carriage wheels trundled onto the grass than she is peeping over the side, checking what impression, if any, the wheels are making on the turf. It is all part and parcel of her horse-racing homework to see if the course is soft or firm. My task was to listen out for the first strains of "God Save the Queen," and then, after a discreet nudge of my fellow footman, we took off our top hats together in unison. All around ladies cheered and the gentlemen tipped their top hats back. As the music died down, and the carriage slowed up in the Royal Enclosure, I had to disembark to assist the Queen. Getting off a moving carriage with aplomb takes some doing, but I never fell flat on my face.

Once in position in the Royal Box, the Queen, armed with binoculars, was at her most animated. She urged on a horse, clapped with joy, and sometimes let out a cheer. It was both funny and endearing to see the monarch watching the race on television inside the Royal Box, then rushing out, with some grace, to the balcony to see the horses tearing up the final two furlongs to the winning post. Lord Porchester was always at her side, advising her on form. I was there, too, ensuring that Earl Grey tea was served between the third and fourth races. Princess Margaret didn't drink tea; she preferred Pimm's.

The Princess of Wales's timing for going into labor could not have been better. Royal Ascot went ahead without interruption and on the night of June 21, 1982, Prince William—or "Baby Wales," as she called him—was born at nine o'clock at St. Mary's Hospital, Paddington. Two miles away, on the Queen's floor at Buckingham Palace, the staff, who were among the first to share the news, cracked open a bottle of champagne in celebration.

Everyone in the household was desperate to see the baby prince, but the heir to the heir spent his initial weeks in the new nursery at Kensington Palace with nanny Barbara Barnes. My first glimpse of Prince William came two months later in August at Balmoral. He was alone, parked outside in his large blue pram, covered with a net, in front of the tower on the lawn. Nanny was keeping a watchful eye on him from the window.

IF ROYAL ASCOT was the time to see the Queen animated, Buckingham Palace was the place to see her utterly mesmerized, on the evening when the latest Madame Tussaud's waxwork of her was unveiled for her inspection in the Chinese Dining Room. "Would you like to come and see it?" the Queen asked me.

Her Majesty, followed by a pack of scampering corgis, led the way. I walked a pace behind, encouraging the more reluctant dogs to keep up. No one else was around: the Marshal of the Diplomatic Corps occupied a small office annexed to the dining room, but he had gone home, and all was in darkness. The room is, of course, Oriental in style, with red, gold, and green decor. The fireplace is carved with entwined dragons and serpents, the central carpet is a Chinese woven rug, and there are Chinese lanterns for light fittings. It is like stepping back into the flamboyance of the Brighton Pavilion in the days of the Prince Regent.

The Queen stepped inside and immediately saw the waxwork standing alone in the center of the room. Before she switched on the lights, she took a step back in surprise as she saw the silhouette of a woman in evening dress. She switched on the lights and the waxwork was cast in bright light. It was an eerie likeness.

I knew the Queen's face so well, and the sculptor had captured every line and angle, even the two wisps of gray hair above each ear. She is well practiced at sitting for portraits and seeing the end likeness, but I wasn't, and I just stood and gawked at the "twin" before me. "It's really very good, isn't it?" she said, peering a little closer at it. It was a strange and intensely personal moment for me to witness the Queen inspecting the Queen. "How could it be so accurate?" she mused.

She stood there for ten minutes, then gave an approving nod. She turned, switched out the lights, and left the room. It was the first and only time that I ever left "The Queen" standing alone in the dark. After our sneak preview, the waxwork was placed in Madame Tussaud's by royal command.

The one royal command that deeply affected the path my life would take came in 1984 when I married my wife, Maria. We had the Queen's unprecedented approval to become the first couple from the Royal Household to wed and remain together in service. It was a decision that undid hundreds of years of royal protocol, and one that gave us our first taste of national newspaper coverage.

FIVE

THE OTHER ROYAL WEDDING

"QUEEN DELIGHTS AT PALACE WEDDING," announced the headline in the *News of the World*. "ROYAL LOVE MATCH FOR PALACE PAIR," screamed the *Daily Mirror*.

Having spent eight years in the anonymity of the background shadows of palace life, Maria and I found the media spotlight sending its full beam into St. Mary's Roman Catholic Church, Wrexham, on Saturday, July 21, 1984. Reporters and photographers from the Sunday newspapers had camped outside Maria's family home all morning and pursued the wedding party to the church to cover what had been dubbed as the "latest royal wedding."

One cunning lady reporter from the *News of the World* broke ranks and, mingling with the constant comings and goings of relatives at Maria's home, penetrated the house, went upstairs, and found Maria's mum, Elizabeth, getting changed in a bedroom. "Get out, you cheeky beggar" was the on-the-record reply.

Outside the church, when my brother and best man, Anthony, and I pulled up, we saw the press pack waiting, cameras at the ready. No royal guests were expected, so it seemed they were here just for us downstairs nobodies: Paul Whybrew, the Queen's footman; Peggy Hoath, the Queen's dresser; and Michael Fawcett, a senior household footman. The Queen's chaplain, Canon Anthony Caesar, resplendent in his scarlet robes, helped officiate at the ceremony with blessings and prayers.

Instead of ensuring everyone got to their seats, ushers became bouncers, to keep out reporters. All I was concerned about was that our big day not be ruined because many friends had traveled north from London. Unfortunately, nine guests were missing: the corgis. Not even Chipper was there. But they sent us a Royal Court Telegram, which read: "Though we corgis weren't invited, In one thing we are united, If you wish us to placate, Bring us back some wedding cake—from Chipper, Smokey, Shadow, Piper, Fable, Myth, Jolly, Sparky, Brush." It had an ink paw print at the bottom.

I have Rose Smith, a housemaid on Princess Anne's floor, to thank for playing Cupid between Maria and me. Rose, like me, was from Derbyshire and had been a fellow student at High Peak College, Buxton, but had started work at Buckingham Palace six months earlier than I. She married my best friend, footman Roger Gleed, and that union brought about her exit from the palace: in those days, it was the rule that married couples were not allowed to work together. She went to work for the Duchess of Gloucester as her dresser at Kensington Palace.

Hanging around with the Gleeds brought me into the same social circle as Rose's good friend Maria Cosgrove, who had worked in the linen room, the Belgian Suite, and then in the Duke's suite; the young woman who had called me a "twopence-ha' penny toff." Then I noticed her. The sharp wit, the infectious laugh, the stunning brown eyes and dark hair, her "mashed-potato dance"—a sort of front crawl in reverse with arms flailing backward over her head. The romantic air around Balmoral played its part as we sat around campfires at badly made barbecues on the moors. Pipe Major McCrae entertained us under the night sky with his bagpipes, while Cyril Dickman rang his handbell and we all sang ourselves hoarse with a collection of Scottish songs. Maria became my friend, then my best friend, and then we fell in love, in the spring of 1983.

On weekend visits to her parents' home in Holt on the English–Welsh border near Wrexham, I saw the same close-knit, working-class values I knew so well. It felt like home. Maria's mum, Elizabeth, told me to call her Betty. She never stopped cooking, and her kitchen was like a pie-making factory. Catholicism dominated Betty's life in the same way that the Queen dominated mine. There were as many images of the Pope as there were pies. Maria's father, Ron, a jovial electrician who was as sparky as his trade, sat and told me all about his "beautiful only daughter" and fired off a round of jokes.

When I next saw him, he was a different man. He sat with a mask over his face, struggling to breathe with two oxygen cylinders propped up on either side of his easy chair. Ron was dying of lung cancer. That June, 1983, Maria desperately wanted her dad to see Trooping the Colour live from her bedroom window at the front of Buckingham Palace. The staff lift didn't reach the top floor, so Roger Gleed and I carried him in his wheelchair up the last flight of stairs. Ron was excited to be inside the palace and so proud of his daughter and what she had achieved. He died four weeks later at the age of fifty-nine.

On New Year's Eve, I took Maria home to Derbyshire and proposed at the country-house hotel of Higham Farm, getting down on one knee with a solitaire diamond ring that cost me every single penny I had. I wanted her to have the best I could afford. Marriage to Maria meant conforming to one protocol outside royal life in order to keep the prospective mother-in-law happy. I had to be confirmed into the Church of England, but pledge that our children would be brought up Roman Catholic. Canon Anthony Caesar contacted me, and I was later confirmed by the Bishop of London. Betty's influence has lasted because, whenever I enter a Catholic church, I always automatically dip my fingers into the font of holy water.

*   *   *

WITH BOTH SETS of parents informed, there was only one more person to tell about this great romance. Dog-feeding chores seemed the best time to break the news to the Queen. I told her that love had blossomed between her footman and her husband's housemaid, and she was delighted for us.

"It is such a shame that she will have to leave service," I said to the Queen.

"Oh? Why is that?" she inquired. I couldn't believe she was unaware of an unwritten rule that had been upheld for hundreds of years. "Is there nothing that can be done about that?"

"Well, with all due respect, Your Majesty, you are the Queen," I said.

A word in the right ear obviously worked. A letter from the Master of the Household arrived to tell us that Maria would not have to leave service. The Queen had intervened and the rule was being relaxed.

A week before our wedding, Maria and I were summoned to meet the Queen. I was off-duty and we waited like visitors in the Pages' Vestibule. It felt strange when page John Taylor opened the sitting-room door and announced us: "Paul and Maria, Your Majesty," in the same way that I had announced, "The Prime Minister, Your Majesty," when Margaret Thatcher once went aboard the royal yacht *Britannia* in the Bahamas.

The Queen was in the middle of the room. It felt equally odd to be with her in civvies. "It's going to be a very exciting weekend for you both," she said. She handed us a small dark-blue box, a gift from herself and Prince Philip. We opened it in front of her, and it was a gold-metal and enameled carriage clock, bearing their personal ciphers. Then she opened the hinged lid of an even larger box and presented us with two china candlesticks, handpainted with flowers. We were overwhelmed. They were our first wedding presents.

"Do have a wonderful time and I shall see you both at Balmoral," said the Queen. Maria curtsied. I bowed.

We would next be working in royal service as Mr. and Mrs. Burrell.

WHEN THE BIG DAY CAME, one special person was missing from church, Maria's dad, Ron. It was a day tinged with sadness for the entire family, but it was also a proud moment when her brother Peter, standing in for their dad, gave his sister away.

As the stirring sound of the "Trumpet Voluntary" on the church organ swept my beautiful new wife and me out of church, we were confronted with a fresh problem. We could not get to our awaiting car because there were so many reporters, photographers and others outside. In stepped Canon Caesar and Michael Fawcett to keep the press at bay. We posed for photographers outside the main door and escaped.

It was a stifling hot summer afternoon when we arrived for the reception at the Bryn Howell Hotel, Llangollen, where the best man read out cards and telegrams from friends. The last one read: "With congratulations and our very best wishes for your future happiness—Elizabeth R and Philip."

That night, Maria and I set off on a two-night honeymoon to Llandudno, Wales, before returning to duty at Balmoral. On Sunday morning, the newspapers were placed outside our hotel door. We were front-page news.

BALMORAL WASN'T PREPARED for the change in protocol to receive a newlywed couple below stairs. Maria's usual housemaid's room was more comfortable, so we decided to share her single bed while corgis Chipper and Shadow slept on the floor. One person eager to find out all about our big day was the Princess of Wales, heavily pregnant with her second child. Maria went to her suite, and the two women sat on the bed, laughing like schoolgirls, as Maria showed off the proofs of our wedding photographs. They had sat there for about ten minutes when they heard a voice calling: "Diana? Diana, where are you? It's lunchtime." It was the Queen.

"I'd better go. I'm late," said the princess, "but leave the photographs and I'll look at them again later."

Through Maria, the princess got to know me better: I was the husband of a staff member she trusted. More important, I was the Queen's footman and had the Queen's ear, so she viewed me as a good ally, though she needed to do more homework first.

That August, the princess still looked for reasons to be among downstairs staff. At Balmoral, she missed London lunches with friends such as Janet Filderman, Caroline Bartholomew, Carolyn Herbert, and Sarah Ferguson, who was then dating Prince Andrew. She began to seek me out more and more in the Pages' Vestibule, near to the main staircase. We exchanged pleasantries and indulged in small talk. The princess, while giving the impression of being super-friendly, was doing what she did to anyone new she met. She was checking me out. She said how much she missed London. I inquired about her health as an expectant mother, spoke about the joys of marriage, and how Maria and I longed to have children. All the time during those snatched conversations, there was a nagging doubt in my mind that it wasn't appropriate to be on such friendly terms with her.

At this time, the princess joked that the constant smiling she did in public would make her facial muscles sag. She was touched that everyone still referred to her as "Lady Di." "That should put the republicans in the shade for a while," she said. She was adamant that her "Spencer determination" would not allow the media to catch her looking fatigued, sad, or nervous. She felt she was growing in stature and confidence, daring to enter social debate about politics. In a letter she sent to a lifelong friend, she reflected on the dichotomy it was to be her: "It is quite amazing the change that is going on inside me—the Diana bit wanting to go and hide rather than be out in the public eye and the Princess who is here to do a job to the best of her ability. The second lady was winning but at what cost to the first?"

It drained the private woman of her energy. The glare of publicity made her even more conscious of her image. Worries over whether she was up to the job made the bulimia worse, but Prince Charles was a crutch. She wrote to a friend:

> *We are moving at quite a pace . . . I have to get used to being here, there and everywhere. Charles is being wonderful, so understanding when I sometimes feel a bit bemused and sad with the pressure. I never realised what a support he could be to me. I am trying to support Charles too and be a mother. Strange to know which should come first. C does actually, but what can I do when the press draws comparisons with us both, making [sic] C into the background?*

The unsympathetic claimed the princess had no consideration for how Prince Charles might be affected by walking in the shadow of his wife during the "Lady Di-mania" of the time, but she wrote to that same friend: "We must also understand it's his first time with another person and crowds scream for me to come and talk to them. Putting myself in his position, it must be so difficult."

It was around this time when the princess first confided in me: her first test to see if anything she told me would reach the Queen. I was alone in the Pages' Vestibule, waiting for the Queen to call, when the princess appeared around the corner. Her pregnancy and health were the main topics of conversation again. Then, out of the blue, she told me: "I'm having a boy."

I don't know whether it was meant to shock me or evoke a response, but it seemed such a personal thing to say. Was it a secret? And why was she being so unguarded? With Prince William's birth, household staff had been taking bets on whether it would be a girl or boy. I think my wide-eyed surprise was clear. "I really don't think you should be telling me that, Your Royal Highness," I said.

The princess laughed. She liked to surprise people.

I asked Maria and she didn't even know. If it *was* a test, I passed, because neither of us said a word to anyone.

On September 15, 1984, a boy called Henry, to be known as Prince Harry, was born at St. Mary's Hospital, Paddington, at 4:20 P.M.

For the princess, it was a special time: "I have to admit, I feel very chuffed with life at the moment."

Around the same time, there was another cause for celebration: Maria was pregnant with our first child.

"PAUL, YOU GO. The poor girl has been there long enough," said the Queen.

Maria was two weeks overdue and in Westminster Hospital. I was in constant touch with the maternity ward and on normal duties at Buckingham Palace, but Her Majesty, who was anxious about our baby's delayed arrival, insisted that my rightful place was at my wife's hospital bedside. The Queen's only instruction was for me to ring her page John Taylor as soon as there was any news.

Best friend Roger Gleed wanted to be with me, and we both ran from the palace to the hospital in a thunderstorm, arriving drenched to the skin. From three o'clock that afternoon until 6:40 A.M. the next day, I never left Maria's side.

On May 22, 1985, I witnessed Alexander Paul Burrell arrive in the world with a piercing scream. The most incredible thing in life is watching your child being born. Nothing could ever match the magic of that moment. I went out into the corridor and Roger was still there waiting for me. I remembered what the Queen had said, so I rang the page with the good news. The Queen, not Mum, Dad, or my brothers, was the first to know.

Frances Simpson and Harold Brown, housekeeper and butler to the Prince and Princess of Wales at Kensington Palace, arrived bearing a bouquet of flowers, bubble bath, and a handwritten note for Maria. It read: "What a clever lady you are! With love from Diana, William and Harry."

The headline in the *Sunday Mirror* was less significant:

"MARIA'S ROYAL BABY," but reporter Brian Roberts labeled Alexander "a new royal child."

The Queen was as amused as we all were by the headlines, and she was keen to see our first child. Not many babies, age seven days old, have an audience with Her Majesty in her palace sitting room. Mum, carrying son, joined an extremely proud dad and stood before a casually dressed Queen, wearing black riding boots—spit and polished by me the previous day—breeches, and long-sleeved shirt. She had just returned from riding Burmese round the gardens. He was a working policeman's horse 364 days a year, but for one day he was the Queen's ride for her official birthday parade, Trooping the Colour, and she had been familiarizing herself with an old friend.

Maria curtsied. I bowed. Alexander was fast asleep, oblivious to the momentous occasion. "It's so good of you to see us, Your Majesty," I said.

She smiled and approached the little bundle in Maria's arms. "What tiny fingers," said the Queen, and she placed one of hers in our son's clenched fist. "I want you to have a little something from me," she said, picking up a parcel from the table. She added: "It's for Alexander."

Maria opened the box, which contained two knitted cardigans, folded neatly in tissue. Our audience lasted five minutes, but for two parents it was a proud, overwhelming moment. As we left, that special moment was spoiled somewhat by a senior male member of staff who passed us in the corridor. He was overheard to snipe: "He could have worn a tie."

WE HAD LEFT the staff living quarters on the top floor and moved into a two-bedroom grace-and-favour flat in the Royal Mews at the rear of the gardens, in the southwest corner off Buckingham Palace Road. Maria had left the service of the Duke of Edinburgh to concentrate on motherhood. Our next-door neighbors were friends Roger and Rose Gleed, and they were happy days. The accommodation, predominantly for grooms and chauffeurs, is situated above ground-floor archways that lead to garages for a fleet of Rolls-Royces and stables for the thirty-five horses that pull the state carriages. Stored in the largest central bay was the spectacular Gold Coronation Coach. The Royal Mews, like the palace, is built round a courtyard and is under the command of the Crown Equerry, whose job is to oversee all modes of transport for the Royal Family and household.

The Royal Mews became a regular stop-off point for the Princess of Wales after her regular morning swim at the palace. A week after the birth, she brought Alexander a knitted, double-breasted matinée jacket. She enjoyed a chat and a mug of coffee with Maria and giggled as she raided our cupboards for chocolate biscuits.

The Queen knew when the princess had come to the palace for a swim; she heard the crunch of the gravel beneath her sitting-room window. Between the swim and seeing Maria, the princess would nip upstairs to the Queen. When she emerged she would say to me: "Is it all right if I pop round and see Maria?" As she drove out of the front gate, round the Victoria Monument and down Buckingham Palace Road, I would call Maria: "Make sure everything's tidy, the princess is coming round." Both Maria's mother and mine were visiting when the princess arrived for a peek at Alexander. She never knocked, just walked in with a cheery hello. When Maria introduced both grandmas to her, they didn't know what to do with themselves. "Ah, he's gorgeous!" cooed the princess, as she and Maria gazed at our new son. When they looked up, Grandmas Burrell and Cosgrove had left the flat and were waiting outside on the balcony. Maria asked her mum why they were outside. It seemed they felt their presence in the room was a bit presumptuous when the Princess of Wales was there.

The princess herself put them at ease. "Don't stand out there, come on in and let's all look at Alexander."

Maria and the princess were like neighbors sharing coffee and chats while their husbands were away at work. The princess always sat back in the sofa and cradled Alexander. Over the spring, summer and autumn of 1986, she had started to wonder aloud how it would be to have Maria and me working for her. It was five years since Maria had been forced to turn down the initial approach from the princess to be her dresser.

"I would love to work for you, but Paul will never leave the Queen. He's totally devoted to her," Maria said. The princess noted the obstacle but was determined. Those weekly chats over coffee turned into virtual lobbying sessions. "It would be so wonderful if you and Paul worked at Highgrove," she hinted heavily.

Week by week, she got the message across. As a mum, the princess also knew Maria's soft spot. She emphasized the quality of life in the countryside compared to the city. There would be a cottage instead of a first-floor flat, a private garden for Alexander instead of St. James's Park and its small playground. She painted an attractive picture of an idyllic lifestyle, which Maria increasingly found hard to resist. When I was away traveling or at Windsor for the weekend, it began to dawn on Maria, who was alone with Alexander, that life at Highgrove would mean her husband would be at home all the time. No more royal tours, no more weekends away, no more Christmases at Windsor, no more voyages on the royal yacht.

As 1986 progressed, Maria began to agree with the princess. Life at Highgrove would be so much better. And the princess would have real friends among her staff.

"Leave it with me. I'll work on him," said Maria.

On July 23, 1986, Sarah Ferguson married Prince Andrew at Westminster Abbey and they became Their Royal Highnesses the Duke and Duchess of York, a week before the fifth wedding anniversary of the Prince and Princess of Wales. Unlike that last great royal wedding, Paul Whybrew had to stay behind at the palace with the corgis and look after the wedding breakfast while I rode out behind the Queen and Prince Philip on the magnificent 1902 gold state landau.

As we rolled along in the bright sunshine, I looked

straight ahead, bolt upright as always, and didn't have time to savor the atmosphere because as the Queen's hand performed the customary wave, mine was tight round the brake cable as we approached Admiralty Arch, the sharp right turn into Whitehall. It was always an anxious moment being in control of the brake's winding mechanism. It was there to ensure, on any slight downward slope, that the carriage didn't run away and crash into the horses. Thankfully, my brake-application record remained intact.

I had forgone a chance to be at the wedding ceremony: as a long-serving member of staff from the Lord Chamberlain's department, I had received a gilt-edged invitation, but I'd chosen the even more privileged seat behind the Queen on the landau. It would be my last ceremonial carriage drive through London, though I didn't know it then. As I rode through the streets, Maria took her place in the abbey as a guest, wearing a hat borrowed from the Duchess of Gloucester.

Sarah Ferguson had moved into Buckingham Palace a few months before the wedding. Unlike Lady Diana Spencer, who had had to have her own separate suite before marriage, Sarah shared with Prince Andrew. They lived in the second-floor rooms in which the Prince and Princess of Wales had spent the early days of their married life. The duchess did not suffer the same isolation as the princess because—such is her bubbly, vibrant personality—she surrounded herself with people. If Buckingham Palace staff viewed the princess as the loner who found friendships belowstairs, the duchess was seen as the gregarious wild one who spent all her time upstairs, entertaining friends and throwing parties.

She and Prince Andrew would order five-course dinners, and the kitchen staff wondered what had hit them. Even the Queen didn't entertain so lavishly, and as a result the duchess didn't endear herself to the downstairs staff.

"At least the Queen eats at a decent hour. Those two can have meals going up there anytime after ten p.m. and we're working ourselves silly to keep up with them," moaned one chef. Since the beginning of 1982, the duchess had shared regular lunch dates with the princess, and became a confidante and friend. They called themselves "The Wicked Wives of Windsor." Together, they discussed the dour men in the gray suits of the royal household: "the enemy within," as they called them. Having married into the Royal Family first, the princess could warn the duchess about the dos, the don'ts, those people she could trust, those she needed to be wary of. The list for the latter group proved rather lengthy.

The duchess, like the princess, had a desire to be genuinely liked and appreciated by their mother-in-law, the Queen. It is sovereign's gift to bestow on a son, on the eve of marriage, a royal dukedom, and it was significant that she conferred on Prince Andrew the title Duke of York, because it had long been associated with her father, King George VI. The poignancy was not lost on the duchess, who took it as a clear acceptance of herself.

In that regard, she misunderstood. The monarch had not bestowed a title on her: she had bestowed it on Prince Andrew, and Sarah, as his wife, would take it too. The subtle difference shows how persnickety protocol can be, but the gray suits picked up on the error when the duchess wrote to the Queen thanking her profusely for the honor. The duchess had intended to be gracious but, as she soon suspected, there were from the very beginning people in the household who were out to bring her down. The warm breath of fresh air that she brought with her mixed with the cool rising air of the household and caused unrest. One aristocrat called her "Vulgar, vulgar, vulgar," and a newspaper dubbed her "The Duchess of Pork." She was discovering how hurtful life could be in royal circles.

Even among the household staff, she couldn't win. From top to bottom in the Royal Household of Buckingham Palace, the duchess was poorly treated. It was determined to freeze her out. In the Queen, Prince Charles, and, of course, Prince Andrew, she had probably her only allies.

One morning, as she walked through the main hall toward the front door at Balmoral, a passing member of staff said, "What does that fucking red-haired mare want?" He said it so loudly that she must have heard, but she kept smiling. The duchess always kept smiling—outwardly, at least.

MARIA WAS ALSO giving the impression of being happy when deep down she was nothing of the sort. Since leaving the Duke of Edinburgh after our son's birth, she missed working in the Royal Household. The ongoing enticement of man-and-wife employment at Highgrove provided the prospect of an escape route.

One evening after work she broached the subject. "Living here isn't easy, and you're always away. We need to start thinking about our future." There was nowhere for Alexander to play. If we wanted a second child, there was not enough space. She could hardly get one stroller up the steps, let alone two. Country life was better than city life. She needed to be happy. All this she told me as a buildup to the main point. "There is a possibility of both of us moving on and working for the Prince and Princess of Wales at Highgrove and having a new life. You as full-time butler and me as a housemaid," she ventured.

Not a second thought was needed on my part.

"No way. There is no way I'm leaving the Queen," I told her.

Over the next few nights, the same conversation ended in stalemate. But Maria's unhappiness played on my mind. I had a duty to the Queen. She was No. 1, and I couldn't contemplate working for No. 2. It was, I thought, a backward career move. Besides, I was a footman and had no idea about running an entire household as a butler. Also, I'd go from traveling the world to being stuck in a mansion. It made no sense.

"Maria, why would I give up the best job in the world?" I asked her.

"For your family, that's why," she said.

That is the one problem with royal duty: its hours, and the dedication required, get in the way of duty to your loved ones.

Maria contested that life at Highgrove would be better for us all *as a family*. She told me how close she was to the princess, and how they had discussed it in great detail.

Great detail? "How long have you two been discussing this?" I asked.

"On and off for about a year," she said. "All I'm asking is that you go to Highgrove and have a look. Go and have a look. Just for me," she added.

I surrendered. Maria informed the princess, and a discreet visit was planned. One afternoon that summer, Harold Brown, the prince and princess's butler at Kensington Palace, agreed to drive me down the M4 to Gloucestershire to see the house, estate, and staff cottage at Close Farm. It was a weekday, and the prince and princess were both out. Harold gave me the grand tour, room by room—what a beautiful house and gardens! It reminded me of another Gloucestershire residence, Gatcombe Park, home of Princess Anne and Captain Mark Phillips, where the princess's first household friend and Big Mac courier, Mark Simpson, had become butler. The large, airy rooms had stunning countryside views and the tranquillity was in complete contrast to the hectic pace of London life. I heard sheep and cattle in the fields, rather than the horns and sirens from the Mall. I imagined Alexander and a second child growing up there. The sense of freedom and quality of life hit home.

Then Harold drove me the half mile to Close Farm to see the potential grace-and-favour cottage. My heart sank. It was a ramshackle, semi-detached house, clearly not lived in for years. It had broken windows, peeling paint, chipped walls, and a jungle for a garden. It was derelict. It needed knocking down, not occupying.

"Don't worry, the prince has every intention of fixing it up for you," Harold reassured me.

Not even my vivid imagination could visualize a satisfactory renovation. How could I leave the splendid world of Buckingham Palace and our first cozy flat for this?

Back at the flat, I conveyed my horror to Maria. But such was her unhappiness with London life that I could have told her it was a grace-and-favour tent, and she would have looked on the bright side.

"We can make it a home," she insisted.

I stood in the palace and saw the Queen, and thought there was no better boss in the world. I stood in the flat, saw Maria, and thought, She cannot remain so unhappy. I imagined working for the Prince of Wales, who had a reputation among staff for being demanding. I imagined Maria working for the Princess of Wales, and knew how friendly and down-to-earth she would be. I looked at Alexander and knew he would be better growing up in the countryside than the city. Above all, I knew family must come first.

Even as I made up my mind and decided to say yes to Maria, I was desperately unsure. I was gambling with a safe, privileged position, trading it for the unknown. People rarely leave such a senior position beside the Queen in exchange for another royal household. If anything, instinct rather than conviction guided me.

"Are you mad?" said colleague Paul Whybrew, when I told him. He could not believe I was leaving, and he implored me to think again. But my situation was different from his: he was single and could pursue his ambitions with tunnel vision. I had a family to consider. My mind was made up. All I had to worry about now was telling the Queen.

In June 1987, at the Epsom Derby, Prince Charles was sitting in a cane chair in the corner of the Royal Box, working on his correspondence. The Queen, the Duke of Edinburgh, Princess Alexandra, Princess Michael of Kent, and the rest of the royal party were having pre-luncheon drinks just a few feet away. I asked the prince if he would like one. He asked for his usual lemon refresher. When I returned with it on a tray, he leaned forward and whispered, "The princess tells me you will soon be coming to work for us."

"Yes," I said. "But please don't mention anything to the Queen, Your Royal Highness. I haven't told her yet and would like to tell her myself."

*   *   *

THE QUEEN, in her green Hunting Stewart kilt and a cardigan, was standing with her back to the open log fire. We were in the ground-floor sitting room at Craigowan House, which overlooked the golf course on the Balmoral estate and is where she stays when the court is not in residence at the castle. She had returned from a walk and the corgis were littered around the tartan carpet. It was two weeks since the Epsom Derby.

"I don't really know how to begin to tell you this," I said, and proceeded to get my next words all mixed up.

As I looked at her a huge part of me wanted to change my mind.

"What is it, Paul?" the Queen asked.

"This is so difficult for me." I had been by her side for ten years and had never found it difficult to talk to her until now. "I have been thinking long and hard about my future for the sake of Maria and Alexander ..." The Queen was still smiling. ". . . and it is the hardest decision I have ever taken ..." She could have taken the corgis for a walk twice in the time I took to get to the point; I cannot have impressed her with my decisiveness. Then I said it. ". . . but I have had a discussion with the Prince and Princess of Wales about going to work for them."

"Paul," the Queen said, "you do not have to tell me. Charles has already told me." She sensed how torn I was, and broke my unease with a few words of reassurance. "Look at it this way. You are not actually leaving me. You are simply moving to one side for now. Charles and Diana need people like you. One day, when I'm gone and they are king and queen, you will be back here again," she said.

As I turned to leave, she added, "Anyway, Paul, you are leaving for the best possible reason, for your family, and I understand that."

FROM THE END OF JUNE to the start of August, I carried on with my duties as normal. Not another word was said by the Queen about my departure. For those two months, a household footman worked in my shadow, training as my replacement to work alongside Paul Whybrew.

One afternoon while I was on duty, Lady Susan Hussey, the Queen's lady-in-waiting, asked to see me in the second-floor ladies-in-waiting sitting room. I had always liked Lady Susan, wife of the then BBC chairman Marmaduke Hussey, and the Queen was fond of her. Lady Susan was an honest, forthright woman whose opinion was respected. Unlike many in the household, she was easy to get along with and not at all stuffy or grand.

She was at her desk, signing letters, when I walked in. She asked me to close the door. She started to say that she had heard I was leaving the Queen and then asked: "Do you think it was the right decision to make?" She went on, "I don't know if you are aware, but everything isn't quite what it seems in the household where you are moving."

Downstairs gossip was already awash with talk of "difficulties" within the Waleses' marriage. Gossip must be taken with a pinch of salt among staff, but the Queen's lady-in-waiting was issuing a friendly warning, and effectively providing confirmation. She had long been a trusted confidante of the Prince of Wales and her "intelligence" was the best there could have been. I told Lady Susan how difficult a decision it had been but that there could be no going back.

At the beginning of August 1987, the Queen's imminent departure for the royal yacht *Britannia* and the Western Isles Cruise signaled my last duty day. Everything I did was for the last time: my last breakfast, my last walk with the corgis, my last walk down the Queen's corridor at Buckingham Palace, my last occasion to say, "Will there be anything else, Your Majesty?" That afternoon, she rang her bell in the sitting room and asked if I could take the corgis for a walk. She said it as if it were any other normal afternoon.

By the time I returned, the Rolls-Royce was waiting to take her to Portsmouth, where she would board *Britannia*. My last duty was to see the Queen to the car, so I stood at the Garden Entrance at the side of the palace and waited.

She climbed in with Lady Susan Hussey, and I offered them both a rug for their knees. I closed the car door and stood there. I looked at the Queen in the hopes that she'd say goodbye. She hadn't said anything about my last day, so maybe there would be a wave or a smile. But there was nothing. The Queen looked down, then straight ahead, and the car pulled away.

Some time later, I saw Lady Susan Hussey again, and asked, "Do you know why the Queen wouldn't say goodbye to me?"

"Paul, she couldn't," she replied. "She just couldn't look at you. It wasn't easy for the Queen either."

SIX

DECEIT AT HIGHGROVE

HIGHGROVE SPRANG ONTO red alert. Armed police, guns cocked, stood in the fading evening light on the doorstep and counted down to the moment of storming the house, all set to flush out the intruder whose shadowy figure had been spotted moving near a window in an upstairs room. Beads of sweat broke out on my forehead, and fear took hold of me. The bulletproof vest strapped round my chest, an addition to my butler's uniform, did nothing to reassure me.

The Prince and Princess of Wales were away. I was the first to approach the back door, and my hand steadied to turn the key in the lock before I stepped aside. Surrounding me were an armed unit from the Gloucestershire Constabulary, dog handlers with Alsatians, and around six police who patrolled the estate. It was their unit that had raised the alarm by telephoning our home in the middle of that evening.

Maria had taken the call. "Hello, Maria, is Paul still up at the house?" asked one of the officers.

"No, he's been home about ten minutes. I'll put him on."

I took the receiver.

"Paul, is anyone else in the house?"

"No. I've just locked up."

Then the policeman knew something was wrong. "Well, a light has just gone on on the landing. One of the guys in the backyard noticed a figure in the window, and he thought it was you. You'd better come up."

As I made my way to the police post near the house, an urgent call for assistance was put out for the attendance of the dog handlers and an armed-response unit. When the entire collection of police came together, bulletproof vests were handed out.

"Right. Keep at the back of us," whispered an officer, as the back door was pushed open. The police went off in different directions. They were armed with guns. I was armed with the layout of the house for what would be a perfectly executed search of the residence. The officers swept through each floor, starting at the basement and walking stealthily, landing by landing, room by room. The nature of the *Starsky and Hutch*–style flush-'em-out operation was funny, looking back, but at the time the police could not have been more dead serious. My heart was in my mouth.

As we crept onto the top floor, I pointed out William and Harry's bedroom, the nanny's room, and the day nursery. Suddenly the two dogs began to snarl. "They're getting something," said one handler.

Everyone was convinced that someone was in the house. Each top-floor room was checked, but there was nothing.

Then the armed officers peeled off and climbed into the loft space. Nothing.

On to the roof. Nothing.

The officer who had spotted the movement in the house was bewildered. He was convinced it had been me, and only a check-call to the house had told him otherwise. He couldn't understand or explain it. Both the prince and princess were informed of the incident, but it was put down to a mistaken report, and remains a rather spooky mystery.

That puzzling incident with the police could almost sum up life at the royal countryside retreat. Ghosts from the past, in the haunting shape of Camilla Parker Bowles, and things that went bump in the night, prompted by the rows she caused, ensured that life could never be as straightforward as at Buckingham Palace. But those sights and sounds would take time to be noticed. Initally, all seemed well.

W HEN I ARRIVED at Highgrove, only one thing re-minded me of "home": the wooden box fixed to the wall in the butler's pantry. Like the Queen, Prince Charles called staff by pressing a bell and a little red circular disk dropped, like a miniature parking garage barrier, into a small round window. At Highgrove, that red disk might as well have been a warning flag heralded by an urgent siren rather than a bell, because Prince Charles never liked to be kept waiting. From the ground-floor pantry, it was a stopwatch dash across the carpeted corridor and into his rooms.

Whenever the princess saw me hurrying to him, it tick-led her. "Go on, run along! Run!" She laughed. "You don't run that fast for me!"

I didn't *need* to run that fast for the princess. Or for the monarch. But everyone in the household staff knew how exacting Prince Charles could be, and so did his wife. She'd tease me, especially when I had to go out on the rooftop in all weather to raise his standard. His flag had to fly when he was in residence. The Queen had a flag sergeant for this job, but at Highgrove it was my task. I had a million and one other duties, but the prince insisted. When word was telephoned through that he was five minutes away, the rooftop circus routine began. I climbed into the dark attic via a ceiling hatch on the nursery landing and then squeezed, on my knees, through another hatch, which led out into the spine of the gray-tiled, sloping roof. A wooden gantry with a handrail to one side ran along the curved ridge for me to walk on. For "gantry," read "plank." For "walk," read "brush with death." In gale-force winds and driving rain, that white flagpole became my stabilizer. I waited and waited, and hung on, for the car or helicopter to come into view, then raised the flag. Thankfully, the standard of the Princess of Wales did not have to fly when she was alone in residence. Of that, she always reminded me.

W HEN THE RED DISK dropped into the box window, I had to drop everything and make my way to the library, whose window, behind Balmoral tartan curtains and limed-wood shutters, looked out on to the immaculate gardens and terrace at the back of the house. The prince was invariably sitting at a round table in the middle of the room in a basket-weave chair. The room was suffused with the scent of white Longi lilies in the table's center, sprouting from a vase hidden by piles of books, with just enough space cleared for him to write letters. He stood up and told me a "very special visitor" was coming to Highgrove that summer's day. "Queen Elizabeth will be arriving this afternoon," he said.

The Queen Mother was always referred to as "Queen Elizabeth" by the family when addressing staff. It was her first visit to Highgrove, in July 1988, an important occasion for the prince, who famously adored his granny. A special five o'clock tea was planned. I set a table on the terrace and put up a parasol to shield the Queen Mother from the hot sun. I wanted it to be perfect.

As the Daimler crawled up the sweeping gravel driveway, I stood with him on the two steps at the central stone porch where white double doors led into the three-story, eighteenth-century house. I opened the car door and the Queen Mother, wearing a large hat with silk roses in its deep brim, climbed out. Her grandson bowed, took her hand, and kissed it. "Welcome, darling Granny," he said, and they went inside before enjoying a slow walk around the prized maze of gardens he had designed and created.

In the kitchen, chef Chris Barber and I busied ourselves with the production of smoked salmon, chicken, ham, and cucumber sandwiches, cut into squares with crusts removed, together with the tiny circular jam sandwiches, known as "jam pennies," a favorite in the royal nursery.

I walked through the French windows and out onto the back terrace where the fanned branches of an ancient cedar tree cast a shadow over the stone flags. Gothic pavilions stood in each corner, and there was an octagonal pond in the middle.

At the table set in the center of the terrace, I offered the Queen Mother a smoked-salmon sandwich. She hesitated. "No, thank you, Paul. Do you know, they are my *least* favorite," she said, tilting her head to one side, as she often did.

The prince looked mortified. "Would you like something else, Granny?" he said.

"No, tea is fine," she said, hand raised, palm forward. She didn't eat one sandwich that day.

A couple of hours later, the Queen Mother got back into her Daimler, took out a cream chiffon headscarf, and draped it out of the partially opened rear window. It signaled the start of the ritual between grandmother and grandson. As he saw the headscarf drop from the window, the prince took the handkerchief from the breast pocket of his blazer, held it by one corner between his thumb and forefinger, and waved it in response. He was visibly moved. "I don't know what I would do without her," he said, as the car disappeared down the drive, its wheels kicking up dust. He stood there, waving his handkerchief, until she had disappeared out of view, and we turned to go back inside.

Then the mood changed from reflection to reproof. "Such a pity that tea was ruined," said the prince. He felt that the Queen Mother's staff at Clarence House—William Tallon, the Palace Steward, and Reginald Wilcox, the page—*should* have been consulted. "Next time, would you please ring William or Reg and find out what Queen Elizabeth likes instead of guessing?"

"I'm terribly sorry, Your Royal Highness. Smoked salmon is always served at royal teas."

It was a futile protest. In his eyes it had been a failure, and his cutting remarks had the desired effect. They made me feel lousy. One smoked-salmon sandwich and a visit from the Queen Mother made me realize the stark difference between life at Highgrove and life at Buckingham

Palace. Serving the heir to the throne was going to be more challenging than serving the monarch.

* * *

IT'S HARD TO SAY what the prince did more of: write memos or shake people's hands. For a man so concerned about environmental issues, a small forest could have been chopped down to supply Highgrove with memorandum pads. The Queen preferred to tell me instructions, but Prince Charles wrote everything down. Memos rained down like confetti at Highgrove:

> Did someone pick up the seeds for the garden?
> Is there a bottle bank in Tetbury?
> Can you get someone to look at my telephone?
> Could the China dish be mended, please?

Nor, it seemed, was he inclined to do much for himself. He wrote once: "A letter from the Queen must have fallen by accident into the wastepaper basket beside the table in the library. Please look for it." Years later, after the Andrew Morton book was serialized in the *Sunday Times,* he left a memo stating: "I never want to see that paper in this house again! As for the tabloids, I don't want to see any of them either. If anyone wants them, they will have to find them themselves—and that includes Her Royal Highness!"

* * *

MY DUTY BEGAN at Highgrove, a mile from the town of Tetbury in Gloucestershire, on September 1, 1987. The Prince and Princess of Wales were in Spain as guests of King Juan Carlos before heading to Balmoral. It would not be until the second week of October that I saw my new employers. I had five weeks to familiarize myself with the strange house and a different way of life.

Without Wendy Berry, the housekeeper, I don't know what I would have done. I knew her son, James, a footman at Buckingham Palace. She had gotten the job at Highgrove when he moved as an under-butler to Kensington

Palace and recommended his mother for the post of house-keeper. Working alongside her was like being on probation again, training in her shadow. I had moved from London without Maria and Alex at first, so I stayed with Wendy at her grace-and-favour single-story, stone-built gate lodge, at the bottom of the driveway.

We held down the fort at Highgrove but, with its master and mistress away, the house was closed down. The furniture was covered with dust sheets. Wooden shutters were latched down for security reasons at the great windows on the ground floor. It was like living in a deserted house. It was strange going from the constant occupation of Buckingham Palace, with its background noise and downstairs life teeming with staff, to the emptiness and silence of an unoccupied Highgrove in the middle of arable countryside. We rattled around the building like lost souls. Instead of wild after-duty parties, I shared a bottle of wine and a quiet chat in Wendy's company.

Among the outdoor staff, there were other friendly faces, especially the estate's groom, Paddy Whiteland, as old as some of the rosewood furniture. In fact, he had come with the furniture, having worked at the house for more than forty years. Or, as Prince Charles put it: "We're going to have you stuffed and mounted when you die, Paddy, and put you in the front hall!"

Paddy's knowledge of Highgrove was encyclopedic, and his duties were varied. If the prince wanted a tree taken down, he told Paddy. If he wanted a fence erected, he told Paddy. If a flower bed was messy, he told Paddy. If he wanted to hear gossip, well-informed Paddy told him. The prince trusted his word as much as he trusted anyone. Paddy was a wily old soul, and everyone, especially the prince, loved him.

Then there were the gardeners. Dennis Brown nurtured his plants and vegetables as if they were children. With a flat cap on his head and shirtsleeves rolled up, he was always found with a spade or trowel in the walled Victorian kitchen garden, which supplied organic vegetables and fruit for the house. Colleagues David and James tended the remainder of the gardens, which, on each side of the house, provided a different colorful vista; an avenue of golden yews stood like giant, balled hedgehogs; boundaries of lush green topiary; the multicolors of wildflower meadows; the carpet of yellow of the buttercup fields; the belts of trees. It was, by far, one of the finest gardens in England.

In September, Maria and Alex joined me. We were now expecting our second child. Our new home, at the ramshackle cottage at Close Farm, was far removed from the estate, but the builders had spent the previous month renovating the interior, and the smell of fresh paint hung in every room. But a lick of paint and a new green carpet couldn't paper over the cracks. The garden was still grossly overgrown, the gutter loose and there were broken panes in the downstairs windows.

My first domestic duty was to patch up the windows to keep out the rain. It was a bleak home, even with Maria's choice of pink-and-white Laura Ashley wallpaper. Although she had been the prime mover behind our relocation, she missed the Royal Mews and was having second thoughts.

Living in that house, working in a residence smothered by dust sheets, being 110 miles away from the friendships and banter of the palace and with a homesick wife, I thought: What have I done? It had been a career gamble and first impressions were not encouraging.

Wax-jacketed Paddy, who brought the smell of stables and horses into our home, was always there to make us smile. "If you'll be having a new baby, you'll be needing fresh eggs," he said. He arrived that afternoon on his tractor, pulling a trailer with a flat-pack shed, which he constructed there and then in our back garden. He also brought Rhode Island Red chickens. "Fresh eggs on tap every morning," he announced. Maria said it was a good thing he didn't see the importance of using fresh milk.

When he saw our new green carpet, he said it was grand. "It's God's color, so it is. God always paints in green—trees, grass . . . carpets!" He laughed.

If the living conditions seemed tough, the job was

tougher. When the prince and princess returned in October, the real test began. The support network of three hundred staff at Buckingham Palace had gone. No longer was I one of two footmen where the duties were shared and two pages provided backup. I was a butler in isolation, responsible for the running of an entire royal residence, not one corridor and one suite of rooms. Burrell and Berry were the only full-time indoor household staff when there were really enough duties to keep five on their toes.

Everyone knew the Waleses' staff were the best-paid in royal service. The switch from the monarch to heir to the throne brought a £10,000 increase, taking my annual salary from around £8,000 a year to £18,000. For that hike, the treadmill went faster. I was thrown in at the deep end. There was no wine butler to decant the bottles of port and claret, no one to wash the dishes, no footmen to greet guests, take their coats or fetch logs for the fire, no florist to arrange flowers for the table, no one to run onto the roof to raise the standard, no one to do the shopping. All of a sudden, it was all up to me. No longer did state livery uniforms hang in the wardrobe, just a simple double-breasted, gold-buttoned dark-blue blazer, with lapel badges carrying the Prince of Wales's three feathers. It was worn with dark-blue trousers, white shirt, and dark-blue tie.

There was one blessing in disguise, I suppose. I went from nine corgis to the prince's two Jack Russells, Tigger and Roo, and the chore of walking them was not, thank heavens, my responsibility. Prince Charles did that. There was no manned switchboard, so even answering the telephone became my job.

One day, I picked up the receiver in the pantry. "Hello, Tetbury [and the number]."

"Hello, Paul."

I immediately recognized the voice. It was the Queen. "Good morning, Your Majesty," and I was thrilled to hear her. It was the first time we had spoken since my departure. I couldn't help but ask how she was. And how was my favorite corgi, Chipper. And how was—

*H*anging off Mum's apron strings in the
backyard of 57 Chapel Road

*S*carborough Beach, 1960

*A*ge eleven

*E*arly days
as a trainee
chef in the
living room
at No. 47

"Is His Royal Highness there?"

She interrupted me in full flow. I had obviously talked too long, and I put the call through to Prince Charles. "It's the Queen, Your Royal Highness."

ON MOVING WEST along the M4, I was told that the prince was "not intending to use Highgrove a great deal." It was like Windsor Castle for the Queen and Royal Lodge for the Queen Mother, a weekend retreat. The prince and princess were supposed to spend Monday to Friday together at Kensington Palace, where Harold Brown was full-time butler. At least, that was the official line.

But from that first autumn Prince Charles began to spend weekdays at Highgrove by himself. The prince, who brought with him a valet, traveling chef, and protection officer, stayed at least three days a week. I got used to the sight of the red Wessex helicopter of the Queen's Flight hovering into its landing position in the paddock a few hundred yards from the front door, and weekend post became a weekday job too. When the prince was alone, life at Highgrove had the atmosphere of a doctor's surgery waiting room: formal, quiet, timetabled. He filled his days with engagements and appointments. His lunch guests included friends such as Vernon Russell-Smith, Camilla Parker Bowles, Candida Lycett Green, the Duchess of Devonshire, Charles and Patti Palmer-Tomkinson, and Nicholas Soames, MP.

When alone, he spent hours in the garden. I remember him digging out the earth and laying a carpet of thyme from the back terrace down to a pond. He called it his "thyme walk" and said he'd almost broken his back making it. Otherwise, he stayed in the library listening to classical music, which drifted through the corridors, so loud that a knock on his door could go unnoticed. I often walked around the house in step to Verdi's *Aida*.

The princess was never a weekday visitor. She stayed in London with the children and lunched at the palace with friends, such as fashion designer Jasper Conran, Laura Lonsdale, or Carolyn Bartholomew, or dined at Harry's Bar, Mayfair, with the ex-King Constantine (whom she called Tino) and Queen Anne-Marie of Greece. Or she went to San Lorenzo's, Knightsbridge, with Lady Carina Frost, wife of television presenter David Frost. In the week, she had riding lessons on two mornings, at 7:30 A.M. sharp, with Major James Hewitt at Knightsbridge Barracks, Hyde Park. At that time of her life she was keen to learn new skills. On other mornings she had what she called "deaf lessons," learning sign language, or dance lessons in the drawing room.

On Friday afternoons, husband and wife came together when the princess drove to Highgrove with William and Harry, then five and two. They then headed back to London every Sunday after lunch, traveling with a nanny, a dresser, and a protection officer. The princess viewed London as her social scene and Kensington Palace as home. Conversely, the prince preferred dining with the "Highgrove set" and used the house more and more as his base, staying the odd night in the capital with his wife.

For royal couples to lead separate lives was not unusual. It didn't seem odd that the prince pursued different interests than his wife, ones that kept him in the countryside. In my early days at Highgrove, the prince and princess always shared each other's company on weekends. Contrary to popular myth, I never had to take a dinner tray to the princess in her room. A card table was set up every evening in front of the television in the sitting room and they ate together. They chatted like any ordinary man and wife coming together after time spent working apart. I read somewhere once that the prince never asked about the princess's week or how she was. Utter nonsense. The prince, civil and talkative, was normally first to start the conversation and took great interest in his wife's work or what she had done that week.

If she wanted to talk to him at other times, she always knew where to find him—the library. He sat up late, listening to music, working on stacks of paperwork. The princess retired to bed, where she had her own stereo and taste in more contemporary music. As Verdi and Haydn played downstairs, Whitney Houston played upstairs. Over and over again, one of her hit songs was played—"I Will Always Love You." (It was not until later years that the princess developed a love of classical music.)

Each night, one of my duties was to attend to the drinks tray in the drawing room, and fill a silver flask with freshly squeezed orange juice for the prince. But, to his mild irritation, the princess liked it and often got there first, as Prince Charles reminded me in an official memo: "Please, in future, could you check the flask of orange juice at the end of dinner because Her Royal Highness tends to drink it all and there's none left for me! C." One more memo.

In the drawing room, one of four main rooms off the central hallway, I had another duty: to set up a small altar each Sunday morning so the prince could take Holy Communion from Bishop Woods. I draped a white cloth over a card table and placed two silver candlesticks, with lighted candles, on each side, then placed a small silver salver, silver chalice, and crystal cruets of water and red wine between them. It was a ceremony the prince took extremely seriously, but the princess never joined him. In the early days, they had attended the local church in Tetbury, and she thought communion was a lazy and pointless exercise if it was not carried out in God's house.

When the princess came with the children, Highgrove burst into life. The house was filled with laughter, the joyful shrieks of the two boys running across the wooden floors, the princess chasing them around the hallway, playing hide-and-seek, the prince growling like the Big Bad Wolf. By day, as her boys stood at her side, the princess played the piano that stood upright against the plain peach wall of the hallway, next to the door into the drawing room. Whatever the warnings of Lady Susan Hussey about all not being as it seemed, I couldn't see huge problems on the surface. As parents, the prince and princess appeared blissfully at ease, and no one worked harder than they to provide a warm, happy home for their children. They were an unbeatable team.

A lively atmosphere returned to the staff dining room too. It was no longer just two people: there were the nannies, Barbara Barnes or Ruth Wallace, dressers Evelyn Dagley or Fay Marshalsea, and protection officers Graham Smith or Dave Sharp. As staff of the princess, they had a shared sense of humor. Mealtimes were fun again. The only person who went into a slight flap with the princess's arrival was Paddy. He knew she liked to take a morning swim in the outdoor heated pool, which, in winter, was covered with a giant inflatable bubble. He worried endlessly about getting the temperature right and never quite knew how much chlorine to use. He often guessed, then panicked when the princess emerged from an early-morning dip with reddened eyes. But she always saw the funny side.

The princess was close to her staff and cared deeply about them, some more than others, but none more so than protection officer Graham Smith, who was unique in being universally liked. He was easygoing and had no airs and graces, and in later years, the princess always said he was her genuine favorite. Graham was the initial conduit between the princess and Maria when she was first offered the post of dresser, and he was delighted to see us both at Highgrove.

Graham developed a cough and a sore throat, then cancer of the throat. Whenever she could, the princess took time out of her morning schedules to accompany him on hospital visits for chemotherapy sessions. His illness ultimately forced him to retire from duty and, some years later, he died. His shoes were never truly filled.

Maria was another favorite of the princess. On her first weekend in October, the princess visited our house and brought us a welcome-to-your-new-home gift: quilted cushions to match the Laura Ashley wallpaper. Our semidetached house was about half a mile away off the estate. "You're a bit too far away for my liking. I must work on that," she said.

Unbeknownst to me at the time, she also had to work on me. I was still Maria's husband, Paul, the Queen's former footman. Now I was butler at Highgrove, which was effectively regarded as Prince Charles's territory. I was, in those early days, marked as the prince's man, regardless of Maria's friendship with the princess. When the prince was alone at Highgrove, it was my duty to serve him and protect his world. But not for long, if the princess had anything to do with it.

At neoclassical Highgrove, there was a simple décor behind the façade of ocher and stone, with its Venetian window above the front door. Inside, there were light yellow walls, lime green upholstery, cane furniture in the library, wooden floors, and green carpets. It could have been any large house in Chelsea. On tables and walls, there were photographs of William and Harry, and Herend pillboxes. Prince Charles's touch was apparent too: his own watercolor paintings were framed on walls, his favorite Wemyss Ware pottery massed in groups on mantelpieces and tables, plants and flowers scattered everywhere. On a round table in the middle of the hallway, a spectacular dried-flower arrangement was the first thing that came into view. On either side of the entrance, large pots contained miniature trees or fuchsia bushes.

It was in the outside appearance of Highgrove that the prince really made his influence tell, showing off his love and knowledge of architecture and gardening. The house didn't look grand enough when he purchased it in 1980, so he added Ionic flat-faced stone columns to the front beneath a new pediment with a round glazed window at its center. All around the rooftop, he created a stone balustrade surmounted by four stone urns on each side. The house was his sanctuary, even though it is only a few hundred yards from the main road, reached by a curving driveway that cuts through a red and yellow meadow of poppies and corn marigolds.

The intricately designed gardens were the prince's escape; his exclusive world where he spent hours digging, weeding, planting, and clipping. Aside from his other passion, watercolor painting, a once bare garden became the canvas for his true, natural masterpiece. Windows and arches were cut into high hedgerows, climbing roses were teased and trained to grow over a pergola to form a rose tunnel, a grass path cut a swath through a wildflower meadow. He restored the Victorian kitchen garden, reached by a pink gate in a brick wall surround, to its former glory. Flowers, fruit, and vegetables filled it, but the centerpiece was a pond and fountain surrounded by a little white picket fence. There was the woodland garden: a mass weave of roots, tree stumps carved into chairs, willow screens, and bark flooring. At its center was a giant, rust-colored Amazonian nude lady. The prince handed me a pot of wax and I had to buff and polish her twice a month.

Perched above the figure, lodged twenty feet up a holly tree, was William and Harry's thatched tree house, painted red and green, with its handmade cupboards and chairs. It would become a hideout and a place of many happy hours for the two young princes and two other boys: Alex and my second son, Nicholas, who was born at sixteen minutes past midnight on April 19, 1988. With the prince's permission, I planted a flowering cherry tree in the garden of our house at Close Farm to commemorate the arrival of our second son.

The prince even had his own environmentally friendly sewerage system installed: a system of tanks and reed beds treated and filtered waste. Not even this part of the natural garden escaped the prince's attention as yet another memo made clear: "Would you please inform guests staying at Highgrove NOT to dispose of tampons or condoms down the toilet as they strangle the reed beds." All I could think of was, How am I possibly going to find the words? I have to admit that, when it came to it, I was too embarrassed to relay that particular order. I merely asked guests to refrain from placing foreign objects down the toilet. I didn't have to be as precise as the prince.

The princess, of all people, knew how important the development of the estate and its gardens was to her husband. From the very beginning, she kept a photographic record—stage by stage, season by season. Carefully, and for the sole purpose of pleasing him, she plotted progress and pasted hundreds of color photographs into leatherbound albums. For those who wrongly believed that she turned up her nose at her husband's love of gardening, those albums are a vivid testimony to the opposite. She took an interest even at a time when, as history has informed us, third parties were involved on both sides of the royal marriage.

A DESK DIARY WAS kept in the butler's pantry so that Wendy and I could keep track of the prince's peripatetic lifestyle. It was our arrivals-and-departures logbook: when a corner of the page-a-day diary was filled in with red felt-tip, Prince Charles was at Highgrove alone. A thick green stripe told us that the princess was in residence alone and a capital *N*, for nursery, meant William and Harry were staying. When red, green, and *N* appeared together, mainly on weekends, the Waleses were there as a family. Through diligence and duty, we religiously wrote down the names of the guests who were expected and at what time so that we could keep on top of a hectic schedule. This diary for staff use was left in the butler's pantry. It was not hidden because, for its intended purpose of the efficient running of the house, I never considered it to be a secret.

In the spring of 1988, with a red colored-in corner denoting the prince was alone, the guests for lunch were recorded: "4 for lunch—HRH, Mrs. Parker Bowles, Mr. Neil Foster, and Mr. Vernon Russell-Smith," alongside a reminder that the electrician was coming to fix lights in the library. Nothing extraordinary. Just another run-of-the-mill lunch appointment. In the same way I wrote down "Emma Thompson and Kenneth Branagh for lunch," "Michael Portillo for lunch," "Jimmy Savile for lunch" (the only person allowed to smoke inside Highgrove), "Selina Scott," the television presenter, or "Mr. and Mrs. Hector Barrantes for lunch"—the Duchess of York's mother and stepfather. And I continued to note down: "Mr. and Mrs. Oliver Hoare and Mrs. Parker Bowles for lunch," "Mrs. Candida Lycett Green and Mrs. Parker Bowles for lunch." Or "Mr. and Mrs. Parker Bowles with their children."

Out of the blue one day in August 1988—three months before Prince Charles's fortieth birthday party—the red disk dropped into the box under the label library, and I went to see what he wanted. "Paul, can you tell me how the princess knows who exactly has visited Highgrove this week?"

It made no sense to me. I had not mentioned a word to the princess. I was confused. "I am sorry, Your Royal Highness, I don't understand," and, at that moment, I truly didn't. I didn't think of the times the princess had joined me in the butler's pantry for a read of a newspaper or a snatched gossip over a mug of coffee or at the kitchen sink where I washed and she dried. I hadn't thought much of it when I came in from the main house and found her waiting for me in the pantry. The princess's had been a familiar face in staff areas since her days at Buckingham Palace. I didn't know how cunning she could be. Not then.

As the prince grilled me, suspected me, and asked me to think, the penny dropped like a lead weight on my foot. "Well, I do keep a record of the lunch guests, Your Royal Highness," I said meekly.

"Why?" We both knew what had happened then. "Why do you write names down in your diary?" he demanded.

It was so that I could tell the police who to expect at the front gate, so that Wendy and I were kept up to date and . . .

"Well, don't. Do not write any more names in that diary," he interrupted.

From then on I abandoned the color-coded page system. The page-a-day entries became just: "4 for lunch."

AFTER THE ANNUAL family vacation to Balmoral, something else changed. The Prince and Princess of Wales no longer came together regularly at Highgrove for weekends. Only on odd occasions did that happen, and only when other guests were present. Throughout the autumn and winter of 1988 and into 1989, the princess was alone with the children from Friday to Sunday or did not come on some weekends when the prince was at the house.

A distinction grew up between what we called the princess's house when she was in residence and the prince's house when he was alone. When the princess arrived with the boys and her staff from London, the atmosphere was lighter, more relaxed. Self-service meals were taken in the dining room, and the long mahogany table had a laminated cloth. When the prince returned, formality walked through the door with him. He was waited on at mealtimes, and a white linen tablecloth was used.

When the princess was there, she came to speak to me in the pantry, nibbling bars of white chocolate, which I kept for her in the wine fridge. As she walked in, she closed the connecting door into the kitchen. It was a signal to the rest of the staff, a sort of Do Not Disturb sign. The other door, into the corridor, was left slightly ajar, and it was not unknown for Prince Charles to walk past and spot his wife leaning with her back against the kitchen top, chatting, or, as he viewed it, gossiping. He told the princess not to listen to staff gossip or tittletattle, and it worried me that these idle chats might reflect badly on me and affect my relationship with him.

At one staff Christmas Ball, held at Buckingham Palace by the Queen, the princess spent half an hour chatting with Maria and me as we stood at the far end of the Picture Gallery. That night, she was wearing a Zandra Rhodes cocktail dress with a ragged hem. I remember thinking that we were monopolizing her company. "Your Royal Highness, you'd better move on," I said. People were staring at us, noting that an acceptable five- or ten-minute chat was turning into a drawn-out conversation, and the princess and Maria were giggling like old friends. I found it both extremely embarrassing and flattering that the princess spent so much time with us.

In the pantry, she dropped by for no longer than fifteen or twenty minutes. She laughed and joked; she spoke about William and Harry and their progress. One day she was excited because William had lost his first tooth. It was then that the lonely princess I had first observed over a Big Mac meal with Mark Simpson reappeared, but this time it was in her own home. She said how lonely she had been feeling, how strong she needed to be, how unappreciated she felt. It was all generally said and rather vague; she gave no details. It was as if she was floating her concerns by me, perhaps fishing for a response or reaction, but none was ever given. I listened. I felt sorry for her, but I just listened. And she ate her white chocolate. She told me she had a "special friend" no one knew about. Again, I said nothing. It would have been rude to ask.

In that room, when we were alone, she seemed vulnerable, insecure, but when she walked out of the pantry door, she snapped back into a princess, and the staff, especially Wendy, were curious. What had she said? What was going on? Family stuff, I said.

What was the prince like with me when he was at home alone? Well, he left me memos.

WENDY KNEW long before I did what was happening. I had to find out for myself. Like a jigsaw puzzle without the front of a box for reference, a picture came together piece by piece. My desk diary might have been devoid of names and color codes but I still wrote the word "Private" on countless days in the spring of 1989: a reminder to butler and housekeeper that Prince Charles was staying elsewhere in a private residence. Only his then–assistant private secretary Richard Aylard, his personal protection officer Colin Trimming, and his valet, either Michael Fawcett or Ken Stronach, knew exactly where he was.

By late 1989 and early 1990, the truce was at straining point. Staff might have been left in the dark, but we were not deaf. On the increasingly rare occasions when prince and princess came together, and when the boys were fast asleep, raised voices were heard in the downstairs rooms, doors slammed, heavy footsteps marched up the stairs and across the landing, and there was a deadly silence in an echoey house.

Nor were we blind. I walked into the sitting room one

Saturday evening and the card table I had carefully set for dinner for two was in chaos. Glasses were overturned and broken, herb salt in a dish had been scattered, and the white linen tablecloth was soaked with spilled water. The prince, in his silk dressing gown with his feathers emblem on the breast pocket, was on his hands and knees, picking up cutlery from the floor. "Oh dear," he said. "I think I must have caught my dressing gown on the table and caused this dreadful mess." The princess was nowhere to be seen.

When the prince was alone midweek, and very often on a Sunday night, the usual dinner time of 8:30 P.M. was brought forward. "I think I'll have dinner early tonight, Paul, and then retire," said the prince. The card table was set for one. As instructed, I also laid out the television page of *The Times* for that evening's program schedule on an upholstered stool in front of the sofa with a remote control to one side, the television on standby. New logs were piled high in a basket beside the open, black-leaded fireplace. The sitting room was laid out to give the impression that the prince was having a quiet night in. One evening, Wendy said: "He'll light it for two minutes and then go out. What a waste." The prince's dinners at these times were rushed. When the red disk dropped into the sitting-room box, it was time to clear the card table. No sooner had I returned with the tray to the pantry than I heard car wheels slowly crunching across the gravel of the driveway and disappearing into the distance. "That's him gone until the early hours," Wendy noted.

Prince Charles had a green Aston Martin car for his personal use that was kept in an outside triple garage, a converted stable to the rear of the house. It lined up alongside a classic Bentley, with a cream interior, and a vintage Aston Martin, with a silver dragon statuette on the bonnet, which the Queen had given him as a present for his twenty-first birthday. It was those wheels we had heard crunching across the gravel.

I never thought anything more of these midevening drives until one day I visited the police lodge, close to the house, where a team of officers from the Gloucestershire Constabulary were stationed on permanent patrol. I had gone there with leftovers from the kitchen as a treat. The comings and goings of the prince were raised in lighthearted banter, and a well-kept secret within police circles spilled out. I think they assumed I already knew it. It was said that Prince Charles, on his mystery drives, consistently performed a twenty-two-mile journey, eleven miles there, eleven miles back. And Middlewich House was exactly eleven miles away. Home of Mrs. Camilla Parker Bowles.

"Oh, come on, Paul, you must have known," said Wendy, when I returned to the main house with the gossip. I thought back to the princess telling me how lonely she was. The warning of Lady Susan Hussey about all not appearing as it seemed. The changed routine of more weekends spent apart. The diary. The names. And the princess had seen this. She had known. And all those realizations combined to leave me with a heavy heart.

On her next weekend visit to Highgrove the princess, then twenty-eight, breezed into my pantry and asked if there was anything to eat in the fridge. Living in two separate worlds—one with the prince, one with the princess— meant that the world of household staff was torn by divided loyalties. It meant abandoning the baggage of knowledge from one camp and picking up where you had left off the last time with the other. Switching effortlessly between modes became a robotic function where emotion and morals could play no part. To be butler at Highgrove was to know your place, to observe every detail and not pass comment. Turning a blind eye is a prerequisite for the job: I had intended to remain impartial, until the day the princess decided to involve me. It was going to be my first test of trust. In that summer of 1989, I learned a secret— until she spoke publicly about it—that fostered a bond forever.

It was a Friday, a hot summer's afternoon. After lunch, William and Harry had returned to the second-floor nursery with nanny Olga Powell. The princess came into the pantry and got straight to the point. "I want to ask you something, Paul. I would like you to run an errand for me. I don't want anyone, and I mean *anyone,* else to know about it." She explained the mission. "Will you go to Kemble railway station tomorrow afternoon and pick up someone for me?" she asked.

"Of course, Your Royal Highness," I replied.

"You will be picking up my special friend Major James Hewitt."

Whatever the prince or princess asked me to do, I did to the best of my ability, no questions asked. But in asking me to carry out such a clandestine pickup, she took a giant leap of faith. It was a risk, however calculated, to ask me, the former Queen's man and the butler who spent most of his time with Prince Charles. She gambled that her close friendship with Maria would pay off. What she couldn't have known was that I was determined not to let her down. I had known her misery and sensed her loneliness. This "special friend" brought her excitement and happiness. That much was noticeable.

After lunch, I set off in my silver Vauxhall Astra on the seven-mile journey to Kemble, turning left out of the driveway and on to the A433, which skirted Tetbury, before turning right into a narrow back road that led to the tiny village where the guest was waiting in the deserted parking lot. I saw him before he saw me: a man leaning back against an open-top sports car, dressed in a tweed jacket with a white, open-necked shirt, and sunglasses. "Hello, Paul, how are you?" he said, with an outstretched hand. He had been expecting me. He got into the passenger seat, and I began the journey back, sensing his slight discomfort.

"I can trust you, can't I, Paul?" he asked. I told him that he could trust me because the princess could.

Privately, the mission excited me. In coming years, arranging secret rendezvous and facilitating male guests became the norm. But this was my first-ever mission of making a meeting happen, and no one would find out about it. Not even Wendy could know. I drove into the backyard, then took Major Hewitt through a side gate beside the swimming pool, through the garden, onto the terrace and into the house via the French windows that opened out from the hallway running through the house from front to back. The princess was waiting for us. She embraced her "special friend," who was leaving for a military posting to Germany that autumn. She was glowing. "Thank you, Paul," she said.

"Just call me when you need me again, Your Royal Highness," I said, and I went back to the lunchtime dishes left in the sink.

It needs to be stressed here that Major James Hewitt was a visitor to Highgrove long after Camilla Parker Bowles. Prince Charles had struck the first blow in that regard. The princess merely rose to equal her husband's level of deceit. Of course, the prince would never know about the visitor—it was something I would never tell him. I was the butler at Highgrove but, on that particular weekend, it was the princess's house. Far from wrestling with my conscience, I felt happy to have been of service. Colin Trimming, Richard Aylard, and Michael Fawcett had helped organize the prince's private life. I was helping to facilitate the life of the princess. More important, I was helping engineer her happiness.

ON THURSDAY, JUNE 28, 1990—seven days after William's eighth birthday—there was an accident, which proved to be a watershed in the royal marriage for the princess. That event made her feel more unwanted than she had ever felt before.

The princess was at Kensington Palace, preparing to go to her sons' school play. Meanwhile, it was a mad day at Highgrove, where the prince had been alone all week. I served lunch for ten and then had to rush around preparing an evening reception in the drawing room and hallway for the Wildfowl and Wetlands Trust at which Michael Caine was to be guest of honor. Prince Charles squeezed in a midafternoon game of polo at Cirencester.

Suddenly a phone rang, and all hell broke loose in the world of the prince's valet, Ken Stronach. He screeched away in his car to dash to the prince's side: Prince Charles had fallen off his polo pony and broken his right arm. In excruciating pain, he had been admitted to the hospital.

As about fifty guests began arriving for the reception at Highgrove, however, the show had to go on. I greeted Michael Caine at the front door, and it fell to me to inform him that he had now to step into the shoes of an absent prince. Hosting a reception on behalf of HRH the Prince of Wales was a new role, but he carried it off with aplomb.

MY USUAL ROLE took me into new surroundings: from a grand country house to a basic room off an NHS ward in Cirencester eleven miles away. I became a royal meals-on-wheels, ferrying the prince's food from the Highgrove kitchen and delivering home comforts, replacing the stainless-steel cutlery with silverware; swapping a plain glass with engraved crystal; substituting ordinary white plates with crested bone china; even taking his favorite framed painting of his two Jack Russells—Tigger and Roo—and placing it on an easel in the corner of his room; a little bit of Highgrove to ease his pain, along with a strong painkiller.

That weekend, the princess celebrated her twenty-ninth birthday by driving to the hospital in her gleaming new Mercedes to pick up her husband, his arm still in a sling, and take him back to Highgrove. For her, it was a chance to nurse and care for him, to mother him. Or, as she put it, do what she does best—looking after people. But as she fussed, bothered, and tried to take control, Prince Charles became irritated. He was in pain; he rebuffed her and said he wanted to be alone. She felt utterly rejected and unwanted in her own home, and fled back to London in tears after less than half an hour. That rejection was, without doubt, the straw that broke the camel's back as far as their marriage was concerned. No sooner had she made her departure later that evening than Camilla Parker Bowles arrived. And Prince Charles was pleased to see her.

CAMILLA PARKER BOWLES was seen more at Highgrove than ever before but, contrary to established myth, she did not effectively move in or host dinner parties. She didn't stay over—in fact, I don't recall her ever staying over. From being a regular lunch guest, she became a regular dinner guest or day visitor, with her Jack Russell, Fred. But over that summer she visited on no more than twenty occasions.

If she had been the only visitor, life would have been easier, but she wasn't. She was one of many friends who came to lift the prince's spirits or official guests who arrived to keep him busy. Prince Charles was an irascible patient who could no longer even write letters, let alone indulge his passions for polo, watercolor painting, or gardening. The accident sentenced him to a tedious spell of rest and recuperation at Highgrove for July and August. He spent his days in his library or reclining on his chaise longue in the sun on the back terrace. He was restless and determined that his private audiences should continue, lunch and dinner parties go ahead, and friends visit him. Some, like Nicholas Soames, MP, or Lord and Lady Romsey, stayed the night, which meant there was another room to attend. The prince was hardly independent at the best of times, but the loss of his right arm meant that his valets and I became even more of a household crutch. His irritability grew worse when he tried to learn to write left-handed, penning short letters and notes in the spidery scrawl of a four-year-old. "I feel so bloody useless!" he moaned one day.

I had never felt so bloody exhausted. It had all combined to create an intense workload. And put me, ultimately, in the hospital. My hours, duties, and endurance were stretched to the limit due to the round-the-clock attention the prince needed. Before, he had spent perhaps three days at the house and gone away for a day or two, providing me with a natural break. After the accident he was there constantly, and a royal duty became akin to looking after an infirm relative. I worked from 7 A.M. to 11 P.M. for almost two months solid.

I had finished at midnight one day and got home with every intention of falling into bed. Maria found me collapsed on the bathroom floor, doubled up in pain. Local GP Dr. Walsh was called and he sent me to Princess Margaret Hospital, Swindon. The consultant said I was totally exhausted and, as a result, had contracted a viral infection. Butler, like prince, was ordered to rest, and I spent the next week in the hospital.

Lying there, all I could think about was getting back to Highgrove. No one is indispensable but, in my mind, no one could run the house better. It is either a strength or a fault, but I remain a hands-on person who strives for perfection and needs to do everything himself whenever possible. On my second day there, as I dwelled on it all with a princelike irritability, three familiar faces appeared at the door: the princess and the boys. William and Harry came in, each holding a helium-filled "Get Well" balloon, and their mother sat on the end of my bed. The princess struggled to contain an infectious giggle. Out of uniform, looking forlorn—the sight of her butler laid up was hilarious. "I've never seen you so still," she said, and, with another giggle, added: "You look so pathetic!"

Then she did what she always did in a hospital: wandered off on her rounds. "Let's see if there's anyone else interesting in here," she said, and went off down the corridor onto the ward with William. I could only imagine patients' reactions, coming round from an anaesthetic to find the Princess of Wales beside their beds. Mother and son met a woman recovering from an operation on her birthday. The princess came back in a buoyant mood to "check on my patient." She was thrilled with William because he had bought some flowers from a kiosk for the woman they had just met. She talked about the imminent Balmoral vacation, Maria, our children, and life at our new home—which the princess had secured us before I was taken ill. It was a gorgeous cottage on the Highgrove estate that she had "officially opened" on August 10, 1990.

THE PRINCESS OF WALES, wearing yellow shorts and a turquoise sweatshirt, stood in the doorway at the back door of the eighteenth-century stone cottage with Cotswold slate on the roof. As she held open a pair of kitchen scissors above a taut section of red ribbon, Harry rode his bicycle on the grass and William ran around, laughing with Alexander and Nick. The momentous ceremony seemed lost on them.

The princess wasn't taking it very seriously either. She stood outside the back door, facing into the kitchen: "I declare this house open," she tried to say formally, but giggled halfway through.

It was a Friday evening, and I had nipped down from the main house before preparing dinner for the prince and princess, who were due to leave for Mallorca that weekend. I left Prince Charles in his library. He had given us a moving-in present: a collection of his watercolors. One depicted tiled rooftops in Florence, a landscape of the Italian countryside; another, a scene from a polo match; and a third, an aged drawing of the HMS *Sirius* sailing ship.

The princess's long-held plan to move the Burrell family closer to Highgrove had paid off. From the basic bleakness of Close Farm, we moved to No. 3 The Cottages. The three-bedroom house had low, beamed ceilings and roses climbing up the front wall. A white gate broke up the Cotswold stone wall that surrounded it. It was the home Maria had dreamed of and it was perfect. Prince Charles had even had a derelict storeroom converted into a playroom for our boys. The princess had ensured Dudley Poplak brought class to it: ropes for the staircase, borders for all the rooms, and new materials for the curtains and cushions, all for free. The property, formerly occupied by the prince's valet Ken Stronach before he moved to London, was a short stroll from the main house. There cannot have been a more beautiful walk to work for any employee in England. From the west side of Highgrove, the scenic route led under a hedged archway, down the grass path through the wild-flower meadow, past the woodland garden, then through the kitchen garden.

I DON'T THINK either the prince or I will ever forget the visit of eccentric comedian Spike Milligan, who stayed over at Highgrove one Saturday night. He didn't want to be valeted, and alarm bells rang when he didn't show for breakfast. We later discovered that he hadn't slept a wink in his four-poster bed because, for some inexplicable reason, he had spent the night stretched out on the hard bathroom floor of the Blue Room. Some weeks later, he mailed us a specially made china plaque with written instructions that it be screwed to the bathroom floor. The plaque read: "Spike Milligan slept here." Prince Charles found it hilarious.

THE BELL RANG AND that red disk fell into the box. The prince was standing in the center of the room with Camilla Parker Bowles. Both of them were looking at framed pictures leaning in a stack against the wall.

"Paul, where are those pictures that were over there the other day?" he asked, pointing to the fireplace.

His guest smiled at me. I knew exactly which ones he was referring to. How embarrassing, I thought. "Do you mean your watercolors, Your Royal Highness?"

"Yes—the ones of the tiled rooftops and landscapes of Florence."

"You gave them to me when we moved into the cottage," I replied.

He thought for a minute. "Oh, so I did." Then he turned to Mrs. Parker Bowles. "Well, we'll just have to find something else for you."

It transpired that the prince and his guest were looking for pictures to hang on the walls of her home. She had received many gifts from the prince over the years. Even today she can be seen wearing a diamond brooch in the shape of the Prince of Wales feathers. Thinking back, I was helping the prince to select gifts for his mistress behind the princess's back, but I was only doing my duty. Blind eye, no opinion. As taught.

An assortment of jewelry arrived in regular dispatches along with a trusted party heading west down the M4, sent by Genevieve Holmes, the prince's personal assistant at St. James's Palace. These boxed assortments, wrapped in crisp white tissue paper, were from Kenneth Snowman, of the London-based Wartski jewelers. He had often visited the Queen with pieces of Fabergé. Now it was my task to unwrap and set out the selection on a wooden tray, which I placed on a stand in the corner of the library, covered with a white linen cloth. With me out of the room, Prince Charles selected an item and the rest was packed away and returned.

Yet the prince never forgot the princess. For their tenth wedding anniversary, in 1991—when the media had us believe that deep loathing existed between man and wife—he sent her a keepsake charm to add to her gold-link bracelet, itself a gift from him to her. When she unwrapped the paper, she found a two-centimeter X in gold, not a giant kiss but the Roman numeral symbolizing the figure ten, to accompany the gold W and H he had sent in 1982 and 1984 to mark the births of their sons. Each year, he had sent her a new charm, always gold: a pair of ballet shoes for her love of dance; a tennis racquet for the lessons she enjoyed; a bear because she always had teddy bears; a polo cap; an apple; and, poignantly, a gold miniature of St. Paul's Cathedral, where they had got married. The princess treasured the bracelet and kept it in her safe. The marriage might have been in trouble, but the bracelet was a special reminder of all the good times, she said.

She continued to send her husband an anniversary card and a Valentine card, even after they separated, in 1992, until the divorce four years later. The last gift the prince ever sent the princess was a straw hat trimmed with seashells. She wasn't sure whether it was a joke or just his bad taste. "What am I supposed to do with that?" She giggled.

* * *

I HAD THOUGHT royal overseas tours for me were a thing of the past; only Kensington Palace butler Harold Brown accompanied the Prince and Princess of Wales abroad. Then one day the princess came into the pantry, told me about a five-day trip to Japan to mark the Emperor's Coronation, and asked me to join them in November 1990. "I don't see why Harold should be the one who always gets to go away," she said.

It was the beginning of the end for Harold and the princess, but it was the beginning of a much closer relationship with her for me, even if I didn't know it at the time.

Japan was not easy for anyone on the royal tour. The divisions between husband and wife were sharply evident even before they arrived at the British Embassy and were allocated separate master suites on the first floor. They were business partners with nothing else in common, together because of the nature of their work. Frostbite had set in on the relationship, and there was no hint of togetherness in anything they did or said. I saw a different princess from the one I had known at Highgrove. There was an unsettled edge to her personality: tetchiness and frustration. She was highly strung in the prince's presence and snapped at me and her dresser Helena Roache over the smallest things: more towels were needed, the hair dryer wasn't working properly, there was a water mark on a dress. The carpet between the prince and princess's rooms might as well have been made of eggshells, and that surprised me because I had never felt uneasy before in her company.

"I want to travel the world and do things my way," she said in her room. Joint tours, with their timetable and protocols, placed a free, spontaneous spirit in a straitjacket. She desperately wanted to break free and do solo tours.

I saw the confidence-crushing effect Prince Charles had on her in Japan when she tried to win his approval. Prince Charles and his staff were checking their watches as they milled in the grand hallway ahead of an official function when the princess, looking radiant, came downstairs wearing a Catherine Walker red tartan coatdress with red velvet collar and cuffs. It was loud but elegant, and she was smiling. I was waiting at the bottom of the stairs when she walked to the prince's side and said, "So, do you like my outfit, Charles?"

His reply was soft and devoid of bitterness, but its effect was brutal. "Yes. You look like a British Caledonian air stewardess." With that, he turned and walked out of the front door to an awaiting car. The smile vanished from the princess's face and she looked down. Then she did what she became expert at: she mustered confidence from somewhere and followed him out of the door.

It was not the only time he crushed her confidence, intentionally or otherwise. Six months later, in May 1991, on a joint tour to Czechoslovakia, the royal party stayed at President Havel's palace in Prague. Not only did husband and wife have separate rooms, they stayed on different floors. The princess had changed for an afternoon engagement and, again, came down the stairs to where the prince was waiting. She wore an off-white jacket and skirt, with black buttons and a black handkerchief in the breast pocket, with black-and-white shoes. She didn't ask how she looked this time, but Prince Charles poked fun at her appearance. "You look like you've just joined the Mafia." He smiled. Perhaps it was meant to be a joke, but no one laughed. The sad thing was that she always looked stunning, but it was other people who told her so.

Only when she snatched the odd few minutes away from the protocol did she revert to the fun, warm princess I knew. Like the time when she led Helena Roache and me out through the French windows into the embassy garden before she left for the Emperor of Japan's garden party. "Come on, you two, let's have a happy snap," said the princess. In all my years with the Queen, I had never been photographed with her informally, and yet there I was, side by side with the future Queen of England. As Helena said "Cheeeese," I was momentarily uneasy about protocol. "I'm not sure this is the done thing. Hope His Royal Highness doesn't see us," I said.

"Oh, don't worry. Now, smile for the happy snap," said the princess, and the camera clicked.

That picture remains a cherished memory. I look at it now and see myself rigid, standing at attention, wearing the Hermès tie the princess had bought me the previous June. (The princess *never* forgot anyone's birthday.) I see her in her three-quarter-length jacket worn over a simple shift dress in the colors of the Japanese national flag, with a red disk on her hat to depict the rising sun. We did the same on a balcony in Czechoslovakia.

Happy snaps, taken at a time when the princess was anything but happy. I couldn't wait to get the film from Japan and Czechoslovakia developed, and they went on proud display on the mantelpiece in our cottage alongside another memory, a portrait of the princess taken in July 1990. She had beckoned me to join her in the dining room, where, on the table, she had spread out a collection of black-and-white prints from her first *Vogue* magazine shoot with photographer Patrick Demarchelier. She looked stunning with tousled hair and a high-necked black sweater. "Would you like one?" she asked, and gave me the pick of the collection. When my choice was made, she took the photograph, leaned on the sideboard, and signed it: "To Paul and Maria, with much love from Diana." One more smile to hide a thousand inner turmoils.

Her generosity matched that of Prince Charles. That same year, for my thirty-second birthday, he presented me with the first lithographic print of his watercolor paintings of Wensleydale. He signed it in pencil "Charles 1990." Every other print thereafter was signed "C." We hung it on the wall above the fireplace where his wife's portrait stood in its frame.

M Y PASSPORT HAD rid itself of the cobwebs. Then, in September 1991, we went to Pakistan, the princess's first solo royal tour. Her wish to travel and do her own thing had been granted, and she was free of the binding, merciless protocol of joint visits, away from her husband's criticisms of her dresses and outfits. She was on the world stage by herself and determined to shine as an independent royal figure, representing her nation. Buckingham Palace and the Foreign Office would be watching. The princess was in a buoyant mood because the tour had been given the go-ahead by the Queen, who had sanctioned one of her BAe 146 jets to fly into the Himalayas. The princess approached me in the pantry at Highgrove. "This tour is so important to me, Paul, and I want the A-team with me," she said.

I joined that team, headed by her assiduous private secretary Patrick Jephson, and including dresser Helena, hairdresser Sam McKnight, and a protection officer. Erstwhile radio journalist Dickie Arbiter was also on hand to handle and cajole the media. He was a huge supporter of the princess, who held him in such high regard that she placed him on her birthday-card list.

It was a privilege to be on such a historic solo tour with the princess, especially when its ultimate success and smooth running exceeded expectations everywhere we went: the mountain village of Chitral, the Khyber Pass, Lahore, Rawalpindi, and Islamabad. As always, she was the consummate professional, loved the people, and made a terrific impact everywhere she went, no more so than in Chitral, in the clouds of the Himalayas, where the entire five hundred–strong village turned out to see her. The laudatory newspaper and television coverage that greeted the trip gave her such a thrill and sense of achievement. From that moment on, she went from strength to strength and grew in stature, with her reliable A-team alongside her every step of the way.

Upon our return from the tour, she presented me with an illustrated book about Pakistan. Inside, she had written a special message to remind me of the depth and humbleness of the people we had met, especially at a center for the deaf. It read: "For Paul. 'There are many whom love God ... they roam the jungles in their search ... but I will love that person who loves all of God's humanity'—Iqbal. With love from Diana, Pakistan 1991." That verse, from the Pakistani national poet Sir Muhammad Iqbal, had been her inspiration and guide on this first solo tour, and it encapsulated the emphasis she placed on the benevolence she took with her everywhere she went.

The memories of that tour were great: the snake charmer, who reduced her to a fit of giggles as he popped a cobra's head into his mouth, her "crowning" with a turban as an honorary scout in Chitral. I will never forget the first day, as I stood among the bleached white headstones of the Commonwealth War Cemetery in Rawalpindi, where the princess paid her respects to fallen heroes. As she laid a wreath on behalf of the Queen, it struck me how odd it was, as her butler, to be witnessing the event. I was not a private secretary or equerry, whose presence was essential. My proper place was back at the residence, preparing lunch or tea, but, more and more, the princess had encouraged me to be part of her entourage. I wore suits, not a uniform, like everyone else. Increasingly, in 1991, I found myself getting to know the princess better, getting closer.

In Pakistan, I began to understand more about what made her tick. She told me about a longtime friend called Adrian Ward-Jackson, introduced to her by Princess Margaret. He was HIV-positive. She confided her troubles to him. He spoke openly about his illness to her. It was from this friendship that her positive campaigning for AIDS began and her awareness of the disease was awakened. She first noticed the impact of the disease, in what she called "a major way," when she visited an AIDS unit and opened a wing at Middlesex Hospital. I will never forget what she said: "Not since TB has there been a disease killing people *before* their parents, and no other member of this family [the Windsors] has taken it up." She felt that too many people took only a temporary interest when an awareness campaign needed to be constant and relentless. She received hate letters asking, "Why are you so supportive of the gay community?" and felt they were indicative of the confusion that education and awareness might end.

Cynics have often cruelly suggested that the princess's

charitable worth was all for PR purposes and she would do anything for a caring photo opportunity. What they never understood was her compassion, her genuine desire to help others, the huge importance she attached to humanitarian work. And when it came to true friends in need, there was no better friend to have on your side than the princess. Adrian Ward-Jackson died knowing that.

He had asked her to be with him at the end, and she considered it a privilege. In mid-August, when their friend Angela Serota rang to say he was gravely ill, distance and duty did not get in the way of her promise. She was at Balmoral, but, after failing to get a flight, embarked on a seven-hour drive through the night to London, accompanied by protection officer Dave Sharp, so that she could be by Adrian's side with Angela.

The princess sat with Adrian for four days. In his final moments, as she asked him a question, he moved his thumb in response. It was one of the most humbling and poignant moments of her life, she said, and she was mesmerized by his peace in suffering. Angela lay on the bed beside him as she and the princess said the Lord's Prayer. To understand what this moment meant to her is to understand the princess. It was when she discovered her inner self, the meaning of commitment, how people faced death, the journey of a soul, she said. If her sense of spirituality came from anywhere, it came from that hospital room when Adrian passed away shortly after midnight on August 23, 1991. Then, as she always did in hospitals, the princess went on a private walkabout and visited the baby unit on another wing, while Angela stayed with Adrian's body. The princess had seen a life end; she wanted to witness a new one beginning. After that night she often spoke about death and the courage of Adrian Ward-Jackson. She bought a book called *Facing Death and Finding Hope,* billed as "a guide to the emotional and spiritual care of the dying."

* * *

IN THE MONTHS following the Pakistan tour, I found myself seconded from Highgrove to Kensington Palace as cover for Harold Brown on his days off. For several weeks during the year, I was back in London in a small room on the top floor of apartments No. 8 and No. 9, down the corridor from the royal nursery. Meals were generally for one, set on a trolley and wheeled into the sitting room. The princess was curled up on the sofa in her white robe, watching *Brookside* or *Coronation Street*. Rather than dismissing me, she allowed me to remain and we chatted. She ate. I stood. When she had finished her meal, invariably salad or fish, I pushed the trolley out of the sitting room, through the drawing room, and into the first-floor pantry. She followed me and the chats continued as I washed, and she dried. Like at Highgrove.

But I was seeing more of her world, and a comfortable rapport was developing. She let me in, while Prince Charles kept me at arm's length. When we stood together in the pantry at either residence, I was chatting idly with Maria's friend, not the Princess of Wales, even though I insisted on calling her "Your Royal Highness." In spite of that, all the barriers were down and the public princess was gone. In her robe, she was scrubbed clean of makeup. At those times, she was so ordinary, so normal. I was serving two different people, the fantasy figure everyone saw on the outside and the little girl no one knew on the inside. I knew where the fantasy began and, within KP, where the reality took over.

I had heard much in staff circles about how difficult she could be, how her moods were unpredictable, but, one-to-one, there was no one easier to talk with or listen to. All I could think was that Harold Brown had a fantastic job and boss. I found myself looking forward to his days off.

Family life in the countryside with Maria and the boys could not have been happier. Alexander and Nick were settled and, on weekends, loved nothing more than being with their best friends, who happened to be Princes William and Harry.

* * *

WILLIAM AND HARRY, Alexander and Nick grew up together. Two sets of boys from starkly different backgrounds who ran around at Highgrove and, in later years, Kensington Palace. The princess gave us the princes' cast-off clothes and shoes. On weekends, they all lived in one another's pockets. Childhood memories for each of the boys will revolve around those happy days and years; the same memories captured in our family photograph albums. From the moment we moved on to the estate, the young princes were under our feet, visiting for fizzy drinks and chocolate biscuits, playing in our back garden, riding through the grounds on their bikes, screaming and laughing in the playroom, digging in our sandpit, making snowmen in the winter, splashing about in the swimming pool in summer. They made us smile as much as our own boys.

William's face was a familiar sight in our kitchen. He would pop his head round the back door, throw a cute smile, and say: "Have you got any chocolate biscuits or sweets, Maria?" He knew we kept a tin of Kit Kats, Twix, and Penguin biscuits, and he raided it as often as his mother did. Alexander's first memory is of his third birthday in May 1988, when we threw a small party at Close Farm and William, then five, and Harry, three, were among the six children who tucked into a blue tractor cake made by their parents' chef, Mervyn Wycherley. As Prince Charles played polo in Windsor, the princess stood with us, marveling over the messy feast taking place on a Thomas the Tank Engine paper tablecloth, and took turns with Maria and Wendy cradling our newborn son Nick, then only a month old. The princess gave Alexander a green soldier's jumper with patches on the elbows and shoulders, along with a plastic toy rifle and burgundy beret from the Parachute Regiment. She knew that, like Harry, he was mad about playing soldiers.

Very often over the years, the young princes were alone in the countryside with no other children to play with, and the princess invited Alexander and Nick to the nursery, which occupied the entire top floor at Highgrove. When I went upstairs, carrying plates of fish fingers and chips for two princes and my sons, I stood there and watched Alexander and Nick munching away with the future King of England.

If the princess and nanny Ruth Wallace took the princes out for a day, Alexander and Nick invariably went along. In September 1989, after the princess had returned from Balmoral, leaving Prince Charles in Scotland, all the boys went to Bristol Zoo. The surprise for me was that I was invited to take an impromptu day off and go on the first of many family days out with the princess. It felt unusual to relax out of uniform as the princess melted into the crowd like any other mother, wearing a blue 492 baseball cap. The princess, Maria, and Ruth, with Nick in his stroller, strolled together as protection officer Dave Sharp and I kept watch on the three other boys. Ever since the days when the princess and Maria first met at Buckingham Palace, marriage and motherhood had always been the common link that bound them, and shared experiences over the years, together with boys who were constant playmates, ensured a lasting friendship. When we moved into the cottage in 1990, Maria and the princess were like neighbors. The princess was both employer and family friend. Alexander and Nick always said, "Hello, Princess," and I thought it odd, in a nice way, to hear them be so informal while their mum and dad insisted on calling her "Your Royal Highness." I'm convinced that our boys grew up thinking that "Princess" was her Christian name.

It helped create an affectionate blend of the formal and informal. When the princess came into our kitchen, Maria flicked the switch on the kettle and asked, as routine, "A cup of coffee, Your Royal Highness?," and then Nick jumped onto her lap, gave her a hug, and asked: "Where you been, Princess?"

It led to some classic moments, the best of which was when three-year-old Nick, in his shorts and T-shirt, wandered from the cottage and up through the meadows to the main house. I was on the front doorstep, waiting for the prince to depart, as his Bentley waited in the driveway.

Then Nick came up the path, ignored me, and skipped onto the step just as the prince appeared in black tie for an engagement in London.

Nick looked him up and down, then piped up: "You look smart, Prince Charles. Where you going?"

It was one of those moments when, as a parent, you cannot believe what your child has said, and a gap in the earth could not open quick enough. Not that Nick sensed his father's horror. Having delivered such childlike audacity in the face of protocol, he didn't hang around. As he asked the question, he was squeezing past the prince to go inside and find William and Harry. Prince Charles couldn't help but smile.

Highgrove, the great house and its acres of land, was a playground for the four boys. I built a ball pool in one of the outside sheds, and it was an often raised debate as to who enjoyed the facility more: the boys or the princess. She would sneak up behind William, Harry, Alexander, and Nick and push them into its multicolored depths, then join them. The Princess of Wales slipped onto her back to "drown" quite regularly under those balls, and the boys would jump on top and tickle her.

When the princess was not around, one of my more casual duties was to keep the children occupied, and we devised a game called "Find as many eggs as you can," an alternative version of the Easter Egg Hunt that the Queen organized in Frogmore Gardens in the grounds of Windsor Castle for the royal children. She took a basket of chocolate eggs down to the gardens and hid them in various nooks and crannies of walls and trees or among the daffodils and primula. It became a race between the corgis and the children as to who would find them first. In the butler's version, I hid clutches of fresh hens' eggs between bales of hay and straw in the barn opposite the stables. Admittedly, it was not half as much fun as finding chocolate ones, but the excitement still propelled the winner, often William, into finding the most eggs.

William had a guinea pig and Harry had a gray, floppy-eared rabbit, which lived in a hutch in a corner of the stableyard where Paddy Whiteland kept two ponies, Smokey and Trigger, for the princes. They were taught to ride by a groom named Marion Cox. There were also their father's two Jack Russells, the Black Aberdeen Angus cows, Prince Charles's polo ponies, and the tawny owls in the barn. Carp swam in a pond in the garden, and William and Harry's tropical fish tank stood in a corner of the kitchen. Then there was the hamster, which traveled with the princes from Kensington Palace to Highgrove. William and Harry came into the kitchen to help chop up apples, carrots, and lettuce for the guinea pig, rabbit, and hamster, and they always cleaned out the hutches themselves.

The best part for my sons about having two princes as playmates was the electrically powered miniature D-registered Aston Martin Vantage soft top, a toy version of their father's car and a gift from the manufacturer. The British racing-green two-seater was, as my boys often told me, the best toy ever, with its cream leather interior, rose-wood dashboard, working headlights, cassette player, and leather steering wheel. Most young boys run round to a friend's house to see if he or she can come out to play. William drove, and we got used to seeing him in the driver's seat with Harry beside him when they appeared outside the cottage to take Alexander and Nick for a spin on the estate. William always argued with Harry about who was driving and, as the eldest, he always got his way. He loved cars and motor racing, and considered himself, at age ten, an expert driver! Until, that is, he tried at snail's pace to squeeze his pride and joy through a narrow gateway that led past a greenhouse to our back door and scraped one entire side of his gleaming car against a stone pillar. Maria was in the kitchen when a panic-stricken William raced in. "Maria, Maria . . . there's been a terrible accident!" She wondered what on earth had happened, especially when he added: "Papa is going to go mad. I need a tin of green paint."

Maria went outside for a vehicle inspection and had to tell William that a lick of paint was not going to solve his problem. The stone had grated into the metal, leaving a deep groove down one side. William was horrified. He thought about parking the car in the garage with the crumpled side against the wall so that Prince Charles would not find out, but Paddy and I ensured he came clean. Prince Charles was not amused that his son had "been so silly," but the car was sent for repair with Aston Martin and returned like new.

William and Harry were confident, expressive boys who were not shy when it came to approaching or talking with the adults around them. Only individual bedrooms separated their lives. They went everywhere and did everything together, even if William was the natural leader by age. They both attended Wetherby's private school in Notting Hill, London, and each arrived home desperate to show their mother the day's artwork. At both Highgrove and Kensington Palace, the princess, who was keen to show she was proud of both boys' work, covered the walls of her combined dressing room and bathroom with untidy pictures of butterflies and flowers made out of egg cartons, crepe paper, and eggshells.

Harry's passion for soldiers came through in his artwork; he was forever depicting pitched battles around castles with fighter planes dropping bombs from the sky, splashing the page with red ink to complete the bloody scene. Harry clearly believed that water balloons were bombs, too, and that his father's prized south-facing garden was the battlefield when a summer barbecue was held. Harry and William joined forces with my brother Graham, visiting with his family for the weekend, and the mischievous trio engaged in a water-balloon bombardment of the princess, who was chased around the garden, failing to escape her sons' surefire accuracy. Staff barbecues were a regular treat staged by the princess, often held when the prince was not in residence so that everyone, the princess included, could let down their hair. Mervyn Wycherley would produce mountains of food for the dressers, protection officers, nannies, housekeeper, and butler. It was our night off, said the princess. Afterward, she helped clear and stack the dirty plates.

Then came her greatest thrill: pushing everyone into the pool. The shrieks of delight and splashing about signaled the start of a caper that I labeled "People Soup." As with the water balloons earlier in the evening, the princess didn't mind getting wet and couldn't resist jumping into the pool to join in.

The princess never tired of indulging in such frivolity. For her, it represented her rebellious streak, defying the impeccable behavior that would ordinarily be expected of a future Queen of England. Splashing about in the pool in her clothes, she was on the same level as her staff. She loved seeing the look on people's shocked faces as she leaped in.

But nothing could have matched the horror on the face of the British ambassador in Cairo on her second solo visit overseas, in May 1992.

W E WERE ON the deck of a riverboat heading for the Philae Temple on a small island near the Aswan Dam when the princess, on looking out across the Nile, turned to me and said: "Time for a happy snap, Paul." She pushed her sunglasses up into her hair. "Now, don't lean in too close," she said from the corner of her mouth as Helena lined up the pose, "it's been a hot day!" Even with a stiff breeze, she was conscious that she had been sweating beneath her taupe coatdress, but it was a mischievous comment, aimed to startle, designed for a laugh, a moment captured on camera.

Seconds later she startled me again. "Now, can you make somebody else happy? I want you to organize a birthday party tonight back at the embassy for Sam."

Floating down the Nile was not the best time to become spontaneous party planner for hairdresser Sam McKnight, but I had learned that nothing was impossible when the princess asked. As the royal party disembarked for a short stopover at a hotel on the banks of the Nile, I commandeered a telephone and plotted a poolside surprise.

That night, in the lush garden of the embassy in Cairo,

Sam walked down the terrace steps into a chorus of "Happy birthday to you" belted out by eleven members of staff, led by the princess, clutching a bottle of champagne in one hand. Then, as sure as camels are born with humps, high spirits led to high jinks, and we all ended up in the pool, fully clothed. The princess was bobbing up and down, letting out drowning yelps, before her blond hair dipped beneath the surface. Patrick Jephson's eyebrows arched: as the man in charge of her public schedule, he was not accustomed to such scenes. Neither was the British ambassador, who, when he learned of the mass dip, frowned. I think he felt such antics were inappropriate and reckless, especially because two days earlier the paparazzi had sneaked onto a neighboring rooftop and photographed the princess in her black swimsuit. Fortunately, the lenses were not trained on the late-night "People Soup," and the headlines focused on another triumphant tour, showing the princess wandering among the giant columns of the Temple of Karnak in Luxor and through the Valley of the Kings, then marveling at the Pyramids and the Sphinx.

The headlines in Britain confirmed that the princess was an ace card on the diplomatic front. Whatever her personal battles at the time, she was becoming virtually infallible as the roving ambassador she had always intended to be. No amount of whispering campaigns from the men in gray suits could dislodge her confidence—or the global esteem in which she was held.

Egypt was a defining moment in my relationship with the princess. She had brought me on the trips, used me more at Kensington Palace, and shared the secret about her "special friend." Now, in the year that the Queen famously described as her *annus horribilis,* she was drawing me further across the invisible line separating her professional from her personal life. Because she had been a familiar face at our flat in the Royal Mews and then at the cottage at Highgrove, because she was a friend of my wife, because she was a virtual auntie to my sons, crossing that line did not seem as problematic as perhaps it should have.

The princess was sitting in her embassy bedroom in front

of a large mirror on the dressing table, fiddling with her hair. I had come from the kitchen with a glass of carrot juice. "How did you manage that in the middle of Cairo?"

"Mervyn Wycherley," I answered. I turned to leave but she swiveled round on the upholstered stool and said, "Sit down, sit down." As she turned back to the mirror, I sat on the edge of the neatly made bed. "Next time you come to London, there is somebody I want you to meet. Lucia is one of the most beautiful and elegant women I have ever met," she said.

Lucia Flecha de Lima was the wife of the then Brazilian ambassador to the Court of St. James's, and she was, first and foremost, a mother figure to the princess. Her ambassador husband, Paulo Tarso, who went on to become the ambassador in Washington and then Rome, was a father figure. The princess regularly used their embassy on Mount Street, London, to meet someone. *Not* James Hewitt. In that room in Cairo, the princess told me all about this someone and the meetings they had been having.

She had confided in me again, and more than that, she wanted me to meet Lucia, a key member of the surrogate family the princess had handpicked to be around her. Anyone could work for the princess. Anyone could feel that they knew her well because her skill was to make people feel that way. But she knew where the professional line was, and, in some notable cases, when to dispose of someone's services. Access to her inner circle was by invitation only. Not even Maria, a friend of old, was included. Meeting Lucia and a handful of the princess's closest friends would happen later, but my invitation into that circle came that morning in Cairo.

On that trip, she was more friendly and open than she had ever been, but there was also sadness behind the confident façade. The bedroom door she normally left ajar was locked. She emerged with reddened eyes. She said she needed time alone to open an emotional valve. With the Queen or anyone else, I would never have dared ask. With the princess, I couldn't help it. "Are you all right, Your Royal Highness? Is there anything I can do?"

She smiled. "Everyone needs to cry now and again, Paul," she said, and then, with a straightening of dress or shirt, she pulled herself together, took a deep breath, and strode out as the indefatigable Princess of Wales.

Her stoicism and bravery were remarkable, considering what she was going through. The princess was under immense pressure. The father she adored, Earl Spencer, had died in the hospital while she was skiing in Austria in March. That same month, the separation of the Duke and Duchess of York was announced. Then Princess Anne started divorce proceedings against Mark Phillips. All eyes were on the publicly strained Prince and Princess of Wales after a disastrous joint tour of India, which was remembered for one image: the princess, alone and isolated, in front of the Taj Mahal.

Also playing on the princess's mind was her collaboration with journalist Andrew Morton and the book he was about to publish: *Diana: Her True Story*. With hindsight in later years, she regretted it, and in Egypt, as the media speculated about her involvement with the project, she might have been having second thoughts.

When I returned to Highgrove, I told Maria how concerned I was for the princess, how she was opening up, how she wanted to introduce me to her friend Lucia. Maria could see I was becoming absorbed with the princess, though my obligation was at Highgrove, not Kensington Palace.

Maria said in bed that night, "You are the butler *here*, not there. You can't afford to get too close."

SEVEN

CAUGHT IN THE
CROSSFIRE

IN 1992, change swept through Highgrove as the gardens blossomed with the onset of summer. Outside, a hysterical media anticipated catastrophic failure within the Waleses' marriage. Inside, there was an unnerving sense of dread. That something was wrong was evident; it was the suspense of what the consequences might be that hung in the air.

There was a change in Prince Charles. He was locked into a period of melancholy and seemed, all of a sudden, rather vulnerable. One night, I had set the card table for dinner for one. As he sat down, facing the television in the sitting room, I stood behind him, unloading my butler's tray. The television wasn't on. All that could be heard was cutlery against the plate and the sounds of the countryside coming through the wide-open windows.

Then the prince said, without turning to face me: "Paul, are you happy here?"

"Yes, very much so, Your Royal Highness," I replied, transferring the main course from the tray to the plate on his table.

"Is Maria happy here too?" he asked.

I was somewhat perplexed as to where his doubt had sprung from. "Yes. We're both very happy here, Your Royal Highness."

"Good. I'm glad to hear it," he said, and that was that. He started his main course.

I returned to the pantry, wondering why he had seemed so concerned. Maria said it was probably because of our ever-increasing closeness to the princess. "Look at it through the prince's eyes," she said. "His wife chatting in the butler's pantry. You covering for Harold at Kensington Palace more and more, requiring an under-butler to replace you at Highgrove. You going on her solo tours. Days out with the princess with our sons and the young princes. And, from the moment we moved into the cottage in 1990, the princess being a constant visitor to our home." Duty had placed me in the most undesirable position, and the prince had been querying which camp I was in.

Of course he had noticed the time the princess was spending at our cottage. "I suppose she's down at your house again, Paul, is she?" he asked when he couldn't find his wife in the main house.

The princess would go for a walk in the gardens, pick a bunch of flowers, sweet peas or lilies of the valley, and arrive at the back door of the cottage. "Maria, are you in?" she shouted, walking in without waiting for a response. She said hello, flicked the switch of the kettle, reached up to take two mugs from an overhead cupboard, and began making coffee. William and Harry, Alexander and Nick were out playing somewhere on the estate. The princess hitched herself up onto the tiled countertop and kicked off her shoes, her legs swinging. She poured out her heart to Maria time and again, talking about life with her husband and how unhappy she was. For Maria it was less awkward to get close because she wasn't in a professional predicament. She was just the wife of the butler, and she listened without offering opinions.

"You don't know how lucky you are, Maria," said the princess one day. "This is all I've ever wanted, a happy home and a loving family," and her eyes welled up.

She had come to know our family well. Mum and Dad and Maria's mum had known her from the days at the Royal Mews. My brother Graham and his wife, Jane, Maria's brother Pete and his wife, Sue, were constant visitors to the cottage too, and the princess eased herself into our family fold. There were no airs and graces when she was around, and whether we were sitting around a wooden table in the garden or chatting in the kitchen, the princess was one of us. When she knew one of the family was visiting, they too would be invited to one of the summer barbecues. I'll never forget the first time Graham met the princess at Highgrove. He shaved four times that day, he was so nervous. Then he met her and realized how breathtakingly normal she was.

Maria's mum, Betty, had a special place in the princess's heart. Once, at a Christmas cocktail party for staff and tradesmen in the state apartments at Kensington Palace, she invited her to join them. The Wales family stood by the door, receiving the guests, who shook hands with William, Harry, and then the prince and princess. When the overawed lady with the white hair and rather large glasses approached the princess, she broke from protocol, grinned widely, embraced her, and kissed her cheek.

The prince looked taken aback. After the elderly lady had shaken his hand, he turned to his wife and said, "Who was that?"

"Oh, that was Betty," said the princess.

On another occasion, she telephoned Betty, knowing she lived alone in North Wales. "Hello, Betty, it's Diana. What are you doing?"

"I'm sitting on the bed talking to you," said Betty. She always managed to make the princess laugh.

The princess had rung because Betty was having central heating fitted in her old people's bungalow, and she wanted to check that everything was in working order.

One day in 1992, the princess made a dream come true for her, a devout Catholic. She called her at home and said, "Betty, I would like you to come and join me and meet Mother Teresa."

Betty nearly fell off her chair. "I can't come out to India!"

She had the princess laughing again. "No, Betty, you won't need to, because Mother Teresa is going to be in London for twenty-four hours. If no one can bring you down, I'll send a car for you," she said. As it happened, a relative drove her to Highgrove, where she met the princess, and the two drove on to London together.

Mother Teresa was outside the mission house where she was staying, waiting to greet the princess. The princess introduced Betty, who the press reported was a lady-in-waiting.

Mother Teresa kissed her, and the three went into a room alone and sat round a small wooden table. They spoke about the homeless and poor in Britain, the sick and dying of Somalia, the need to say the rosary as often as possible. Mother Teresa was holding something in her hand. As she opened her palm, she revealed two medals and a set of rosary beads. "What would you like?" she asked Betty.

Betty took the medals. The princess took the rosary beads. She did not know how to say the rosary, but Betty assured her that she would teach her. In fact, the princess followed Betty's lead that day: as they walked into the chapel where the novice nuns were waiting, Betty turned to her and said, "Do what I do."

Following her example, the princess dipped a finger into a font of holy water and blessed herself, then removed her shoes. The three knelt with the nuns and prayed. Betty said she was on a spiritual high for weeks afterward.

In February 1992, after her tour of India with the Prince of Wales, the princess gave Betty a special present: the garland Mother Teresa had placed round her neck in front of the world's media. Betty treasures it to this day.

PRINCE CHARLES was living full-time at Highgrove and had effectively abandoned Kensington Palace, although the princess still came down on odd weekends. The prince had started to change the Dudley Poplak–inspired décor. He hired Robert Kime, interior designer and friend of Camilla Parker Bowles, and the house switched from light pastel greens and yellows to richer reds and browns. It was dark, somber. Large pieces of rosewood and mahogany furniture arrived: a grandfather clock for the hallway; a new brass fender with an upholstered seat to surround a slate hearth for the fireplace in the drawing room. A gilt overmantel mirror was placed on the wall; rush matting replaced the green carpet; and new curtains were hung in the windows. In the hallway, a huge William Morris tapestry was draped from a brass rail. In the sitting room, the portrait of Lord Byron that had hung over the fireplace was sent away on exhibition and replaced with an oil painting of Windsor Castle. Bit by bit, month by month, the prince was making the interior his own.

When the princess visited one weekend, she spotted a dark wood sideboard in the dining room and winced. I told her that two marble statues were being considered for the alcoves beside the fireplace. She grimaced.

But the princess was making her own fundamental decisions about the interior of Kensington Palace. She removed the Victorian mahogany half-tester marital bed from the master bedroom and consigned it to the Royal Collection at Windsor.

ON MY THIRTY-FOURTH birthday, June 6, 1992, the Queen's private secretary, Sir Robert Fellowes, telephoned the *Sunday Times* newspaper, demanding to know the contents of its serialization of the Morton book. But the real storm had brewed at Highgrove on the previous day, when Prince Charles and his private secretary Richard Aylard set out on their own fact-finding mission.

That morning, the princess was at Kensington Palace, first with her personal trainer, Carolan Brown, and then with her beauty therapist and friend, Eileen Malone, for her usual 10 A.M. facial.

Unbeknownst to the princess, as she relaxed, Prince

Charles's camp was working up a sweat over a fax sent from Broadlands, the home of Lord and Lady Romsey. Two sheets of paper had spewed out of the machine under my desk in the pantry. I saw the word "Broadlands" first. Thought Romseys. Thought trouble. It was a transcript from a broadcast interview with Andrew Neil, then editor of the *Sunday Times:* he had said, on tape, that the princess had given her tacit approval for the book and Prince Charles had every right to feel betrayed. More than ever, my loyalties were split, but one event would end the dilemma once and for all.

IT WAS THE END of a particularly exhausting, warm day. Lunch had been taken outside on the terrace in the sunshine. In the evening, Prince Charles had his dinner for one on the card table in the sitting room, early again, so that he could disappear on another of his twenty-two-mile drives to Middlewich House and Mrs. Parker Bowles. The phone had been ringing all day. As the sun set, Gerald Ward, a local landowner, had left a message for the absent prince, as had many others, including his press secretary, Dickie Arbiter. With the washing-up still to be done in the pantry, the phone rang again.

"Hello, Paul, how are you?" said the princess. She laughed when I told her I had been run off my feet all day. "I don't suppose the hubby's around, is he?" she said. She never referred to him as His Royal Highness, as protocol dictated, when talking to members of staff.

I wished she hadn't asked that question. It was the first time she had rung Highgrove when he was away "privately." Now what did I say? Should I lie? I couldn't lie to the princess.

She asked again: "Well, is he?" This time she sounded impatient.

Thinking on my feet, I was honest if inexact. "I'm sorry, Your Royal Highness, he's not. He's gone out."

Out. It was past eight o'clock in the evening. Damn. Shouldn't have said that.

"Well, where's he gone?" she insisted.

"I don't know, Your Royal Highness."

"*Of course* you do, Paul." And she had me. "You know everything that happens down there. Now, where has he gone?"

If the princess knew anything about me, she knew honesty was my strength as well as my weak spot. Trapped between duty and loyalty to both parties, my instinct was a plea, for her sake as well as mine. "Please don't ask me, Your Royal Highness. The best person to ask would be His Royal Highness, not me," I said. I felt awful. I didn't want to land the prince in trouble, or lie to the princess. She had been too good to me.

She changed the subject, but only to another form of questioning. "Has anyone else phoned this evening?" she asked.

I failed to see the danger in telling her that Dickie Arbiter and Gerald Ward had left messages. It seemed harmless on the face of it, but not when the princess could use such information as proof that she knew *exactly* who was calling the house, creating the impression with Prince Charles that she was not missing a trick. I had given her ammunition and suddenly knew it.

"Please don't say anything, Your Royal Highness. I could get into terrible trouble, you know that," I said.

She told me not to worry, but I knew it was not going to be forgotten. That night I went to bed worried sick.

Maria was unsympathetic. She scolded me for opening my mouth. "You should have thought, you should have thought," she said.

The next morning I walked to the main house accompanied by dread. An ordinary morning passed and provided false belief that, perhaps, the princess had kept silent. That was until the prince's valet Michael Fawcett came into the pantry as I prepared for lunch. He had a face like thunder. "He wants to see you and he *isn't* happy," he said.

For once, the red disk hadn't dropped into the box. A messenger had been sent: it was a summons, not a duty call. From my pantry, I heard the thuds of the prince's footsteps coming down the staircase, across the polished boards of the hallway. I heard the library door open and slam shut. I waited a few seconds, my heart racing. I went and knocked on the door of the library with a deep sense of foreboding. I could lose my job. That was all I thought.

Prince Charles was standing near his round table. "Close the door behind you," he said in a clipped voice.

The door clicked shut. "Your Royal Highness?" I inquired.

He was indignant. "Can you tell me why—*WHY*—Her Royal Highness is constantly aware of whoever visits or telephones Highgrove when she isn't here?"

"I don't know what you're talking about, Your Royal Highness."

"Have you spoken to Her Royal Highness recently, Paul?" His voice was quavering with anger.

I told him that the last time I had spoken to her was the previous evening. "When you were out," I said.

"And *what* exactly did you say to her?" He was on the edge now. His notorious short fuse was burning out. I could almost hear it fizzing to its end.

"That you were out, Your Royal Highness." Even I noted the tone of resignation in my own voice.

His face was puce red. "WHY?" he bellowed.

"Because you *were* out, Your Royal Highness."

Puce now turned practically purple. "And did you tell her who rang the house last night?"

"Well, I said Mr. Ward had rung but that you were out because, that way, it confirmed I was telling the truth," I said.

The prince was incredulous. My stupidity was now mutually recognized. He could not believe what he was hearing. "Why on earth couldn't you simply have said that you just couldn't find me?"

Something told me to stand up for myself. I was not Michael Fawcett. Or Richard Aylard. Or in the camp that willingly covered his tracks. "Are you asking me to lie, Your Royal Highness?"

And then, with the temerity of that question from a servant, he exploded: "Yes! YES! I am!" His bellow bounced off the walls and watercolors. In a flash, he picked up a book from his table and hurled it in my direction. I can still see its fluttering pages whirring through the air. I don't think it was intended to hit me, and it didn't. Prince Charles ranted: "Yes, I am! I am the Prince of Wales," he screamed, and stamped a foot to emphasize his authority, "and I will be king! So yes. YES!"

I didn't dare ask if there would be anything else. I made a sharp exit. I was stunned. His temper was legendary, but until then I had never had the misfortune to witness it. I pulled out a chair in the pantry and sat down with my head in my hands, cursing myself for my own stupidity.

Minutes passed and then the bell rang. The red disk dropped into the box under LIBRARY. Scene two.

I opened the library door and entered awkwardly. Before me was a starkly different picture. The anger had abated and the prince was sitting at his table. I should have been the one who was embarrassed, but it seemed that he didn't know where to look. He could not have been more contrite. "Paul, I'm terribly sorry. I really didn't mean to do that. I do apologize."

On the floor, the literary missile he had thrown in my direction was splayed out, pages down. As I bent down, picked it up, and returned it to the pile, I told him: "If you can't vent your feelings on me, Your Royal Highness, who can you vent them on?"

He sat back in his chair, forlorn, as if his anger had sucked all the energy out of him. He nodded, and that was my signal to leave again. I had tried to pretend to the prince that everything was all right, but I knew it wasn't. Both of us had been wrong for different reasons but, from that moment on, things could never be the same again.

No longer was the sense of divided loyalties merely a psychological dilemma; I had been caught in the crossfire. In my own mind, I already knew where allegiance and instinct would take me. I just couldn't tell Maria. She loved life at the cottage in the countryside.

*   *   *

THE BOOK *Diana: Her True Story* was published on June 16, 1992. The princess went to Royal Ascot appearing ultraconfident. She knew all eyes would be on her, but such an experienced public performer gave no reaction. Behind the façade, though, she was crumpling when she walked into the Royal Box. It was there that the enormity of the damage the book had caused struck her. She felt the rest of the royal party ostracizing her, she said, and conversations were stilted, awkward, and cold.

As she did her public best, she saw that Andrew and Camilla Parker Bowles were guests, laughing and being jolly, performing another charade of marital happiness. Then she witnessed Princess Anne posing for a photograph with her old friend Andrew Parker Bowles. She found it offensive to see her sister-in-law cozying up to him.

LATER THAT YEAR, Princess Anne assuaged the princess's hurt. Indeed, she took the princess aside and offered words of comfort. In 1992, Princess Anne was in love with Commander Tim Lawrence following her divorce from Captain Mark Phillips, and a new royal marriage was nigh. It was wrongly reported at the time that the princess had "snubbed" Princess Anne by not attending her wedding, but nothing could have been further from the truth. Princess Anne herself offered an escape clause. She felt guilty that she was so in love at a time when the Prince and Princess of Wales were finding life so difficult, and told her, "A lot of us in this family are praying for you." Princess Anne understood that her sister-in-law might not want to attend the ceremony because it would be too painful, and her compassion was appreciated by the princess. The only reason she did not attend was because she had the Princess Royal's prior consent.

AFTER THE ASCOT MEETING, there was a hastily arranged summit at Windsor Castle where the Queen and the Duke of Edinburgh sat down with the Prince and

Princess of Wales. The atmosphere was tense, but the views exchanged were frank and honest. The princess told me: "Mama despaired as she listened to me. I think she aged at that time because all I seemed to be doing was relaying to her my anguish."

At Windsor, Prince Philip made it clear that everyone was upset by the biased account in the Morton book, and suspicious of her involvement. The princess, by then in denial, insisted that she had not assisted the author. I honestly believe that she was taken aback by the scale of what she had unleashed.

"The publication of that book was an unbearable time. Only my friends guided me through," she later said. But, deep down, she knew that, devastated and angry as she was at the state of her marriage and still grieving for her father, she had been rash, impulsive, and confused in cooperating with Morton. Her friends had been given permission to get across her case that she was a victim and isolated. In doing so, she had wrecked any chance of a reconciliation and the small prospect that Prince Charles might change his ways.

The self-imposed damage was something she struggled to accept in later years. She had wanted the truth to be known but, essentially, she was making cries for help, hoping to win sympathy and be rescued. But no one, especially the one man she wanted to rescue her, Prince Charles, was going to help. She still loved him, and in her eyes—which had a tendency not to see the other side of many stories—she had been abandoned in favor of Camilla Parker Bowles.

Even when she knew she was wrong, the princess marched on with purpose, and there was no abatement in her anger and sense of injustice. She told the Queen and Prince Philip that she had tried to be civil to her husband but she had come up against a stone wall and, regrettably, she felt separation was the only answer. A trial separation. Not a divorce. She wanted freedom. Not a severance of ties.

The Queen and Prince Philip did not countenance the suggestion of a split. Both the prince and princess were told that they must learn to compromise, be less selfish and try to work through their difficulties for the sake of the monarchy, their children, the country and its people. At the Windsor meeting, as Prince Charles listened, the princess made her loathing for Camilla Parker Bowles quite clear. She later said that being able to express her anger openly to her in-laws was a huge relief: "Everything was out in the open, then. In the book and within the family."

Indeed, there was one positive aspect about the book: the princess's bulimia stopped for a time, at least, after the book came out. "I think that whole episode represented the biggest challenge of my life," she said.

THE QUEEN FELT the candid discussion had gone well and suggested a follow-up meeting the next day. But the princess failed to take up the invitation. In fact, she refused to stay at Windsor that week, breaking with tradition, and attended the Ascot meeting on only two out of the four scheduled days.

The Duke of Edinburgh fired off a letter, making clear his disappointment that the princess had not turned up for their second meeting when he and the Queen were taking the time and making the effort to listen to the couple's marital problems. But the princess, upset by the presence of Camilla Parker Bowles at Ascot, had retreated to Kensington Palace, wounded and angry. It began a stream of correspondence between her and the Duke of Edinburgh.

The Queen and Prince Philip had the best intentions: to save the royal marriage. They had decided that a delicate, volatile situation required a wise head. Oddly, that wise head was deemed to be Prince Philip's, whose reputation for tact did not augur well. Nevertheless, he stepped in as mediator. The significance of the counseling role that he and the Queen adopted cannot be overstated: until then, as a mother and father, they had never interfered in any of their children's marriages, believing that wisdom is only learned through life experience. But they clearly decided that on this occasion they could not stand by and watch the

Prince and Princess's marriage disintegrate. Like Her Majesty, Prince Philip tried hard to remain impartial and understanding of the princess's plight, but, as with all mediators, his role required him to be candid and impart some harsh truths. "How many other wives would have to discuss their marital problems with their father-in-law instead of their husband?" the princess said, in her frustration.

For her it was another indication of the Royal Family behaving abnormally when it came to personal relationships, of Prince Charles putting his head in the sand. To be fair, Prince Philip was doing more to save the marriage than Prince Charles, and whether his motivation was to protect the institution or the individuals, he acted with good faith. No one was better qualified than he to understand the sacrifices required to marry into the Royal Family. The inherent problem of using Prince Philip as mediator was that he rarely pulled any punches.

In the bombardment of correspondence that followed the Royal Ascot week, Prince Philip upset and infuriated the princess with comments she described as brutal. She never shredded the letters. Instead, she tied them into a bundle and kept them, a deliberate preservation of the truth, and to back it up she made several photocopies that she dispatched to friends she trusted. Others, like television interviewer Martin Bashir and me, were shown the originals; I saw them in 1993, Bashir in 1995. Even a year after she received them, she still shook her head over their contents.

A lot of nonsense, and plain lies, have been written about them. Much later, newspaper reports aided by wild exaggeration from dramatic sources claimed that they were "the nastiest letters Diana had ever received," and that they were short and curt and written on small note paper. Such gross inaccuracies cannot be allowed to linger. The letters offered some harsh truths but they were never poisonous. Indeed, in time they grew understanding and sympathetic. Nor were they curt and rude. They were long and rambling, and some were four pages long. All were written on regular letter-size paper.

What I can also say, contrary to those same newspaper reports, is that I never recalled Prince Philip ever using the words "harlot" or "trollop" in any of the correspondence. Nor, in what I witnessed, did he ever accuse the princess of damaging the monarchy.

When he sat down to write them, Prince Philip was clearly bristling from the revelations of the Morton book, which he had digested, page by page, in full. He, too, was suffering from wounded pride on behalf of his son and family. That placed him on the defensive and, I believe, hampered his objectivity. However much he tried to be evenhanded, an accusing finger tended to leap out of the pages.

His intention was clearly to put his thoughts on paper and demand that the princess do some soul-searching. He wanted to jolt her into thinking more about her marriage, her behavior, her motives. On reading them, one conclusion could be drawn: he felt he had to be cruel to be kind. On one hand, he praised the princess for her solo tours and charity work, then said that being the wife of Prince Charles "involved much more than simply being a hero with the British people." The remarks kept punching away at the princess's ego and spirit, and they were delivered by the man she had held in great respect ever since she married into the family. That was what bothered her most.

It got worse before it got better. Prince Philip said that jealousy had been the cancer within the marriage. The princess took that as an attack on herself. He also said that following the birth of William, her irrational postnatal behavior had not helped matters. My role as an interfering butler had not been forgotten. I winced again as the duke recounted, as one of many examples, the time she had quizzed me over the telephone about where Prince Charles went after he had left Highgrove in the middle of the evening. He said his son felt that the princess was a jealous spy: listening at doorways and questioning the butler about his whereabouts.

"If Charles had been honest with me from the start, I wouldn't need to be suspicious of him," she told me.

It is hard not to sympathize with the view that when a husband continues to see an old flame, it is hard for any woman not to attempt to reassure herself. Just as the actions of the princess had made Prince Charles suspicious, his sneaky private life made her doubt him. The irony of the vicious circle seemed lost on both Prince Charles and the Duke of Edinburgh. Blow by blow, the parental advice came wrapped in barbed wire: she had not been a caring wife; while she was a good mother, she was too possessive with William and Harry.

I had seen her with her boys, and all she had ever done was smother them with love and affection; she wanted to be there for them twenty-four hours a day, seven days a week. On weekends, she had ensured that they went to Highgrove to see their father. Only in a royal world, where the nanny's hand rocks the cradle, could the attention and love she gave those boys ever be misconstrued as overly possessive.

But what stunned the princess was when Prince Philip raised the thorny issue of her husband's mistress. He wrote that she should have been grateful that her husband had, initially, cut himself off from Camilla Parker Bowles. Prince Charles felt he had made "a considerable sacrifice" in cutting ties with her and that the princess had "not appreciated what he had done."

Then came the knockout blow that had left the princess sobbing. Prince Philip had written: "Can you honestly look into your heart and say that Charles' relationship with Camilla had nothing to do with your behaviour towards him in your marriage?"

The princess was being accused of driving Prince Charles into the arms of the one woman she had tried to keep him away from. Even a year on, the idea made her blood boil. "They are all the bloody same—looking after one another!" she said.

On one hand, Prince Philip was telling her that he was not apportioning blame, but, on the other, he was laying responsibility at her door.

* * *

THAT SUMMER OF 1992. Highgrove was not a place where I saw much of the princess. The marriage had irretrievably broken down, although communication was maintained into the autumn with the Duke of Edinburgh. Where one letter had made the princess despair, a new one arrived and lifted her hopes. The princess always wrote back, firing off an angry response to the first few letters. One letter from the duke famously started: "Phew!!! I thought I might have gone a bit too far with the last letter . . ." Eventually, he accepted that Prince Charles shared equal blame for the marriage breakdown and had been equally stubborn.

As his attitude changed, so did that of the princess. However hard she found her father-in-law's opinions and observations, she learned to respect his honesty. After she had challenged some of his comments, his letters became warmer, kinder, and more considerate. More important, for the first time since her troubles had begun in the mid-eighties, she felt someone from the House of Windsor was taking the trouble to listen to her without dismissing her as unhinged or emotionally hysterical. In meeting each other head-on, the princess and the Duke of Edinburgh had broken down barriers and brought many unspoken issues into the open. The princess saw the effort her father-in-law was making, noted the length of his letters, and admired him for it. It was a marked shift from the rash assumption of others in the Royal Family, who were too quick to dismiss her concerns as the rantings of a madwoman. Had anyone stopped to think her mood swings, bulimia, and screaming fits were born of a maddening frustration at simply not being heard? A wave of relief, almost of vindication, swept over her when the duke made it clear that he didn't subscribe to the belief, peddled by the warped ignorance of some in Prince Charles's camp, that she was "mentally unbalanced" or "unstable."

The princess's memory was sullied later *after* her death, when she was unable to defend herself, with the appalling suggestion that she had suffered from borderline personality disorder. Royal author Penny Junor researched the illness for her 1998 book *Charles: Victim or Villain?* and "discovered it was spot-on for the behaviour Diana exhibited." It is worth remembering that, in reaching such a speculative conclusion, she was aided by the unused research of Jonathan Dimbleby for his 1994 book *The Prince of Wales.*

The princess juggled a hectic life in the full glare of the world's media. If she had suffered from BPD, she would never have coped with such a burden of duty in such a demanding environment. Take it from someone who lived with her—who witnessed an ordinary human being struggling with an extraordinary life—she suffered, quite simply, from an eating disorder.

Thankfully, the Duke of Edinburgh acknowledged that simple fact. In one letter, he recognized that bulimia could affect a sufferer's behavior, and he said she could not be blamed for the "behavioural patterns" the disease had caused. That admission was of huge significance to the princess. At a stroke, Prince Philip had dissociated himself from the venomous off-the-record briefings that had left her feeling, for so many years, that no one cared or understood. For the sake of her memory today, the world should rely on the conclusions of the duke, stated when the princess was alive, rather than those of a royal author, put forward when the princess was dead.

WHAT PROVIDED HER with even greater hope was that both the Queen and Prince Philip still shared the belief that the marriage could work if compromises were made on both sides. The duke even made a numbered list of common interests and activities, which might bring the couple together again. This bolstered the optimism that the princess still felt. Beneath all her bitterness and anger, the princess still loved Prince Charles and believed, naïvely or otherwise, that one day they could try again. In 1992, she recognized that separation was inevitable and might even be healthy. She did not, as some royal autobiographies have suggested, believe the marriage was dead.

Just as the duke had made the princess cry with some of his words, he also made her laugh. Indeed, she had leaped around her room with unbridled joy when he expressed his private thoughts about Camilla Parker Bowles. Both he and the Queen had long been deeply worried about their son's friendship with a married woman, and they had strongly disapproved, he said. Then he wrote: "We do not approve of either of you having lovers. Charles was silly to risk everything with Camilla for a man in his position. We never dreamed he might feel like leaving you for her. I cannot imagine anyone in their right mind leaving you for Camilla. Such a prospect never even entered our heads."

That confirmed everything the princess needed to know. Nor did it escape her notice that the Duke of Edinburgh had begun signing off his letters "With fondest love—Pa."

The correspondence became a roller-coaster ride through despair, hope, tears, then laughter, defiance, and concessions. In sharing with me what she was going through, it was almost as if the princess was looking for an independent witness to prove that her view of the royals— the family, the marriage, the household, the way she was treated, her perceived injustices—was not an insane misinterpretation that suited her own agenda. Perhaps she also wanted to share the vindication the letters gave her, as if proof was needed of what the Duke of Edinburgh had written. She was also aware, of course, that I knew the Queen and her husband.

It was true that the princess did not take criticism well but, on balance across the months, she felt she had made progress and got her points across. When she died, she was a great admirer of the Duke of Edinburgh. Despite the hurt his initial missive had caused her, she said she would never forget the role he had played as counselor.

Generally, the well-intentioned intervention of the Duke of Edinburgh reached an impasse. More scandal appeared in the newspapers, and the princess did her best to quell the media's thirst for tabloid headlines. She released a statement following speculation about Prince Philip's letters. It read: "The suggestion that Her Majesty The Queen and HRH The Duke of Edinburgh have been anything other than sympathetic and supportive is untrue." The princess was again putting on a brave face at a time when all sides recognized that the marriage was at the point of no return. Nevertheless, the Duke of Edinburgh continued to plug away, determined to ensure that the business relationship between the Prince and Princess of Wales trundled on, wearing its mask of togetherness, for the sake of the monarchy and the country. Indeed, it was Prince Philip who, during a private conversation at Balmoral, gently persuaded the princess to accompany Prince Charles on the tour to Korea when she had said she would prefer not to go. It was a disastrous trip in terms of PR for the marriage. On November 27, I penned a letter to my Kentucky friends Shirley and Claude Wright: "It will take a major scandal or a public statement to change this situation, none of that is likely to happen this year unless there are dramatic weeks ahead. I will always be at Highgrove to look after whoever lives here. I'm sure 1993 will be an eventful year, but my job is quite safe and I very much doubt our life styles will change."

Little did I know that, earlier in the month, the offices of the prince and princess had been arranging a separation. At Highgrove, we were all in the dark, and the princess had had good reason for not informing me, because she knew the impact it would have on all our lives.

I HAD ORDERED the Christmas trees for Highgrove. Prince Charles was staying away "privately," and the princess was in Tyne and Wear with her friend and secretary, Maureen Stevens. Wednesday, December 9, dawned as any other. Then news came through that, at three o'clock, we should expect the arrival of Jane, Countess of Strathclyde, palace personnel officer. We knew she was the bearer of bad news as soon as we saw her face—it seemed unfair that someone of whom we had become fond should have to carry out such a task. She looked flustered and, instead of exchanging small talk and pleasantries, she had been instructed to ring the prince's private secretary, Richard Aylard, as soon as she arrived. As she made the call, she told me to gather all the staff—Wendy, Paddy, Lita and Barbara (the daily ladies), and Maria—in the kitchen.

Jane had timed her arrival to coincide with the announcement by Prime Minister John Major that the Prince and Princess of Wales had, regrettably, decided to separate.

As John Major delivered his statement to the House of Commons, Jane emerged from the dining room, with a look of sorrow on her face, already regretting the upheaval she was about to cause.

"Can I see Paul and Maria first?" she said, and we followed her into the staff dining room. "Please, close the door behind you."

I sat there, holding Maria's hand tight. Then Jane, in a somber voice, started: "I have only this minute learned myself. I had driven to Highgrove not knowing why I was coming here. But it has just been announced that Their Royal Highnesses the Prince and Princess of Wales are intending to live apart . . ."

It had been inevitable, but the sadness of hearing it made our hearts sink. Yet Jane hadn't finished.

". . . and Her Royal Highness the Princess of Wales wants you both to go to London and look after her." Princess Diana wanted me on her team, to work alongside the existing butler at Kensington Palace, Harold Brown.

Maria burst into tears and wailed: "I don't believe it. I don't believe it." Jane and I sat in silence as Maria wept. "What are we going to tell the boys? Their friends are here, their school, our cottage. No. No!"

Jane crouched down and put her arms round Maria. "I don't know what to say to you," she said.

My thoughts raced, too, but for different reasons. The inevitability of the announcement was matched, in my mind, by the inevitability that our future lay with the princess. I felt strongly convinced that things were happening for a reason. If anything, I was puzzled about why the princess had not informed us earlier. That was all I couldn't understand.

As we walked out of that room and into the kitchen, with Maria in pieces, Wendy saw us first. "What on earth . . . ," she said, racing over to Maria.

"Can I see you now, Wendy?" said Jane. Ten minutes later Wendy emerged. She had been let go. It is a tribute to her that she remained philosophical—"I'm nearing retirement anyway"—and was more concerned about us.

We sat around the kitchen table for most of that afternoon, long after Jane had gone, all of us contemplating change over many glasses of gin and tonic. Paddy's role was unaltered, and he returned to the stableyard. The two daily ladies had gone home in a state of shock.

Wendy offered Maria a cigarette. "We're not supposed to smoke in the kitchen, but I can't see that it matters now," she said, and they chain-smoked a packet of twenty. Back to London. Another duty. Another royal residence. We would never see the princess or William and Harry again at Highgrove.

That night, after she had returned to Kensington Palace from the northeast, the princess telephoned the cottage. She, of all people, knew how upset Maria would be at the prospect of leaving the countryside—and the life she had always dreamed of—for London. "Don't worry, Maria," the princess reassured her as she wept again. "You and Paul will be better off here with me. I know you don't want to come back to London, but I will take care of you all."

Maria put down the phone feeling so sorry for the princess. She knew how lonely her life was at Kensington Palace, and that all the princess was doing was ensuring that the family she had grown close to went to work for her, not her husband. In the separation of the royal marriage, the princess had included the Burrells among the possessions she wanted to keep.

Meanwhile, the princess was dealing with her own domestic bombshell, delivered in another envelope from Buckingham Palace and penned by the hand of the Duke of Edinburgh. As the lawyers and advisers from both camps held summits to negotiate the terms of the separation, Prince Philip came out with his own suggestion: that the princess move out of Kensington Palace apartments No. 8 and No. 9, her main home for the previous ten years, so that Prince Charles could keep the residence as his London base.

As alternative accommodation, more appropriate for a mother with sons at boarding school, the duke suggested, was apartment No. 7: empty, derelict, and previously occupied by distant relations of the Royal Family. The princess said it was a shoebox and not a fitting home for two royal princes. Apartment No. 7 had more significance to the Duke of Edinburgh. It had been the apartment where he had stayed on the eve of his wedding to the Queen on November 20, 1947.

The duke called it a "semi-detached" arrangement. But the woman whom I was about to start calling "the Boss" dug in her heels and refused to move an inch. The benefit of frank communication with her father-in-law allowed her to tell him exactly how she felt without fear of causing upset. She told him there were no circumstances in which she was going to make way for Prince Charles.

So he remained at Highgrove and settled for a new apartment in St. James's Palace. The princess remained in No. 8 and No. 9, where my sole employment with her would begin. Maria joined her, on a part-time basis, as a housemaid.

EIGHT

KP

"WOULD YOU LIKE to watch a film?" asked the princess.

It was a Saturday afternoon at Kensington Palace and we had returned from shopping in the nearby high street. The chef had been sent home for the day, having left a salad in the refrigerator for dinner, and the "house" was quiet. It was a free afternoon with nothing scheduled, and the princess had a couple of hours to spare.

She was standing in the doorway of the ground-floor pantry as I made two cups of instant coffee. "You choose the film. Give me five minutes," she said, and went up the angular staircase that hugged the half white, half yellow walls.

Both of us could talk endlessly about movies and, as I stirred the coffee, I knew exactly which to select. Her collection was not a patch on the vast hoard of films William and Harry had amassed, but she had a number of fine classic movies, most with a heart-tugging romantic theme. "Weepies," she called them.

In the sitting room, I crouched down and scanned the the spines of the VHS video cases that filled two shelves of a white cabinet: *Gone with the Wind, Silk Stockings, My Fair Lady, Top Hat, Carousel, South Pacific, Ghost.* My eyes stopped on *Brief Encounter.* A guaranteed weepie, which she had watched more times than I had made her black coffee or carrot juice. "I think this one," I said, as she came into the room, and pushed the tape into the VCR. Princess and butler sat down at either end of a pink-and-cream-striped three-seater sofa that backed onto her mahogany desk, facing the gray marble fireplace at the opposite side of the room. Daylight flooded in from behind us through the white-framed sash windows. A box of Kleenex lay on the cushion between us. "I always blub at this!" she said, snatching a tissue, and the movie began.

She shifted into a more comfortable position, and sniffled her way through a chance meeting turning into a love affair.

Ask anyone who ever sat with the princess through a concert or joined her to watch *Brief Encounter*—the strains of Rachmaninoff's *Piano Concerto No. 2* reduced her to tears every time. As the steam train pulled away in the climactic scene, and that stirring music filled the sitting room, sobs broke out beside me. The princess half turned to me, and tears were streaming down her cheeks. She rocked backward with laughter when she noticed that I, too, had a tissue in my hand. "We're both so silly!" We laughed—God, how we laughed.

To this day the strains of Rachmaninoff make me smile. That night, and on countless other occasions, she played the concerto endlessly on her portable CD player, which she carried from room to room. Or she would sit at the grand piano, next to the window looking out onto the rear of the palace gardens, and play the *Brief Encounter* theme. I would creep upstairs and stand at the door unnoticed to watch her play the dark-wood piano; lost in thought, eyes closed. Forget about possessions or items. That sound was the most important thing I took away from Kensington Palace.

But before either she or I could feel comfortable enough together to share such tear-jerking movie moments, I had had to earn my stripes. Trust came with time. After leaving

Highgrove, duty, shared initially with fellow butler Harold Brown, came first.

T HE FURNITURE VAN stacked with all our worldly goods pulled up outside the Old Barracks where first-floor flat No. 2, with two bedrooms, bathroom, sitting room, and kitchen, became our new home. Its broad back stood on the periphery of the capital's hustle and bustle, insulating us from the congestion of Kensington High Street, and it looked out over a wide expanse of lawn. The three-story red-brick rectangular frontage of Kensington Palace, or "KP" as it was known to staff, stretched out in the south-west corner of Kensington Palace Gardens, set back from the western edge of Hyde Park. It was a planet away from the Gloucestershire countryside. We had arrived on a warm spring day in April 1993, and found ourselves in a London oasis, surrounded by green spaces.

A familiar face was waiting to greet us. The Princess of Wales was smiling, and holding a bunch of flowers for Maria. What other boss would take the time and trouble to do that?

As Maria opened the car door, the princess bounded over with excitement. "Welcome! Welcome! Welcome! You're here at last," she said, hugging Maria, as Alexander and Nicholas ran up to her and clung to her legs.

As the removal van was emptied, the princess stood outside in the sunshine, intrigued by our household goods. "Oh, that's nice, Maria, I didn't know you had that." Then she clapped her hands together, "I'm off now to leave you to settle in," and walked off, across the grass, back to the palace before she headed off for Easter to stay with her sister Lady Sarah McCorquodale in Lincolnshire. She had Easter eggs to pack for her nieces and nephews.

We inspected the flat. There were new carpets, and a new tiled floor in the kitchen. The Old Barracks is a converted stable block that once housed the grooms and soldiers who guarded the palace, which was bought by King William III and Queen Mary II in the late seventeenth century. In modern times, it had been divided into grace-and-favour accommodations for the royal household and staff. Our neighbors were the princess's sister Jane and her husband, Sir Robert Fellowes, the Queen's private secretary; Brigadier Miles Hunt-Davies, the Duke of Edinburgh's now knighted private secretary; Jimmy Jewell, the duke's accountant; and Ronald Allison, the Queen's press secretary. Fellow butler Harold Brown didn't have staff quarters. Somehow, through well-connected friends in high places, the onetime under-butler at Buckingham Palace had secured himself a royal apartment within Kensington Palace. He was known as the servant who lived like a royal, and apartment No. 6 was his grand home. We worked separately, splitting the day into two shifts to attend to the princess's every household need.

BUT MY FIRST DAY of work at KP had been four months earlier.

As I walked through the palace doors on that day, the princess shook my hand and said: "You're now part of my team. Welcome to the A-team!"

I settled into a routine of working in the city during the week and going back to see Maria and the boys at our cottage at Highgrove at the weekends while the flat was made ready for us. It was a tiresome journey, but no more than the princess had done for the previous few years. It was awkward for Maria to be living on the Highgrove estate. She and the boys were told they were not allowed to go up to the main house anymore. Anyone would have thought that our cottage housed the plague, because we were treated like outcasts. In the eyes of the household, we no longer belonged. I cannot say that we were not warned: Prince Charles's valet, Michael Fawcett, had said before the separation, "Be sure which side you back. Remember, the prince will be King one day."

He was devoted to the prince, but I had been chosen by the princess. She didn't inherit me, nor was I an appointee, like an equerry sent for service or a protection officer sent by the police. She had requested me, and I wasn't going to let her down.

But Maria, still living in Gloucestershire, suffered. In the first weeks of 1993, Lita Davies, a daily lady at Highgrove, was approached by someone from Prince Charles's camp who wanted to speak to her about why she was maintaining her friendship with Maria. Lita was told that it was "probably for the best" that she stopped having contact with her. Lita was adamant that she would not be told which friends she could keep.

Then she faced another, stiffer warning. She was told not to discuss anything that went on at Highgrove with Maria.

Lita handed in her resignation the following day.

There was clearly deep concern in the prince's camp that the princess still had eyes at Highgrove. It was a sign of how difficult the situation had become. It convinced Maria that we had made the right move.

In our first week as a family at KP, the princess was extra hospitable and generous, as if she wanted to erase any doubts we might have had about leaving the countryside. The day after she returned from visiting her sister at Easter, she treated William and Harry, Alexander and Nick to a day out at Thorpe Park in Berkshire. The princess, dressed in black leather jacket and black jeans, gave them all a memorable day of fun, buying all four boys water pistols and joining them on the rides. Little Nick was only five and didn't let go of the princess's hand for most of the day. She called him her "little sexpot," and, that day, as press photographers followed them everywhere, she gave him piggyback rides and carried him on her shoulders.

The following day, the *Sun* dedicated a whole page to the trip with the headline: "WILLS AND HARRY LEARN COMMONER SENSE WITH BUTLER'S SONS AS PALS." The article quoted royal photographer Jim Bennett, who had said what we already knew: "The princess treats the butler's boys like her own. If you were a casual observer and you didn't know she was the Princess of Wales, you would imagine it was a young mum out with her four kids."

That same week, I joined the princess at the Royal Opera House, Covent Garden, to see the ballet *Don Quixote;* I served dinner in the back of the Royal Box for the princess and a party of friends. From the shadows, I witnessed my first-ever ballet performance, and the costumes and music were spectacular.

Back at KP, I was busy in the pantry washing up when the princess popped her head round the door. "What did you think?" she asked.

This was my chance to impress my more worldly-wise boss with my basic review and prove that her new recruit was no Philistine. I told her I thought it was amazing. Then I asked her what she thought. "Rubbish," she said, and burst out laughing when she saw the surprise on my face.

I had started work for the princess four months before moving into the Old Barracks, sleeping in a simple single room in the top-floor nursery. Apartments Nos. 8 and 9 occupied three floors at the heart of KP in an L-shaped layout, overlooking the back of the palace. In total, KP housed a hundred people and four royal households, all living their own independent lives with their respective private secretaries, equerries, ladies-in-waiting, butlers, chauffeurs, maids, dressers, chefs, and police protection officers. The princess's apartments were tucked behind the palace front, out of sight, on the north side. They were accessed via the long drive that passed the Old Barracks and continued straight ahead, passing a row of cottages for other household staff, before a sharp right turn brought visitors to the rear of the palace and the front door of No. 8. It faced onto a small green. Its Georgian windows had a view, to the right, of the princess's private walled garden, where she retreated in the summer months. It was her sanctuary in the center of the capital. Every day, when the sun was out, I would set out a lounge chair, spread a towel, and place a cooled bottle of Volvic water underneath it in the shade. "It is so peaceful in there—there is a tranquillity which is hard to explain," she said. She could spend hours topping up her tan, reading or listening to her CD Walkman.

Her privacy, and that of visitors she didn't want to be spotted, was also protected by a secret passage into her apartments, accessed through an archway, topped with a white-painted tower and black-faced clock, into the cobbled square of Clock Court. It was the one area of the palace not covered by CCTV cameras, on the insistence of Princess Margaret, who guarded her privacy vehemently too. That way, visitors were kept away from the monitoring eyes of the police. It became a well-trodden route of mine in my duty to meet certain guests.

KP was not the cozy home the princess had often dreamed about, but it was a fortress she regarded as ultrasafe for herself, William, and Harry. After 1992, when it became solely her home, she ensured her decorative stamp was placed on every room. She got rid of carpets that bore the Prince of Wales feathers. But she did not, as the misinformed have suggested, match Prince Charles in expunging all memories of her estranged partner. She respected that it was also her sons' home, so it was only right to have photographs of "Papa" in many rooms.

But when it came to photographs, images of William and Harry had the monopoly. On the peach walls of the dressing room, which she walked through to get from bedroom to bathroom, there were around twenty official portrait photos of the princess with William and Harry, taken over the years by Patrick Demarchelier: black-and-white images of unguarded moments in a photo studio, both boys' arms slung around their mother in almost every shot. The opposite wall was covered with framed montages of their school artwork.

Wherever you looked around the apartments, images of William and Harry, at all ages, stared back from virtually every flat surface: on the piano in the drawing room; on the princess's desk in the sitting room and on a table in the corner; on the walls of the corridors. These boys were, quite simply, her life.

She turned Prince Charles's study into William and Harry's own sitting room, just a few yards down from hers. In this room, there were hours of fun. My sons joined the princes there to take one another on in combat games on the PlayStation. The boys sat on a green sofa, facing the television, entranced for hours. In her own sitting room, the princess loved nothing more than to hear the excited shrieks of the children. In the evenings, she and her sons would sometimes eat together in the boys' room. William loved watching the BBC hospital drama *Casualty* because of all the blood and gore, while his mother and Harry writhed on the sofa in mock horror. Or they'd watch *Blind Date* and try to match unfortunate couples. "Pick number one!" the princess would scream, while the boys would deliberately choose a different one. "No, number two, number two!" they yelled.

I think there was a natural low whenever the boys left to visit their father or went to boarding school. As the princess stood, waving them off from the doorstep, she said, almost without fail, "I'll miss ma boys!"

She hated them not being around, and Alexander and Nick often stepped into the void. The princess would ring the Old Barracks and invite my sons up for tea and to play with William and Harry's things. It wasn't the company she wanted; it was the comforting noise of playing children. "Get the boys to come up, it's dead in here. Get them to come up and make some noise!" A royal palace became my sons' part-time playground.

When the young princes were away, the princess wrote to them endlessly. Almost every day, sometimes two or three times a day. A letter. A postcard. Every letter expressed her excitement at seeing them again so that she could shower them with hugs and kisses.

THE PRINCESS EMBRACED the start of 1993 as if it was going to be the best year of her life. She was a new woman, no longer having to keep up appearances. She embarked on successful solo tours to Zimbabwe and Nepal, where Baroness Chalker went along in her capacity as minister for overseas development. Prime Minister John Major and the Foreign Office supported her missions. She might have been separated from the heir to the throne, but she had the full weight of the government behind her. She was a roving ambassador and a prized asset for Britain. So much for the jealous snipers of the old guard, with their futile attempts to brand her a "loose cannon." She had left them behind in a different age.

The princess was working more and more with the International Red Cross and pricking consciences about the AIDS epidemic and the poverty-stricken. She was taking lessons to become a better orator when she spoke about the homeless, HIV, mental health issues, and the plight of those who suffer, as she had, from eating disorders. In this, she was like my mother, giving so unsparingly of herself to others. She juggled public duty with private joys: an Elton John concert, the ballet of *Romeo and Juliet,* the movie *The Jungle Book,* and the theater production of *Grease.*

Her high spirits were infectious, and where there had been gloom at Highgrove, sunshine radiated through KP. Life was flexible and unstuffy. At the end of the month, to boost staff morale, she threw what she labeled in a staff memo a "celebration lunch party for the A-team." She played the piano. We drank. We sang. We danced.

As if to emphasize her newfound freedom, 1993 was the year she parted company with police protection officers, shedding the final remnants of the establishment she had left behind. She felt that they were duty-bound to report to their superior about their whereabouts. That superior officer was none other than Inspector Colin Trimming, the Prince of Wales's senior protection officer. So, in her independence, she sat at her desk and made a decision. That weekend, as I brought her coffee, she made an instant note to herself. "Self-esteem," she scrawled. Ticked it. "Confidence." Ticked it. "Happiness." Ticked it. Then she wrote "Police"—and put an "X" beside it.

I BECAME ACCUSTOMED to the princess's high voice, a chirpy sound that traveled down the wide staircase with its white balustrade and polished wooden banister. "Are you down there, Paul?" she would shout. That staircase became her calling point for me; the "catwalk stairs" where she would stand and twirl in a new outfit she wanted to show off; or the place where we would sit together—the princess always sat one step above me—talking or going through the correspondence she had received, or a letter she wanted help in composing.

I often waited there for her to arrive. She would burst in through the black front doors, walk along a narrow entrance corridor, turn left, through an arch into the inner hallway, then pass through another arch and on to the stairs, which took her to the first-floor landing and her private rooms. Often, her voice beckoned me from the landing as she leaned over the banister. "You coming shopping, Paul? Give me five minutes."

I grabbed my coat and walked with her down the drive, across Kensington Church Street, down Church Walk, and out on to the high street opposite Marks & Spencer. "Let's go to WHSmith's. We'll get some CDs for the boys," she said, referring to both her sons and mine. En route to the album chart, she stopped beside the large racks of humorous cards, read one punch line and laughed. I can hear her now. "Look at this one! Have you seen the picture on this?" Sometimes she was doubled up with laughter.

Wherever we went, we attracted a following. There was no missing that mental registration as the princess laughed at the cards. Tall. Blonde. Beautiful. Unmistakable. In Kensington. I could almost hear jaws hitting the floor. Then, as we nipped into the chemist or Marks & Spencer, she became the Pied Piper as a small entourage scurried behind her, pretending to shop.

Some people simply didn't believe it.

Two ladies stood beside us one day in WHSmith, whispering with the clear intention of being heard.

"It is, you know—it's her," said the first lady.

"Of course it's not—it's a look-alike," said her friend, and carried on shopping regardless. The princess? In WHSmith? Like the rest of us? Never.

Each time we shopped, we returned to the palace with a

few magazines—*Vogue, Tatler*—for her light reading, and then she wrote the cards she had bought and sent them to William and Harry at their boarding school, Ludgrove, with a few CDs and a collection of videos. One particular day, she yelled the usual shopping invitation and we trotted off again to WH Smith's. Unbeknownst to me, it was a visit with a purpose: to introduce me to a trusted ally, Richard Kay of the *Daily Mail*. We had bought more CDs and cards, and were leaving when who should be entering but "Ricardo," as she called him. The princess went through the Oh-fancy-meeting-you-here charade, blushed and giggled. In my job, I had long been wary of reporters, but this one was different. Good eggs do exist in Fleet Street.

"Oh, I'm sorry," said the reporter, whose supportive pieces I had read over the years, and he held open the door for us.

"I trust him," said the princess, as we walked away. Message received.

BEING AT KP meant becoming accustomed to yet another royal figure's routine. Every morning, between 7 and 7:30 A.M., a dresser went into the princess's bedroom to "call" her, although she was invariably already up and about.

I stood in the corridor between the dining room and the kitchen, where Mervyn Wycherley or Darren McGrady would prepare breakfast. The barefoot princess appeared at the far end of the corridor, in a white robe. Even half awake, devoid of makeup and with unkempt hair, she still looked every inch a princess. As soon as I saw her, I moved into the kitchen to make a pot of coffee.

By the time I had carried the hand-painted Herend coffeepot to the dining room, she was settled into one of the four bamboo latticed chairs around the table, which was covered with a white linen cloth. She was tucking into half a fresh grapefruit, flipping through the daily newspapers, which I had spread flat in the same order as I had for the Queen. From the bottom: *The Times,* the *Daily Tele-graph,* the *Daily Express,* the *Daily Mail,* and the *Daily Mirror.* But no *Sporting Life* on top. I would enter the room, whose magenta walls provided an early-morning warmth, and stand in the half-open doorway until I saw the princess raise her eyes from the paper.

That was my signal. I gave a short, sharp bow from the neck down. "Good morning, Your Royal Highness." As time went on, my insistence on tradition and using YRH clearly irked her: "Paul, please don't do that. There's only the two of us in this room. There really is no need," she said.

But I insisted on keeping to protocol. It was the only time when I didn't listen to the Boss. If she wanted to in-vite me across the professional line to share her world, that was fine. But, by addressing her as Your Royal Highness, I showed respect and defined my role. I *needed* to show her that respect even when, at her down-to-earth best, she did not require me to do so. Each morning, from 1993 until the day she died, I called her "Your Royal Highness."

I walked across to the sideboard and popped a slice of granary bread into the toaster. Then we chatted about the previous night and what lay ahead that day. Often I turned round to find she was twirling a spoon, with a silver bee-hive on the top of its handle, into a jar of white honey, then popping it into her mouth. Sometimes she asked if I had seen the newspapers. It was not always easy to answer, es-pecially if I had spotted a negative article. If a particular paper was missing, she knew I was protecting her from a bad press. "Oh, you don't want to see that," I would tell her, knowing full well that I had ignited her curiosity and she would go looking for it. One paper she never looked at over breakfast was the *Sun.* But that did not stop her tak-ing a sneaky look at chef Mervyn's copy in the kitchen, where it was left in his dispatch tray above the telephone.

Mondays, Wednesdays, and Fridays were exercise days, sometimes at Chelsea Harbour Club, sometimes in the drawing room, where Harold or I had pushed back the fur-niture to make room for the princess and fitness instructor

Carolan Brown or Jenny Rivet. In later years I had to drive the princess in one of her cars to a gym in Earls Court. The fitness classes sometimes took place before breakfast.

Following the separation, the KP timetable had to be flexible, because it was dependent on whether William and Harry were back from Ludgrove and with their mother or at Highgrove with their father. Prince Charles ensured that the visiting arrangements were set in stone, writing to the princess every two or three weeks with lists of his available dates, for months in advance. It was in 1993 that he appointed Tiggy Legge-Bourke to help him look after William and Harry. She was more nursery assistant than nanny, but the princess was infuriated when the media began describing her as a "surrogate mother." In countless newspaper images, Tiggy—a good-natured young woman who lived the quiet life in a terraced property in Battersea—was seen larking about with William and Harry. In time, she became a confidante and personal friend of Prince Charles, and the princess began to view her as a threat. As part of her daily routine, the princess said that her one true extravagance was having her hair washed and blow-dried every weekday morning, first by hairdresser Richard Dalton and then in later years by Sam McKnight, and both men became trusted confidants. All women gossip to their hairdresser and the princess was no different. There were many lighthearted moments between princess, hairdresser, and butler, and she always SPOKE LOUDER SO HER VOICE COULD BE HEARD OVER THE HAIR DRYER!

When she saw my reflection behind her in the oval mirror on the dressing-table, she would shout, "LOOK AT THIS!" It might be kind correspondence—or otherwise—or a magazine photograph or comment by a newspaper columnist. Nobody but dresser, butler, hairdresser, and housemaid was ever invited into this inner sanctum. At these times, she was at her most natural, most relaxed, most easygoing: the princess the world never got to see. To me, at home, she was a fresh-faced girl stripped of the mask of royalty, as vulnerable as the next person. As soon as she was outside the front door, immaculate in one of her many stunning outfits, she drew on her inner reservoir of strength and strode out with majestic confidence. From white robe to Catherine Walker dress or Chanel suit, I witnessed that remarkable transformation each morning, and it never ceased to amaze me.

An L-shaped room the size of a small bedroom was needed to accommodate the hundreds of day dresses, blouses, suits, jackets, trousers, and cocktail dresses that constituted her wardrobe; a multicolored assortment, all hanging from rails above the racks of her hundreds of pairs of shoes, hidden behind floor-to-ceiling curtains. Even the wardrobe layout was immaculate. A blue-and-white-fleck Chanel suit hung directly above matching blue suede shoes; a pink Versace suit above matching pink leather shoes; a scarlet Catherine Walker coatdress above a pair of red satin shoes.

The princess's week could be filled with "away days," when she had engagements outside London or was busy at charity meetings in the capital. When her diary allowed, lunch was either taken at the palace or a stone's throw away at Launceston Place or San Lorenzo, in Knightsbridge. Lunch was a social occasion for the princess, and she preferred to dine one-to-one, with guests from her close-knit circle of friends: Lucia Flecha de Lima, Rosa Monckton, Susie Kassem, Lady Annabel Goldsmith, Julia Samuel, Laura Lonsdale, astrologer Debbie Frank, or, her closest royal ally, Sarah, Duchess of York. The princess surrounded herself with her kind of people. On many Sundays, she went to the duchess's home at Virginia Water, near Windsor, or to Lady Annabel Goldsmith's in Richmond. Both homes had ample security and swimming pools to keep William and Harry safe and occupied.

If the princess had lunch by herself at the palace, she often sat on a high stool at the open breakfast bar, looking into the kitchen, sharing jokes with the chef and me. It was a one-course meal that always incorporated a salad, washed down with iced Volvic water. If there is one image I remember from those rushed lunchtimes, it is of the princess with her mobile telephone balanced between shoulder and neck, speaking from the corner of her mouth as she used her knife and fork.

Whenever she left KP, I followed her out to the car. Whether she was a passenger or the driver, I waited until she was seated, then leaned in, grabbed the seatbelt, and pulled it across her.

If she had been out, she would invariably have returned by 7:30 P.M., and I would make her a cup of her favorite gingerroot tea. Dinner would be grilled trout or a pasta dish; or a plain baked potato with a scoop of caviar, served with a vinaigrette dressing. It was often a solitary meal, served on a wheeled wooden trolley that I pushed into the sitting room before the striped sofa where the princess sat in her white robe. I had already pulled the television out of its cabinet at the bottom of the bookcase and into position. Evenings were the loneliest, quietest times for the princess. The chef had gone. Her dresser had gone. And her private secretary, Patrick Jephson, never penetrated her private world at these times. His office was at St. James's Palace, where he worked from nine to five. At the day's end, as the princess wound down from a busy morning and afternoon, I got to know her better on a personal level. She was relaxed, not fraught and talkative. It became clear, as I wheeled in her two-course evening meal, that with William and Harry at boarding school she preferred not to be left alone. "Stay awhile," she said, more times than I can remember.

I stood, leaning against an upholstered chair, and we talked about her day, my day, the week ahead, what he had said, what she had said. Or the plot lines in *Coronation Street* or *Brookside*. These nighttime chats might be brief or extend into a chat that lost all track of time. Sometimes the ITN news at ten o'clock was the signal for bed. As I wheeled away the trolley, she got up from the sofa and followed me into the anteroom that acted as a first-floor pantry. There, I washed up and the princess dried.

"What do you think tomorrow's going to bring?" she'd ask.

"Whatever happens, we'll tackle it," I told her.

When bedtime came, she disappeared down the corridor with a girlish skip and hop, as if she was suddenly full of energy again, looking forward to the next day. I followed a few paces behind, switching out the lights along the way, in the dining room, drawing room, sitting room, and then the landing. All lights would be turned out except one: the light in the corridor outside her bedroom. She had been scared of the dark as a child and, throughout adulthood, preferred to sleep in half-light.

As she disappeared into the bedroom, her final words each night were exactly the same: "'Night, Paul."

"Good night, Your Royal Highness," I said.

Sometime before eleven, I would leave the palace, walk through the darkness of the grounds, and into No. 2 of the Old Barracks, where my wife and two boys were already asleep.

HAVING LEFT HIGHGROVE to Prince Charles, the princess had no weekend retreat, which she missed. There was no question of her leaving Kensington Palace, but from the start of 1993 she had been on the lookout for a private bolt-hole where she and the boys could spend long weekends. She could go, of course, to the Duchess of York and Lady Annabel Goldsmith, but "It is such an imposition relying on them all the time," she said. "I want my own country retreat away from London."

Suddenly an escape route was provided from the unlikeliest source—her brother, Earl Spencer. It seemed strange that he was coming to his sister's rescue, because they were not especially close. Since her marriage in 1981, brother and sister had seen each other fewer than fifty times. A distance had crept between siblings who had been close in childhood. However, following a request from the princess, the earl offered her the use of the Garden House in a corner of the estate at a rent of £12,000 a year. "The dream solution," said the princess. It guaranteed privacy, and there was also a swimming pool near the main house; her brother promised a cleaner and a gardener.

In a letter to his sister on June 3, 1993, the earl wrote: "I see your need for a country retreat and I am happy to help, provided there aren't too many disruptions on the estate. The Garden House seems to suit your needs perfectly. It would also make sense to have your own pool." He even suggested erecting a new security gate to keep photographers at bay.

As she read that letter, the princess was already mentally decorating the little cottage. So excited was she that she visited Althorp one day with her interior designer, Dudley Poplak. She set off with a picnic lunch, prepared by her chef, and on that sunny afternoon she relaxed outside on the grass on the estate, dreaming of idyllic weekends at her new home with William and Harry.

Fifteen days later, the dream was shattered when her brother suddenly withdrew his offer. He wrote: "I'm sorry but I've decided that the Garden House isn't a possible move now. There are many reasons, most of which include the police and press interference which would inevitably follow. I am now bringing in a senior agent and need an extra house for him. I know I am doing the right thing for my wife and children. I'm just sorry that I can't help my sister! In theory, it would have been lovely to have helped, and I am sorry I can't. If you're interested in renting a farmhouse [outside the park], then that would be wonderful. . . ."

The princess read that letter over and over again, mystified by his about-face. "How can he do this to me?" she raged, then dissolved into tears. What puzzled her most was that he knew she had set her heart on moving in to the Garden House. When he telephoned the palace a few days later, she slammed the phone down on him. "I cannot bear to hear his voice," she said. Almost immediately, she spilled her anger on to her red-edged, letterheaded writing paper, telling the earl exactly what she thought of him as a brother and how hurt she felt. Earl Spencer, probably suspecting the vitriol contained within the envelope, returned the letter unopened. He sent it back with a third letter he wrote on June 28: "Knowing the state you were in the other night when you hung up on me, I doubt whether reading this will help our relationship. Therefore, I am returning it unopened because it is the quickest way to rebuild our friendship."

But that friendship had been damaged forever. How ironic, then, that in death, Earl Spencer chose to accept his sister and bury her on an island grave. Suddenly, the outside "interference" that had so bothered him no longer seemed a concern. Nowadays he encourages the press and thousands of visitors each year to pour through his gates to see his own Diana museum and buy souvenirs.

The 1993 rift widened as the princess refused to take her brother's telephone calls. Earl Spencer had to resort to writing to her private secretary, Patrick Jephson, to communicate with her. Then, in September, he dealt his sister another crushing blow by demanding the return of the Spencer family tiara, which she had worn on her wedding day in 1981 and which was precious to her. As Princess of Wales, it was an essential part of her regal uniform, and she wore it to state banquets at Buckingham Palace, state openings of Parliament, and diplomatic receptions. When he wrote to Patrick Jephson, Earl Spencer made it clear that the tiara had only been "on loan" to the princess, because his grandfather had bequeathed it to him in the 1970s. "It should now be returned to its proper owner," he wrote. For twelve years, possession of the tiara had not been in question, and the princess felt the timing of the request related directly to their disagreement over the Garden House. The earl felt that his new wife, Victoria, should wear it.

It was not merely a symbol of the princess's royal status; it was a memory of her wedding day. But the princess would not give her brother the satisfaction of knowing it bothered her. That October, the tiara was handed back to him, and it was my duty to remove it from the safe where it had sat in a box alongside what she called her "spare"— the lovers' knot pearl-and-diamond tiara that the Queen had given her as a wedding present. At least she was able to keep the Windsor tiara.

Meanwhile, in the KP household, there were staff changes that affected life at the Old Barracks. Maria, who had been a maid with little responsibility since we moved from Highgrove, was promoted to dresser following the resignation of Helena Roache. She would work part-time alongside the senior full-time dresser, Helen Walsh. The appointment posed some domestic difficulties in the Burrell household, because Maria suddenly went from 9 A.M. to 1 P.M. housemaid duties to an erratic timetable, sometimes having to rise at 7 A.M., or work in the evenings. We had to arrange our lives so that when she worked evenings I swapped shifts with Harold Brown to be at home with the boys. Maria knew it would be a strain, but she wanted to help the princess. She said she would try the job for a year and thought that was an established agreement with the princess.

The Boss proved flexible, even allowing Maria to wake her with a telephone call at 7 A.M. instead of walking in personally, as normal duty would have required. But the daytime hours got longer and longer. Maria had never before spent an evening away from Alexander and Nick, and she missed them. When she went shopping for the princess late in the afternoon, she would see the boys playing on the green in front of the Old Barracks. More often than not, when she worked evenings the boys were asleep by the time she finished. But if Maria was working hard, Helen was toiling harder.

The princess recognized the sacrifices they were both making and attempted to compensate. She gave Maria bags full of unwanted designer shoes—Chanel, Ferragamo, or Rayne—because they were the same size 6½, plus handbags and discarded suits by Catherine Walker, Versace, and Chanel. Helen also found herself the grateful recipient of unwanted clothes and gifts. It was the princess's way of making space in an ever-expanding wardrobe and saying thank you. Her sister, Lady Sarah McCorquodale, also benefited from this generosity.

Generosity in a royal household was nothing new. In my time with the Queen, I had been given gifts from foreign tours. In my time at Highgrove, Prince Charles had given me a table carved from a redwood tree trunk, books, a silver box with an enamel lid, and a pair of Lalique crystal grouse. The only time I had ever helped myself to the prince's possessions was when I joined the princess on a Highgrove raid. Harold Brown, Dudley Poplak, the Boss, and I went there, post-separation, to remove items of furniture, lamps, pictures, and ornaments. "This is our one and only chance to take what we want!" We piled the items high in a removal van.

Prince Charles was placing his own decorative stamp on his home, bringing in more dark-wood furniture. The princess was in hysterics when Dudley commented: "It looks like he's returning to the womb!"

IF 1993 HAD GOT OFF to a flying start for the newly independent princess, it ended in a series of blows. First came the falling-out with Earl Spencer. Then, in November, the *Sunday Mirror* published photographs of the princess working out in her leotard at the LA Fitness centre in Isleworth, London. Gym owner Bryce Taylor had planted a secret camera in the ceiling. The princess instructed lawyer Anthony Julius of Mishcon de Reya to pursue legal recourse, and the newspaper was condemned for a blatant breach of privacy by the Press Complaints Commission. It also led the princess to make a dramatic announcement on December 3 during a speech she was giving at a charity lunch for head-injury victims. She stunned the world when she said: "I hope you can find it in your hearts to understand and give me the time and space that has been lacking in recent years. When I started my public life twelve years ago, I understood the media might be interested in what I did ... but I was not aware of how overwhelming that attention would become."

The Royal Household, which felt it was an unnecessary,

melodramatic statement, offered its usual amount of sympathy: the princess's name was withdrawn from the Court Circular and she was not invited to Royal Ascot. The princess had only asked to step away from the spotlight but found herself unceremoniously ejected from the stage door.

The breach of privacy at LA Fitness—which was settled out of court with an apology from the *Sunday Mirror* in 1995—had deeply upset her. When she was hurt, she would retire to her bedroom, where she knew no one could get to her. She cursed herself over the gym pictures because, in cooperating with the media over the years, she felt she had given them the inch that had been extended into a yard. I was reduced to leaving messages on pieces of paper in her sitting room and on a stool at the top of the stairs. She surfaced for her meals, but they were subdued occasions. When I was downstairs in my pantry, she reflected alone on what she felt were her mistakes, playing requiem masses at full volume. When that happened, I knew she was drowning her sobs, ridding herself of the hurt. As she often said: "I only feel fully protected when retreating into my shell. No one can hurt me there."

But she bounced back every time, which was why her withdrawal from the public stage was never going to last long. The people who mattered to her most, the general public, were shouting "More, more" the moment she walked off.

But with all official public engagements canceled, she had time for what she enjoyed most: socializing over lunch. The afternoons from January 1994 through to the spring were filled with appointments at her favorite eateries: San Lorenzo, Le Caprice, the Ritz, Claridges, the Ivy, Bibendum, or Launceston Place. Australian television presenter Clive James and friend Lord Attenborough were regular fellow diners, and she must have seen Lucia Flecha de Lima and Rosa Monckton twice a week. KP became her luxury decompression chamber, and I could almost see the stresses of her high-profile life lifting. The coiled spring unwound as she played lots more tennis, went to the ballet or the cinema, stayed with friends. Warm, carefree, energetic, and good company, she was back in top form.

One day, she treated her staff to a trip to Alton Towers theme park because William and Harry wanted to try out Nemesis, the new thrill ride. It was one of her "let's be normal" days out, and there were thirteen of us, including me, Maria, our boys, nanny Olga Powell, chauffeur Steve Davis, and the young princes, shadowed by their police protection officers, Graham Craker and Chris Tarr. One notable absentee was fellow butler Harold Brown, who was rapidly falling out of favor with the Boss. As if to emphasize the normality of the day—which was never going to be achieved—the princess decided we should travel to Staffordshire by public transport. Dressed in a green-and-white American football jacket, she marched the party to Euston railway station and we boarded a first-class carriage. Maybe it was the continual fitness program she was on, but I didn't realize until that day how fast she could walk. Keeping up with her around the park was like being on a nonstop ride in itself. Nick was the only one in the party who got a respite because he rode on the princess's shoulders. She stopped once, for lunch, tucking into burgers and fries with the rest of us.

"Come on, Mummy, come on this ride," said Harry, tugging at his mother's sleeve. She looked skyward to the twisted metal of the suspended roller coaster Nemesis, and shook her head. "No, I'll be sick," she said, and stayed with Maria. The sedate pace of the River Rapids was more her style.

But no matter that the day was intended to be normal; the press had got wind of her visit and followed us everywhere.

Another little person tugging on her arm was Nick, who wanted to go on the Mad Hatter's Tea Party ride. "Giant teacups, I want to ride on the giant teacups, Princess!" he begged. That was why the princess, the young princes, and our boys appeared in the following day's newspapers, whizzing around in the giant teacups. Sadly, nowadays Nick cannot remember being carried around by the princess, even though a framed photo of them takes pride of place in our house.

The newspaper coverage showed that the press would never give her the time and space she had requested the previous December. Denied images of the princess performing her duty, "Her Majesty's Reptiles," otherwise known as the press, spent every day searching for her going about her everyday life. Journalistic curiosity intensified and, day after day, the newspapers were full of images: the princess at McDonald's; arriving at the Chelsea Harbour Club fitness center; walking along the street; eating in a restaurant; shopping with friends; in the back of a taxi; driving her car. If the princess stepped outside KP, it was a picture. In 1994, the media, with its voracious appetite, ratcheted up Di-mania to another level.

If there was a time when the princess attempted to "find herself," it was 1994. I seemed to open the door to an ever-growing band of lifestyle gurus, health experts, healers, astrologers, and psychics. Friends offered counseling services, ears and shoulders to cry on. She placed the well-intentioned advice from people who genuinely cared in the same melting pot as the zodiac information, the power of the crystals, the messages from the spiritual world, and the "energies" around her. She mused about them long and hard while undergoing acupuncture, massage, or workout.

The scent of incense from burning joss sticks in the princess's bedroom wafted through the first floor, overriding the air fresheners the maids had used earlier in the morning. I became used to the immaculately turned-out astrologer Debbie Frank arriving at the KP front door. The floor of either the drawing room or the sitting room became scattered with zodiac charts as Debbie and the princess sat on the carpet, plotting the movement of the planets and what it all meant for the royal Cancerian. She felt that Cancerians, like their symbol, the crab, had a hard outer shell but a soft center, and wanted instinctively to skulk sideways into the shadows. She also felt that it explained her fascination with water and her dream to live, one day, in a house on a coast. She told Debbie: "This house is full of Geminis. William's Gemini, Paul is Gemini—and it's not easy!"

Debbie was keen to offer me the expertise of her readings, but I declined. "You really must have your chart read," implored the princess. "It's riveting stuff."

Once, an acupuncturist from whom the princess had just returned telephoned. If acupuncturists are meant to be calming, this call was anything but. In fact, the practitioner was on the verge of panic. "I'm a needle short. I think I may have left one in the princess's head!" I walked up the staircase and into the sitting room, where she was writing at her desk, half expecting to find an antenna protruding from her scalp. I started to chuckle, and the princess looked up.

"I've just taken a call," I said. "Apparently, you might have an acupuncturist's needle still in your head."

The princess patted it all over, then burst out laughing. "Put the poor woman out of her misery and tell her I'm okay, I feel a lot better for meeting her again!"

The princess never failed to see the funny side of her therapies and treatments. Some were more bizarre and self-punishing than others. Twice a week it was my duty—and not the chauffeur's (because of its private nature)—to drive the princess to a clinic in North London for colonic irrigation. "You *don't* want to know, Paul!" she said.

She drove herself to the home of Susie Orbach, a psychotherapist who specialized in eating disorders and played an important part in helping the princess bring her bulimia under control. Dr. Mary Loveday, a small, soft-spoken lady, addressed the chemical balance in the princess's body and prescribed vitamin supplements that she would take three times a day.

The growth of the human spirit and the spiritual side of life, "the other side," as she called it, fascinated the princess. Psychic Rita Rogers, based near my hometown of Chesterfield, was a constant guide to her, but Simone Simmons, a faith healer, was a true friend. Some nights, it was not unusual for the princess to spend up to five hours on the telephone to her. I had Simone to thank for the smell of joss sticks.

My view was that these alternative therapists provided the Boss with a release that made her happy, each in its own different way. But in time she would overrely on them in a way that disturbed me.

What was also disturbing was the way the paparazzi stalked her wherever she went. Once, when she was leaving the London home of Susie Orbach, the princess, wearing dark glasses, was reduced to tears as freelance photographers, working for foreign magazines and agencies, surrounded her, poking fun at her and bullying her with comments such as "Look at you, you're a wreck" or "You're nothing but a tart, Diana." When the princess burst into tears and ran to her car, the next day headlines screamed, "DIANA WEEPS," and suggested she was sobbing over her marriage.

Few women would have coped in the eye of those daily storms. On many occasions in central London, I witnessed what it was like to be at the center of the mêlée. I would park the car at a meter and wait for the princess to return from a health clinic, shop, or restaurant. I would catch her eye in the side or rearview mirror as she was pursued by the "rat-pack," lean over, with the engine running, and push open the door so she could leap inside: "Drive, Paul, drive."

But the photographers were already around us, leaning from both sides across the hood, banging on the windows. The princess, holding a hand to her bowed head, said once: "We're going to kill somebody one day." She found it all extremely distressing.

The best times when I was driving with the princess came on sweltering summer days when we stopped at traffic lights with the Mercedes roof down. She loved the shock on motorists' faces when they glanced to one side and recognized her; glum faces were suddenly brightened with delight. Once, the traffic lights turned red and we pulled up alongside a building being renovated in the Mayfair district. One of the builders on the lowest level of scaffolding noticed the princess. Within seconds, word had leaped up to every level, and it seemed as if the entire site's staff had downed tools and burst into a chorus of wolf whistles and colorful support.

The princess was embarrassed and pretended not to hear, but as we drove off, she lifted a hand into the air, waved, and giggled all the way home.

ONE IMAGE THE PRESS never captured was when the princess turned up at Maria's surprise fortieth birthday party held at Café Rouge, a short walk from the palace, on February 1, 1994. It was a costume party; the fancy theme was "famous people." Maria and I went as Antony and Cleopatra. Former Highgrove housekeeper Wendy Berry was Cruella De Vil, brother-in-law Peter Cosgrove was Al Capone, and my brother Graham and his wife, Jayne, came as Napoleon and Josephine. When the princess walked through the door to join us, my other brother, Anthony, masquerading as General Custer, shook hands with the Boss and asked her, rather bluntly: "What have you come as?"

In a black suit with a black-and-gold-embroidered waist-coat, she replied: "A princess, of course!"

That Saturday afternoon, as fellow staff and friends prepared their costumes, the princess had gone secretly to meet Mother Teresa. She was eager to join the revelers later that day, because many would be household staff she knew from either KP or Highgrove—even her old friend from Buckingham Palace, retired palace steward Cyril Dickman, was there. The princess wanted "to do something normal for a change," although the prospect of walking through a public restaurant and into a private room was never going to be regarded by anyone else as normal. Perhaps it was my Roman centurion–style outfit, but I assumed the role of protector for the evening, and arranged to meet the princess with a small group of other costumed guests at the police barrier on the palace drive at eight o'clock.

The princess appeared out of the darkness and couldn't

believe the sight before her. "Look at you all!" she said, and doubled up with laughter. She walked to the venue in the middle of this crowd: the Princess of Wales encircled by Antony, the Three Musketeers, Batman and Robin. Friends and family had traveled south from North Wales, and their false mustaches and wigs almost dropped off with shock when the princess walked through the door. A senior royal at a costume party in a public restaurant! Stuffy courtiers trapped in a different age might have disapproved, but I had never seen the princess have such fun at a social event. She sat in a chair, drinking water, giggling over the high-spirited antics as the crowd sat in a row on the floor, performing the boat dance, before a conga snaked its way round the upper floor.

Then the princess took center stage near the red DJ booth: she had agreed to hand out the prizes for the costume competition. It made my brother Graham's night when he won first prize as Napoleon and she presented him with a CD stereo.

After two hours, the princess decided to leave; as she continued to enthuse about what a wonderful time she had had, I walked her home—the Princess of Wales was escorted through Kensington with a Roman centurion at her side.

It was a joy to watch the princess joining in with Maria's birthday celebrations, especially when she was dreading her own. She hated the birthday focus turning on her: she felt uncomfortable because she feared that friends and associates might feel compelled to spring treats or give gifts. She gave generously to so many people on their birthdays—she noted her friends' on a calendar. But receiving presents embarrassed her. As she said so often: "It's much easier to give than receive. There's no strings attached to giving."

Each July 1, knowing her enjoyment of WHSmith's humorous cards, I would slip one, signed by the Burrell family, onto her desk. In fact, there was lighthearted rivalry among the staff as to who could buy the funniest, most daring greeting. She opened them after breakfast and stood them all on the round table in her sitting room. Then the flowers started to arrive. Twenty-four long-stemmed yellow roses from a secret admirer the world never got to know about. Red roses arrived from friends. Then white flowers—tulips from Elton John and more roses from Gianni Versace—arrived in vased displays. Anna Harvey, the editor of *Vogue* in London, sent a gift-wrapped blouse or dress. There was always a generous gift from Catherine Walker and from Jo Malone. All her female friends sent flowers or presents. At the police box, well-wishers left cards, presents, and flowers. By the end of the day, apartments No. 8 and No. 9 resembled a florist's shop, and every conceivable flat surface was covered with cards.

If the princess dreaded July 1, so did her butler. I would be running up and down those stairs for hours on end. A delivery from Selfridges, from Harrods, from the royal grocers Fortnum & Mason, from Harvey Nichols. And then, without fail, a bunch of flowers from Prince Charles, who addressed every letter and card he sent her, every year until her death, "Dearest Diana."

For the remainder of her birthday, from late afternoon until she went to bed, she wrote letter after letter to say thank you to relatives, friends, associates, and organizations. I have never seen anyone write so many or respond so quickly. But the princess never forgot the strict discipline instilled into her as a child by her father.

In the KP sitting room, she removed sheets of her red-edged paper, with a scrolled *D* below a coronet, from the central drawer of her mahogany desk. She sat there, with her back to the window, as if it were a correspondence production line: write, fold, envelope, seal; write, fold, envelope, seal. Hour after hour she sat there, dipping her black fountain pen into a pot of blue-black Quink, penning her appreciation in the distinctive heavy handwriting that flowed across the paper. Then, after underlining her signature as she always did, she flipped over the letter and pressed it lightly onto the pink blotting paper, which, by the end of the night, was smudged with black. I had to ensure that a pristine sheet was in place for the morning. She folded the letter in half, popped it into a cream envelope lined with red tissue, addressed it, then placed it on top of an ever-growing stack. "I *have* to write thank-you letters. If people take the time and trouble to send a gift, the least I can do is thank them," she said.

Before she went out for dinner on any other day of the year, she prepared her thank-you letter. The envelope would be addressed and propped against a silver ink stand, and on her return she would write the letter, regardless of the hour, so that it could be sent the following morning.

AFTER SIX MONTHS away from the official world stage, the princess began to tread, gingerly, back into the spotlight. The Red Cross, through its director general Mike Whitlam, who became a firm ally, coaxed her into joining a special commission to advise the International Red Cross Federation. In May 1994, the role took her to Geneva. Her private secretary, Patrick Jephson, claimed that the princess's eyes were glazed with boredom, so she soon stepped down. The real reason for her departure was that she didn't want to be an executive in the boardroom but liked to be among the people, in a hands-on approach. She left because of frustration, not boredom, and, as time would prove, she maintained strong ties with the organization in future missions.

The princess returned to London and attended the unveiling of the Canadian War Memorial in Green Park, and then, on the eve of the fiftieth anniversary of D-day, she went to a church service in Portsmouth before joining other senior members of the family on the royal yacht *Britannia*. The princess was slipping back into the groove, but never forgot the causes she was passionate about: she attended the launch of the thirtieth appeal for the mental illness charity Turning Point, went to a concert to raise money for AIDS charities, supported the homeless charity Centrepoint, and then, later in the year, was at the Palace of Versailles outside Paris for a French Foundation for

Children dinner, drawing a standing ovation from almost a thousand guests.

She still walked beneath the halo of worldwide acclaim. Crowds cheered wherever she went. At dinners, galas, and state functions she dazzled everyone, from presidents to ordinary people. She demanded no special treatment, yet her presence, her magical aura, commanded respect and attention.

And yet all the support and encouragement did little to boost her confidence. At KP, she needed constant reassurance. Her inner strength remained, though, and she counted on it to build her confidence. She never needed it more than on June 29, 1994, when an eagerly anticipated television documentary about Prince Charles, made by broadcaster Jonathan Dimbleby with the cooperation of the prince, was screened ahead of a book. Entitled *The Prince of Wales,* it was a riposte, with the royal seal of approval, to the Andrew Morton book of 1992. It had been in the making with the prince's cooperation for eighteen months. So, as the princess had faced royal wrath for her cooperation with Morton, Prince Charles's office, with his say-so, had been making his friends available to speak on his behalf, dressed up as a twenty-fifth-anniversary celebration of his investiture as Prince of Wales.

Jonathan Dimbleby claimed later that the prince had not wanted anything to go in the book that would hurt the princess.

But the prince confessed on television to adultery with Camilla Parker Bowles. The princess had no idea that such an admission was coming. How on earth that could be construed as not hurtful to her was bewildering to all at KP.

As the documentary was trailed in the preceding days, the princess had worried about the program's content. She found refuge and advice in the company of Lucia Flecha de Lima, Lady Annabel Goldsmith, Susie Kassem, and the Duchess of York, who came to KP to support her. On the day of the evening screening, there came crucial support from another quarter: St. James's Palace. That afternoon, the Duchess of Kent—a shining example of warmth and grounded humanity—visited the princess, urging her to be strong.

"How am I to go out there and face everyone?" the princess said that afternoon. If only the misinformed cynics who painted her as a hard-nosed media manipulator could have heard her.

That evening, as Britain settled down in front of the television, she was committed to a long-standing engagement to attend a dinner at the Serpentine Gallery in Hyde Park. She was the gallery's patron, a friend of its chairman, Lord Palumbo, and guest of the then newly appointed chairman of the Arts Council of England, Lord Gowrie. She prepared for the engagement racked with nerves, half of her mind on the documentary, the other half on whether her chosen dress was suitable. Outside the gallery, television cameras focused on her arrival, desperate to capture her reaction to the Dimbleby documentary.

The princess was dressed and ready to go an hour before her intended departure, pacing up and down the first-floor landing. In the pantry downstairs, my ears monitored the creaks in the floorboards.

Then they stopped. "Paul, are you there?"

I bolted up the first flight and stood, looking up to the landing where the princess stood, hands on hips, wearing a midnight blue cocktail dress, nipped into the waist with a belt, white satin cuffs and a tight white collar that hugged her neck. "Well, do you like it?" she asked. My delayed response wasn't spontaneous or enthusiastic enough. "You don't, do you?" The hands dropped off her hips.

Despite the expert female dressers, a male opinion in the household often became her most reassuring sounding board. She wanted to gauge the wow-factor. At KP it was usual for her to appear halfway down the stairs, posing like a model in a new hat or suit. "What do you think?" Or draped in a new dress, with one leg in a pair of stockings and one leg out. "With or without?" Or one foot in a flat shoe, one in a pump. "Heels or not?"

Once, during a dress fitting with designer Jacques Aza-gury, the princess stood with him in the sitting room as his fitter, a woman named Salonge, was pinning the hem of a red dress with matching chiffon scarf. "Isn't it beautiful, Paul? Isn't Jacques clever?" she said, having called me in.

It was virtually impossible not to give a favorable reaction when the princess was dressed to impress. But I had warned her: "If you want an honest opinion, ask me. I'll give it. If you don't, don't ask me."

The evening of the Serpentine Gallery event was a time for unfavorable honesty. "Tonight of all nights I think you should look a million dollars, and that isn't the dress. Sorry."

"Well, I haven't got anything else to wear!" she protested.

I flew up the remaining two flights of stairs, and, with the princess, went into the wardrobe room. We slid back hanger after hanger of evening wear. "What about this one?" I asked, pointing out a sparkling black dress.

The princess screwed up her nose. "No. Too much of an old friend."

Then, in the black section, I found a short cocktail dress designed by Christina Stambolian. The princess liked it but doubted whether she would still get into it because she feared her constant workouts at the gym might have broadened her shoulders. "There's one way to find out." She left the room, holding the latest suggestion by its hanger.

She reappeared in off-the-shoulder black silk crêpe. And she looked spectacular.

"Now, *that* is the dress," I said.

"You don't think it's too much?" she said, jabbing a finger toward her cleavage.

"It's perfect," I said, and then we went to the safe near her bedroom. She pulled out a choker of pearls, which bore a large oval sapphire surrounded by two rows of diamonds, an engagement present from the Queen Mother.

As departure time neared, she was still pacing the landing. "Why do I feel so nervous?" she said, irritated with herself.

Reassurance was needed. "You look fantastic. You'll knock them all sideways," I said.

"Mmmm." It was incredible that she didn't think so.

The princess had long drilled into me the importance of how to arrive and how to depart: "Arrivals and departures—the most important time of any event." I reminded her of this just before she left. Then I added: "Remember, when you arrive, stride out, walk tall, firm handshake, and say to yourself, 'I am the Princess of Wales.' Don't forget that."

There was a characteristic sharp intake of breath. "Here goes then, Paul." I followed the chiffon fishtail down the staircase and along the hallway to the front door. As I shut the rear door of the chauffeur-driven car, she beamed. I waved as the car pulled away.

I watched the television bulletins later that night showing her arrival on that balmy summer's night: striding enthusiastically out of the car, bounding over to Lord Palumbo, shaking his hand, and smiling as if she didn't have a care in the world. It became one of the most famous images of the princess and was captured on all the front pages the next morning. "TAKE THAT!" said the *Daily Mirror.* And Charles? "NOT FIT TO REIGN," it cried.

The princess returned to the palace, already aware of what Prince Charles had said about being unfaithful. The smile was gone. She was quiet. No snack. No hot drink. She went straight to her bedroom and I turned off all the lights. Bar one.

NINE

THE BOSS

N O ONE COULD EVER pretend that duty within the walls of KP was easy. As in countless other relationships—in family, marriage, friendship, or business—happiness can sometimes wrestle with the reverse. Life with the Boss was a roller-coaster ride. Those with lesser stomachs would describe it as a white-knuckle experience. The highs were tremendous but the lows were desperate, and, for many, the ride went too fast, seemed out of control. But the princess *was* in control, and she decided, with the capricious ruthless streak that was part of her character, who rode with her and whom she left behind. The key to longevity with the princess was emotional stamina; you did not judge or question, just accepted the whole package, warts and all, as the complex, flawed but loving, wonderful human being that she was.

Unswerving support and loyalty carry no conditions, especially when they are expected. The going clearly got tough for those who felt sidelined, and they jumped ship far too readily, some before they were pushed. Others, with a consuming devotion, tried to hang on; their exits were terrible to witness. Some true friendships were terminated for good in a knee-jerk reaction based on misunderstanding or misinformation. There was always an inherent risk in growing too close to the princess: the heartbreak of knowing, loving, and then losing the intoxicating friendship of a phenomenon, either by choice or otherwise.

I know that heartbreak, because Maria experienced it between late 1994 and 1995. Maria had said she would try the post of dresser for a year, but the hours got longer, the demands greater, and she could not bear another year of hardly seeing Alexander and Nick. The boys were used to Dad working all hours, but not Mum. "It will get better. Don't give up," I implored her time and again, trying to avoid the inevitable. I knew that if she stepped down, the princess would view it as abandonment. In her life, she saw such rejection as if it were an enemy stalking her. She had felt rejected by her family, who had yearned for a boy, rejected in marriage by Prince Charles, rejected in the search for refuge by her brother, Earl Spencer. The saddest irony of all was that the princess could be equally harsh in handing out rejection. With Maria's experience, I found myself—not for the first time in a royal duty—caught in the middle of the crossfire between the two women I cared most about.

When my wife went to meet the princess at KP to announce her reluctant resignation because she wanted to spend more time with her family, I was the coward who fled and hid, unable through fear to act as peacekeeper. I placed my hands over my ears in the hope that the inevitable din would disperse by itself. Later that night, in December 1994, the conversation was relayed to me by a devastated Maria.

"What? After all I've done for you?" said a livid princess. "I've bent over backward to accommodate you and be flexible, and this is how you repay me."

Maria attempted to get a word in edgewise and explain that the agreement had been for a year and she had honored that, but her boys came first. "But she wiped the floor with me. She had me in tears," she told me that night.

The following day, the fallout was still evident from the black cloud that hung over the breakfast table.

"Good morning, Your Royal Highness," I said, armed with a pot of coffee.

On this occasion, there was no bright response. "Paul. Can you have a word with your wife?"

For once, I had hoped for a huge headline in the papers to divert the princess's attention, but there was nothing. Meekly, pathetically, I said Maria had made up her mind, tried to explain the family-based reasons, and reassured the princess that it had been a difficult decision for my wife, but that she had made it in the full knowledge that I would be giving 200 percent effort for both of us. The princess was unforgiving. For the remaining four weeks of Maria's notice period, the princess never said a word to her. It was known as a "no-speaking spell" among palace staff.

By 1995, others had fallen out of favor, and it was sad, as well as unfathomable, to see chef Mervyn Wycherley leave KP after a nine-month no-speaking spell. Another casualty later that year was my fellow butler Harold Brown, who leaped before he was pushed after enduring his own no-speaking spell. He landed comfortably in the service of Princess Margaret and, therefore, kept his living quarters in apartment No. 6. His departure left me as the sole butler, with an ever-shrinking staff and an ever-increasing trust with the Boss.

But even I was not immune to criticism and the princess's cold shoulder. The blackest period of my time with the Boss was when she began to tighten her financial belt at around the time of her divorce. The expense of running a household dawned on her, and I think she saw the KP telephone bill for the first time. She had a printout of the itemized bill and all staff were asked to write their names next to personal calls they had made. My fraction came to around £300. I wrote a check and thought that would be the end of the matter. But it wasn't.

My usage of the telephone had clearly rankled the Boss. As I presented the check, she wanted to know why I had been running up such a bill. I made the mistake of speaking my mind. "As I am working such long hours, I don't see the harm in me calling my family. I'm working almost sixteen-hour days, Your Royal Highness."

It was taken, wrongly, as a complaint. For the next two weeks, she stopped speaking to me. It was a deeply upsetting time. I felt cut off, deprived of her special friendship, and isolated. It became so bad that I had to resort to leaving Post-it note messages around the apartments. She, in turn, wrote her replies by memo.

The obvious silliness of the situation came to a head when an important message went astray, and she asked for an explanation: "Why couldn't you just tell me, Paul, instead of writing it down?"

"Your Royal Highness!" I said in exasperation. "How could I? You haven't been talking to me!"

She looked almost resigned to the point I had made, so I continued.

"I cannot do my job properly like this. Please, let me function properly."

The ice melted there and then. A huge wave of relief swept over me as I was brought back in from the cold. From then on I was careful about how often I used the KP telephone.

"IN FROM THE COLD," said the *Daily Mirror* headline to mark the defrosting in relations between KP and Buckingham Palace when the princess was invited to spend Christmas with the rest of the Royal Family at Sandringham in December 1994. The press believed, wrongly, that it was Her Majesty's private secretary and the princess's brother-in-law Sir Robert Fellowes who had extended the invitation. The truth was much warmer. In a handwritten letter, the Queen said that she and the Duke of Edinburgh would like the princess to stay with them on Christmas Eve with Princes Charles, William, and Harry.

I became used to witnessing important correspondence:

from the Queen, the Duke of Edinburgh, Prime Minister John Major, and numerous other people, including the princess's family. I was her permitted witness to many things, even her will and legal divorce papers, that she didn't want her private secretary, Patrick Jephson, to see. I wasn't the only friend to view the correspondence. She took advice on speeches and letter-writing from her journalist friend Richard Kay, but my "correspondence sessions" took place either on the stairs or in the sitting room, where the princess sat at her desk. Letters composed officially by Patrick Jephson would be sent for her perusal in a folder. She would shout my name from the top of the stairs and we would meet halfway and sit down. "What do you think about this?" she would say, or she would shriek, "Have a look at this!" Sometimes she would leave a letter on the desk in my pantry with an attached note, saying, "Let me know your comments."

It was on such an occasion that she showed me the letters from the Duke of Edinburgh and her brother, Earl Spencer. In time, she wrote private letters to me: thoughts she wanted to get down on paper, truths she wanted to record and leave in my trust, or philosophies about inner strength that she wanted to share.

My duty evolved until the princess would share her most sensitive letters and let me listen to her most private phone calls. In witnessing all her lines of communication, I know that, until her death, the Queen and the princess were in touch and on the best of terms. And, as an independent witness, I know the history, the traumas, and the nightmares she lived.

THE QUEEN'S CHRISTMAS invitation led the princess to take to Norfolk a present for every member of the Royal Family. In the weeks before the holiday, she had sent me to Kensington, Knightsbridge, and Mayfair to buy gifts for family, friends, and staff. Her generosity knew no bounds so, with her approval, I spent thousands of pounds. Relying on my knowledge and time with the

Queen, I chose for her practical gifts—a cashmere cardigan, a Hermès scarf, or a tartan rug; for the Duke of Edinburgh, a cartridge case, a shooting stick flask. I spent hours wrapping the presents, leaving the princess to write a personal note for each before she left for Sandringham. Privately, she loved the buildup to Christmas even if the actual day was, by her own admission, "a bit grim."

Had I failed to put up a tree two weeks before the big day, she would have been the first to complain. But each year, I ordered an eighteen-foot Norwegian spruce from the royal estate at Windsor, which was set up on the landing between the first and second flights of stairs. It was decorated with ten sets of white lights, adorned with crystal and glass ornaments with white cotton icicles dangling from each branch, and topped with a silver star. There was a smaller spruce for the nursery on the second floor. William and Harry were in charge of its decoration, using handmade ornaments crafted at school.

Christmas was also a magical time at our own home, and our tree, decorated in red, green, and gold, sat in the corner of the sitting room that looked out toward the palace. I dressed up as Father Christmas and delivered the boys' presents from behind a huge white beard and red-hooded tunic, complete with black Wellington boots. They didn't guess it was me until they spotted the same Wellington boots in the outside shed! Nick, then six, wanted to be the center of attention, doing cartwheels in the bedroom, shouting, "Look at me! Look at me!" Those few magical minutes gave Maria and me—and our annual Christmas visitor Betty, Maria's mother—so much pleasure.

But I knew that, come midafternoon on Christmas Day, the princess would be back at KP, alone, having left her boys at Sandringham. By the time she arrived, I was waiting at the door; the thought of her returning to an empty home on such a day seemed so sad. "You can't spend Christmas here by yourself. Come down and spend some time with us," I urged her.

"No, Paul. You don't want me spoiling your Christmas. It's a family time. I'll be fine here." She wanted to be alone.

...cess did what she always did every Christ-
...on. She sat at her desk, got out the fountain
...bottle of Quink, and started writing thank-you
...for the presents she had received. But first, before
I le..., she penned me a festive greeting. "To Paul: Wishing
you a very Happy Christmas. With love from Diana."
Then she addressed her first envelope and wrote her first
note: to Her Majesty The Queen, Sandringham House,
Norfolk.

I returned home almost reluctantly. "If you want anything, just call me," I said.

THE PRINCESS'S ADDRESS BOOK was packed with
names from all walks of life. Whenever she met anyone
for the first time, she could make them feel as if they had
been a friend for life. Articles began to appear in newspapers,
detailing her "charmed circle." If the princess was spotted socializing with someone or attending a therapy session, journalists concluded there was a deep, lasting, best-of-friends
association.

The Boss had many friends, but there was only a small
inner circle, headed by Lucia Flecha de Lima, who was best
friend, mother figure, and counselor rolled into one.
Lucia's husband, Paulo, had been transferred from London
to the Brazilian Embassy in Washington, but even the different time zones failed to send the friendship out of sync.
Lucia would set her alarm for three o'clock in the morning
so that she could talk to the princess at the start of her day.
If the princess needed advice or consolation, she rang
Lucia. I faxed a never-ending stream of letters and messages across the Atlantic to her. Being a friend to the
princess meant being a friend on twenty-four-hour call,
and Lucia accepted this. She was there every single time
for the princess.

"I couldn't cope without her. She's marvelous. She's like
a mother to me," the princess said, time and time again. In
August 1994, the princess went to Washington. In May
1995, Lucia came to London. At Christmas 1996, the

princess stayed with Lucia. Back and forth across the Atlantic, that friendship bridged its long-distance divide and became stronger as time went on.

In London, the princess's surrogate family came in the form of Rosa Monckton, Susie Kassem, Lady Annabel Goldsmith, Richard Kay, and Dr. Mary Loveday. These people, like myself, saw the princess at her most raw and knew *everything*. They understood her better than anyone else and loved her for the person she was.

The Duchess of York's presence was a guaranteed pick-me-up for the princess. Wide-eyed and bounding up the stairs, full of energy, she was a survivor, like the Boss, and there were constant phone calls of support between the two. They'd huddle in the sitting room, deep in serious conversation or laughing, comparing the knife wounds left in their backs by the Royal Household. I built up a vicarious trust with the duchess through the princess, and a friendship developed. Even when she knew the Boss was out, the phone would ring in the pantry and the familiar, Sloaney voice would cheerily say: "Hi, Paul, it's the duchess."

She could be as confused about people's motives as the princess. "Why do people say such hurtful things about me all the time? I don't know what's expected of me," she would say.

Like the princess, she believed in karma. "What goes around, comes around," they both said.

I listened to her like I listened to the princess, and felt terribly sorry for her. "Look," I said, "remember what the Boss says—kill people with kindness and never let them know they're getting you down."

I recall those conversations, over the phone or at KP, fondly every time I look at a framed picture the duchess sent me at the end of 1994, showing her with her little daughters, Beatrice and Eugenie. At the bottom, she wrote me a special message: "Dear Paul and Maria. Thank you so much for your incredible kindness and support. Words are not enough but thank you. With bestest [*sic*] wishes— Sarah."

Outside the trusted circle of the princess's closest friends, she knew exactly what to tell and what not to tell. Everyone brought a specialism or an experience to the table, which meant she counted on their advice or wisdom. The princess compartmentalized her friendships and preferred to meet individuals one-to-one. Each friendship was like an assortment of boxes, and I knew which box she was opening, why she was opening it, and where it was ranked in her life. Being at the center of her world meant becoming a trusted messenger. When the princess was away, she gave me permission to look through her address book, find a name, ring a number.

With Harold Brown gone and the princess wondering who around her she could trust, my role as butler began to evolve in 1995 into personal assistant, messenger, driver, delivery boy, confidant. I stepped in at times when she chose not to use her chauffeur, PR guru, or private secretary because she didn't want professional eyes witnessing certain friendships, messages, or private missions.

"Paul, stand by the fax machine now and don't leave it until it's all come through." The voice of the princess traveled down from the first floor and reached me in the pantry.

Nineteen ninety-five was the year when the princess trusted me to handle her correspondence, from the professional to the most personal and secret. She started to shield information from Patrick Jephson's eyes and divert faxes from his office at St. James's Palace. She had heard a rumor that he was growing dissatisfied and seeking employment elsewhere. She confronted him with it and his response didn't convince her of the longevity of his service at KP. She became wary and put a distance between them that was never bridged again. "How does he expect me to communicate with him on highly delicate and detailed discussions regarding my marriage and my future when I don't even know whether he will be here in the future?" she said.

A new fax machine for the princess's personal use was installed in her sitting room, placed on the carpet under her desk, hidden by the sofa positioned directly in front. There were numerous occasions when I walked into the sitting room to see her and found no one there.

"Your Royal Highness?" I called, turning to go into the drawing room.

"I'm down here," said a voice from out of nowhere. The princess was on her hands and knees under the desk, trying but failing to operate the fax machine. Technology, like cooking, was not one of her strong points.

"It's hopeless. I'm hopeless!" She would laugh with self-mocking humor.

After a few more weeks of facsimile frustration, the machine under the desk was abandoned. Instead, she started to utilize my machine downstairs, underneath my desk in the pantry. She handed me sensitive documents to send and would wait for the replies to come through.

On one occasion, she trusted neither the fax nor the post. "Paul, I would like you to deliver this by hand," she said, handing me a letter. I looked at the sealed envelope. The name was familiar, and so was the address—overseas.

My eyes conveyed my surprise. "I know it's a long way, but it *is* important," she said.

"Consider it done," I told her. The next time she was away, I boarded another plane to a different destination and dropped the letter into the hand that would pen the reply. By the time the princess returned to KP, I was back on duty to welcome her home.

"Mission accomplished," I said.

IN JANUARY 1995, the chattering classes were still ruminating over Prince Charles and his relationship with Camilla Parker Bowles, with whom he had confessed to having an affair. Speculation intensified when, eleven days into the new year, her divorce from Brigadier Andrew Parker Bowles was announced. It followed a two-year separation. But the princess's attention and serious concern had been diverted elsewhere—to the relationship between her husband and his assistant Tiggy Legge-Bourke. Even the press was training its sights in her direction, further arousing the suspicions of the princess.

"THE KISS" was the front-page headline in the *Daily Mirror,* showing Prince Charles skiing with friends, which included Tiggy Legge-Bourke. In a series of photographs, the prince put his arm around her and kissed her "in a show of affection." His private secretary Richard Aylard explained to reporters: "It's not unreasonable for him to kiss her on the cheek; it is perfectly ordinary."

The princess didn't agree and she felt the relationship was crossing the line far too soon after the assistant's recruitment. In fact, so suspicious was she that she regarded Camilla Parker Bowles as yesterday's news. She felt Tiggy Legge-Bourke was getting too close, as well, to William and Harry. As far as the princess was concerned, she was still married, and two other women were circling dangerously around her territory.

DON'T ASK ME WHY I did it, but as everyone sent me cards and presents for my thirty-seventh birthday on June 6, 1995, I decided to send a gift to Mum in Grassmoor. I wanted her to receive a little something to mark the anniversary of my birth. Via a garden center in Derbyshire, I arranged for the delivery of a stone trough filled with flowering plants. A simple message dictated over the phone was written on a card and placed among the greenery.

Dad later told me that when she opened the door, she said to the delivery man, "I think you've got the wrong house, duck. It's not my birthday."

Then she started to read my message and was overwhelmed. When I heard her tearful joy over the telephone at KP that afternoon, I vowed to do the same every year.

Two weeks later, she was still raving about her blossoming trough in the garden. She and Dad had come to the Old Barracks for the night, before I drove them to Heathrow Airport and waved them off on a dream holiday to America and Canada.

When the telephone rang at two o'clock in the morning

on June 15, my subconscious state told me it would be the princess, who was away on an engagement in Russia. She was the only person who ever phoned at such an unearthly hour. A crisis, personal or otherwise, must have happened. Maria got up to answer the telephone. Moments later, she was sobbing. "How am I going to tell him? How am I going to tell him?"

The princess! What's happened? I shot out of bed and bolted across the landing into the sitting room, where Maria was still on the telephone.

It was my brother Graham. Mum had collapsed in the street in Ottawa, Canada, and died instantly from a massive heart attack. She was fifty-nine.

The next morning, the princess rang to check on life at KP, where she was due to return two days later on the Saturday to be with William and Harry. As soon as I heard her voice, I broke down. "What on earth's the matter, Paul?" she asked.

In my devastation, I explained how Mum's heart had given way, how she had seemed so healthy before she left. Then I told her how lost Dad was, stuck in Canada, struggling to organize the release of Mum's body to return home.

"Leave it to me, Paul. We'll get on it straightaway."

One call from the Princess of Wales's office to the British High Commission in Canada sorted out all the technicalities that surround a sudden death in a foreign country. In the middle of a hectic schedule in Russia, the princess took charge of events in Canada to help. She even took the trouble to ring and speak to Dad in his hotel room in Ottawa. She spent around thirty minutes comforting him, reassuring him that someone from the High Commission would be with him at all times, the release of the body was being organized, and his flight back to Britain was paid for.

"On your return, I would like you to come to London with your sons. I would like to see you," she told Dad.

As soon as the princess arrived back at the palace that Saturday, I was with her in the sitting room. I sat on the sofa, cried and apologized, and she sat down with a comforting arm round me. I had known how good, how strong, how compassionate she had been with others, and there I was, embraced by that caring nature that had touched so many strangers over so many years.

She spoke about fate, the meaning of life, the meaning of death, her spiritual beliefs, the final moments she had shared in that hospital room with her friend Adrian Ward-Jackson, experiencing "the journey of his soul." "Paul, the spirit stays around after death. Your mum is still with us. Believe in that. You're strong. You need to be strong," she said.

The next day was Father's Day. Dad and my brothers Graham and Anthony drove to the palace for that desperate weekend. Mum's body was still in Canada, due to return the next day. We ran into the princess at the police barrier on the drive. She was wearing a sweatshirt, purple cycling shorts, and trainers, and she had left William and Harry in the nursery. She embraced Dad and my brothers one by one. Then, linking her right arm with Dad's left, she said, "Let's go for a walk."

On that warm afternoon, Dad and the princess walked in front, we three brothers walking close behind. We went into Kensington Palace Gardens, walking and talking, all five of us, for forty-five minutes. Without a baseball cap, the princess was instantly recognizable. When a passer-by tried to take a photograph, she extended her arm politely and asked, "Please don't."

Despite his grief, Dad was concerned about the princess being exposed in a park. "You don't have to do this for us. You're being noticed. We should go back to the palace," he said to her.

"Graham, I think I'll be okay with your three strapping sons around me." I think that was the only time Dad smiled all weekend.

We walked back with the princess to the orangery beside the state apartments. "If there is anything I can do, Graham, just tell Paul." She embraced my family one last time, then disappeared through a door set in the brick wall.

Later that evening, Dad wanted to be alone, and he went outside to sit on the bench on the green that stretched out in front of the Old Barracks. I looked down from the first-floor sitting-room window and there he was, with his back toward us. And the princess was beside him again. She had been returning home in her car when she spotted him from the drive. She had pulled over and walked across the green to join him. I looked down, thinking how odd it was to be watching my dad with her. I watched his head moving as he talked, wiping his eyes with his handkerchief. Then he broke down, weeping on the princess's shoulder.

Mum came home on the Monday. We buried her that same week. On the eve of the funeral, her coffin rested on the altar at Hasland Church, where she was christened and married, and where Grandma and Grandad Kirk were buried. We filled the church with white flowers of every description. We lit candles in her memory. Each one of us then had a private moment. I stood and placed my hand on the polished wooden lid, bowed my head, and closed my eyes, remembering what the princess had said: "Your mum is still with us."

At the funeral, we couldn't see the coffin because it was covered with a wild garden of flowers. As the other relatives and friends drifted away after the service, I stood by the graveside with Graham. That was when he told me about Mum's secret: her decision to burn Cunard's job offer. He had kept his secret nineteen years, and only now told me of the day she'd received two letters, and burned the one that wasn't from Buckingham Palace. I was stunned.

We went back to No. 47 Chapel Road. Mum's handbag and knitting were on a chair in the back near the fire.

As Dad flicked on the kettle and my brothers, sisters-in-law, nieces, and nephews milled around the house, I sat down and opened her handbag. Inside, there was a powder compact with a royal yacht *Britannia* crest on the lid, a present from my days with the Queen, and a lipstick. The only other item was her battered red purse, which, typically, contained not one penny. But there was a folded card.

It was the message I had sent in the stone trough on my birthday: "Mum, just a little something for suffering so much pain to bring me into the world on this day 37 years ago. With all my love, from your eldest—Paul X."

FAMILY WAS IMPORTANT to the princess, but it was unfortunate that hers was not as close-knit as her inner circle of friends. Her sister, Lady Sarah McCorquodale, was a regular visitor from Lincolnshire—out of all the Spencers, she was the closest. Her mother, Frances Shand Kydd, was a virtual recluse on the Scottish island of Seil but visited when she could. In fact, the princess saw more of her stepmother, Raine Spencer, than she did of her own mother and lunched with her at least once a month, sometimes at Cecconi's, just off Bond Street, because that had been her late father's favorite restaurant.

But while there was a constant stream of visitors to KP, it did nothing to fill the silence in the late afternoons and early evenings when the princess might find herself alone. With William and Harry away at school or at Highgrove, the void had to be filled.

"I hate the silence in this home," she said, as she sat reading *Vogue* or *Harpers & Queen* on a Saturday morning. Music filled some of the space, but she missed the physical presence of what she called "the small people." "Paul, ring your boys and ask them to come up," she said.

The sound of feet running around the apartment, the childish screams, the videos playing on the television, Harry's video games being hijacked— all helped take away the loneliness. Alexander and Nick got the free run of a palace without knowing that, just by being there, they made the princess feel happier. "Do you want something to eat?" the princess would ask them, leaning against the doorway of her boys' sitting room, and she would go to Darren McGrady in the kitchen and ask him to feed two hungry boys their usual—burgers and chips.

Alexander and Nick loved going to KP. They ran up the front drive, racing each other to the back door of apartment No. 8 and into my pantry before bolting up the stairs to where the Boss would be waiting, more often than not on the telephone to a friend.

"Hi, Princess."

"Hi, Princess."

The double yell of my two boys would echo back down to me in the pantry.

With each visit, they returned home full of excitement to the Old Barracks, where Maria was still frozen out by the princess. These visits thrilled the boys but hurt Maria. "She's got you up there, and now she's got my boys," she cried one night.

It didn't help one Sunday morning when Nick, with a child's innocence, asked Maria: "Why don't you work for the princess anymore, Mummy? Why don't you like her?"

"Paul, whatever she has been saying, it's got to stop. Why did Nick ask me that?" demanded Maria. It was as if I was caught between an ex-wife and a new girlfriend. Later that summer, though, Alexander and Nick effectively brought the old friends back together. Somewhere along the mad dash between KP and the Old Barracks, our sons became keepers of a royal peace.

Nick was sitting with the princess, and she asked after his mummy. "She wants to be here, too, Princess," he said.

That night, I was at home after being released early from duty, and the phone rang. Maria answered; it was the princess. In a marked change from previous calls that year, she didn't immediately ask for me. She started chatting, and the two were soon talking as if nothing had happened. Maria had been brought back in from the cold. She was one of the lucky ones.

BRIDGES NEEDED TO BE strengthened between KP and Fleet Street, so the princess—who was intent on avenging her husband's public admission of adultery—went on a charm offensive to woo the media. She invited newspaper editors and columnists to private lunches at the palace. She felt it was a good opportunity for her to be seen in her natural environment, and would give journalists a chance to understand her a little better. She, in turn, would attempt to discover what made them tick, what they knew, and why certain angles had been adopted in certain articles. It was a mutual fact-finding mission.

"If BP [Buckingham Palace] finds out, the press office will go into its usual blind-panic mode!" She laughed.

The great, the good, and the not so good of Fleet Street wiped their feet at the front door of No. 8 and, no matter how brave they had been with their newsprint columns within the safe confines of their empires, it was fascinating to watch them walk with clear trepidation into the disarming territory of the Boss. For so long, she had been only a captivating image that, day after day, had helped them sell their headlines from the newsstands. Now it was her turn to confront them in the drawing room and over lunch. She was in brilliant form. How she and I laughed as we dissected each guest after they had left.

"How funny to see that I can make such powerful people so nervous," said an amused princess, then added, "How enjoyable!"

One by one, journalism's luminaries arrived on different days: Charles Moore, editor of the *Daily Telegraph;* Paul Dacre, editor of the *Daily Mail;* Piers Morgan, editor of the *Daily Mirror;* Stuart Higgins, editor of the *Sun;* Lynda Lee-Potter, columnist on the *Daily Mail;* and even the BBC's royal correspondent, Jennie Bond. The Boss, who was dressed to kill on each occasion, asked me to linger in the doorway of the dining room. We had secret signals, which had been well rehearsed—and well used over the years with any dinner guest. One furtive look of those blue eyes beneath a raised eyebrow was her way of telling me to serve the three courses more quickly. One unfortunate lunch guest, a famous TV personality as well as newspaper columnist on non-royal issues, was served the fastest lunch on record. He was received, fed, watered, and dispatched in forty minutes, never to be seen again.

"I almost slipped into a coma through boredom, Paul. He was *so* boring!" She was disappointed because her illusions had been shattered.

Editors and columnists enjoyed the off-the-record opportunity to chat with her and ask questions. The princess was the perfect diplomat. When Stuart Higgins of the *Sun* asked about her thoughts on Camilla Parker Bowles, she responded, "Well, I actually feel quite sorry for her." He had been expecting scorn and bitterness to pour forth and nearly fell off his bamboo chair. Then the Boss added, "The woman has lost almost everything in life and gained what, exactly?"

When Piers Morgan of the *Daily Mirror* pitched in with his forthright "Do you think Charles will become King?" she answered: "Well, he thinks that, but I think he would be happier living in Provence or Tuscany."

The lunch and good-natured banter with the *Daily Mirror* editor was joined by William. He sat beside his mother, listening intently, and his age belied the maturity he showed.

Piers Morgan turned to him and asked him: "What do you think of the press?"

William looked up to his mother, who gave him a nod for him to answer. "They are okay. I have begun to recognize them and know where they will be, so that means I can avoid them. It's not the British press that are annoying; it is the photographers from Europe. They sit on the riverbank at Eton, watching me rowing, waiting for me to fall in!"

The BBC's Jennie Bond was the only journalist lunch guest who benefited from the princess's generosity. In what was probably the most relaxed conversation of them all, the off-the-record chat turned into women's talk as the well-groomed royal correspondent took advice from the world's best-dressed woman. Jennie had commented on the stunning sheen of the princess's hosiery, and, later that evening, I had to gift-wrap six new pairs of stockings and forward them with a note. During that lunch, the princess also advised Jennie on the best colors to wear for television.

On another occasion, the princess's private courting of the media backfired and handed her sternest critics a golden opportunity to whip up an anti-Diana storm. She had been photographed in a car, secretly meeting *Daily Mail* reporter Richard Kay down a side street. The hysteria that followed represented rank hypocrisy. The princess, for so long in her life, had been undermined by officials from the Royal Household or Prince Charles's catty friends. All she was doing was taking charge of her own PR machine, ensuring she was understood, not misunderstood, and she chose to channel truth through a trusted ally. She was doing no more than Prime Minister Tony Blair's team of spin doctors, or Prince Charles's onetime aide Mark Bolland, who, by courting the media after the princess had died, led a PR strategy to "sell" Camilla Parker Bowles to the public. What clearly rankled with the press offices at Buckingham Palace and St. James's Palace was that the princess was one step ahead—and winning the game.

A S THE CAR CROSSED the Shepherd's Bush round-about and headed onto Bayswater Road to the north of KP, the male passenger with the furtive eyes dived rather dramatically to his right on the back seat and lay on his side, pulling the green tartan rug over him. I rolled my eyes as I concentrated on the road ahead. It wasn't the first time I had had to sneak a secret visitor past the police, but this passenger seemed to enjoy the cloak-and-dagger operation more than most.

I flicked the turn signal and turned right, passing the foreign embassies on the "Millionaires' Row" running parallel to the palace. To anyone looking on, I was alone in the car, heading as normal to my workplace.

"Where are we now? Have we gone past the police post yet?" asked a muffled voice from under the rug.

"No. Stay under. I'll tell you when," I said impatiently, sticking to the strict instructions from the princess to "keep him hidden on entry."

As the car slowed up at the security barrier, the uniformed guard recognized me and waved me on.

"I can't believe they never stopped you," the muffled voice said again.

I drove under the arch of the clock tower at the side of

the palace into Clock Court and parked adjacent to the secret doorway into apartment No. 9.

"I can't believe how easy that was!" exclaimed the passenger, casting aside the rug and stepping out. Martin Bashir patted out the creases of his jacket and shirt, picked up his briefcase, and followed me through the door, up the stairs, past the princess's bedroom, down the corridor, and into the boys' sitting room, where she was waiting for him. It was midsummer 1995, and the wheels were being put in motion for the filming and broadcast of a royal *Panorama* interview for BBC1.

I have to be honest, I had no idea then that the *Panorama* project was being planned. It seemed that only Bashir and the Boss shared this secret. But getting the television journalist in and out of KP became a well-rehearsed routine, no questions asked, only small talk exchanged. It was a mission carried out in either my blue Vauxhall Astra or the princess's dark-blue BMW. "The beauty of a BMW is that it melts into the crowd in London," she always said. The instructions were easy to follow. Park outside the white office building that sits alongside BBC Television Centre, wait in the car park, and Martin Bashir would emerge and get into the left rear seat. When approaching KP, "keep him hidden." I had become expert at keeping visitors a lot more sensitive than Bashir hidden, visitors who made much less fuss than he did. But in delivering him unnoticed to the princess, my job was done, and I returned to the pantry until I was needed for the return leg.

"Paul, are you there?" shouted the princess.

"Yes. Is he ready to leave?"

"Mr. Bashir, your chauffeur awaits," said the princess.

On those visits, there was never a hint that a project was being covertly planned; it was one secret the princess was not going to share with me. Not until it was "in the can." Bashir was a clever man and, in time, he learned the insecurities of the princess and no doubt convinced her of the wisdom of doing such a frank television interview. The princess listened to the charming, smooth-talking operator, who somehow convinced her that what became a PR disaster would be a good thing. Instinctively, the princess *wanted* to trust him. He played the pity card and talked to the princess that summer about how life "hadn't been great" for him recently, his marriage and the pressures of living in a terraced house in the Wimbledon area of London. As she told me afterward: "He's not had an easy life. I enjoyed talking to him." I think she even convinced herself that he was a friend.

What she didn't know was that Bashir phoned me regularly, on the hunt for inside information. What he didn't know was that once, when he rang, the princess was standing next to me in the pantry, some time after the interview had been broadcast.

As I went through the routine of batting away his small talk, she mouthed to me: "Who is it?"

Covering the receiver mouthpiece, I mimed back: "Martin Bashir."

"Put it on the speaker." She pointed at the button on the telephone. I pressed it, and, within seconds, the irreverent voice of the journalist echoed around the pantry. After that conversation, the princess saw her "friend" in a different light.

With the *Panorama* program, Bashir had tapped into the princess's vengeful streak at the time she wanted to get even with Prince Charles over his adultery confession in the Dimbleby documentary. Filming took place on a Sunday when she could be assured of being alone. No dresser, no chef, and it was my day off. The princess had to cope with salads in the fridge and notify the police of visitors she expected. The camera crew, under the direction of Martin Bashir, set up its equipment in the boys' sitting room. The next morning, when I asked why the furniture had been moved, the princess said it hadn't been.

Then, a week before broadcast, the princess told me she had filmed *Panorama;* it was all top-secret stuff, and she felt Britain would understand her better at the end of it. "I'm sure many people will support you. As long as you are happy with the end product," I told her.

On the night of Monday, November 20, I sat at the Old Barracks and joined more than twenty million viewers in watching the princess speak about how she wanted to be "the queen of people's hearts," how Prince Charles would not suit the "top job" of being king, how there had been "three people in our marriage," how she had adored James Hewitt, and how she would not go quietly. The interview told me nothing new, but my concern for her image was great. I watched *Newsnight* on BBC2 and saw Nicholas Soames, the politician friend of Prince Charles, tear into the Boss with the kind of hypocrisy that both she and I had come to expect and loathe. When Prince Charles needed defending, Nicholas Soames would be wheeled out to make an articulate argument with his anti-Diana ramblings.

The next day, the princess was in high spirits, buoyed by the adrenaline rush of her latest surprise move and also by the positive reaction and sympathy she had received in the morning newspapers. She had taken a huge PR risk, and her reputation among the British public as a royal survivor was intact. But in her headstrong decision to cooperate with Bashir, she had never considered, perhaps naïvely, the implications that *Panorama* would have on her marriage. Divorce would be rushing to her door.

But, momentarily, she was on the crest of a media wave. There was almost an air of invincibility about her. She felt she could take on all comers, and next in line was Tiggy Legge-Bourke.

IT WAS DECEMBER 14, 1995, and the staff Christmas lunch, combining the offices of both the Prince and the Princess of Wales, was being held at the Lanesborough Hotel on Hyde Park Corner. It was the day when the Boss was going to come face to face with Tiggy Legge-Bourke.

"Come with me in my car," the princess said. We drove the short distance together, past the Knightsbridge Barracks, through Hyde Park and the stone arch, pressing the button inside the car that remotely activated the barrier in the archway. "I love this little shortcut." She beamed. By the time we arrived, we were late, and the hundred or so guests were already enjoying the prelunch reception.

As we entered the room, heads turned to the princess. "Keep standing by me and just watch," she said, through her smile. Those elegant legs strode purposefully as she cut a swath through the crowd. She was making a beeline for Tiggy Legge-Bourke, who was chatting at the far end of the room. I was walking in her wake.

"Hello, Tiggy. How are you?" said the princess, smiling. Before she could answer, the princess adopted an air of mock sympathy *"So sorry* to hear about the baby."

Horror paralyzed Tiggy's face. Tears welled in her eyes, and she left the room, accompanied by Prince Charles's valet Michael Fawcett. I turned to find the princess. She was mingling with the rest of the crowd, having fired her message across the bows of her husband's camp.

"Did you see the look on her face, Paul? She almost fainted!" said the princess afterward.

The thunderbolt delivered at the Lanesborough had sent tremors across Hyde Park and into both St. James's Palace and Buckingham Palace. Prince Charles was livid. Word even reached the Queen, and she was aghast. The fallout of the princess's barbed greeting sent aftershocks through the system for the following week, as Tiggy Legge-Bourke instructed lawyers to deny the allegation, and the statement said "that a series of malicious lies are circulating . . . which are a gross reflection on our client's moral character. These allegations are ultimately without the slightest foundation."

The actions of the princess had the desired effect, precipitating the most discreet behind-the-scenes investigations, led by the Queen's private secretary. Sir Robert Fellowes personally telephoned the princess—also his sister-in-law—four days after the confrontation to get to the bottom of whatever it was she had been alluding to during the conversation with Tiggy Legge-Bourke. She had put the cat among the pigeons and, during that phone call, she reported her allegations to Her Majesty's right-hand man: that Tiggy had been having an affair with Prince

Charles, and she had undergone an abortion. She even furnished the Queen's office with a precise date.

"There, now it's all official. Robert has promised to investigate," she told me after the phone call.

Back at Buckingham Palace, Sir Robert Fellowes was the perfect man to handle such a sensitive issue. After putting down the telephone, he set out to ascertain the truth. He discovered that Tiggy Legge-Bourke—who was "carefully questioned"—had been to see her private gynecologist twice, once in the summer, once in the autumn of 1995, for what was described as "women's problems." She had been to the hospital on two separate occasions in the autumn of that year. But Sir Robert Fellowes concluded that the allegation made by the princess was false. His dismissal of her claim was delivered by a uniformed orderly who rang the bell and handed me the official letter.

The princess opened it with her silver paper knife and shook her head disapprovingly as she read the words. "Typical!" she said. "Paul, look at this."

He had written: "Your allegations concerning Tiggy Legge-Bourke are completely unfounded. Her relationship with The Prince of Wales has never been anything but a professional one. On the date of the supposed abortion, she was at Highgrove with William and Harry. It is in your own best interests that you withdraw these allegations. You have got this whole thing dreadfully wrong."

The thorough inquiry was emphatic that there was no truth whatsoever in these allegations. Indeed, Robert Fellowes attached his own personal note to his sister-in-law, emphasizing how wrong she was: "This letter is sent from one who really believes that you have got this whole thing dreadfully wrong, and that you *must* realize it—please. Love Robert." With hindsight and with any objective assessment of the facts, the princess simply could never have been right.

By THE END OF 1995, the princess's own private secretary was also drafting a letter; Patrick Jephson had decided to quit KP. Another member of staff who leaped before he was pushed. All lines of effective communication had been cut between him and the princess. It was sad to witness the demise of that relationship because not only had he been expert at his job, he had been close to the princess. I was once dispatched to Asprey & Garrard, the Crown jewelers, to choose a pair of gold cuff links for him, bearing his initials. But by 1995 he felt snubbed by every private decision she had taken, and was blind to the correspondence she had diverted through my fax machine. There is no future for an unhearing, unseeing employee in a royal household. The *Panorama* interview and the Tiggy Legge-Bourke incident had been the final straws. His curt resignation letter, which dropped into KP the following month, summed up his bitterness: he told the princess that she had denied him all normal means of communication with her, leaving him to feel unwanted.

"The rats always jump ship, Paul," she mused. "Looks like you'll have to be butler, lady-in-waiting, and private secretary rolled into one. You're at the helm now!"

The herculean task of managing the princess's PR was, thankfully, not my responsibility. That burden fell to a new recruit, Jane Atkinson. She was charged with handling the continued fallout from the Tiggy Legge-Bourke incident. Prince Charles's assistant demanded an apology, but the princess refused to back down. By then, the princess's mind was elsewhere. She had received her own bombshell, hand-delivered again by a uniformed orderly. The Queen and Prince Charles had fired a double salvo into KP just before Christmas. A divorce was demanded by both the sovereign and the heir to the throne.

"DIVORCE" was a word, not a prospect, to the princess. It was something she had often used to threaten Prince Charles during the latter years of their marriage. She had screamed it to get his attention, to wound, like a child in a tantrum threatening to run away, knowing she didn't really mean it. In getting to know and understand the princess, I talked with her about how misunderstood she felt, how much pain she had endured, how she felt her "personal torture"—because that was what she called it—had helped her grow into a stronger person. But one thing that shone through each heartfelt conversation was the love that lingered for Prince Charles, no matter how much hurt she felt he had caused. She had found freedom and relief in the separation, but she was adamant about one thing: "Divorce is a nonstarter."

Then, on December 18, 1995, a week before the princess was due at Sandringham House with William and Harry for Christmas, she received a lengthy letter that made the first official mention of a divorce. It did not come from Prince Charles, but from the Queen. It was a crushing blow; the first time the princess had ever heard the word "divorce" on Windsor lips.

The Queen had seen one book from the princess, another from the prince; one television confession from her son, another from her daughter-in-law. The disintegration of the marriage between the Prince and Princess of Wales was being played out in public. As head of state, she felt she had to take control. I had taken this letter to the princess in her sitting room, and returned to the pantry. Minutes later, a familiar cry traveled down the staircase: "Paul, come here."

She was on the sofa, and looked on the verge of tears. With an air of resignation, she rolled her eyes, beckoning to the desk behind her. "Look what's arrived," she said.

On the desk, left exactly where it had been read earlier, was a letter with the red crest of Windsor Castle. I recognized the distinctive handwriting of the Queen. It began, as always, "Dearest Diana," and ended, "With love from Mama." This letter, though, was different from any other I had read, and, as the Queen's former footman, I felt uncomfortable as I read it.

I was talking to the back of the princess's head as she remained on the sofa, but I needed to express my discomfort. "I'm not sure I should be reading this; it says 'in the strictest of confidence.' "

"Oh, Paul, just read it. What am I going to do? What

will everyone think?" She sighed. She jumped up, agitated, and began pacing. "The Prime Minister and the Archbishop of Canterbury! My divorce has been discussed with John Major and George Carey before it has been discussed with me." The princess was infuriated that the Queen had consulted the government and the Church first. The constitutional issues did not concern her. "This is my marriage and it is no one else's business!" she yelled. Recalling another part of the letter, she said: "In the country's interests, is it? What about the interests of me? What about the interests of my boys?"

She felt that her divorce, just like her marriage, was being handled as if it were a business. The tone of the Queen's letter was sympathetic, delicate, and devoid of anger, but it did smack of a mother-in-law frustrated with the behavior of both parties, emphasizing that a divorce could not inflict further damage on the two sons who had suffered enough over the previous years.

The princess was having none of it. She immediately telephoned the Queen at Buckingham Palace. In a polite conversation, the princess questioned the haste for such a monumental decision. The Queen calmed her and tried to reassure her that she would not be rushed into any decision.

The Boss was not reassured. She sat down at her desk and dipped her fountain pen into her bottle of Quink. She penned an instant reply to the Queen, telling her that she needed time. But there would be little time to reflect. The next day a second bombshell landed on the doormat: a letter from Prince Charles requesting a divorce.

Again, I was invited to read the letter. Prince Charles said the marriage was beyond repair and that that represented both "a national and personal tragedy." Divorce was inevitable, and it needed to be done quickly, he wrote. The princess suspected that the letters were a two-pronged assault from Buckingham and St. James's Palaces, intended to make her buckle.

She placed both letters on the desk, the red of Windsor and the blue of Highgrove side by side. "What do you see?" she asked. The obvious didn't strike me. "Look."

One finger underlined a sentence used in the Queen's letter. Then the same finger pointed to a sentence in the prince's letter. Both were the same, word for word, referring to the "sad and complicated situation" of the royal marriage. "Those letters have been drafted and advised by the same people," she said, with the excitement of someone who had just made a vital discovery. "They must think I'm stupid."

She sat down and fired off a response to her husband, unable to write fast enough to keep up with her anger. Her response was unequivocal: "Your request has utterly perplexed me. I do not consent to an immediate divorce!"

THAT WEEK, events and emotions reached a boiling point, with the Tiggy Legge-Bourke allegations coming to nothing, and the letters from the Queen and Prince Charles. Ahead of her, there was another difficult festive period, made even more awkward by the divorce requests. Prince Charles had clearly reached the end of his tether, and I doubt I had ever seen the princess so heartbroken.

Communication between the prince and princess was at its weakest. The princess requested one-to-one meetings, but the prince wanted someone to sit in and take notes. She refused, and 1995 ended in stalemate. The prince wanted a divorce. The princess wanted to remain married.

At this time, I became a crutch that the princess leaned on. She was despondent and felt her world was about to be turned upside down, her role taken away from her. The divorce letters left her in pieces. She curled up on the sofa, put her head in her hands, and sobbed. As butler, what was I supposed to do? Stand there?

In William's absence—he was a great source of comfort to his mother when she was distressed—I made sure the supply of Kleenex was plentiful. I made sure I was there to listen. I made sure she was not moping in her loneliness. I didn't see the Princess of Wales crying: I saw a vulnerable, hurt woman crying and in need of comfort. The Queen would never have displayed such emotion before me, and no footman would ever have had the temerity to place an arm round her. But I had a much warmer, closer relationship with the princess, who was a tactile person. When she was hurt, she was like a little girl, and the sight of her compelled me to do something other than stand awkwardly by. I sat beside her, put an arm round her, and tried to tell her that everything would be all right; that she was strong, a survivor, that the British public was behind her. I listened for many hours, and, as we did when we watched *Brief Encounter,* we ended up laughing over the silliness of the situation.

As I got closer, I would remain with her until I knew that she was going to be okay by herself. But even when I left to return home, I worried endlessly. On some occasions, she would wake at 2 or 3 A.M., and feel the need to talk. I would listen, and be back at work for breakfast.

That Christmas, the princess penned me a letter, dated December 27, 1995, which I treasure to this day. When the misinformed, the embittered, and the ignorant attempted, during my Old Bailey trial in 2002, to suggest that I was nothing more than a butler to the princess, that my closeness was a figment of my imagination, I read this note over and over again. At the toughest time of my life, the princess's own words comforted me:

A letter that is long overdue to thank you profoundly for everything that you've done for me and, in particular, since August. Your presence through the tears and frustration has proved invaluable, and I did want you to know how enormously I appreciate your support. 1996 will be a happy one and I look forward to it . . . thank you. With love from Diana.

TEN

HANDLING THE DIVORCE

ACING THE QUEEN in a one-to-one meeting at Buckingham Palace, the princess knew she would never have a better opportunity to ask the one question that had constantly chipped away inside her mind since Prince Charles had publicly confessed to an affair with Camilla Parker Bowles. "Does this mean that Charles is going to remarry?" asked the princess.

"I think that very unlikely," replied the Queen.

If the Boss had gone into that meeting looking to emerge with concessions, that one reassurance from the highest level made her feel more secure.

It was midmorning on February 15, 1996, and the princess had come to Her Majesty's sitting room for a discussion that Prince Charles hoped would end the stalemate. On the previous day, she had sent her estranged husband a Valentine's card, signed: "With love from Diana." Cupid had long since deserted them as a hopeless cause, but the princess was defiant until the end, even as the system prised her fingers off a marriage on which she had so stubbornly refused to loosen her grip. She never stopped loving Prince Charles. She felt she was being forced to let go. Even when she stared irreparable damage in the face, the inevitable never dawned on her.

But the summit with the Queen was her first opportunity—since the divorce letters had dropped onto her mat—to speak openly and frankly to her mother-in-law, and she didn't want to leave anyone any illusions. "I do not want a divorce. I still love Charles. None of what has happened is my fault," said the princess. Her stance was crystal clear from the outset, in what turned out to be a businesslike, but friendly discussion. It couldn't be anything other than businesslike because the Queen's deputy private secretary Robin Janvrin was there to take notes. The gray suits at Buckingham Palace had been worried because "Bulimics rewrite history in twenty-four hours."

The princess didn't want a note taker at a private family discussion, but it was feared that she might brief allies in the media. The Queen had Robin Janvrin by her side to preserve the truth. When she got back to KP, the princess had me for the same protection.

As the princess spoke of being profoundly upset over the marriage breakup, the Queen apparently listened sympathetically. Indeed, she emphasized how over the years, she had tried to do everything she could to help, as had the Duke of Edinburgh.

But the princess, who never doubted that her parents-in-law had made a substantial effort even if their son had not, felt that others were only too happy to see her cast adrift, that they had been jealous of her work in public life. She unbottled years of suspicion and emotion before the Queen, and not for the first time. Over the years I despaired when journalists and "in the know" royal "experts" had claimed that the princess and the monarch spat venom at each other or, as the *Daily Mail* once suggested, "Diana spurned the Queen's hand of friendship . . . turning the two women into enemies." They were never enemies.

Until the princess's death in 1997, the Queen and the princess exchanged numerous letters, two royal icons from different generations trying desperately hard to understand each other. The one area on which they shared common ground was the welfare of William and Harry. In that meeting, the Queen reassured the princess that she must not worry about the welfare or custody of the two young princes. "Whatever may transpire in the future, nothing will change the fact that you are the mother of both William and Harry. My concern is only that those children have been in the battleground of a marriage that has broken down," she said.

As the meeting continued, and Mr. Janvrin's pen remained poised, the princess ultimately agreed to a divorce. But she wanted to record her hurt too. She said: "Mama, receiving your letter and Charles's letter on almost the same day before Christmas was tough. It was the first time Charles had actually mentioned divorce, and the letters I have received since have not helped."

The Queen agreed. "The recent exchange of letters has not led anywhere, but what I wrote before Christmas remains my view. The present situation is not doing anybody any good, either country, family, or children." The monarch was insisting, at her diplomatic best, that divorce proceedings should start soon. There was no turning back.

But she more than understood the princess's concerns for the future. Afterward, the princess said that she had displayed the same sensitivity and kindness that the Duke of Edinburgh had shown in 1992. By the spring of 1996, the princess felt she had had far more constructive talks with her mother-in-law than she could ever have had with her husband.

Then the meeting addressed the issue of the future and title of the princess, a sensitive question that became the subject of intense media speculation in the following days. The princess insisted that she had not offered to drop HRH, because it was too important to her. Then Buckingham Palace issued a statement: "The decision to drop the title is the Princess's and the Princess's alone."

It is true that the princess first raised the issue of her future role. She said to the Queen: "I have worked hard for sixteen years for you, Mama, and do not want to see my life taken away from me. I want to protect my position in public life. I want to be able to stand up for my own life." She then added: "I have real concerns about the future, and all the answers lie with you, Mama."

The Queen accepted that, but said: "I would like to decide things in consultation with Charles. The title is also a matter to be discussed with Charles." Then she added: "Speaking personally, I think that the title 'Diana, Princess of Wales' would be more appropriate."

The issue of HRH status remained uncertain until both the Queen and the princess could discuss it with Prince Charles. What is certain is that the idea for the title by which the princess would later be known was a seed sown by the Queen.

Many things were discussed that day: the princess was refused an office inside Buckingham Palace, and she told the Queen the reasons behind Patrick Jephson's departure. As the lengthy meeting continued, the princess expressed her concerns about William. She was worried about her eldest son and Prince Charles flying on the same aircraft: if a disaster or midflight incident occurred, they would both be affected.

The Queen replied: "That is only a problem on holiday and then it is only a question of who flies on public aircraft. The royal aircraft are safe. That is probably not a big worry."

By the end of the meeting, the Queen was anxious to let the princess know that she was always there for her. "This is a very difficult issue for me personally, but the situation does need resolving for everybody's sake," she said.

Duty and protecting the country's interests had placed the Queen, yet again, in an unenviable position as mediator between son and daughter-in-law. The princess accepted that the Queen needed to be firm, and she could not get over how considerate she had been. "I just want an amicable agreement, Mama," said the princess. "I do not want to be difficult."

I COULDN'T IMAGINE life without the princess.

"Diana's rock" has been a phrase used to describe me that some will believe and others will pour scorn on. But it was a label she attached to me in conversations with her friends, though she never expressed it directly to me. In KP, she described me as: "You are my third eye, Paul"; "You are at the helm of my ship." Or, when she was with her friend Susie Kassem, I was "Magic Merlin." It is also true that she often said to me, "Oh, you're such a pain in the arse!" when I offered an unpopular suggestion, fussily arranged the flowers in the sitting room, or just got in the way.

But I also knew when to be there when she wanted company and to talk. It was the same instinct that told me when she wanted coffee or carrot juice. The art of being a good servant is to anticipate the next move, and to know what the master or mistress wants before they know it themselves. Or, as housekeeper Mrs. Wilson put it in the movie *Gosford Park:* "To be the perfect servant is to have no life." Maria would probably have agreed with that.

I knew when the princess was down, when life was getting on top of her. At those times, I would merely make my presence known: appearing in the sitting room as she sat on the sofa, waiting by the arch leading into her dressing room, standing near the sideboard in the dining room as she ate, leaning against the banister on the first floor as she dashed from bedroom to sitting room. At these times she used to call me her "emotional washing machine." "I can come home, tell you everything and tip it all out," she said.

She went out and sucked up grief, pain, plight, and suffering on her visits to the homeless, the sick, the dying, and the poor, and returned to KP burdened with it but satisfied that, in a day's work, she had showered love and affection on the people who mattered. Put that with her own insecurities, fears, and problems, and emotional overload was the result. She used to arrive at KP and rush up the stairs, shouting: "Give me five minutes. I must talk to you—I *must* talk to you."

I flicked on the kettle and made two cups of coffee, and we would sit for beyond an hour, chatting. Or, rather, I would listen as the princess told me of the saddest things she had witnessed, or a thrilling moment when a sick child's eyes widened to look at her. The princess's eyes often welled up as she recalled traumatic experiences at a hospital, hospice, or medical center. It was as if talking to me became an emotional release. Then she would pick up the phone and call a friend, or call healer Simone Simmons or psychic Rita Rogers.

As William grew up, the princess decided to have serious mother-to-son conversations with him. She felt he was a wise head on young shoulders, and she had brought up both her boys to be sensitive, caring, and in touch with their emotions. But she confided in William about her problems and her life. He got used to comforting her. He had to take on a lot of his mother's emotions at a tender age, but the princess didn't want to hide anything from him. She wanted him to know all, so that he wasn't presented with a distortion of the facts from either the press or the wider family.

One Friday, William came home as usual for a weekend from school, accompanied by his friend Sam. Police protection officer Graham Craker had brought them to the palace and William darted through the front door and up the stairs, shouting, "Mummeeee!"

By then, he was almost as tall as the princess, and his smile showed off his metal braces. His mother, who had been listening out for the car's wheels on the gravel, rushed out onto the landing and gave him a hug. No matter how old they were, the princess smothered her boys with love and hugs. That weekend, he bounced off his mother and dashed into the boys' sitting room to slouch on the green sofa stationed in front of the television with his friend. The noise of an action-packed PlayStation game and competitive shouts suddenly broke the quiet of KP. The princess loved it when her sons came home, with their natural exuberance bringing joy back into the apartments. "It always feels so empty without them," she said.

William's friend Sam saw the world of KP through a young outsider's eyes. William and Harry were used to me—I was part of the furniture. It was their school friends, people like Sam, who seemed to find it odd that the butler was a regular face in the private living quarters of the princess. From Friday through to their departure on Sunday, Sam saw me here, there, and everywhere. William burst into the sitting room, unannounced, with Sam trailing behind him. "Oh, sorry, Mummy," he said. I was sitting on the sofa beside the princess, who was perched on the edge of the seat, half facing me. We were deep in conversation.

As William retreated politely, we heard Sam ask: "Why's *he* always in there?"

William's reply was matter-of-fact: "Oh, that's only Paul. He's here all the time."

THE ONE PLACE to find the princess was her writing desk. As a prolific letter writer, she was at home there. In our conversations, she sometimes struggled to articulate an experience or her emotions. But with a pen in her hand, she found the words to express herself. If she taught me anything, it was the same lesson she taught William and Harry: always write thank-you notes for people's time, gifts, hospitality, advice, or friendship.

She said that the one thing I taught her was to write down her thoughts at the end of one of our many conversations. "Let yourself know how you feel. It can be therapeutic," I had said. I knew the importance of writing everything down because the Queen kept a diary, with her unique perspective on history. The princess was also living extraordinary episodes as a royal icon, never more so than in the mid-nineties. When it seemed that many were plotting against her, she needed to keep an accurate record of the truth.

On the mornings after one of our sessions, I would walk into the pantry and find an envelope on the green leatherbound blotter on my desk. Inside, the princess had written her thoughts on her red-edged paper. She had mulled over our conversation, the advice given, the opinions she refused to change. Those letters became an official addendum to our talks.

Most often, she would show me a letter, like the divorce letters from the Queen or Prince Charles, and take it back;

but, on occasion, when she felt "the truth needs to be kept safe," she wrote it down and gave it to me. I became the repository for royal truths; quite separate from the intimate secrets that were never written down and remain locked inside my head. Each letter invariably started: "As I sit here today . . ." Those notes are her legacy, and are crucial to the truths that enshrine her memory and debunk the damaging myths that seem to have been peddled since the day she died.

O N FEBRUARY 28, 1996, KP issued a statement: "The Princess of Wales has agreed to Prince Charles's request for a divorce. The Princess will retain the title and be known as Diana, Princess of Wales."

The announcement followed a meeting between Prince Charles and the princess. But it was a letter from the prince, received earlier that week, that had finally convinced the princess to raise the white flag. Nothing would change his mind, and she was exhausted from arguing about what had gone wrong and who was to blame. "Let's move forward and not look back, and stop upsetting one another," he urged her, and the princess agreed.

With obstacles removed, lawyers began work on the severance of the fairytale.

Once a decision had been reached, the Boss seemed mentally stronger. After years and months of being in denial over divorce, she seemed to have garnered some extra mental strength from somewhere. "I'm focused, Paul," she said. "I have a strong sense of public duty. I am clearheaded and motivated and want to get on without obstruction."

I N MAY, as the lawyers thrashed out an agreement and divorce settlement, the Prince and Princess of Wales put on brave faces as they attended the annual parents' day at Eton for William. The princess wanted to be there for her elder son but had been dreading the occasion because she knew that her husband's friends, the Knatchbulls and the Romseys, would also be there—they, too, had children at

$\mathcal{F}$rom Buckingham Palace to Highgrove,
and our new home!

$\mathcal{R}$oyal mealtime—Alexander's birthday party with the young princes, and dinner for the grown-ups at Sandringham

*T*he official opening
of our cottage on the
Highgrove estate,
with Harry looking on

The Royals and the Burrells at Bristol Zoo

Playtime at Highgrove

$\mathcal{B}$oys and their toys

$\mathcal{M}$aria's birthday party

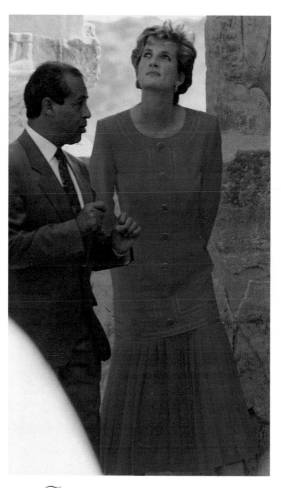

*T*raveling the world with the princess

The royal conversation that led to the collapse of my trial

Walking to freedom . . . and into a media frenzy

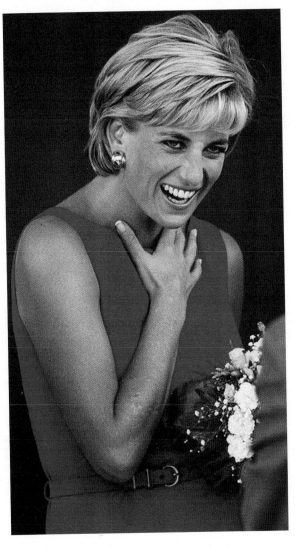

$\mathcal{T}$he infectious giggle . . . how I remember her best the school. The princess had wanted to arrive with her husband, but her request was declined. "I was cold-shouldered the moment I got there by everyone, including Charles," the princess told me afterward.

At the preluncheon drinks, she had mingled by herself, smiled, and chatted with everyone, every inch the strong and confident princess, masking how uncomfortable she felt. At the concert that followed, a seating plan was the final straw. She had wanted to sit next to Prince Charles, but she found herself beside the provost, while the prince sat on the other side of the aisle with the provost's wife.

I'm not having this, she thought.

The princess got up, crossed the aisle, and approached the provost's wife: "Excuse me, do you think I could possibly swap places with you so that I can sit next to my husband?"

The provost's wife could hardly refuse and the princess had deftly pulled off a little coup that had gone unnoticed by everyone but her husband.

Nor had she finished upstaging him. The humiliation was not going to be hers. She made sure of that outside the school, where the BBC and ITN television camera crews were waiting.

As the Prince and Princess of Wales emerged outside as proud parents and parted to go their separate ways, the princess rushed to her husband's car, placed a hand on his shoulder, kissed his cheek, and whispered to him: "Goodbye, darling."

That moment of a rare, united front made all the news bulletins that night, and the following day's headlines screamed: "A KISS IS JUST A KISS."

"Now Camilla knows what it feels like to be on the receiving end," said the princess, at breakfast the next morning. She was civil throughout the divorce proceedings, but she didn't have to be forgiving as well.

ON MAY 30, 1996, the divorce of the Duke and Duchess of York became absolute. The duchess came bounding into KP, stripped that day of her HRH status and living with the new title of Sarah, Duchess of York. She laughed over that morning's headlines. "We'll show 'em!" she said. At what was a somber time for both ladies, their shared laughter was a tribute to two people who refused to lie down and give up before "The Firm."

Like the princess, the duchess felt liberated by that sense of newfound freedom. She had faced a poisonous press and vicious enemies within the Royal Household, but she was always one of life's survivors. The duchess seemed to know that even on the day divorce was granted. "We'll win in the end, won't we, Paul?"

"Just keep smiling and hold your head up high," I replied, and she breezed into the sitting room to join the Boss. That summer, the princess and the duchess went on holiday to a mountain hideaway in the South of France with their children. In sharing their experiences, their struggles, and their pain, they had never been closer. They were more like sisters than onetime sisters-in-law; each learning how to survive in her own indomitable way. Besides, each had a new man in her life and seemed happy again.

PART OF THE PRINCESS'S own survival plan was to find a new future and head off in a different direction. She would always be anchored in London and KP for William and Harry, but she began to search for a holiday home and a foreign base from which she could project a humanitarian campaign on a global scale. "Do you like Australia, Paul?" the princess asked me, at the start of an exceptionally hot June in 1996. She asked me what I thought about a life Down Under, and I reminisced about my travels to the other side of the world on tours with the Queen. "I've been to every state, and New South Wales is probably my favorite," I told her.

She was sitting on the sofa, flipping through a collection of real estate brochures. "Would you ever consider living there?" she asked.

I knew the princess liked to shock but over the years

nothing she had done had truly shocked me. Until then. I looked at her as if it was a joke. "I'm serious!" she added.

"Well, it's a bit too far away from home for me," I said.

"I know, I know," she said, clapping shut the brochure, and then she changed the subject.

THE LAUGHTER OF KP was in sharp contrast to the silences at the Old Barracks. With no second butler to fall back on, no full-time lady-in-waiting and no private secretary, work was like a constant treadmill. I was, and I knew it, spending far too much time at work: out by eight o'clock in the morning and not back until beyond eleven. When I returned, all Maria welcomed home was an emotionally drained, exhausted, and irritable husband. Alexander and Nick only saw me on Sunday or when the princess invited them to play at the palace. Family life was suffering. Since the day the princess had announced in February that she had agreed to a severance of her marriage, I had lived, eaten, and slept the divorce drama by her side, sharing with her the traumas, the legal meetings, and the unsettled feeling that the tumultuous change can bring.

"While you watch over the destruction of one family, this family will need to be reminded what you look like," said Maria. "Forget about there being three people in the marriage of the Prince and Princess of Wales. There are three people in our marriage: you, me, and the princess. I'm sick of it, Paul."

Another Burrell marriage was in a far graver state. My brother Graham had confessed to an affair, and his wife, Jayne, had left the family home with the two children. He rang me in my pantry, full of remorse and shedding tears, and the marriage seemed well and truly over. We were a close family, and that marriage breakdown occupied my thoughts more than the divorce of the prince and princess. The Boss noted that I was down when I served her dinner on the day Graham had telephoned. She knew how close I was to my brother.

When she had finished, she said: "Can I have Graham's telephone number? I will ring him."

That night, she sat at her desk and dialed his home in Grassmoor. My brother was on the sofa in front of the television when he answered.

"Hello, Graham, it's Diana. Paul's not all right, so I don't expect you are either," she said.

Graham could not believe who was speaking to him, and no one at work would believe him if he told them the Princess of Wales had rung him to act as a virtual marriage counselor. He said the Boss was brilliant. She listened and offered words of comfort, sharing her own feelings about how difficult it can be when a marriage falls apart. She asked him about love, marriage, his other woman, the future, and she telephoned him on three more occasions over the following fortnight. She didn't mince her words. She told Graham how foolish he had been but, if he still loved his wife, he should persuade her to come back. Assisted by the princess, Graham did just that. To this day, my brother credits the princess for helping save his marriage.

One marriage that could not be saved, to her eternal regret, was her own. Each Tuesday night since February, Lord Mishcon had arrived at the front door. He was a small, gentle man who, according to the princess, had a genius of a legal brain. He was also extremely charming. In those early winter months, when I opened the door, he'd step in and remove his hat. Shaking the princess's hand, he often said, "Excuse the cold hand of an old man, ma'am. I assure you that the heart is warm." Before he had issued his latest briefing on negotiations with her husband's office, he had already got her smiling. By the summer, Anthony Julius, another lawyer from the same firm, was the bearer of good and bad tidings. By the end of June, only small technicalities had to be ironed out.

The divorce settlement stated that the princess would receive a £17 million lump sum payment. In return, the Prince of Wales had made his demands clear: he wanted back a pair of watercolors of distant German relations, a pair of chairs (circa 1780), and all of the George III silver, which we had used on a daily basis.

On July 1, there was a constant stream of flowers, presents, and cards for the princess's thirty-fifth birthday. One smitten individual sent two bunches of long-stemmed red roses, thirty-five in total. But two days earlier, on the Saturday, there had been an even greater surprise. The front doorbell rang. No one was expected and I turned the brass knob, wondering who it could be. The last person I expected was the heir to the throne. Prince Charles had popped in unannounced.

"Hello, Paul, may I come in?" he said. He had been due to catch a helicopter from the paddock beyond the upper stables at the rear of the palace, but was early, so he had decided to visit his estranged wife.

"Your Royal Highness, I think you know the way." He smiled and went up the stairs. If I was surprised, I couldn't wait to see the reaction of the Boss.

"Diana, are you there?" Prince Charles called, walking up the stairs as I followed behind.

He was met by the rather stunned princess on the first-floor landing, and they greeted each other with a kiss on both cheeks. She looked over his shoulder at me and her eyes widened with mock horror. Then she couldn't resist breaking the ice with her usual humor. "I suppose you've come to take the furniture away, then, Charles!"

Husband and wife, in the throes of a rather awkward divorce, laughed together for the first time in an age. If only they could have done that more in public, I thought. These two people got along, even if it was as friends. It was sad to detect a surge of excitement in the princess; I could see her reenergizing on the spot. It was all very cordial, relaxed, and civil. I went downstairs to make the prince a cup of tea, just how he used to like it at Highgrove: Earl Grey, strong, with a dash of milk.

IN MID-JULY, Buckingham Palace announced that a decree nisi had been granted. It left one outstanding issue: the princess's HRH status. The Queen had first suggested the title Diana, Princess of Wales, but the matter of HRH had remained unresolved. The princess rang her brother-in-law—the Queen's private secretary, Sir Robert Fellowes—to ask that she be allowed to retain the title HRH. Her request was declined. She would receive a £17 million lump sum payment, but the price would be the loss of her royal status. The princess was not someone to stand on ceremony, but it was an important title because, in her eyes, it was a special title given to her upon marriage, and it seemed spiteful to take it away. It was, she felt, part of her royal identity, and she had worked tirelessly as a royal highness for many years. When the final decision was made behind the scenes, the princess was devastated.

She turned to William in her distress. She told me how he had sat with her one night when she had been upset over the loss of HRH, put his arms round her and said: "Don't worry, Mummy, I will give it back to you one day, when I am king." That had made her cry even more.

When the tears had subsided, the princess began signing more than a hundred typed letters to charities, regiments, and organizations to which she had an affiliation, explaining that, because she would no longer be HRH and a member of the Royal Family, she felt unable to be a royal patron. She severed links with the Red Cross and Help the Aged. Instead of spreading herself so thin, the princess felt she would be more effective concentrating on a small nucleus of organizations, so she kept her ties with the National AIDS Trust, Centrepoint, Great Ormond Street Hospital, the Leprosy Mission, and the English National Ballet.

Meanwhile, the princess's office moved lock, stock, and barrel from St. James's Palace to the ground floor of apartment No. 6 in KP. She had been refused an office at Buckingham Palace because the Queen felt it was better that she remained independent. So apartment No. 6 became known as the office of Diana, Princess of Wales, headed by the comptroller Michael Gibbins.

One of the complications that the loss of HRH brought the princess was that protocol dictated that she would be an outsider required to curtsy to those members of the

Royal Family who still carried the title. The onetime future Queen of England now faced the humiliation of curtsying to the Duke and Duchess of Gloucester and Princess Alexandra. But she found support from an unlikely corner of the Royal Family. Her next-door neighbor from apartment No. 10, HRH Princess Michael of Kent, wrote a sincere letter that touched her.

"Paul, look at this. What a sweet, sweet thing to say," said the princess.

> *I was horrified to learn in the Press that after your title was removed, you would be expected to curtsey in public when meeting me . . . I insist that this would cause me the greatest embarrassment, so please do not even consider it. I have always admired your courage and strength. If only Charles had loved you from the beginning, then this situation would never have happened. You will always have my support.*

The letter from Princess Michael of Kent was a shot in the arm. All I could do, together with the rest of her friends, was reassure the princess that she was far greater than any combination of three initials. I told her: "You don't need a title. Wherever you go in the world, you are known as Lady Di—and no one can take that away from you. Besides, you will always be HRH in my eyes."

And I remained true to my word for what would be the final year of her life. Each morning, when I greeted her at breakfast, I placed the coffeepot on the table and said: "Good morning, Your Royal Highness."

IF THERE WAS ONE blessing in the loss of her HRH status, it was that she was free to chart her own path in life and concentrate on her humanitarian projects. And others, in the world of movies and cosmetics, had different offers to throw her way.

One evening in July, the telephone rang. It was the film

actor Kevin Costner. The call came through on the direct line into my pantry. As I placed him on hold, I rang the princess on her extension in the sitting room. "It's Kevin Costner. He would like to speak with you," I told her. There was a shriek of excitement. "Put him through, Paul, and come up."

I walked into the sitting room and the princess was at her desk, listening intently. She saw me and waved me over. "But I can't sing!" she said, giggling. She paused. "What would I be expected to do?" Another pause … "I'm not sure but, yes, okay, send it and I promise I will have a look." When she ended the call, she told me: "He wants me to star in his next film—*The Bodyguard II*!" It was to be the sequel to the first film that had starred Whitney Houston. She would play a princess. He would save her life. He promised it would be tastefully done. He would look after her. He would send her the script.

"Can you believe it?" she said. "He was so charming, but he *cannot* be serious."

Mr. Costner could not have been more serious. It had been an informal approach, but the princess—although it flattered her ego and she had been charmed by him—dismissed it. "It is simply impossible," she said.

The proposed script for *The Bodyguard II* eventually arrived, though. I'm not sure that she managed to read it.

The movie offer followed a more suitable suggestion from the American cosmetics giant Revlon. They had approached the princess with a proposal for a multimillion-dollar deal to head a charity organization on its behalf. "Cindy Crawford will continue to be 'the face.' They want me to be the 'spirit and style,'" she told me.

FROM MID-FEBRUARY, we had all been working toward and building ourselves up for the morning of August 28, 1996, the day the divorce became absolute, the day the Prince and Princess of Wales became single again. When that day dawned, the atmosphere was a mixture of sadness and anticipation. As I stood in the corridor waiting for the princess to come for breakfast, it struck me that while she was letting go of her marriage, I was cutting ties with the Royal Household, which I had joined in 1976, and beginning a new adventure. The sadness was balanced with the excitement of a new challenge.

When the princess appeared, she was full of energy, determined to make a success of her independence. She tucked into grapefruit and honey and talked about the tours that were planned: Washington in September, Australia in November. She was still thinking about moving to Australia.

Later, she paced the sitting room, preparing herself for a day of being besieged by the world's media outside. The telephone rang. It was Sir Robert Fellowes, in his capacity as her brother-in-law rather than as the Queen's private secretary. "I wanted to ring just to say good luck for this difficult day ahead. It is a tragic end to a wonderful story," he told her, but the princess was in no mood to wallow in pity or sympathy.

"Oh, no," she said, looking at me. "It's the beginning of a new chapter. And remember, Robert, I do still love my husband. That will never change."

The princess looked so elegant that day in pastel blue. She picked up her handbag, took a deep breath, and strode along the landing, down the stairs and to the front door with determination, still wearing her engagement and wedding rings. "I'll take them off eventually," she said. "But not now." She remembered only too well her reaction when divorce ended the marriage of her mother and father, and how traumatic it was for her as a child to see the rings removed. "A ring is so small but it signifies so much," she said. She walked out the door to fulfill an engagement at the English National Ballet.

She returned later that day, wanting to talk. Over coffee in her sitting room, she said, "I'm now a very rich lady, and I think you deserve a wage rise." My salary was increased from £22,000 to £30,000, and the rest of the household—chef Darren McGrady, secretary Caroline McMillan, comptroller Michael Gibbins, and personal assistant Victoria Mendham—

were rewarded too. The Boss was thanking us for sticking with her over the past few months, through thick and thin.

She seemed quiet when I left her. We had spoken about the significance of the day, her love for Prince Charles, how she wished the British public knew how much she hadn't wanted a divorce, how she wished things could have been so different. She delved into the myriad philosophies that, as she put it, "help me do the mental housecleaning." Philosophy arrested her insecurities, worries, and doubts, and the words of others gave her strength.

> Be more concerned with your character than your reputation, because your character is what you really are while your reputation is merely what others think you are.

> The self must know stillness before it can discover its true song.

> Success is the result of good judgment. Good judgment is the result of experience. Experience is the result of bad judgment.

> Use problems as opportunities to change our lives.

> Problems call forth our courage and wisdom.

> Learn to adapt.yourself to the demands of such a creative time.

> From a correct relationship to yourself comes a right relationship to all others and to the divine.

Or she quoted Benjamin Franklin: "Those things that hurt, instruct."

On the night of the divorce she repeated another to convince herself that she had done the right thing: "There needs to be a meeting of heart and mind which allows one to love and let go. I know that, Paul. I know that now," she said.

So much nonsense has been written about the princess and her divorce. So-called friends and advisers have lied to the world, saying that she had wanted to divorce Prince Charles from as early as 1990, that she bore a hatred for her husband that never existed. "Charles and I are friends and are civil to one another. I think he realizes what he lost in me. I have no hatred for him. All the suffering has made me into the person I am," she said. When it came to Camilla Parker Bowles, she harbored resentment but not hatred. She had another philosophy to help here: "Resentment is trying to change something that is just what it is. When we can't change it, we resent it."

The princess spent many hours trying to fathom why her marriage had failed—and hours analyzing herself, trying to understand her own mind. The bottom line was that she suffered from low self-esteem that ate away at her and then at her marriage. As she explained it: "High self-esteem doesn't protect you, but it does allow you to entertain self-doubt without being devastated!"

She felt her low self-esteem had taken root in childhood when she had acquired many of her ideas about herself. She had taken that poor self-image into the marriage with Prince Charles. In him, she focused solely on deriving a boost to her ego, through his attention or her achievements. When it was not forthcoming, she said she felt rejected. "As if the entire foundation of my self-esteem had been demolished," she said. Citing someone she called Mevlana, "the best poet and mystic ever," apparently, she said, "It is said that 'patience is the key to joy'—if only I knew that back then!"

The princess also needed to realize, and I think many people told her this, that anger was a natural emotion, but she felt many women found anger distressing. I told her that Prince Charles did too.

She even hired a boxer to come to KP with his punching bag so that she could rid herself of that anger. Diana, Princess of Wales, could certainly pack a mean punch.

We discussed all those emotions that night of the divorce. After our discussion, I left to go to the kitchen. When I returned to the pantry, there was a little note saying thank you, with a few other thoughts.

All she had ever wanted was for the British people to understand what she had gone through, how difficult it had been. And while she felt that Prince Charles had truly made her suffer, she had learned from her suffering. She went to her grave loving the prince. I know that because it is the truth she left on my desk that night. Prince Charles has often said that, within the next twenty-five years, the royal archives will prove the truth of his relationship with the princess. It seems wrong to allow the world to labor under illusions for the next quarter of a century. The princess's own words can debunk the lies now. That night, she wrote to me:

> It's the 28th August 1996—15 years of marriage have now been signed off. I never wanted a divorce and always dreamed of a happy marriage with loving support from Charles. Although that was never meant to be, we do have two wonderful boys who are deeply loved by their parents. A part of me will always love Charles, but how I wish he'd looked after me and been proud of my work.
>
> It has been a turbulent 15 years, having to face the envy, jealousy, hatred from Charles's friends and family—they have so misunderstood me and that has been painful and brought enormous heartache.
>
> I want so much to become Charles's best friend as I understand more than anyone what he is about and what makes him tick.

ELEVEN

✣

A MATTER OF TRUST

"**H**URRAY, YOU'RE HOME!"

Those words leaped from the red-edged cream paper. We had pushed open our front door at the Old Barracks, dragging our suitcases behind us, after a two-week holiday to Kentucky, which had given me the chance to catch up on lost time with Maria and the kids. Amid the mail spread out on the mat was an envelope that immediately grabbed my attention. It was addressed to "Paul" in the princess's handwriting.

On the eve of our return, she had nipped down and pushed the letter under the door. As I read on, there was clearly lots to tell: "Dramas galore during the past two weeks and you'd be impressed by these ones! It's wonderful to know you've returned. See you Monday! Love from Diana."

I returned to work with a tan that made the princess jealous. She went on her sunbed at least twice a week. It was as big as a spaceship, situated on the ground floor next to the dresser's room and the wardrobe room. "You go and warm it up, Paul, I'll be down in half an hour," she used to say. She never liked using the machine cold and the benefit of being the official "warmer-upper" was that I had a fifteen-minute stint in it before leaving it ready for the princess. She once remarked that she felt "like a sandwich in an ultraviolet toaster."

When William and Harry returned from their summer vacation at Balmoral, their mother thought William had been placed on a rack and stretched. He stood next to her in the sitting room and she couldn't believe how much he had grown: he was fractionally taller than she was when they stood back to back. He needed new rugby boots and I was sent out to purchase a size 13 pair for a boy who was aged fourteen and still growing.

"Height. It's a Spencer gene," said the princess. "The Windsors are PORGs—People of Restricted Growth."

William knew he was growing fast too. "I couldn't believe it. Granny and Aunt Margot seemed to have shrunk. And I'm taller than Papa now," he boasted.

Little Harry looked up at his brother and mother expectantly, and the princess said: "Oh, Harry, you've got the Spencer gene too. You'll be as big as your brother one day."

William will be king one day, King William V. In the summer of 2003, in an interview to mark the celebration of his twenty-first birthday, he spoke of how seriously he took his role, and how much he wanted to become king. I knew the boy, so it was heartening to hear him say this. I suspect it would also have been a nice surprise for his mother, because she knew how much the shy, introverted schoolboy had dreaded the prospect of ascending the throne. He was reared with huge expectations, and yet he didn't want the spotlight. As he went around Wales on his twenty-first birthday engagements, I know the princess would have been brimming with pride at the adjustment he seemed to have made.

I know how proud she would have been because of her concern for his future. "William doesn't want to be king, and I worry about that," she told me one night in the sitting room. "He doesn't want his every move watched." She went on to telephone her American friend Lana Marks and express the same worries. The princess empathized with her son, who, like his mother, was naturally shy and retiring. He had been born second in line to the throne. At the time, Harry's attributes and attitude almost made him more of a realistic prospect to take on the onerous duties of the monarch. He was more outgoing and pragmatic.

"Harry would see no problem in taking on the job," said the princess. "GKH. That's what we'll call him. GKH, for Good King Harry. I like that!" From then on, whenever Harry was visiting for a weekend, we used those three initials to refer to him. It was an affectionate nickname she shared with two other close friends, even if Harry never knew. "Where's GKH?" she'd ask, when looking for him around the house.

Of course, whenever the boys were in the house, staff had strict instructions on how to address them. We were not to bow, despite their HRH status. We were not to call them "Your Royal Highness." We were not even to refer to them as princes. They were, quite simply, William and Harry. It was all part and parcel of the princess's determination to ensure they were treated normally.

As a teenager, normality was all William longed for. He longed to be cool and ordinary, not unique and destined for a life of privilege and duty. His mother had been thrust, unprepared, into the royal spotlight as the future Queen of England, so she understood his fear, but she didn't want it to take root and grow into his adulthood. She coached him, prepared him, and spoke at length to him about his birthright. William could also count on the wisdom and support of Prince Charles and the Queen. At Eton, he regularly crossed the bridge across the Thames into Windsor and walked up to "Granny's castle" to have tea with Her Majesty, joining her for lengthy discussions about what the future held, what his role would entail, how important his duty was to the country and its people.

The princess began the life-of-duty grooming process at an early stage, as has been done for generations of royal children. But she did not want advisers from the Royal Household molding her son. She wanted to do it her way, just as she had taken charge of his upbringing, virtually making the nannies redundant.

I was at KP when the princess encouraged William to make his first-ever speech at the age of ten. It was Christmas 1992, and tradesmen and servants had gathered in the state apartments for the annual staff cocktail party. Earlier, William had drafted a few words to say to us. He had sat at the princess's writing desk in the sitting room, giggling nervously as he wrote his debut speech on a sheet of pink paper. Then his moment came. He stood on a box so that he could be seen, and around a hundred people fell quiet. "Ladies and gentlemen . . ." he started. His mother's eyes were on him. "I know how busy you must all have been," and he had the room laughing at the ironic remark aimed at a notoriously overworked joint household, "so I would like to thank you all for coming." Then, in a reference to the protection officers in the room, he said, "I should warn you, there are enough policemen in here to Breathalyze you all twice over! Merry Christmas and a Happy New Year." The place erupted into a roar as he stepped down to a hug from his mother and a ruffle of his hair from his father.

Harry's trademark was his kindness. Once, when Alexander went to play on the prince's PlayStation, he said that he was saving for a console of his own. Harry, who appreciated that royals wanted for nothing, said he felt sorry for him. He went to his bedroom on the nursery floor and returned in a few minutes with a five-pound note. "Here you are, Alexander. Put this toward your savings."

Meanwhile, William was still joining the princess at KP lunches at which she encouraged him to join in conversation with adults: with Elton John, discussing and asking questions about AIDS; with *Daily Mirror* editor Piers Morgan, to foster better relations with the media; with Sarah, Duchess of York, chatting about the problems and pressures of duty.

One day, William received special permission to take the afternoon off lessons at Eton because his mother had arranged a surprise. As he waited upstairs at KP, a black stretch limousine pulled up outside the front door. Out stepped supermodels Naomi Campbell, Christy Turlington, and Claudia Schiffer, who were in London to open their Fashion Café. William, who had posters of them on his wall, had longed to meet them, so the princess had arranged for them to come to KP, just a few months after she had organized a meeting for him with Cindy Crawford.

William, excruciatingly self-conscious about his braces, sat down uncomfortably on a sofa in the drawing room as Campbell, Schiffer, and Turlington all leaned in around him, posing for the camera the princess was holding. William blushed. "Mummy, stop it!"

The supermodels tried to put him at ease with polite conversation, and the princess was delighted with how her son coped. If he can handle himself in the company of beautiful women today, I suspect that is thanks to his mother.

When Claudia Schiffer asked him about Eton, he replied, "I don't much like the heavy mashed potato, but the lady maths teacher, Miss Porter, is very attractive," which she and the others found very funny. He went on to talk about life at Balmoral, the Queen's corgis, and his likes and dislikes. When they swept out the front door, the princess asked him what he thought. "Not as nice as Cindy Crawford," he said.

W ILLIAM SHARED the desire to be normal with his mother. The most photographed woman in the world longed to taste anonymity. She loved doing "what everyone else does." If she walked around a zoo or park unnoticed, she was delighted. Sometimes, she went out at 7 A.M. to jog or Rollerblade around the paths of Kensington Palace Gardens, knowing she could glide gloriously in a rare freedom when no one was around.

When she was feeling particularly daring, she opted to wear an elaborate disguise, and dressing her up soon became part of my duty. Once I was sent out to buy a long, shoulder-length, straight brunette wig from Selfridges.

Then I had to go to an optician in Kensington High Street and purchase a pair of large, round-rimmed spectacles, asking the optometrist to ensure that he fitted clear glass for the lenses. When I got back to KP, the princess couldn't wait to try on her new look.

I was in my pantry when she came downstairs as a different person. She tried to keep a straight face but I couldn't help gawking. "Nobody's going to recognize you! Look at you!" I said. The princess was shrieking with laughter, tears rolling down her face.

That night, in wig, glasses, black Puffa jacket, and denim jeans, Diana, Princess of Wales, joined a queue with friends outside Ronnie Scott's jazz club, in London. The next morning, she couldn't wait to talk about it over breakfast. "The smoke in that club got into my eyes—even with the glasses on!" she explained. She went on: "When we were standing outside, we queued far too long for my liking. I started to chat up a man next to us and he didn't have a clue who I was. It was so funny. I could be me in a public place!"

The paradox was evident to me, even if it was lost on the princess, because she wasn't "being me" at all. She had needed to become a different person before she could be herself, and as she marveled at the freedom of disguise, I thought about how terribly sad her statement was.

"COME ON, I want to show you something," said the princess in late September 1996. I followed in her wake, trying to keep up with her rapid strides downstairs and into the dressers' workroom and wardrobe room, with its floor-to-ceiling white doors. She flung them open one by one, exposing rails of long evening dresses, arranged in the color spectrum, starting with black at one end, through color in the middle, and white at the end.

"Just look at all these dresses!" she said. "How many ballgowns do you think there are in this room?" She began walking down the line, using one finger to count them all on their velvet hangers. There were sixty-two in that room alone, which did not take into account the dresses that hung in the L-shaped wardrobe room on the first floor.

"Each one of these is a memory and an old friend," she said, "but now is the time to sell them all."

In late summer this represented shock number two. First, the suggestion about moving to Australia, then selling off her wardrobe. The princess was taking charge of her world. Out with the old, in with the new. It had been a conversation with William, and then Elton John, that had prompted her into thinking about a charitable dress auction. The divorce settlement had left her with millions. Auctioning her dresses would ensure that others benefited, too, especially AIDS charities, which needed money for hospices and research.

We stood in that room as the princess picked out dresses and reminisced. She took a hanger, held it high, arm extended. "Ah. My *Gone with the Wind* dress!" She held out a full, off-the-shoulder floral-print gown. Then she pulled out another. "Worn at the White House, dancing with John Travolta when it was someone else I had my eye on!" It was an ink blue velvet creation.

Then she spotted an oyster satin dress with a bolero jacket, made by Victor Edelstein and worn at the Elysée Palace, Paris, at a state banquet given by President Mitterrand. "Not sure I can part with this. When I wore it, I actually felt like a princess." The following June, her reluctance was clear when the final selection was made for the New York auction: that dress was the last lot, No. 80.

Nostalgia did not stop the princess in her mission. She grabbed two hangers, I did the same, and we went upstairs, back and forth, back and forth.

"Ring Maria and ask Betty to come and join us," said the princess, knowing that Betty was staying with us at the Old Barracks.

By the time Betty arrived, my shirt was stuck to my back. I had been up and down those stairs as I carried around fifty dresses to the first floor, then dismantled and reconstructed a rail in the boys' sitting room. It now resembled a cluttered secondhand-clothing store. The princess treated the auction idea a little like she did her personal life: she wanted advice from everyone. Betty, an expert with knitting needles at home in North Wales, suddenly found herself as the voice of reason on haute couture at the palace. How the princess laughed! Betty was not ruthless enough for the task: all she saw was the most beautiful collection of dresses being thrown out and she was horrified. She had visions of them appearing at a jumble sale. "Ooo," she said, visibly shocked, her hand at her chest, "you mustn't throw that one out!"

One by one, I held up the dresses, and the ruthless selector, the princess, disagreed with the hoarder, Betty.

"Ooo, no. You don't want to be giving that one away either!" Betty kept saying. "Oh, now, that's a nice dress. What a waste!" she went on . . . and on. Before long, the princess was crying with laughter.

That weekend, William brought some tough decision-making to the process. He flicked back the hangers on the rail that had appeared in his room and made his selection. Another person whose input was precious was Aileen Getty, granddaughter of American billionaire J. Paul Getty. She had full-blown AIDS and came to lunch several times at KP. The princess couldn't wait to show her the dresses that were being sold to raise money for people in her position.

Christie's sent its costume expert, Meredith Etherington-Smith, to whom the princess took a shine. It was her job to catalog and describe each dress. Seventy-nine dresses—cocktail and evening wear—ultimately went under the hammer and raised $3,258,750, around £1.85 million, for AIDS and cancer charities on both sides of the Atlantic.

One cupboard in the downstairs wardrobe room was left untouched. On the day of the auction's conception, the princess had lifted back the tissue covering one particular dress: the wedding gown she had worn in 1981. "This is one dress I can't sell," she said, and remembered how her mother, Frances Shand Kydd, had paid for it in guineas. "I want to donate it to the Victoria and Albert Museum for its national dress collection," she said. She expressed that wish a year before her death. She did not mention it exclusively to me: during a lunch with *Daily Telegraph* editor Charles Moore, she had told him too. Today, that wedding dress stands on display in the Diana museum at Althorp, her ancestors' home.

Some dresses were never destined for auctions or museums. Some unwanted designer wear went to female staff, but other suits and dresses were taken to secondhand-clothing stores in Knightsbridge or Chelsea, where they would be handed over in exchange for cash when sold. This was done at the princess's behest, to raise spending money for her because royals rarely carry hard currency. The princess tended to use a credit card, which she signed as "Wales," not "Diana." By generating cash, she could spend it as she wished without trace, and take William and Harry to the cinema or to McDonald's. In the biggest paradox of their opulent royal life, the young princes were fascinated by money and how the Queen's face adorned every note of every denomination. A five-pound note became known as a "blue Granny," a ten-pound note was a "brown Granny," and a fifty-pound note was a "pink Granny." When the princess handed out money, it was a joy to watch the boys jumping up and down, clutching the notes, invariably requesting a "pink Granny."

Both personal assistant Victoria Mendham, who left palace service in early 1997, and I took around twenty outfits to the secondhand-clothing stores, which suddenly had labels such as Catherine Walker, Versace, Chanel, and Armani hanging on their rails, without knowing the name of the donor. An outfit worth £2,000 would be sold for around £200, and somebody, somewhere, would be walking around in the princess's clothes.

These regular sales netted the princess around £11,000, which she kept stuffed into an envelope in a bottom drawer. One day, in April 1997, she decided to hand it over to comptroller Michael Gibbins, whose jaw hit the floor when he opened the envelope, the princess said. He took the money and banked it, unaware of how such a sum had been raised. Even the accountant had been left in the dark about the princess's most private finances—until then.

THE PROBLEM WITH being a newly divorced princess and the most beautiful woman in the world is that men across the globe are aware that you are single again. His eligibility is a problem William will have to contend with. By the end of the summer of 1996, many high-profile or wealthy men began to make their intentions known to the princess. She was flattered, of course, but she already had feelings for someone. Not that her suitors were aware of that, because her recent happiness was a secret. They kept knocking on the door, undeterred by polite refusals or constant excuses. Being butler at KP at this time was like being a flatmate with a platonic female friend, sharing with her the flattery and thrill of the chase, knowing that she was unattainable. My duty now involved fielding calls from the smitten, the downright persistent, and the unhappily married. It was my job to know whom she wanted to speak to and whom she didn't, who had to be let down gently, who had to be told "No!"

One day, out of the blue, fifty long-stemmed red roses arrived with a rather overfamiliar message attached. The princess first sought my opinion, then gossiped about the gesture with Katharine Graham, publisher of *The Washington Post,* who was nearing her eightieth birthday but never lost her elegance. The princess admired her strength—"She went out into a man's world and came out on top"—and Miss Graham became a key ally in America along with Anna Wintour, editor of *Vogue;* Barbara Walters, the doyenne of U.S. television interviewers; and New York–based photographers Patrick Demarchelier and Mario Testino.

The princess adored life in Manhattan: shopping on Fifth Avenue, lunching at the Four Seasons, staying always at The Carlyle hotel. She became a regular visitor to America, spending a lot of time in Washington, where, of course, she stayed at the Brazilian Embassy with her number one friend, Lucia Flecha de Lima. It was Lucia who introduced the princess to Lana Marks, who became a friend in the final year of the princess's life—a psychiatrist's wife who lived in Palm Beach, Florida, and ran exclusive leather boutiques across the States. She shared the princess's sense of humor as well as her passion for fashion and ballet.

One Oscar-winning Hollywood actor's confident image suddenly disappeared when it proved he was too shy to call the palace himself and ask the princess for a date: he got a friend to write a letter on his behalf. When the princess wrote back, politely refusing, he returned with another request a month later. She had a drink with him, to be polite, but chose never to meet him again.

He wasn't the only one with honorable intentions. There was a sporting legend, who made a living out of racing in a field of competitors; a leading musician; a novelist; a lawyer; an entrepreneur; a billionaire who ran his own empire; and one extremely famous politician. They may have been enthralling company, but her heart lay elsewhere.

The princess called me the "steward of the racecourse" because I helped control the men in her life: deciding, after some serious consultation, who was in the running and who was lagging behind. I was now organizing virtually every aspect of her life, but I carried out the duty in a light-hearted manner. I teased her. She teased me. Just as she had compartmentalized certain friendships, she controlled the position of her gentleman friends. We called it "the trap system," as if the men were competitors on a racetrack, running round after the princess with their gifts and flowers. The occupant of Trap No. 1 never changed. He remained in pole position in the princess's eyes, not threatened by those on the periphery. Throughout the day, I kept the princess informed about which trap had phoned, and at what time. "Trap No. 5 has rung, he wants you to ring him back. Trap No. 8 wants to speak to you. Shall I put him off again?" On her writing desk, the princess kept a list of the trap system and its occupants. In my pantry, a duplicate of the same list, which changed as men fell in and out of favor, was tucked into the back of my desk diary.

Sometimes the princess could not believe how many suitors were making their intentions known. She used to joke that the racecourse was getting "a little overcrowded." Once I wrote to her: "There is still serious overcrowding on the racetrack. After further consultation, I have been informed that Traps 8 and 9 are void and have been declared non-runners. One failed the random drug testing; one failed the strict medical examination."

Then the princess wrote to me: "Due to serious overcrowding on the racetrack, the judges have asked for a reevaluation on the contents of the traps and have asked Mr Paul Burrell for his valuable assistance on this sensitive issue!!"

Following what I would call "a steward's inquiry," it became rather empowering to strike a line through the traps containing the lawyer and the politician.

The drawback of being sucked into this royal vortex and being so close to the princess was that my life merged into hers. When friends said they would always be there for her, it meant on call twenty-four hours a day. Being butler and friend placed an even greater expectation on my time. In September 1996, I had got home late, beyond eleven o'clock again, and was sitting down to a bottle of red wine with Maria at the Old Barracks. Just after midnight, the princess rang, in tears, after a little setback in her personal life. As I spoke to her, Maria tutted. The princess was asking me to go out and deliver a message to someone following an altercation over the telephone.

Hearing how upset she was, how could I refuse? Even at that late hour, even though I was exhausted, I had to—I wanted to—oblige. As I put down the receiver, I had to tell Maria that the princess needed me to run an errand.

"That's it. I've had enough. You—are—pathetic!" she spat.

"But you've got to understand that she needs me. No one else can help her at this hour," I said.

"Paul. You baby her. She clicks her fingers and you go running. Well, I've had it. I've had it with you and I've had it with her!" Maria stormed off to bed. I put on my shoes, pulled on my jacket, and went out into the night.

Mission accomplished, I got to bed in the early hours. That morning, I went to work as usual at eight o'clock, wondering if I had ever been to sleep. But the tiredness was worth it when I reached my desk in the pantry and found a note from a far happier boss.

Dear Paul. Not many people would venture out late at night to sort a heart out . . . but then, not many people have the kindness and qualities you possess . . . I am profoundly touched by your actions last night, and very much wanted you to know that. Times are challenging in this particular home, but one thing is for sure, that is without you at the helm of this ship, we'd all be in bad shape and the laughter gone! So thank you very much for coming to my rescue once again. Love from Diana.

Once, one of her suitors had persuaded the princess to accept a dinner invitation when she didn't really want to go, and I teased her endlessly about being on her guard. "Don't worry, Paul, I can look after myself," she said.

When she left, I stayed at the palace and spent half the evening worrying about her, wondering if she was going to be okay. I had told her to ring me on her cell phone, which she kept in her handbag at all times, if there were any problems. She was due back by eleven o'clock, so I decided to leave a mischievous note on her pillow, wondering, as a man, if I could second-guess the suitor's every move. The princess often said I had an annoying habit of always being right.

When she got back, she filled in my joke questionnaire and left it on a stool at the top of the stairs to ensure it was the first thing I saw when I arrived before breakfast. My questions were written in black; the princess penned her answers in green.

YRH . . .
IF . . . you had a candlelit dinner for 2? Correct!
IF . . . there were roses on the table? Correct!
IF . . . he had lizard lips and drooled all evening? Deaf instead.

AND insisted on you drinking a glass of champagne?
2 glasses.
THEN I WAS RIGHT!

That morning, at breakfast, we laughed so much. After serving her, I pulled up a chair, sat down at the dining table, and said: "Come on, then, tell me all about it."

Those were exactly the same words used by one national newspaper journalist who had obtained the telephone number for the direct line into my pantry. He rang to inquire about a tip-off he had received that I had been offered a position as butler, in America, to movie actor Mel Gibson. By 1996, the press was beginning to analyze the relationship between me and the princess. First came the *News of the World* on January 14 with a headline "BUTLER IS THE ONLY ONE DI TRUSTS," followed by a full page in the *Daily Mail,* asking, "IS THIS THE ONLY MAN DIANA REALLY TRUSTS?" and telling how I was assigned "to stand guard over her fax machine back home and act as her most personal of go-betweens." But the unexpected call about Mel Gibson was the first time I had been put on the spot by someone I didn't know.

The truth was that an American agency had tentatively suggested that I might work for Mel Gibson, but I wasn't going to tell that to this persistent reporter. In a ten-minute phone call, he pressed for the truth, but I said: "I am happy working with the princess."

The reporter kept on: "But will you deny that Mel Gibson has approached you to be his butler?"

"I am happy working with the princess," I repeated.

It threw me, and I panicked, because I hadn't told the princess about Mel Gibson. It was a nonstarter, so I hadn't mentioned it. Now the newspapers could cause trouble for me, I thought. I went upstairs and immediately told the princess about the call.

She was furious. "I'm not having this! I'm not having them ring you here like that!" and she stormed downstairs, out through the back, and into the adjoining office, where she made Caroline McMillan ring back the reporter, scolding him for breaching accepted protocol, asking him to refrain from contacting her staff, and repeating that her butler was going nowhere. I dreaded the next morning's newspapers and, with the princess, I read the rather embarrassing headline across two pages that announced, "I'M DI'S GUY," and the story telling how I had snubbed Mel Gibson to pledge my future to the Boss. A potentially negative situation had been turned into a positive story, and the princess spent the day teasing me about being her guy.

I thought all talk about being poached was over, until the day American chat-show host Oprah Winfrey came to lunch at KP. The princess was really nervous about meeting her because, she said, "She is such a big name." It didn't cross her mind that perhaps Oprah would be nervous too.

I took Oprah into the drawing room and offered her a drink. She accepted a glass of water. Then I returned to the princess in the sitting room. "What's she like?" she whispered.

"She's taking everything in, not missing a trick. She's extremely smart and wearing the *most* enormous diamond studs in her ears!" The princess seemed impressed.

She made her typical confident entrance. "Sorry to keep you waiting, sorry, sorry," she said, as she walked over to greet the U.S. television star.

I served lunch in the dining room and soon became part of proceedings as conversation turned to America.

"We love America, don't we, Paul?" the princess said. "He goes there every year for a holiday."

Oprah to the princess: "So, would you ever consider living in the United States?"

"It would be a wonderful place for my boys to visit," she said diplomatically, not mentioning that she was still considering a move to Australia.

Then I chipped in: "I would pack my bags and go and live in America tomorrow." I looked at the princess and winked.

Oprah saw her opportunity. "We could do with a butler. Why don't you come to Chicago and look after me?"

The princess suddenly straightened in her chair. "Look, Oprah," she said laughing. "He's *my* butler and he's staying here." It became a friendly tug-of-war all the way through to coffee: Oprah kept returning to it to embarrass me.

After lunch, the princess and I walked her to the front door, where her car was waiting. Just before she pulled away, Oprah opened the window, leaned forward, and said: "This is your last chance, Paul!"

The Boss, standing beside me on the front step, threw a possessive arm round me and shouted out: "Hey, he's mine—and he's staying here with me." The lunch appointment ended on laughter as we stood there, waving her goodbye.

I SEEMED TO BE constantly beside the princess— morning, noon, late at night.

"Come on, Paul, we're going for a drive," said the princess, one summer's evening after dinner.

We jumped into her BMW. She headed out down the backstreets of Bayswater and Queensway, and toward Paddington Green, near the railway station. Right. Left. Right. Left. Side street after side street. She knew all the shortcuts. "You don't need to do the Knowledge!" I joked.

"I could take on any London cabbie." She smiled, the peak of her baseball cap shadowing her face.

We arrived at a street corner. The princess pulled over but kept the engine running. Then she dropped the electric window on my side. Two heavily made-up girls in short skirts had been talking to each other on the corner. When our BMW pulled over, they stopped, looked, caught my eye, and tottered over in their high heels. The ladies of the night were working their corner.

The larger maintained eye contact with me as I shuffled in my seat. She placed both hands on the roof of the car, bent down, and leaned in. "Hi, Princess Di. How are you?" she said, speaking across me.

My head swiveled right and the princess was leaning in

toward me. She called the girl by name and said, "I'm fine. Have you been busy?"

The second, slimmer girl bent down to join in the conversation. "Nah, it's been quiet, but we'll stick around. Gotta work, Princess," she added.

Good God, I thought. The princess knows them.

"Who's this, then?" said one, looking at the rather nervous character who was saying nothing.

"This is Paul." She introduced me. We shook hands. It was all very polite.

The Boss reached into her pocket and got out two crisp £50 notes. "Look, girls, have the night off. Go home to your children," she said, stuffing the notes into two eager hands. The princess asked about their children. One had been coughing. Was he better?

After a brief conversation, the larger woman patted the roof of the car, and the two girls were off, lured away by a pair of braking headlights a few hundred yards down the road. A load of good that £100 handout just did. What a waste, I thought. "This is absolutely crazy. You cannot afford to be here, Your Royal Highness," I said. "DI AND BUTLER CAUGHT KERB-CRAWLING" was the imaginary headline that had raised my voice by a panic-stricken octave or two.

"Oh, Paul," said the princess, as she pulled away, "lighten up. Those girls need help, and that's all I'm doing—helping them."

The naïveté of her mission was astonishing, but her heart, as always, was in the right place. If the princess had been faced with an avalanche, I think she would have tried to stop it. She wanted to help everyone. The sick. The poor. The homeless. The starving. AIDS sufferers. The infirm. Prostitutes. Drug addicts. Drunks. If it was up to her, and increasingly it seemed that it was, her mercy missions would have been endless. How many times during my duty did I hear those earnest words: "I feel I can help . . ." or "I want to go where hearts need mending"?

We returned to the Paddington area several times in the summer and winter of 1996. In November, we pulled over at the same street corner. This prostitute with two children at home was working the streets to provide for them and couldn't even afford a coat on such a cold night.

The princess, in one of her roadside "counseling" sessions, had given this woman £100. "Now, buy yourself a coat, and I want to see you in that coat the next time I'm here," she said, almost motherly. Within a few weeks, we saw the woman again looking a lot warmer—wearing a thick waist-length black coat.

In the princess's wardrobe, there was a floor-length fur coat that she had once been given. She had accepted it graciously as a gift, but she never wore fur. One afternoon, I saw her leave KP with it tucked under her arm. She returned home without it. She told me how she had been driving through Victoria when she spotted a Dumpster on the side of the road. She stopped the car, dropped the window, and hurled in the coat. "You never know, a tramp might pick it up. That should keep him warm!" she said.

I GOT USED TO SITTING in that BMW, sometimes in the passenger seat, sometimes behind the wheel, often after midnight. There was a practical reason for making it so late: not only were the streets of London quieter, but the princess knew that photographers, should they be watching, could not get sneak photos with long lenses in the dark.

Parked in an alleyway just round the corner from the Royal Brompton Hospital in Chelsea, I could be waiting for an hour, listening to late-night radio. I had dropped off the princess, who left, armed with magazines, videos, and CDs, for the heart and lung transplant patients or those suffering from cystic fibrosis. These hospital visits were not new, even if the *News of the World* drummed up hysteria about them and cynics dismissed them as publicity stunts. The princess was there because she had a contact at the hospital, and she genuinely cared and took an interest. She was doing nothing more than she had done when Adrian Ward-Jackson died in 1991 or when I was in the hospital in Swindon in 1992.

Sometimes waiting in the car for the princess was not so boring. Once, when she was lunching with her friend Lord Attenborough at Tante Claire in Chelsea, sitting in the window, I arrived in the BMW to pick her up at two-thirty. Luckily, there was a parking space directly in front of the restaurant, and I could see Lord Attenborough's back, with the princess facing the window. She had seen me pull in.

The car stereo was playing the CD soundtrack from *Aladdin*. Our family friends in Florida, Chuck Webb and Ron Ruff, regularly sent the princess CDs of the latest Disney movies: *The Lion King, Pocahontas, Beauty and the Beast*, and *Toy Story*. I have long been a collector of animation art and visited New York for its annual animation sale to purchase cels—individual frames from the movies with their original production backgrounds. The princess had her own cels, most famously from *Who Framed Roger Rabbit?*, presented to her at its royal film premiere in Leicester Square, London. She also bought William and Harry all the Disney videos, and she often drove to Disney soundtracks—*Beauty and the Beast* and *Aladdin* were her favorites. The in-joke between butler and princess was one particular track on *Aladdin*—"A Whole New World"— which she played over and over again. She knew the lyrics by heart and, whether with me or alone, she sang them out loud when driving. This song was playing as she was finishing her meal with Lord Attenborough. I started to mouth the words and gesticulate in an exaggerated manner. When she saw me, no doubt Lord Attenborough thought his jokes were working a treat. On the way back to the palace, we sang that track together.

BY NOVEMBER 1996, after the princess had visited Sydney, Australia, to help raise $1 million for the Victor Chang Cancer Foundation, she returned and waved good-bye to dreamy thoughts of living Down Under. She decided she would have felt so isolated there. Instead, her attention turned to a new potential home: South Africa.

Christmas 1996 would be the princess's last Christmas,

and she spent it in another corner of the globe, in the Caribbean. The press was convinced that she was heading to Australia to enjoy the festive period with a male companion, so it was my job to keep them under that illusion, booking two seats on a Qantas flight for Sydney, knowing that reporters would be checking the flight passenger list. As the media stalked the Qantas desk at Heathrow, the princess sloped off on Christmas Eve to the opposite side of the world and the exclusive K-Club complex on the tiny island of Barbuda, near Antigua, accompanied by her personal assistant Victoria Mendham. The ploy worked, but only for a day or two.

William and Harry had delved into their Christmas stockings on the Sunday before Christmas. William was overjoyed with his stereo system. Harry started hooking up his PlayStation 2.

On Christmas Day, the telephone rang constantly at the Old Barracks. Maria told me not to answer it. We both knew it would be the princess and, for once, I obeyed, so that I could give all my time to my family. On Boxing Day, I took the calls. The princess rang every day for a chat until her return on New Year's Day, and she couldn't wait to get back. Unlike Harry, who had gone to Klosters in Switzerland with Prince Charles and had the time of his life skiing, despite the presence of the press, which he later described as a "nightmare" to his mother, William had refused to go with them: age fourteen, he was already beginning to loathe the media spotlight.

My own next destination would be Angola. I would walk beside the princess as she came into her own as a true philanthropist, championing the humanitarian causes that meant so much to her.

TWELVE

SIDE BY SIDE

I FOLLOWED ON THE HEELS of the princess as we walked out of the squinting brightness of the African sun and into the gloom of a village hospital. I say "hospital" because that was what it was to the locals, but really it was a bare room with six metal-framed beds. The walls had once been plastered but never decorated. With the media pack jostling and shuffling behind us, we walked to the bedside of a young girl, a thin white sheet pulled up to her neck, her wide eyes staring up at us.

Then a nurse pulled down the sheet to the girl's waist to expose the most horrific sight. Her entire insides were spilling out of her gaping abdomen. She had gone to fetch water for her family and stepped on one of the millions of land mines that remained buried and live under Angola's scorched soil.

It was impossible to connect the two sights: the pretty face on the pillow, the bloodied entrails at the midriff. The most instinctive thing to do was recoil, but the princess kept herself focused on the girl's eyes. The princess placed her hand in the girl's and bit her lip to keep herself from crying. Then she pulled the sheet up to the girl's neck,

281

turned to the press and said: "Please, no more." The camera lights flicked off.

It was January 15, 1997. The day is remembered for that famous image of the princess walking through a minefield being painstakingly cleared by The Halo Trust, treading along a safe path in her white shirt and cream chinos, wearing a green flak jacket and helmet with clear visor. It was a photo opportunity that led cynics back home to suggest that the princess was meddling on the political stage, and call her a "loose cannon." Her campaign would sharpen the world's focus on the global land mine treaty on which Britain, Canada, and America had been stalling. The cynics in Fleet Street accused her of having seized another well-rehearsed, attention-grabbing photo opportunity in the minefield. But they hadn't seen that little girl in the hospital bed, because the princess didn't wish them to see her. It was one of thousands of profound moments I witnessed during my duty. For those who don't want to believe that she made a difference, they should have read the *Sunday Times* article filed by its reporter Christina Lamb. That day she stayed behind to interview the little girl.

The journalist, hardened by war zone experiences, cynical by nature, had tried to explain to the child who had just visited her bedside. "She is a princess from England," said Mrs. Lamb.

"So is she an angel?" the little girl asked. That afternoon, the girl died from her injuries.

Outside, the princess provided her own answer. Responding to reporters' questions about being a "loose cannon," she replied: "I am a humanitarian—always have been, always will be."

I HAD NOT BEEN ON a tour with the princess since Egypt in 1992, but she had asked me to join her on the trip to Angola from January 12 to 17. The request came out of the blue. "There will be just you, me, and people from the Red Cross," she said, as well as two police protection officers, on whom the government insisted on an overseas trip.

I wondered what use I could be.

"You will come everywhere with me, as assistant, lady-in-waiting, secretary, and dresser!" she joked. So I woke her, ironed her clothes, and shadowed her every move on engagements. My enforced versatility once again provoked the press to ask questions about the significance of the butler being the princess's constant shadow, and I sensed among other royal household staff that my role was putting a few noses out of joint.

The princess had rebuilt bridges with the Red Cross since her withdrawal as its patron, and had consulted Mike Whitlam, its then director-general, about its anti–land mine crusades. He had sent literature and videos for her to watch, and that was what had fired her desire to do something. In Angola, mines killed one in four of its twelve million people, and the country became the launching pad for the princess's anti–land mine crusade, with Mike Whitlam by her side.

Armed with the itinerary for the trip, I had gone shopping for the dress-down clothes the princess would require. First stop was Ralph Lauren in Bond Street for shirts, chinos, and three-quarter-length trousers. (She even bought me some new shirts.) Then there was Armani for jeans, and Tod's for flat leather footwear. All had to be packed with the dresses and skirts needed for the embassy and dinner with the first lady, Ana Paula dos Santos. I also went to Boots for the essentials, including vitamins.

Bill Deedes, a veteran columnist from the *Daily Telegraph,* was to join the press pack in Angola, but the princess insisted he travel with us to and from the capital, Luanda, because he had been such an influence on her thinking, having been involved with the anti–land mine cause since 1990. He had been a regular visitor to KP, where we had a standing joke about the difficulty of the *Daily Telegraph* crossword. "My butler still thinks your crossword is so unfair," the princess said, every time she welcomed Bill, highlighting my intellectual shortcomings for the puzzle rather than her own.

On the flight to Luanda, she was endlessly scribbling notes and redrafting her speech, which was delivered amid the rubble of the run-down airport. She declared that she wanted "to ban, once and for all, antipersonnel land mines." As we drove to the British Embassy, bumping around the potholed roads in a Land Cruiser, the princess was shaking her head at the pitiful sights she witnessed: almost every other person we passed had just one leg; only the façades of buildings remained—homes, shops, offices—peppered with craters from mortar fire. It was like driving through a movie set.

IT HAD BEEN a long road that the princess had traveled since she had visited Calcutta in 1992 to visit Mother Teresa. That trip had been a life-changing experience for her, placing her on a humanitarian and spiritual path at a time when she had found zero fulfillment in an ending marriage. "That was when I found my direction in life," she told me.

Before we left for Angola, she presented me with a copy of a record of her thoughts on that trip to India, as if she wanted me to understand what the humanitarian cause was all about and why such work was important to her. The princess's vivid account explains how she experienced a spiritual awakening in Calcutta that became the driving force behind every mission and campaign she worked toward.

She had gone to visit Mother Teresa's home, and when she arrived, the sisters sang the Lord's Prayer in the chapel, then knelt with the princess to pray. The princess viewed those women as saints.

Angola 1997 would mirror Calcutta 1992 in how the princess reached out to the sick. India acted almost as a template for her to rely on in future humanitarian missions, because she could never forget how important a simple, sincere gesture could be when dealing with the young, the sick, and the poor. She carried with her in her heart the lesson she had taught herself in one instinctive moment when, as she visited Mother Teresa's home for children, she picked up a blind and deaf boy. As she wrote: "I hugged him so tightly, hoping he could feel my love and warmth." She spoke about the experience with passion, belief, and with a conviction that made me understand where she was coming from.

Her written account of her experiences in Calcutta told of a visit to a hospice for the dying. On reading it, I knew that her time there, coupled with the experience of witnessing the death of Adrian Ward-Jackson, had made the greatest impact on her, which was why she gave me such strength after my own mother's death. In that hospice, she had been confronted with row upon row of beds, each filled with a man, woman, or child facing inevitable death with courage. "Dying with dignity," she called it; individuals were "happy" to pass away under Mother Teresa's roof.

I read what she had written about the entire experience, and how it had so profoundly changed her outlook on life—and death. On returning from Calcutta, she was driven by a deep feeling to help the sick and dying on a global scale. It was her responsibility, she felt, to use her position as the Princess of Wales to make a difference.

In Angola, I read that account over and over again. Each morning, the princess couldn't wait to get out and see the victims of the land mines. Eager, once more, to make a difference.

"Come on, let's get to work," she said, and we went to visit the villages of Huambo and Kuito, following the path that she had embarked on five years earlier.

Later that year, in June, the princess visited New York to meet Mother Teresa in the Bronx. A headline in Britain read: "ANGELS IN THE BRONX."

Angola represented the apogee of my years in royal service, when I transcended all personal and professional expectations. It was the time when, with encouragement from the princess, I felt confident enough to leave behind the self-imposed limitations of being "butler" and become her right-hand man. I finally discarded the remnants of the butler's uniform in the second week of January at the

British Embassy in Luanda: when the princess told me that she intended to take me everywhere, she meant it. I just didn't realize that it would involve walking through marble corridors of the government building to meet the country's first lady, Ana Paula dos Santos, and her foreign minister.

In Pakistan, Czechoslovakia, and Egypt in 1992–93, I'd known my place on the sidelines as an observer. In Angola, I became a participant, beside Diana, Princess of Wales, and was received after the princess by our hosts. I don't think the first lady even knew my job title was "butler." As far as anyone in that room was concerned, even the Angolan staff, I was her private secretary or equerry-in-waiting. It was a bizarre feeling for me.

A private secretary should be doing this, I thought, but she didn't have one. A lady-in-waiting should be doing this, but she didn't have one. So it was left to the man who had pressed her dress, carried her luggage, and hand-washed her garments to have a formal audience with the first lady, listening intently to the discussions on land mines and the country's politics.

At least my training stood me in good stead. I had been used to announcing the heads of Commonwealth countries to the Queen on the royal yacht *Britannia,* so I knew the protocol and exactly how to behave, one step behind the princess.

As I stood there in those first few anxious minutes, I remembered my first duty at Windsor Castle back in 1976, and how I hadn't been trusted to handle the meat or vegetable trays. And there I was, beside the Boss, the woman who had engineered my career advancement. I felt proud. And, if I'm being honest, rather smug, too, knowing that if the Royal Household could have seen me, they would not approve. It made the experience even more enjoyable, imagining the suits sniffing down their noses that I didn't "belong" or didn't "know my place." It was an accusation I would face when working for the Diana, Princess of Wales Memorial Fund.

I'm not even sure Her Majesty's ambassador Roger Hart grasped what on earth my role was. As we stayed in his official residence, he often saw me emerging from one-on-one meetings with the princess. Then there was dinner, when the princess requested that my name be included on the seating plan. So there I was, making polite conversation at the dinner table with Her Majesty's representative in Angola, his wife, and the princess.

The best bit for me, and what made the princess really giggle, was when it came to the end of the evening and she announced that she was going to retire for the night. It was a rehearsed departure, so, as she stood and pushed back her chair, so did I. We retreated simultaneously and broke into raucous laughter later as we remembered the raised eyebrows we had left at the table. She loathed the claustrophobia of stuffy formality, even though the ambassador and his wife were great company.

We only had a formal dinner once. After that, it was a cold snack in her room. Each night, the princess, wrapped in a robe that covered a swimsuit, went with me through the official residence, down the back passages, through the kitchen, and out into the garden to the swimming pool. I sat on the tiled edge with my feet dangling in the water, counting the lengths the princess swam. End to end, motoring along in her front crawl, she did twenty before stopping to catch her breath.

Then she stood in the shallow end, pushing back her drenched hair. "How do you think today went?" she asked, leaning against the side of the pool. We discussed how it had gone, what tomorrow would bring, and her concerns. Then she did another twenty lengths beneath the stars and the moon.

LORD ATTENBOROUGH was about to release his latest film, *In Love and War*. At its premiere in London in February, it would be trailed by a ten-minute documentary to raise money for the British Red Cross Landmines Appeal. That was why a production team had exclusive access to our Land Cruiser to shadow the princess in Angola.

On this occasion, the princess didn't mind having a camera crew breathing down her neck, because she knew it would highlight the cause around the world. But it required one technical practicality: the princess had to be "miked up." A microphone was attached to the front of her shirt, leading to a transmitter pack on her belt at the back of her trousers. I think it was on day two of the trip when the sound recordists got more than they bargained for. Forgetting that she was wired for sound, we made what the princess referred to as "a pit stop" at a remote garage. I wandered off with her for a private chat away from the cameras, behind the building. She wanted to discuss personal issues, and whom she would call when we got back to the official residence. Then we gossiped about the camera crew: the characters, the way they worked, the silly incidents, and she was giggling mischievously. Finally I spotted the microphone and it dawned on her at exactly the same time. Her laughter turned to horror.

"Check it!" She panicked.

Sure enough, the little light on the transmitter pack was blinking red. Our gossip had been transmitted live. Returning to the vehicle like two naughty schoolchildren, we felt our guilt was as glaring as the sun. To this day, I still don't know if the production company picked up on that moment. We never dared ask.

Angola was an exhausting, emotionally draining experience, but everyone involved returned with a feeling of triumph that we had bounced an important issue onto the world stage. At the end, the princess, with her usual generosity, presented a thank-you gift to all those who had participated and made the trip such a success. All the staff at the British ambassador's residence—the drivers, the chef, the maids, the office staff, and the ambassador himself—received wallets and leather memo pads, embossed with *D* and a coronet. When I returned to KP, a gift from her was waiting for me—a marble bust of an African woman that she had been given in Angola.

*   *   *

THE GENEROSITY of the princess ultimately led me into the number one court at the Old Bailey when the outside world, and especially Scotland Yard, could not grasp how much senior royals gave to members of their staff. It was incomprehensible to those who didn't understand a world behind closed doors.

The previous September, my son Alexander had gained a place at the London Oratory School beside the mighty stadium of Chelsea Football Club. The princess asked about his progress at school. I happened to mention that he seemed to have a lot more homework.

"So he's locked away in his room for hours on end, is he?" she asked.

"No. He sits at the kitchen table while Maria's making tea," I said.

The princess couldn't believe that he didn't have a desk. Kitchen tables were for family eating. Desks in a quiet corner were for homework. "I have just the thing," she said.

In 1981, to mark the marriage of the Prince and Princess of Wales, the city of Aberdeen had presented them with an upright writing bureau, but it had never been used. It had been in storage for all those years, so the princess saw the opportunity to put it to good use. My brother Graham and I went down to a storage cupboard in the inner hallway on the ground floor at KP, and loaded the desk into the back of my Vauxhall Astra. It was one of the items I was said to have stolen after the death of the princess.

In the final year of her life, the princess was constantly getting rid of items that reminded her of her marriage. The carpets and china bearing the Prince of Wales feathers had already been thrown out. Now circumstances were different. While part of her would always remain in love with Prince Charles, a fresh clearing-out process began of the more sentimental items, as if she was mentally shedding a past that had been crammed into her emotional baggage. Genuine happiness lay with someone else. She had finally persuaded herself to move on and let go. It wasn't a process carried out with any animosity, because relations with Prince Charles had never been more civil. As with the dress auction that would be held in June 1997, the princess was giving up her past. It was a personal triumph, for at the height of her bulimia, the past had haunted her, and she said the condition made her "bring up my past." But she had survived, and she had grown strong. And she was heading in a new, exciting direction.

"In our new world, we won't be needing all this," said the princess, standing in the boys' sitting room. She was emptying boxes full of clothes, trinkets, ornaments, CDs, books, cassettes, unwanted gifts. This was her "nesting" process, which took place either late in an evening or on a Sunday afternoon.

She gave me a Cartier clock. It had been a wedding present but she thought its mother-of-pearl face and orange-and-black marble base were "hideous." A pile of things was heaped in the center of the room, and the princess invited members of staff to help themselves. Lily Piccio, a Filipina maid, could not believe her eyes, and carried whatever she could to the modest flat she shared with her sister. Aromatherapist Eileen Malone, mother of the cosmetics entrepreneur Jo Malone, received another ornate carriage clock that had been a wedding gift. "It will always remind you of me," said the princess. Psychic Rita Rogers was presented with a beautiful eighteen-carat gold Van Cleef & Arpels necklace in the shape of intertwining hearts, worth at least £8,000. For her eightieth birthday, *Washington Post* publisher Katharine Graham received a silver box from Asprey jewelers with *K* inscribed on the lid, and inside with "Devotion and admiration, from Diana." Even Christie's expert Meredith Etherington-Smith knew the kindness of the Boss. As a thank-you for cataloging and supervising the dress auction, the princess, who knew her love of starfish, had the Crown jewelers at Garrard create a solid gold starfish scattered with diamonds, and inscribed on the underside, "With fondest love from Diana."

Bags filled with clothes went begging, and healer friend Simone Simmons, who was visiting the princess almost every day, was another beneficiary. One afternoon when

Simone was there, the princess asked her to help herself. "What? You want me to take *all* these bags of clothes?" said a somewhat surprised Simone.

"No," said the princess, "those bags are for Paul," and I took at least three filled with clothes, handbags, and shoes for Maria.

Like the Filipina maid, Scotland Yard could not believe its eyes, or the truth, when officers entered our bedroom and found designer suits, which the princess had once worn, hanging in the wardrobe; when it found CDs in a box; when it found ornaments on our shelves; when it found the writing bureau. When it found around four hundred items that the princess had given me.

Nor could the Spencer family judge as credible the prodigiously giving nature of their own sister toward non-relatives. Lady Sarah McCorquodale would later say that she expected me, as the butler, to have nothing more than a signed photograph and a pair of cuff links. They wonder why I have always maintained that friends knew the princess better than her own family did.

A T EASTER, the princess returned to the K-Club and Barbuda with William and Harry. In May, she went on a three-day trip to Pakistan to visit Imran Khan and his wife, Jemima, daughter of her friend Lady Annabel Goldsmith. The princess wanted to learn more about Islam. On each visit, she rang me three times a day as, I'm sure, she did other friends. I honestly don't know what she would have done if she had lost her mobile telephone. It seemed to be permanently attached to her right ear.

While she was away, I was showing a new recruit the ropes at KP. The princess had hired an under-butler to carry out the duties I no longer had time to perform. Craig Weller, then twenty-three, had been trained by the team at Buckingham Palace, and his arrival made my life much easier.

The princess returned from Pakistan, and I learned a big secret. It was one that she should not have told me, but one that she was bursting to share. I think she managed to keep her lips sealed for all of five minutes.

"Paul! Paul!" she shouted from the first-floor landing before she ran down the stairs to my pantry. "I've got a secret! I've got a secret!"

By the time she reached the bottom step, it was a secret no longer. I was perplexed. This was not the normal manner in which she imparted information. She was wearing a pale blue Chanel suit when she told me: "You're going to get a medal, Paul!" Then she broke the news that I was to be decorated by the Queen at Buckingham with the Royal Victoria Medal, Her Majesty's personal order. "And it's about time too. It's all supposed to be a secret but, hey, you know all my secrets. I had to tell you. I'm so pleased for you, Paul," she said.

I was stunned. The Queen was going to decorate me in her birthday honors, to be announced in June, in recognition of my twenty-one years in royal service. Finally, she was rewarding me for all those years of walking recalcitrant corgis.

The princess seemed more excited than I. She told me: "After the investiture, I'll take you out to lunch and we will have champagne to celebrate at Mara's [San Lorenzos restaurant]. We'll make an occasion of it."

When the official announcement was made on June 17, the princess was in Washington attending the eightieth birthday party of Katharine Graham, but she still sent a congratulatory telemessage. It read: "A million heartfelt congratulations on your RVM—it's wonderful news and the boys and I are absolutely thrilled for you! Love from Diana, William, and Harry."

ON THE MORNING OF my thirty-ninth birthday, on June 6, I walked into my pantry and found an envelope on top of a gift-wrapped box on my desk. Inside was a gold, black-leather-strapped Longines wristwatch, and the attached note read: "Happy, Happy Birthday. With love from Diana."

On July 1, as the princess turned thirty-six, KP resembled a florist's shop again: around fifty separate arrangements of fresh flowers, dried flowers, and plants took over every vase and pot. They included sixty white roses from Gianni Versace and a dozen trumpet lilies from Giorgio Armani. The Prince of Wales sent a perfumed candle from Highgrove. Mohamed al-Fayed, owner of Harrods, sent a leather handbag. The princess's stepmother, Raine Spencer, was the first telephone caller of the day, followed by Lucia Flecha de Lima—waking in Washington at 3 A.M. so she could be among the first to wish the princess a happy birthday at eight, British time. That is the devotion of a true friend.

If my duty involved being one step ahead of the princess, it also required me to act on instinct for the young princes. William and Harry knew that every Christmas their mother and I would choose their presents, and, at the same time, I would be secretly selecting presents from them to the princess. I acted on their behalf for her thirty-sixth birthday. I knew exactly what to buy. Her collection of crystals was growing as she tapped into their healing and calming "energies," encouraged by friend Simone, who always wore a huge crystal pendant round her neck. On her advice, I went to a fossil and crystal expert in Chelsea, beside the London Oratory School, and entered a multicolored crystal maze. On a shelf stood an eighteen-inch stone tower, whose front section had been removed to expose its sparkling purple-and-violet crystal interior. I knew immediately that that was the gift, even if it did cost £500. On a weekend prior to her birthday, William was back from Eton and he sneaked down to my ground-floor storeroom while the princess sat upstairs in the sitting room. With both hands, I lifted this thick icicle-like rock out of the box, and William's face lit up. "That's brilliant, Paul!" he said.

Once it was wrapped, William cradled it in both hands and heaved it up the stairs. "Are you sure you can manage it, William?" I said, as he staggered under its weight.

Minutes later, I heard the tearing of paper, the rustling of tissue, and then a shriek of delight.

DOWN AT THE Old Barracks, my son Nick treasured his own crystal collection, inspired by what he had been shown by the princess, who had sat with him in the sitting room, leaving him spellbound with tales of what the magic crystals could bring. He had taken his little box, with tiny crystals embedded in cotton, to show to the princess. It made me smile to see my nine-year-old son in conversation with the princess. She sat on the edge of the sofa, peering into Nick's box. Both of them were engrossed. Nick told her how important it was to wash, clean, and reenergize the crystals.

"They need to be put under a bright light, Princess," he advised her.

So the princess decided to give her butler's son a duty to perform. She gave him some of her crystals and he brought them to the Old Barracks to wash them in a bowl of warm, soapy water. At night he left them to dry under the bright light of his bedside lamp. The next day, he went up to the palace to tell the princess that her crystals were fully recharged.

As a reward, the princess gave him a rose crystal and told him to place it on his bedside table, where it would soothe him as he slept. "I have exactly the same rose crystal next to me when I sleep," she told him, "so now you can have one too." Then she made him a promise. "After we all come back from our summer holidays, I will take you to the crystal factory and we will choose a nice big crystal for you."

Nick couldn't wait.

FOR THE PRINCESS'S BIRTHDAY, dress designer Jacques Azagury had created the most stunning, sparkling, beaded black evening gown, with low-cut neckline and black satin straps and bows. "You *must* wear that tonight!" I said, as she paraded up and down the sitting room. I went across the landing to the safe and pulled out some sapphires and diamonds.

"No, Paul, not those. I want to wear emeralds."

That night, she wore the dress to the centenary dinner of London's Tate Gallery, with the emerald-and-diamond bracelet Prince Charles had given her as a wedding gift, the emerald-and-diamond earrings he had bought for her twenty-second birthday, and Queen Mary's cabochon emerald-and-diamond choker, a wedding present from the Queen.

IT WAS DECIDED, after much doubt and discussion between the prince and princess, that Harry should follow in his brother's footsteps and go to Eton after he finished at Ludgrove.

"He will look good in a tailcoat, won't he, Paul?" said the princess. "Like a little penguin!" Harry had longed to go to Harrow so that he could be with a friend from the van Straubenzee family, so the news that he was going to look like a penguin at Eton hardly put a sparkle in his eyes.

Nor was William getting his own way: there was a pro-hunting rally in London and the young prince was eager to get out there, join the crowds, talk to the people and mix, but the princess would not allow him to go. She didn't "feel it was appropriate." Strangely, Tiggy Legge-Bourke joined the crowds, and her presence made the next day's headlines instead. William realized his mother's point.

There were three children who couldn't smile enough inside the palace, though. A sweet family came to visit for tea: a mother, a father, and their ten-, seven-, and five-year-old children. Since the age of four, the seven-year-old girl had had a brain tumor. It had been removed twice but had returned, and her parents had been told it was inoperable a third time. It had been the child's wish to have tea with the princess. I was sent out to get Barbie balloons and little toys for the table, and that family left with their memories captured in a disposable camera.

The treat for William and Harry was a summer holiday in Saint-Tropez on July 11 after the princess had turned down an offer to holiday with them on the island of Phuket in Thailand. Mother and sons jetted off to the South of France and the coastal home of Mohamed al-Fayed, his wife, Heini, and three of their youngest children. The princess was taking up an invitation extended to her in the spring; she had decided to say yes after lunching with her stepmother, Raine Spencer, at the RAC Club in the first week of July.

The Harrods owner—who lived the high life in London's Park Lane, complete with his own butlers—was by no means a close friend of the princess. He had been on the periphery of her life, with strong links to her family; he had been a friend of her late father, Earl Spencer, and Raine. Indeed, Raine was a regular visitor to his residence in the Bois de Boulogne district of Paris. This property was known as the Villa Windsor because it had formerly been the home of the Duke and Duchess of Windsor following the duke's abdication in December 1936.

Al-Fayed's fascination with all things royal led him to purchase the impressive property when the duchess, Wallis Simpson, died in 1986. Eleven years on, he was making his move on another figure blamed for bringing turbulence to the Windsor dynasty: Diana, Princess of Wales. For many years, he had made known to her his presence and hospitality. Whenever she shopped at his Knightsbridge store, he always popped up at her side. Every Christmas, without fail, he sent a Harrods hamper to KP. On birthdays, he sent the princess and the young princes a generous gift. In the eyes of the Boss, he was a true gentleman. He had learned from Raine Spencer all about the difficult times the princess had faced in the mid-nineties. All he wanted to do was help and be there if she needed him—out of respect for his friend, her late father, he had always told her.

Until that summer, the princess had always politely turned down his offers of hospitality. But the offer of a break in a villa overlooking a bay on the Côte d'Azur, with rigid security and private staff, proved irresistible. For

William and Harry, there was also the prospect of jet skiing, speedboat rides, and scuba diving. A near two-
hundred-foot yacht, the *Jonikal*, serviced by its own crew,
awaited them. It was the Egyptian multimillionaire's own
version of the royal yacht *Britannia*. What the princess
didn't know as she flew out there was that it had been
specifically bought to accommodate her and the princes.
No sooner had she said yes to his holiday invitation than
Mr. Al-Fayed took out his checkbook and purchased it for
an estimated £15 million. Nor did the princess realize that
her host would be providing something else to help lift her
spirits: the presence of his eldest son, Dodi, a film producer
who was engaged to be married later that year to American model Kelly Fisher. Mohamed al-Fayed requested his
son's company on the boat on July 15.

WHEN DODI AL-FAYED arrived on the *Jonikal* on
July 15, the press besieged the princess from a boat. I
was holding down the fort back at KP, overseeing a redeco-
ration of the princess's sitting room. She had brought in her
old friend Dudley Poplak once more to work his magic and
transform her favorite room from pink and cream to something "a little more professional and mature"—creams,
golds, and blues. The striped sofas were reupholstered in
cream; peach cushions replaced with blue and gold. A new
cream-upholstered long stool arrived, on cabriole legs. The
princess loved pink—even the paper used for her internal
memos was pink—but that summer she was erasing it from
her world.

As the upholsterers, carpet fitters, and curtain makers
moved into the sitting room, the princess rang me constantly. She was regretting a spontaneous drop-in she had
made on the press boat to ask them how long they intended to remain in position taking photographs. Before
leaving, she had teased them. "I'm going to shock the
world when I make my next announcement!"

At KP, comptroller Michael Gibbins was dealing with
the fallout, and the princess instructed him to issue this

statement: "Diana, Princess of Wales wishes to make it clear that she did not give any exclusive interviews to reporters yesterday. Her purpose in talking to some journalists was merely to enquire how long they intended to remain in the south of France as the oppressive media presence was causing great distress to all the children. There was no discussion of the possibility of any statement being issued in the future."

The princess was ringing me at KP up to eight times a day from the *Jonikal*. In one typically marathon call, she told me that she was going to get back at the media—using her leopard-skin-print swimsuit. "I'm going to wear it for the rest of the holiday. That will annoy them because they'll get the same picture every day!" she said. Sure enough, the papers were filled that week with her on the beach, on the boat, on the jet ski, diving into the water always wearing her leopard-skin swimsuit.

What shattered the fun was the news that her friend Gianni Versace had been shot dead outside his mansion in Miami. At the end of the autumn, he had been due to send an entire winter wardrobe to the princess. For that month's *Vanity Fair* magazine, she was pictured wearing a Versace dress on the front cover. News of his death sent the princess into overdrive. Every hour, I had a frantic call from her. "We must get hold of Elton John!" she said. "He's somewhere in the South of France. His home in Windsor will have the number."

I didn't get the chance to say that Elton had called KP the previous day, leaving his contact details. The tragedy of Versace's murder had ended a nine-month silence between the princess and the singer, and brought about a long-overdue reconciliation. She had fallen out with him after a donated photograph of her and her sons had been used "inappropriately" in Versace's book, *Rock and Royalty*. The princess was horrified when she saw that the family image had been used among photographs of semi-naked male models. She was deeply worried about what the Queen would think. The use of the photographs had nothing to do with Elton, but because he had been the go-between, she had blamed him, and the dispute had festered on both sides. That rift was healed in shared grief, and the princess comforted Elton at Versace's funeral on July 22, as she sat with an arm around him.

In a phone call, she told me that speaking to Elton again was "like old times." She added: "He has been so understanding and told me that isn't it ironic that we can make something good out of tragedy and mend our friendship. He said Gianni would like it. Wasn't that sweet of him?"

THE BOSS WAS PANICKING. The private jet that was due to bring her and the boys home had a mechanical fault on the airport tarmac in Nice. "I must come back, Paul. I have a serious public engagement at a hospital tomorrow," she said, on Sunday, July 20. They should have been back for 6 P.M. but she was on the phone, stranded, at 8:30 P.M. Eventually, they made it back at midnight. "Oh, it's so good to be home," she said. She always liked coming home.

"So, how was it?" I asked.

"Wonderful. We had a great and normal time." Then she went to bed.

The next day, normal duty would resume: Meredith Etherington-Smith for lunch, and Mike Whitlam from the British Red Cross for tea.

THAT LATE SUMMER I read the tabloid newspapers with incredulity as two names occupied all headlines, Diana and Dodi, and with disbelief at the journalists' assertions that this was the princess's "first serious relationship since her divorce." It was an absurd thing to suggest and the princess was worried that many people "would read too much into this." She had known Dodi for less than two months, and she *never* rushed into making up her mind about any man.

All the princess's closest friends know the identity of the only man with whom she had enjoyed a happy, long-term, serious relationship since her divorce. And it was *not* Dodi al-Fayed. It was someone whose relationship with her was formed on foundations far deeper and more meaningful than the brief spiritual connection she had made with the soft-spoken Harrods heir. He spent a total of ten minutes at KP in their entire time together. It is wrong—and therefore not true to the memory of the princess—to allow the world to accept the notion that the princess had decided Dodi was "the One." It is true that she was captivated by his company, enthralled by his charm, excited at the novelty of his lavish romance. But "the One" he most certainly was not. In fact, while her head was dizzy from jetting around Europe, her heart was, I am convinced, still in London.

Mohamed al-Fayed himself joined the speculative frenzy. He was reported as saying, "I'm like a father to Diana." With all due respect to him, that was never the case and, in the solitude of KP, it seemed to me that this entire Diana-Dodi relationship was heading into fantasyland. Lucia Flecha de Lima's ambassador husband, Paulo, was a father figure. Lord Attenborough was a father figure. Mr. Al-Fayed could only claim, at best, to have had a distant avuncular role in her life. He was exceedingly kind, but he was as much a father to the princess as Dodi was "the One."

In fact, to me, Dodi wasn't even Dodi. He was called "Sister." That was the code name given to him by the princess so that we could refer to him openly. When the princess said, "What do you think my sister would say?" or "Has my sister called?," she was not referring to Lady Sarah McCorquodale or Lady Jane Fellowes, but him.

She had been swept off her feet, intoxicated by Dodi's extravagance and his generous nature. He had a jet-set life and toys that offered a royal lifestyle without the suffocating restrictions.

"Can I take you to dinner?" he had asked in a phone call to KP.

"Of course," replied the princess. "When?"

"Tomorrow night."

"Where are we going?"

"Paris," he said, and the princess was high with excitement.

Dodi was going all out to impress her: arranging a helicopter to whisk her across the Channel, accommodating her in the family-owned Ritz Hotel and its Imperial Suite. I packed everything she would need into her Versace shoulder bag. She left for the night, leaving nanny Olga Powell and me to look after William and Harry.

That Saturday evening, July 26, she rang me from the suite. "Oh, Paul, it's wonderful. Wonderful!" she squealed. "And he's just given me a present. I couldn't wait for him to leave so that I could tell you. He has bought me the most beautiful gold watch surrounded by diamonds. I've *never* seen anything so beautiful."

She was like a sixteen-year-old girl, and her happiness was contagious.

It was on that day that she had visited Villa Windsor—where it was suggested that she and Dodi had been making plans to live. Not according to the princess. "We didn't stay long. The rooms are like a mausoleum. I couldn't live there! It's full of ghosts," she said. She asked me to buy a black crocodile picture frame from Asprey so that she could send Dodi a photograph of herself. He had requested one.

"You can't dedicate the photograph to him. You don't know who it will be shown to," I warned her. The frame was bought and she put the photograph in it. But, tellingly, she heeded my cautionary advice and didn't personalize it with a message or her signature.

She arrived back at KP, bearing gifts for Maria and me. She pulled out of her shoulder bag two peach robes, each with an embroidered crest of the Ritz Hotel. "I'm sure they'll suit Maria. Just not sure how you'll look in peach!" she joked.

That final week of July, the princess chose to make a hard decision. Her head told her to break off her previous relationship. Dodi, too, had decided to call off his engagement to Kelly Fisher. Both were single adults again. William and Harry were to spend August with Prince Charles in a vacation that would end at Balmoral. The princess joined Dodi, this time alone, from July 31 to August 4, back aboard the *Jonikal* in the Mediterranean, cruising from Corsica to Sardinia, then returned home to get back on the humanitarian path.

A GLOBAL MAP PEPPERED with red pins was affixed to cardboard and propped against the back of a chair in the corner of the KP sitting room. With the help of Mike Whitlam, the princess had identified the most land-mined countries of the world—from Georgia to Korea, Angola to Vietnam—and each pin denoted a danger area, and a mission to be accomplished.

Following up the Angola trip, the princess had planned to take her anti–land mine crusade to Georgia in the former Soviet Union, but the British government had deemed the trip too risky, so plans had to be canceled. Instead, the tour switched to the former Yugoslavia and Bosnia from August 8 to 10, accompanied by the Landmine Survivors Network (LSN) and Bill Deedes from the *Daily Telegraph*.

On the first night, we stayed in private accommodation provided for us in the hills of Tuzla. That night, the capacity of princess and butler to deal with anything remotely hi-tech was put to the test. Give me a knife, fork, and seating plan, and I will take on the best. Give me an electronic gadget, and I'm useless. When Dodi provided a satellite telephone for the princess to keep in touch from Bosnia, the two of us had looked at it helplessly. There we were, outside a mountaintop house, the princess holding out a compass to tell me the direction of the satellite, while I, having unpacked the machine, rushed into the undergrowth to find a signal.

"Is it working yet?" I called, and the princess could hardly speak for laughing. Then, at last, we found a signal and she made contact.

T HE NEXT DAY, we traveled in a group of five in a Land Cruiser, and the princess insisted on riding in the front passenger seat. Beside me in the backseat were

Americans Jerry White and Ken Rutherford, who had founded the LSN after they had become civilian victims of land mines. Jerry had lost a leg; Ken had lost both. They shared the princess's sense of humor. As she got into the front seat, they would start to clamber awkwardly into the back, and she would swivel round and say to them: "You can take your legs off, boys!" and that broke the ice for the two men. They'd felt that because she was "royalty," they had to keep their artificial limbs attached.

As we traveled toward Sarajevo along dusty, primitive roads, the princess nibbled fruit or sipped Evian water from a plastic bottle. Talk focused on the known fact that a land mine victim can recall exactly where and when—date and time—the accident happened. "It is etched on their memories forever," the princess added.

Jerry told of his accident, then Ken recalled his. The princess said: "My accident was on July twenty-ninth, 1981."

There were puzzled looks all round. Not even I knew instantly what she meant. Then the penny dropped and everyone laughed. Until the princess spotted a lady carrying a bunch of flowers, walking through the gate of a cemetery.

"Stop! Stop now!" The vehicle pulled onto the side of the road. The princess slid back the door, jumped out, and galloped through a hole in a brick wall, weaving through the rows of headstones until she reached the lady. It transpired that she had lost her eighteen-year-old son in the former Yugoslavia's civil war. While the grieving mother arranged the flowers at the graveside, the princess sat with her and talked. After about five minutes, the princess stood up, and both women cupped each other's faces in their hands and said farewell.

We went on to stay at the Elephant Hotel in Sarajevo. The princess wanted to use the satellite telephone again, so I spent half the evening hanging out of the window, waving the receiver around. "No . . . Yes . . . no . . . Yes," said the princess, indicating whether or not she had a signal.

Dodi had been shopping for a new car, even though he had enough to fill a parking lot. Now he wanted to buy a silver Lamborghini, and he told her that he was going to buy her a surprise present. His father was parading himself at the Craven Cottage home of Fulham Football Club, which he had purchased for around £7 million, pledging to invest more than £20 million in the transfer market. On a less grand scale, he sent a £5,000 wide-screen Sony television from Harrods to KP as a gift for William and Harry, together with two laptop computers, one of which the princess gave to my boys. With Mr. Al-Fayed making it clear that money was no object, and his son flaunting his extravagance, a niggling doubt wrestled with the princess's excitement. It was all becoming a bit too much.

We drove into Sarajevo and visited a hillside shantytown with a priest as our escort. There, we met a fifteen-year-old girl in a home crudely constructed out of brick and topped with corrugated tin. She had no parents and had lost a leg while foraging through a refuse pile to find a meal for the younger brother and sister in her care. The press, and indeed the princess, thought the plight of this teenage girl was harrowing. But while the reporters and photographers focused their attention on one more land mine victim, I caught the princess's eye and drew her attention to a curtained-off back room. The two of us managed to step into it without being followed by a lens. As our eyes adjusted to the darkness, we saw the teenager's skeletal four-year-old sister on a stinking mattress in a corner of the room. She was severely mentally handicapped. She had soiled her bed and was drenched in her own urine. Her eyes were closed.

We didn't say a word. I just watched as the princess walked over to the bed, crouched, and picked her up. She cradled the tiny frame to her and stroked the wasted arms and legs.

The child opened her eyes, which had no pupils. She was blind. As I stood at the Boss's shoulder, I witnessed something very special, a simple act of humanity, an action that personified the woman I knew so well. Now I could see for myself the worth of those notes she had given me from Calcutta.

She performed countless other humanitarian acts on that brief mission, but that one I shall never forget.

On the flight back to Britain, the princess, Bill Deedes, and I sat together. The Boss decided to make a short toast. Raising a glass, she said: "Here's to our next country."

When we returned to KP, she was already focused on her next land mine mission: to Cambodia and Vietnam, in October 1997.

THIRTEEN

GOODBYE,
YOUR ROYAL HIGHNESS

RAPTUROUS APPLAUSE erupted around me as "Beauty" and "the Beast" took their bows on stage to a standing ovation at London's Dominion Theatre. It was the night of August 30, 1997, my final chance of relaxation, and I had taken in a musical with my family before the Boss returned from Paris the following day. She was spending her last night of an impromptu summer holiday with Dodi in the Imperial Suite of the Ritz Hotel.

Back at the Old Barracks, Maria, my brother Graham, his wife, Jayne, and I sat in the lounge, clasping mugs of coffee, reliving the highlights of one of the princess's favorite musicals.

I was the first to retire to bed, ready to return to 7 A.M. starts at KP, looking forward to seeing the princess for the first time since August 15 and catching up on all her gossip. She had plenty to tell me. She had made that clear in our last telephone conversation. There was also a lot to be planned before an autumn land mine mission.

Shortly after midnight, the telephone rang. It was Lucia Flecha de Lima, and she was frantic. She had been at home in Washington when Mel French, chief of protocol for

President Clinton at the White House, had rung to inform her about a car accident involving the princess. She had seen the reports on CNN. Lucia didn't yet have the new number for the princess's mobile. I knew that the princess never went anywhere without it. So I rang it, not even considering that she wouldn't answer. She always answered. It rang, then clicked into the automated answering service. Maria made more coffee. I rang again. And rang. We sat around the kitchen table. And I rang and rang and rang.

Over the years, I had repeatedly told the Boss that if she was ever in trouble, she should get to a public restroom, lock herself in a cubicle, and call me. "I will always come and get you, no matter where you are," I told her.

Now on the fateful night of her accident, August 30, she was in trouble. Her phone was ringing without answer, and I felt helpless.

I left the Old Barracks and ran across the green, up the road alongside the palace, and into the office. Comptroller Michael Gibbins, personal assistant Jackie Allen, driver Colin Tebbutt, and secretaries Jo Greenstead and Jane Harris were there. Anxious faces everywhere. Someone made coffee. Michael, who was chain-smoking, manned the telephone on the desk in his private office, liaising with the Queen's private secretary at Balmoral, while Jackie and I sat outside in the general office.

The first call came through at about 12:30 A.M., and it confirmed what Lucia Flecha de Lima had told me: there had been a car accident in Paris. But it didn't seem to have been serious.

Within the hour, there was a second call. It *was* serious. Dodi was dead. The princess had suffered injuries, believed to be a broken arm and a fractured pelvis. I must get there, I thought. She'll need me. Jackie Allen started to book flights for me and driver Colin. He was chosen because, as a former royalty protection officer, he was well used to making unemotional decisions. All British Airways offices in London were closed, so the tickets had to be booked via its offices in New York.

At four o'clock, Michael picked up the telephone again.

Jackie went into the room. Minutes later, she emerged. She told me to take a seat, and put an arm around me. "Paul, you're going to have to be strong. I'm sorry to have to tell you this, but the princess has died."

THE PRINCESS HAD BEEN pronounced dead an hour earlier, at 3 A.M., after failing to survive emergency surgery. An invisible force knocked me back and winded me. If I had screamed, no sound would have come out. Complete emptiness. Raw pain. Jackie and I sat there and cried.

Then duty, engaged on some kind of autopilot, kicked out emotion. She needs me more than ever now, I thought.

I RANG MARIA at the Old Barracks. "The princess has died. I'm going to Paris." The plane tickets were booked. I rushed home to pack a small overnight bag, then ran back to Nos. 8 and 9. I walked through the back door into a home that had been expecting her. Its silence hit me. Within twelve hours, her voice and giggling would have filled that void.

I walked around. Everything was how she had left it. I went to her desk. All neat and tidy: three miniature clocks ticking quietly, telling the same time; a dozen pencils in a beaker; the Quink bottle to one side; the fountain pen in the inkstand; a memo sheet containing her "word list" of good vocabulary to use in correspondence. She had no qualms admitting being a bad speller.

Then my eyes found what I had been searching for: the rosary beads given to her by Mother Teresa, draped round a miniature marble statue of Jesus Christ, that stood next to two statuettes of Our Lady, one white, one ocher, beneath the lampshade. I picked up the rosary beads and slipped them into my pocket. I went into the dressing room and approached the table in front of the mirror where she got ready every morning, where the hairdressers styled her hair. There was the miniature clock, which told her whether she was late or not; half-used bottles of her fa-

vorite perfumes, Faubourg 24 by Hermès, and Heritage by
Guerlain; her Pantene hairspray; a glass full of cotton buds;
rows of lipsticks in a plastic container. I took one lipstick
and powder off her dressing table and placed them inside
a leather Gladstone bag with the gold *D* and coronet emblem, especially made for her in the previous year. I did *not*
take any clothes. I drew all the curtains, then took the
princess's jewelry and placed it in the safe.

I walked outside to join Colin Tebbutt. There was one
last thing I needed to do, because I knew we couldn't
leave these most private rooms—the sitting room, bedroom, dressing room—unguarded as we flew to Paris. It
was her world. It needed protecting. Colin and I went
around, shutting the doors and sealing them with thick
parcel tape. We added labels, which we then signed, denying access to the all and sundry I feared would come
marching through within the next twenty-four hours.

Colin and I drove to Heathrow for the first flight to
Paris. Thank God he was there, with his knowledge of the
protocols of VIP airport procedures. On the flight over, I
hardly said a word. All I could hear was the princess's
voice. The last conversation. The last time I had seen her.
Her laughter. Her eagerness to come home and see
William and Harry.

How would I find her? How would I cope?

Paris. She hadn't even wanted to go to Paris.

Why? Why? Why?

As I flew across the English Channel, Lucia Flecha de
Lima was boarding the first available plane from Washington to London.

M ARIA WAS WAKING our sons. Twelve-year-old
Alexander had heard the news from the conversations on the landing, and was sitting up in bed, saying nothing. Nine-year-old Nick had also heard. He was lying on his
front, the pillow over his head, sobbing his little heart out.
"She was going to take me to the crystal factory. She was
going to take me to the crystal factory."

That Sunday, Maria never got dressed: the telephone rang constantly.

I arrived in Paris to do what the princess would have expected.

BRITAIN'S ASHEN-FACED ambassador to France, Sir Michael Jay, and his wife, Sylvia, met us at the British Embassy. After coffee, I took Mrs. Jay to one side. "I am worried that the princess will be dressed in an awful shroud, and she wouldn't like that," I said.

Mrs. Jay understood. "Come with me, and we'll do something about it," she said.

She took me to a rather grand suite of rooms, and opened a large Louis XIV–style wardrobe. "If there is anything suitable in here, please take it," she said.

"It has to be black, and possibly three-quarter-length with a high neckline," I explained.

Mrs. Jay riffled through her hangers and pulled out a black woolen three-quarter-length cocktail dress with a shawl collar. "That's perfect," I said, and we slipped a pair of black shoes into the princess's Gladstone bag. The dress was placed in a hanging bag, and we set off on the short journey to the Pitie-Salpetrière Hospital. As we arrived at the front entrance of the eight-story hospital, Mrs. Jay, who had seen the princess in the early hours of the morning, squeezed my hand. "Be brave," she said.

I remember the muggy heat and endless empty corridors, as if the whole place had been evacuated. On the second floor, we walked out of the lift into a hive of activity. Doctors milling around in white overalls. Nurses rushing around. Policemen standing guard. We were ushered into a small office. In broken English, the chief surgeon expressed his sympathy and explained that nothing could have been done to save the princess. Then we were led down yet another corridor with empty rooms at either side. At the end, two gendarmes stood to either side of a doorway. That's where the princess is, I thought.

We passed the policemen, entered the next room on the right, and were introduced to a Roman Catholic priest, Father Clochard-Bossuet, and an Anglican priest, the Reverend Martin Draper. It had been Father Clochard-Bossuet who had administered the last rites, and he told me how he had anointed the princess with holy oil. My mind flashed back to all those times when the princess and I had gone down to the Carmelite Church in Kensington Church Street, lit candles, and prayed together.

In Paris, Colin and I drank coffee and waited with the priests. Chief nursing officer Beatrice Humbert walked into the room, wearing her white coat. It was about eleven o'clock. She told us we would be going in to see the princess shortly.

I said: "I really do not want this to turn into a peep show. I need to be informed of everyone who wants to enter the room where the princess is lying." The nurse completely understood my anxieties about privacy, and left the room to make sure the instructions were kept.

Eventually it was time to see the princess. I don't know how I stood up. Nurse Humbert held my hand tightly, and Colin took my arm. We went out and past the two gendarmes, who bowed their heads. The door opened into dimness. Daylight sneaked through the slits of the almost-closed Venetian blinds over the windows. One wall light provided the only illumination. A lady and a gentleman undertaker stood like statues in the corner. The silence was broken only by the whirring of a large fan.

Then I saw her. The woman I had looked after for so long was lying on a bed with its headboard to the wall. A white cotton sheet was pulled up to her neck. Nurse Humbert and Colin took my weight as I leaned into them, wanting to look away, needing to be by her side.

The reality struck me in that room, and I sobbed. I approached the side of the bed, wanting her to open her large, blue eyes, wanting to see her smile, wanting her to be asleep. What I witnessed before me was indescribable, and it is not appropriate to explain further. But, regardless of how she looked, I wanted to hold her, as I had so many times before. I wanted to make things better, as I had so many times before. The draft of the fan came across me as it turned slowly: the princess's eyelashes moved. What I would have done for those eyes to open.

I looked up and noticed that the only flowers in the room were two dozen roses from the former French president, Valéry Giscard d'Estaing, and his wife. All that kept me strong in that room was the spiritual belief the Boss had fostered in me. She had not been afraid of death since she had witnessed the passing of Adrian Ward-Jackson. "When a person dies, its spirit hangs around to watch for a while," I heard her say, from long ago when my mum had died. That thought was my only comfort. I believed that her spirit was still in that room above her broken body, a soul waiting to begin its journey, as she would have put it.

I wiped my eyes, gathered my strength, and informed Nurse Humbert that I had brought a black cocktail outfit and shoes in which to dress the princess, along with her lipstick and powder. Then I took Mother Teresa's ivory rosary beads out of my pocket and gave them to the nurse. "Can you please place these in the princess's hand? Thank you."

I had another task to perform: I had to go to the Ritz Hotel and collect the princess's possessions from the Imperial Suite. Colin Tebbutt, who was selflessly dealing with my grief and shock before his own, had organized transportation. It was only a short drive through Paris, and we were soon in the lobby.

I asked if Mr. Al-Fayed could be informed that I was there to collect the princess's belongings. Reception told me he was upstairs. We were left waiting in the main reception corridor for around forty-five minutes. Eventually we were informed by a messenger that Mr. Al-Fayed was too busy, and the princess's belongings had already been dispatched to England, via his country estate, Oxtead.

We headed back to the hospital, which was thronging with press. Colin and I sat in the room where we had met the priests. A telephone rang on a side table. I picked it up and recognized the voice of the Prince of Wales, ringing from Balmoral.

"Are you all right, Paul?" he asked.

"Yes, Your Royal Highness, thank you." I remember thinking, what an idiotic thing it was to say—I had never felt so bad in my life.

"Paul, you will come back with us on the Queen's Flight. We will be with you about six o'clock. Jane and Sarah, the princess's sisters, are coming with me," he said.

Then he said something that left emotion strangling my goodbye. "And William and Harry send their love, and the Queen wants me to extend her sympathy to you."

I asked Nurse Humbert if I could see the princess again. I composed myself, this time knowing what to expect. Yet, when I walked in, a different sight confronted me, one that brought dignity in death—something else the princess would have said. She now wore the black dress and shoes, her hair had been beautifully blow-dried and, in her hand, she held Mother Teresa's ivory rosary beads.

That afternoon Prince Charles arrived. He walked up to me, and the grief we both felt didn't need to be expressed. He stood opposite, touched my lapel, and said: "Are you sure you're all right?" I managed a nod.

When Lady Jane Fellowes and Lady Sarah McCorquodale saw me, they ran to me, flung their arms round me, and sobbed. In a way, one Windsor, two Spencers, and a butler were a great comfort to one another.

SHORTLY BEFORE SIX O'CLOCK I entered the room for the last time. The princess's body had been placed in a coffin. Much nonsense has been written, on both sides of the Atlantic, that she had told me she wanted to be buried in a casket with a window so that her face could be seen. She never said any such thing. Her body *was* placed inside a gray casket with a window, which was then placed inside a French oak coffin with a solid lid; I was told that the window was to meet French customs regulations.

I boarded the Queen's Flight BAe 146 with Prince Charles, Colin Tebbutt, Lady Jane, and Lady Sarah. All of us bringing the princess home.

How ironic that I took my seat on the plane next to Mark Bolland, the prince's aide, who was then his deputy private secretary; the media Svengali who, in later years, would be charged by St. James's Palace to create a proactive press strategy to make Camilla Parker Bowles acceptable as the partner of Prince Charles. I wondered what on earth he was doing on the plane, and hardly said a word to him. As tea was served in the cabin, I felt sick at the thought of the princess below us in the hold. Reduced to precious cargo.

The plane touched down at RAF Northolt, North London. We disembarked from that somber flight, stepping down metal stairs into a stiff, warm breeze that lifted everyone's hair. The evening sun was shining. We stood in a silent line on the edge of the airfield's apron. Almost in slow motion, eight airmen gently pulled the coffin out of the belly of the plane, the Royal Standard draping it. They walked in slow steps across the tarmac to the waiting hearse. Prince Charles headed north to be with William and Harry. Two sisters and a butler were charged with ensuring that the princess reached her next destination: first an undertaker's, and then the Chapel Royal at St. James's Palace.

The three cars in our cortège pulled away from the airfield and out onto the A40 dual carriageway to take us into the center of London. The most amazing sight brought me out of the blur and back into focus. As we drove, other cars braked and stopped. Every single motorist, on both sides of the road, on one of the busiest routes into the capital, stopped, turned off their engines, climbed out, and stood by their vehicles, heads bowed. People lined the footbridges and dropped flowers into our path. All I could think of was what the princess would have thought. "They're not stopping for me! Oh, no!" She would have curled up with embarrassment.

We arrived at an undertaker's in London, and the next person I saw was the princess's doctor, Dr. Peter Wheeler, who comforted everyone. "I have to attend an autopsy now," he said, "and it is not going to be easy."

"Why does she need another autopsy?" I asked, knowing she had already undergone one in Paris.

"The one performed in Paris was conducted on French soil, under French law. For our government's satisfaction, we have to do the same," he said, mentioning something else about forensic inspections and necessary procedures. An autopsy was held in 1997, and yet, by the end of 2003, no British inquest has been held. The princess's body rested overnight at the undertaker's.

The next day, there was only one place for me to be— back at KP as usual. Butler to a household without a mistress. At eight o'clock on that Monday morning, my first duty was to remove the parcel tape from around the doors. I was now back to guard her world. I was the only person who remained in apartment Nos. 8 and 9, save for Lily the maid, who tried to keep cleaning but sat there breaking down.

Michael Gibbins came to see me, armed with a difficult task. "Paul, I've been asked by St. James's Palace to collect all back-door keys." I refused, and it wasn't challenged.

The coldhearted treatment of the princess's staff was evident later that day when I learned the fate of dresser Angela Benjamin—whom the Boss had admired for her fresh approach, casual manner, and sense of humor. When she showed up for work like the rest of us, she found herself being escorted off the premises by policemen. She was told to gather her belongings, and was even watched as she unloaded her laundry from the tumble dryer. Her own grief didn't seem to matter. She was back on the train to Devon by lunchtime, wondering what on earth she had done wrong. The answer is clear: she was a warm human with genuine feelings in a robotic world run by a cold, unfeeling household that brings about banishment as easily as it commands loyalty.

THAT MORNING, I was unaware of what had happened to Angela. I had been at my desk in the pantry, staring out of the window into the courtyard. The desk diary was open in front of me. William and Harry's tailor was due. Then the Armani fitting. From upstairs, all I could hear was the princess's telephone ringing off the hook. Then, within the next hour, mine began to shrill: two lights blinking for both direct lines into the palace. I answered calls all day long. No sooner had I placed the receiver on its hook than it rang again. Another friend turning to me, as the closest person to the princess, to share their grief: the intimate friends, celebrity friends, alternative therapists, astrologers, psychics, fitness instructors, hairdressers, dress designers, members of the Royal Family. The list was endless. Anybody and everybody who had shared the princess's world rang that day.

Even her own family—Lady Sarah, Lady Jane, and their mother, Mrs. Frances Shand Kydd—came to me with their grief, all wanting to unload their feelings, ask their own questions, what had been the princess's innermost feelings about them. Some remembered. Some smiled at the memories. Some felt guilty and needed almost to absolve themselves. It was like being a priest, listening to a day of confessions and thoughts.

Eventually, by the second day, it was all becoming too much. Michael Gibbins and Jackie Allen decided, for my own good, to take messages on my behalf.

That week was the most distressing period of my life, and only a sense of duty got me through it. I had much more important things to occupy my mind than embittered family politics. From the very beginning, the Spencers included me in *every* decision, trusting my judgment and knowledge. I drew up my recommendations for the guest list for the funeral at Westminster Abbey, taking the princess's address book and making lists for her family of all her friends. Lady Sarah looked at it and questioned some high-profile names: George Michael, Chris de Burgh, Tom Hanks, Tom Cruise, Steven Spielberg. "But they *are* friends of the princess," I told her. I felt it summed up everything that I, the butler, not the family, knew who the princess's real friends were.

Back at the Old Barracks, Maria was attempting to comfort Mrs. Shand Kydd, who had descended, chain-smoking and drinking copious amounts of wine, saying how her daughter should never have been on that boat with the Al-Fayeds. She also felt that as a family, the Spencers should be in control of arrangements, not the Windsors. She said her son was going to make a speech "to be proud about." She talked of what a good mother she had been to the princess.

But I knew the truth of this family's relationship with the Boss—and it emerged some years later. If ever there was a real mother figure in the life of the princess, it was Lucia Flecha de Lima. There is absolutely no doubt that the princess viewed the relationship she shared with her as that of mother and daughter. Lucia treated the princess as if she were one of her own, and the comfort she gave the Boss in her most troubled times was enormous. On the Monday morning, the one person I longed to see was Lucia, and she arrived at the palace to be with me, accompanied by her daughter Beatrice.

Over four nights of that week, the princess—by now in an English oak, lead-lined coffin—lay in the Chapel Royal at St. James's Palace, whose rear walls backed onto the Mall. Mourners from all over the world began to gather, laying flowers and lighting candles. It was a public vigil that mirrored those that took place outside the gates of Kensington Palace.

I couldn't think of another person I would rather have been with at that time than Lucia, and we decided to go together to the chapel, she in a black dress, me in a black suit. The door creaked open and we looked down the nave, with its wooden pews on either side. There, ahead of us, in the chilly gray of that holy place, was the coffin, resting on a trestle before the altar. It struck me how lonely, cold, and unfamiliar it all was, but Lucia had spotted something else awry. Not one candle was lit. Not one flower was to be seen. Outside, the most spectacular remembrance garden was being laid by the public, and there were more flickering candles on the grass verges than there were stars in the night sky. Inside, there was nothing.

Lucia immediately found the Queen's chaplain, the Reverend Willie Booth. "Please, please, put some flowers from the people in here," she said. He said he would see what he could do.

For Lucia, it was not an emphatic enough response. The ambassador's wife clicked into assertive diplomacy. "I can only say that if there are no flowers in here when we return tomorrow, I will walk outside and tell the people that the princess has no flowers!"

At a time when the Queen had not yet traveled south from Balmoral, and harsh questions were being asked about the Windsors' distance from the mourning capital, the prospect of Lucia revealing the cold bareness of the chapel was the last thing a troubled monarchy needed. To ensure that her request was met, she took it upon herself to arrange for bouquets to be brought in by the princess's florist, John Carter. The next day, a bunch of white trumpet lilies lay on top of the coffin, sent by Prince Charles, and Lucia brought more flowers, white roses from the garden of Lord and Lady Palumbo. Lady Annabel Goldsmith spoke to me every day by telephone, and Rosa Monckton, who was the princess's best friend and sister rolled into one, came to KP with her husband to sit with me. We reminisced and cried together, and she, too, visited the chapel.

Susie Kassem came to the palace. She brought with her a candle. Together we went to the stairs, a landing point on one of the turns. We stopped beneath the huge Nelson Shanks portrait of the princess. Susie bent down and placed the lit candle on the carpet. We knelt together and prayed, sharing our own memories in silence.

Sources of strength from within the princess's inner circle were around me. Her friends, the people who knew her best, were rallying round as a team, ensuring that the farewell went perfectly.

WILLIAM AND HARRY came home with Prince Charles. As they met the crowds outside, and inspected the flowers left in tribute to their mother, I was waiting for them in the inner hallway. Harry rushed through the door and hugged me, his tears soaking my shirt. William reached out and shook my hand. The outward courage both boys were displaying was incredible, and they suddenly seemed so grown-up in their black suits and ties.

"We've come for a few things. We're just going upstairs," said William, and the two brothers went to the nursery and their sitting room.

"How are you coping, Paul?" said Prince Charles, who was clearly struggling with the enormity of events. He spoke politely and calmly, but he looked distant as he wandered around the apartment, lost in thought. He went upstairs. I followed, without being asked. At Highgrove, this would have been the height of presumption, but in a domain that was no longer his, I could not be dismissed. He was now in *my* territory. Whether a friend or the future King of England, no one was left out of my sight. I followed him into the sitting room, and he walked to the writing desk, standing over it. He opened a top drawer, looked up, saw me watching his every move, and closed it again.

William's voice broke the awkwardness. "Are you ready, Papa?" All four of us went down the stairs together.

"We'll see you soon, Paul. We'll be back," shouted Harry, before they all disappeared out of the front door.

A CLEAR, forensic-like bag arrived at KP. It contained the clothes the princess had been wearing when the chauffeur-driven Mercedes smashed into the thirteenth pillar of the Place de l'Alma. Lucia was with me at this most harrowing time. We now had something of the princess from Paris: a black top and white trousers. We stood at the bottom of the stairs with the bag. It didn't seem to matter that they were bloodstained and shredded by the surgical procedures. It was her. In my grief, I couldn't let go. I placed that bag in the refrigerator on the ground floor to preserve them.

Somehow, the thought of her spending the eve of her funeral in the Chapel Royal didn't seem appropriate, and I made my feelings known to both Lady Sarah McCorquodale and Michael Gibbins. KP was the princess's home; it was where she had spent most of her adult life. It seemed only right that she should come home for that final night and leave through the front door en route to Westminster Abbey. "Let me look after her one final night, and let her leave from the front door one last time," I pleaded. Lady Sarah wanted to bring her sister home, too, and the Queen approved the request.

The princess would spend her final night in the square room of the inner hallway on the ground floor. On that day, I had asked the police to bring flowers in from the street. I spent two hours arranging those flowers with the bouquets sent by friends—white lilies, white tulips, and white roses. These were placed in urns, perched on ornate pedestals and on the carpet. I also brought out every candlestick in the house, interspersing them among the greenery.

Then Roman Catholic priest Father Tony Parsons, from the Carmelite Church where the princess and I had prayed, arrived. He had with him two huge ivory church candles, which I placed on silver stands, and anointed the room with holy water. He handed me photocopies of appropriate prayers to read, and a text from the Gospel according to St. John. The two of us said a prayer together before he left.

I was left by myself in the middle of that room in my black suit, breathing in the thick scent of the flowers. In those silent minutes before the princess's coffin arrived, it was like waiting for her to come home on her birthday, with flowers everywhere. The double doors of the front entrance were open, and I heard the tires of the hearse approach. Her Royal Highness was carried into her home, the coffin draped in the red, gold, and blue of the Royal Standard.

I didn't light the candles, not then; I kept the ceiling lights on. Mrs. Shand Kydd visited with her grandchildren, spending time beside the coffin with Lady Jane and Lady Sarah, but there was no Earl Spencer that night.

The one person who wanted to be there—who *should* have been there—was Lucia. All week she had been asking to join me for the vigil. "Can I come and join you in prayer, Paul?" she asked, over and over again. But when I told Lady Sarah how important Lucia was to the princess, and how much she needed to be there that night, Lucia's request was denied. Lady Sarah only felt it appropriate for family to attend. The one woman, in my opinion, who was more family than any of them was refused her final, most personal of farewells.

Maria didn't want me to be at the palace by myself. "You look exhausted, and it's a big day tomorrow. You need to sleep," she protested, knowing it was in vain.

"She cannot be on her own. I *have* to be there."

All relatives had visited the princess by ten o'clock that night. I closed and bolted the front door, ready for the long night ahead with the princess. Instead of Lucia by my side, there was a stranger: the Right Reverend Richard Charteris, Bishop of London. He sat in prayer on a chair in the corridor leading to the front door. In the inner hallway, I turned off the lights and lit the candles, all fifty of them, creating dancing shadows on the surrounding yellow walls. I sat on a chair with my back to the bishop, my left hand on the coffin, my right hand supporting the prayers and biblical text on my lap. Despite my grief, and knowing that about thirty thousand people were also praying for her outside, I never slept a wink. I had a final special conversation with the princess, knowing she was listening. I talked to her, read to her, and prayed for her until 7 A.M.

When morning came, I left for the Old Barracks, showered, and changed for the funeral, then returned to the palace. It was a beautiful morning. The flowers still gave off a scent. The candles had burnt out. I waited to hear the slow, rolling wheels of the King's Troop gun carriage pull up outside. Eight soldiers, in scarlet Welsh Guard uniforms, filed in, lifted the coffin onto their interlinked arms, and took the first steps on the two-mile journey to Westminster Abbey. It was 9:10 that Saturday morning as they prepared to leave.

It was a sight to behold on our front doorstep: six black horses, mounted by men in ceremonial uniforms, wearing caps with a single gold feather, the First World War gun carriage behind, carrying the coffin, white lilies spilling over its sides. Then came the 1st Battalion Welsh Guards, standing at attention in their red tunics and bearskins. I looked across the road. Maria, Alexander, and Nick were huddled with the rest of the household staff.

The horses moved off, and the wheels of the carriage began to turn. I had stood in that same spot two weeks earlier, waving off the princess in her BMW. Now she was leaving again. For the last time.

FOURTEEN

A VERY
STRANGE BUSINESS

EARL SPENCER STOOD, looking down on the coffin from his elevated position in the ornate pulpit at Westminster Abbey. As he spoke, his words of a year ago rattled around in my mind, words he had directed at his sister: "Your mental problems . . . Your fickle friendships . . . I'm on the periphery of your life . . . and that no longer saddens me. The weakest of relationships out of all the sisters . . ."

That was what *I* heard as he delivered his emotionally charged masterpiece of oratory, speaking, as he said at the outset, "as the representative of a family in grief, in a country in mourning, before a world in shock."

I wasn't really listening to his public funeral address delivered in September 1997. As his voice echoed through God's house, I sat in the choir stalls, head bowed, suppressing disbelief. His carefully crafted words leaped from the pages in his hand and grabbed the monarchy by the throat, leaving the crowds outside applauding its public humiliation, while the master of the "blood family" seized the most inappropriate moment to claim the moral high ground. The hypocrisy masked by his eloquence was only known by the princess's real family: the people like me who knew her best, the surrogate family of chosen friends and confidants who knew the truth of this alienated brother-sister relationship.

I didn't see the closest of brothers walking to the pulpit that day. I saw a man who had once been close to her, in a faraway childhood; someone speaking on behalf of a remarkable adult he clearly loved, but didn't know. In a 1996 letter to her, he himself mentioned that he had only seen the princess around fifty times since she got married in 1981. As the abbey and the nation were riveted by his funeral address, I found myself caught between two flashing images: the earl speaking fondly in the elevated pulpit above me; the princess on the stairs, holding one of his letters, entirely different in tone.

In the abbey in 1997, he said, "Fundamentally she had not changed at all from the big sister who mothered me as a baby."

Then my mind flashed back to 1996: "After years of neglect on both sides, our relationship is the weakest I have with any of my sisters ... perhaps you have more time to notice that we seldom speak." And "I ... will always be there for you ... as a loving brother; albeit one who has, through fifteen years' absence, rather lost touch—to the extent I have to read Richard Kay [in the *Daily Mail*] to learn that you are coming to Althorp ..."

Back in the abbey: "Diana remained throughout a very insecure person ... most childlike in her desire to do good for others so she could release herself from deep feelings of unworthiness of which her eating disorders were merely a symptom." In 1996: "I fear for you. I know how manipulation and deceit are parts of the illness ... I pray that you are getting appropriate and sympathetic treatment for your mental problems."

The princess felt she was over her bulimia, but what upset her most was the suggestion that she was mentally ill. "Mental problems" was a phrase she had thought she would only ever hear from the sniping friends of Prince Charles.

Back in the abbey: "The world sensed this part of her

character and cherished her vulnerability, while admiring her for her honesty." In 1996: "I long ago accepted that I was a peripheral part of your life, and that no longer saddens me. Indeed, it's easier for me and my family to be in that position as I view the consternation and hurt your fickle friendship has caused so many. . . ."

Then he referred to William and Harry. "We will not allow them to suffer the anguish that regularly used to drive you to tearful despair. . . ." Another flashback: "I'm sorry but I've decided that the Garden House isn't a possible move now." That letter had driven the princess to tearful despair, not to mention his request for the Spencer tiara to be returned.

MANY COMMENTATORS viewed his speech at Westminster Abbey as the expression of his pain for a sister badly treated by the system. In my eyes, it was the words of a man riddled with guilt, focusing on childhood because of the distance that had come between them in adulthood. But he included some apt tributes, too, describing the "unique, the complex, the extraordinary, and irreplaceable Diana, whose beauty, both external and internal, will never be extinguished from our minds. " And he captured the "joy for life, transmitted wherever you took your smile, and the sparkle in those unforgettable eyes . . ."

I couldn't help feeling, though, that this man, who had caused his sister so much heartache in recent years, was not the man to speak on her behalf, to be the standard-bearer for the princess. He had turned down her plea for sanctuary at her ancestral home, yet was preparing to accept her into the grounds now that she was dead. I sat there thinking, How can he be so hypocritical in God's house?

Nor could I believe that, on a day of remembrance for a remarkable life, the earl had chosen such a moment to make a veiled attack on the Royal Family, reminding the world that he, his sisters, and mother were the blood family who would protect William and Harry "so that their souls are not simply immersed by duty."

At that point, I lifted my head and looked over at the Queen. Harry was stroking his face. William gazed ahead: pawns in a Spencer v. Windsor tussle. I thought of how the princess would have cringed at such a public declaration of ownership when she, of all people, respected the influence that Prince Charles and the Queen had over her sons.

I stared at the coffin draped in the Royal Standard, with a candle at each corner. On it, propped in a wreath of white roses, was a card from the young princes: "Mummy" had been written on the envelope. I clutched Maria's hand to my right and Nick's to my left. He was crying his heart out, and Alexander, on the other side of him, was doing his best to be strong. I looked straight ahead of me and saw Hillary Clinton. Then came another flashback: the princess telling me how, on a visit to the White House earlier that year, she had talked to Mrs. Clinton about one day living in America, and how the first lady had said the American people would embrace her. I choked back the tears once more.

Then Earl Spencer finished his address, and then came the sound of rippling applause, rolling in from the streets, through the Great West Door and down the nave. I looked around and saw Elton John and George Michael clapping. Euphoria was greeting a travesty of the truth, and the Queen's humiliation was complete.

An emotional outburst from a Spencer was received warmly by a people who, that week, had turned like never before against the House of Windsor. I felt a profound sense of injustice. The Queen had been a firm favorite of the princess, who corresponded with her until her death. She admired the Duke of Edinburgh for his cruel-to-be-kind mediation during the separation in 1992. But if that year had been the Queen's *annus horribilis*, then the six days before the princess's funeral in 1997 were the worst of weeks for a family that dithered in its transfer from Balmoral to London, hesitated over whether the Union Jack should fly at half-mast over Buckingham Palace, and was paralyzed by the enormity of the grief at the loss of the princess.

Never, it seemed, had the monarchy been in such a perilous state, thrown into a state of rare introspection and a review of its protocols. The address by Earl Spencer, followed by its rousing reception, exacerbated the crisis. Commentators rambled on about how the death of the princess had crystallized the gulf between an anachronistic monarchy and its modern-day people; how in death the princess had brought the House of Windsor to its knees, having proved to be no more than a nuisance in life. Even more dangerously, the republican arguments gathered momentum. In the maelstrom of that week, the saddest thing, and the truth that no one stopped to consider, was that the princess would have been turning in the coffin that had not yet been laid in the ground.

Columnists and television pundits seemed to relish the thought of her looking down from above, gleeful that an institution perceived as at the root of her isolation and suffering was floundering. Yet no one could have been more devoid of hatred than the princess, and no one wanted to see the House of Windsor survive more than she.

The fundamental point is that she did not blame the Royal Family for her isolation. The cause of her suffering and misery was Prince Charles, but she harbored no hatred toward her ex-husband or his parents. Indeed, if the princess could have spoken up that week, she would have *defended* the Windsors.

Of all the speeches that could have been made that week, the princess, in her simple terms, would have taken the attitudes of the mourners in a totally different direction. "I can never find the words to do justice to what I want to say," she often moaned (hence the "word list" on her desk). But in the October before her death, we had sat on the stairs at KP, trying to do just that. Over an hour we had sat, ruminating over her future, her fears, and the state of the monarchy. Teasing out her thoughts, putting them on paper. The next day, as was becoming usual, an envelope lay on the desk in my pantry. It contained a letter, written on her red-edged paper, which she gave to me.

If that letter could have been produced at her funeral, it would have thrown the weight of the "People's Princess" behind the Royal Family at a time when it needed it most. I reproduce it now to remove all doubt, and they are the thoughts, devoid of animosity, of the only Spencer whose views count:

> *I just long to hug my mother-in-law, and tell her how deeply I understand what goes on inside her. I understand the isolation, misconception, and lies that surround her and feel very strongly HER disappointment and confusion. I so want the monarchy to survive and realize the changes that will take [sic] to put "the show" on a new and healthy track. I, too, understand the fear the family have about change but we must, in order to reassure the public, as their indifference concerns me and should not be.*
>
> *I will fight for justice, and fight for my children and the monarchy . . .*

* * *

THE ROYAL TRAIN was waiting for us in London, and I was invited to the family-only burial service, seventy miles away in Northamptonshire at the Althorp estate. As the hearse carrying the princess collected a shower of flowers on its crawl through London and up the M1, I joined the Spencer family, Princes Charles, William, and Harry aboard the train in its smart burgundy carriages, pulled by the two locomotives named "Prince William" and "Prince Henry."

It was a strange, subdued, awkward journey, which took one and a half hours. I must have nodded off as soon as we pulled away, catching up on the sleep lost during the all-night vigil. I woke up at a station near Althorp. After a short drive to the family estate, we assembled in the drawing room before being taken into the grand dining room. It struck me, as we walked through the hallway, that the black-and-white marble floor was similar to that at Westminster Abbey.

Earl Spencer stood at the head of the long rosewood table, telling everyone where to sit. I found myself positioned rather awkwardly between the Boss's mother and

ex-husband, Mrs. Frances Shand Kydd to the left, Prince
Charles to the right. It wasn't easy for the prince to be sitting there on Spencer territory, having endured the anti-
Windsor tone of the earl's funeral address, knowing that
all eyes were not looking at him kindly. Conversation was
difficult and stilted, but, as the only one around that table
who knew how civility had been restored between the
prince and princess, I kept the small talk rattling along,
knowing that a conversation about Highgrove and its
gardens would see us through the three-course meal.

"You must come down and see the gardens sometime,"
said Prince Charles.

"I would love to, Your Royal Highness," I replied, knowing that it was unlikely.

William and Harry sat on the other side of their father,
nearer the foot of the table. Both boys were quiet, chipping
in with the polite conversation now and again.

As coffee was being served, a butler approached the
earl and whispered in his ear. He stood and left the room,
and he must have been gone for about five minutes. When
he returned, he announced: "Diana is home."

We crossed the chessboard hallway. I was walking just
behind Prince Charles and the boys. Looking down the
hallway from over their shoulders, I saw the hearse—and
something else. The Royal Standard that had been
draped over the coffin was gone, replaced by the white,
red, black, and gold of the Spencer flag, which only half
covered it. In the five minutes when the earl had been
out of the room, he had made the swap. Until my trial in
2002, everyone had believed that the princess had been
buried as they had last seen her, her coffin wrapped in
the standard. Buried as a royal. Buried as a princess. As
she would have wanted. Yet the carefully orchestrated
dignity of that day altered when the earl switched flags,
and the inappropriateness of such a petulant gesture
seemed lost on him. For the princess had been proud to
be royal, and had wept over the loss of her HRH status.
It seemed ironic that the Royal Family, having denied the
princess her HRH status, had respected her role and

given her a royal send-off with a state funeral, and her brother had reversed the gesture.

Eight soldiers from the Princess of Wales Regiment suddenly appeared and carried the princess on their shoulders, one step at a time, down toward the lake, across a temporary pontoon, and onto an island where a grave had been prepared. There was no carpet of flowers, only grass and the shadows of the trees, as shafts of sunlight shot through the canopy of leaves. All I could think was, What a lonely place to bury a woman who couldn't bear loneliness. It was as if a stranger had been planning the funeral and was getting it all terribly wrong. There is not a friend from the inner circle of the princess who agrees that it is an appropriate place for her to be buried. Like all her true friends, I knew there would be no returning to this island for me.

The burial service was thirty minutes long. What happened and what was said should remain private. At the end, I crouched down, picked up a handful of earth, and dropped it onto the gold plate that read: "Diana—Princess of Wales 1961–1997."

Then I stood, and said aloud: "Goodbye, Your Royal Highness."

AFTERWARD, I sat with Mrs. Frances Shand Kydd in the little white temple overlooking the lake. She smoked a cigarette and reflected: "Well, at least I had her for nine months, Paul. All on my own. She was mine for nine months."

I unknotted my black tie and undid the top few buttons of my shirt. Then I removed the gold cross and chain that she had given me to wear on the eve of the vigil. "This has protected me, but now it belongs with you," I said, and dropped it into the palm of her hand.

After she had finished two cigarettes, we all reconvened in the drawing room for a cup of tea. Everyone stood, huddled in little chattering groups. Then Earl Spencer approached the television in the corner of the room and switched it on. All eyes turned to the screen. The highlights of the funeral were being shown. Prince Charles and his sons stood there in silence. *Why are we watching this now?* I thought.

Then Earl Spencer's voice came out from the back of the television, filling the room. His echoing voice from Westminster Abbey. His speech from the pulpit. I have never been caught in such an awkward moment. But Prince Charles was clearly not standing for a repeat performance of the humiliation. He put down his cup and saucer and said to William and Harry, "I think it's about time we were leaving." As the earl's speech carried on in the background, the Windsors politely shook hands and said goodbye. I left shortly afterward.

I MUST HAVE WANDERED, lost, around Nos. 8 and 9 throughout September and October. I wasn't sleeping well, and when I did, I had a recurring nightmare: the princess was with me at KP, saying, "When are we going to tell people that I'm still alive?," and I would wake, convinced she was there. Or, Maria told me, I would cry in my sleep. At that time, I couldn't sit and grieve at the Old Barracks. I *needed* to be up at KP; it was the only place where I felt close to the princess.

I went from room to room, imagining the princess everywhere. In the sitting room curled up on the sofa. At the piano playing Rachmaninoff. At the dining table, wrapped in her robe, at breakfast. In the wardrobe room doing a catwalk pose. At her desk, head down, writing letters.

I sat on the newly upholstered sofa, holding a cushion with a *D* embroidered on it. I looked across at the fireplace and saw signs of the princess's humor: a red-and-white "I LIKE DI" sticker slapped incongruously onto the gray marble surround; a sign above it saying "CAUTION: PRINCESS ON BOARD." Two pairs of pink ballet shoes hung on the hook on the back of the door. In one corner on the floor, there was her school lunch box, with "D. SPENCER" on the lid.

I sat on the stairs, imagining her leaning over the banister—"Paul, are you there?"—the times we had composed letters together, the sound of the door closing, of her rushing in with her latest piece of gossip.

I sat on the chaise longue in her bedroom, staring at the small mountain of teddy bears on a sofa against the wall, with a gorilla, a panda, a rabbit, a frog, a pink elephant, a black panther, a hedgehog. There must have been about fifty.

On both bedside tables, there were pictures of William and Harry. And then I went over to the round table near the window, where there were five framed photographs of her husband with the boys, and one just of him, with other treasured images: her beloved father, Earl Spencer, a night out with Liza Minnelli, dancing with Wayne Sleep at the London Palladium, her sisters Jane and Sarah, her friends Lucia and Rosa.

Maria came up to visit me one day with a sandwich. "It's not doing you any good being here," she said. But it was. Somehow.

In the middle of one night, after experiencing the same recurring nightmare, I left the Old Barracks and went up to KP. Having just dreamed about the princess, I needed to sense her presence. Those who have experienced loss might understand what I did next. Those who have not might consider my action to be that of a madman. It seemed right at the time. I went into the L-shaped wardrobe room, pulled back the curtains where her dresses hung, and crawled into the gap between the floor and the clothes. I could smell her scent. In that position, I fell asleep for the night.

IN MID-OCTOBER, I was in that same wardrobe room with the princess's sisters and mother, Lady Sarah, Lady Jane, and Mrs. Frances Shand Kydd. The family was going through the clothes, deciding what to take. They asked me to fetch the princess's luggage, a matching set of three black leather suitcases. Each one was packed with blouses, skirts, cashmere cardigans, and shoes; cosmetics, bubble baths, and perfumes; then loaded into the back of estate cars outside the front door. None of these items had been valued before probate, but, as executors of the estate, the family was doing as it wished.

I had already been busy cataloging the entire contents of the apartments: linen, ornaments, jewelry, clothes, and personal effects. It was a painstaking task carried out with the help and expertise of Meredith Etherington-Smith from Christie's, who had cataloged the princess's dresses for the hugely successful auction in New York earlier in the summer. David Thomas, the Crown jeweler, also visited to finalize an inventory of the princess's collection. As I stood beside Lady Sarah in the wardrobe room, she removed a silk blouse that the princess had worn. Still attached to each sleeve were silver-and-red enamel heart-shaped cuff links. Without saying a word, Lady Sarah removed them, pressed them into my hand, and smiled. "If there is anything else you want, Paul, you only have to ask," she said.

I clasped the cuff links and said, "I have all that I need, and the memories are in my heart, but thank you."

Lady Sarah, who I knew had been closest to her sister of all the family, was an executor of the will, together with her mother. Such was their generosity at the time that they had used their discretion to vary the will, bequeathing to me £50,000 "as recognition of my duty and loyalty towards the princess." Lady Sarah continued rummaging through the clothes. Then she took out a black Versace dress and jacket, handed it to me, and said: "That's for Maria. She can wear it for the investiture."

The date had come through. The Queen was going to decorate me with the Royal Victorian Medal on November 13. I would return to Buckingham Palace for the first time since I had left the Queen's service ten years earlier.

IT WAS STRANGE to drive through the front gates of Buckingham Palace, across the forecourt, through the archway, and into the quadrangle, the red gravel raked flat for another event. I got out of the car, looked up to the top-floor windows, and showed Alexander and Nick where

Dad's first living quarters had been. I arrived there as a re-cipient in morning dress like everyone else, not as a servant in livery. I had not felt so nervous since my first day at work as a footman in 1976.

It was a bright, crisp winter's morning as we approached the glass veranda of the main entrance and entered the palace. Maria and the boys peeled off to take their places in the Ballroom. I could hear a string orchestra playing in the background as I joined the hundred other recipients of honors, all gathered in the Queen's Picture Gallery—where I had seen the princess cuddling her bridesmaids at her 1981 wedding. That day, the memories stalked me down every corridor and in every grand room as clocks and watches ticked toward 11 A.M. Then, in groups of ten, people were called to proceed through the gallery and wait at the threshold of the Ballroom, where an audience of five hundred people was witnessing a very British spectacle.

As I waited, I noticed a young lady sitting all alone on a sofa, directly beneath a Van Dyck portrait of King Charles I. "So what are you here for?" I asked, after introducing myself.

"The George Medal," said the soft-spoken twenty-two-year-old.

It is the highest medal that can be bestowed on a civilian for bravery. I wondered what on earth she had done. She was Lisa Potts, a nursery nurse who had used her body to shield children at a picnic while a deranged intruder wielded a machete, slashing her in the playground at St. Luke's infants school in Wolverhampton.

I looked at her hands, which were terribly scarred. "That's nothing compared to the injuries suffered by some of the children. Some of them were cut from their mouths to their ears," she said.

Burrell and Potts were asked to proceed to the Ballroom together. She was the star of the investiture, and it was a privilege to share the occasion with someone so coura-geous. I watched and waited as she approached Her Majesty and said a few words.

Then it was my turn to accept an honor that the princess

had said was in recognition of my twenty-one years in royal service, serving the Queen, Prince Charles, and herself. But then I got a surprise. The Lord Chamberlain's voice came across the microphone: "To be decorated with the Royal Victorian Medal for services to Diana, Princess of Wales, Mr. Paul Burrell."

No one had told me, but the Queen had felt it fitting that the award should focus on my loyalty to the princess. I bowed, shook her hand, and she pinned the medal to my lapel. "You don't know how happy I am to give this to you," said the Queen. "It means an awful lot, and thank you for all that you have done. What are you going to do now?"

I glanced over her shoulder and spotted an old colleague, Christopher Bray, the Queen's page. "Perhaps Christopher might need an extra hand, Your Majesty?"

She chortled. We shook hands again, I took two steps back, turned, and walked out of the room.

That night, a group of ten family and friends went to celebrate with me at San Lorenzo restaurant. Just as the princess had planned.

TWO WEEKS LATER, a letter arrived at the Old Barracks from the Chancellor of the Exchequer, Gordon Brown, informing me that I had been chosen as a member of the Diana, Princess of Wales Memorial Committee to help advise the government as to how the life of the princess could best be commemorated. I would be working alongside the princess's friends Rosa Monckton and Lord Attenborough on the committee set up to complement the work of the independent and recently established Diana, Princess of Wales Memorial Fund.

If there was a moment when the critics believed that I was nothing but a butler with "ideas above his station," then I suppose my appointment to the committee was when people who were not close to the princess began to snipe behind my back, misunderstanding my relationship with her. Such a misunderstanding perhaps wasn't helped by a comment piece in the editor's leader column of *The*

Times, headlined: "BUTLER POWER: PAUL BURRELL IS THE
BEST MAN TO SELECT THE DIANA MEMORIAL." It read:

> No man is a hero to his valet . . . nor no princess ei-
> ther a heroine to her butler . . . but the butlers and
> valets are the unsung and offstage heroes. They are
> among the select few to be admitted to the private
> reality behind the public masks of ceremony and
> razzmatazz. So the appointment of Paul Burrell . . . is
> a rare instance of life imitating art. For once, the but-
> ler is being consulted officially . . . Jeeves would have
> approved. But this is a problematic assignment . . .
> the Government is following wise precedents of fact,
> folklore and fiction. When in doubt, consult the but-
> ler as the discreet insider who really knows.

I think understandable pride made me somewhat deaf. I
couldn't hear the knives being sharpened behind my back.

WILLIAM AND HARRY returned to KP two weeks
before Christmas 1997. I had prepared the apartments with flowers and plants, to make them look as
homey as possible, and nanny Olga Powell was with me in
the sitting room, awaiting their arrival. The boys burst
through the front door in a jolly mood, looking forward to
Christmas at Sandringham.

I walked around the apartment with them, holding a
handful of yellow Post-it notes to label what should go
where, and who owned what item. The boys were moving,
with Prince Charles, within St. James's Palace, from an
apartment to York House, their new London base. William
and Harry scurried from room to room, gathering books,
cuddly toys, photographs, posters, videos, and paintings,
then decided which sofas, chairs, and rugs they wanted to
take with them. William was the more methodical of the
two. He mentioned jewelry, then dismissed it. "Oh, we can
do that in the new year, there is no rush," he said.

The one thing that struck me was how polite he was,

even when it came to selecting his *own* possessions. "Can I have this? . . . Would it be all right if I have this?"

"William," I said, "everything here is yours and Harry's. You can have whatever you want. There is no need to ask."

He walked into the L-shaped wardrobe room, and stood, facing a collection of Chanel, Versace, Jacques Azagury, and Catherine Walker creations. "What should we do with all of Mummy's clothes?" he asked.

"I'm not sure whether you are aware," I said, "but the Spencers are planning an exhibition at Althorp, and they very much want key possessions and costumes to be included in that—including the wedding dress."

"No!" William retorted sharply. "I definitely do not want them to have that."

"Why not?" said Harry, chipping in.

"I just don't, that's all," William snapped, "but they can have some of Mummy's dresses. We can do that in the new year too."

It had been the princess's wish for her wedding dress to be sent to the National Dress Collection at the Victoria and Albert Museum. Her elder son was making it clear that he didn't want it to go to Althorp. So where is it today? It's on display at Althorp.

Then William continued around the nursery corridor. "I'd like that rug, that sofa, that chair . . . those curtains, that drinks table . . ." And we remembered how the princess had spent £30,000 on new carpets two years earlier.

It was poignant to watch the two brothers going around their rooms, selecting items, and watching William take charge of his younger brother.

"Can I have my bed, please, Paul," Harry asked, "and that chest of drawers?"

"Oh, you don't want that, Harry!" said William, getting all paternal. "There's not enough room for *that*."

"Yes, there is," Harry shrieked, and I could see the princess shaking her head and smiling.

There was no dispute when they entered their sitting room downstairs, the location of their huge wide-screen television. "It's far too big for Highgrove. Can it go to York

House, please? It will fill one wall!" William said. He was always in charge of the electronics. I smiled because I sensed that Prince Charles would not approve. He hated the boys sitting in front of the television, watching mindless programs. He rarely watched television, except for documentaries.

Then we entered the sitting room, and I think that was when memories stopped them in their tracks, because this had been their mother's room, and they felt it. Silence descended. William stood looking at the photographs on the table. Harry stood over the writing desk, touching everything, in a daze.

After a few minutes, William's voice halted the reflection. "I want the giant hippo, Paul," he said, pointing at it. Mother and sons would all lie back against it to watch television.

When the tour was finished, the apartments were littered with yellow Post-it notes, items or furniture labeled "W—York House" or "H—York House."

As they searched through the video collection and flicked through the CDs, I remembered that 1997 was to be the first year *ever* that the princess would have had the boys to herself for Christmas Day; she had agreed in the summer with Prince Charles and the Queen that they could break away from the tradition of Sandringham. She had planned to spend Christmas with her sons at the K-Club in Barbuda.

But even though the princess was no longer with us, I still wanted them to have a reminder of a KP treat: a tradition they could take with them to Sandringham. I had prepared a Christmas stocking for each of them. As the boys were saying goodbye and rushing down the stairs, I stopped them. "Because I have always been responsible for making up your stockings every year, I could not let this year pass by without doing the same," I said. Surprise registered on both their faces. "I have even sewn up the tops so that you cannot get to the contents! I rather doubt they will survive, though, until Christmas morning," I said, handing over the knitted stockings the princess had used every year.

"Oh, they will, Paul," said William, "and thank you so, so much." And Harry ran to me and gave me a hug.

Together, we walked to the front door. "Now, you know exactly where I am. If you want *anything,* then all you have to do is call me," I said.

"We will, Paul," said Harry, "and we will see you in January when we return from skiing with Papa."

When their stockings were tucked safely into the back of the Land Rover Discovery with the rest of the belongings they had collected, they wound down their windows, William in the front, Harry in the back.

"Bye, Paul!" they shouted, as protection officer Graham Craker drove them away.

I had stood there so many times with the princess, waving them off. She always turned to me and said: "The house will be quiet now. I'll miss ma boys."

FROM THE CENTER of the princess's world at KP, I looked outward with dismay.

In its infancy, the Diana, Princess of Wales Memorial Fund was run by the princess's divorce solicitor, Anthony Julius. It seemed to me that he was taking charge of every aspect of her life, with Lady Sarah McCorquodale and Michael Gibbins following in his wake. I saw three people who didn't know the Boss intimately suddenly running her affairs. An independent charity set up in memory of the princess had none of her closest inner circle of friends helping to steer the project. I suddenly found myself on the periphery.

At the palace, I was getting used to visits from Mrs. Frances Shand Kydd. She would be in the sitting room with a bottle of wine, going through her daughter's correspondence, making unilateral decisions over what should be destroyed. She shredded more than fifty letters, and I witnessed history being destroyed. I felt it was wrong.

The Fund. The shredding. By the end of 1997, I felt I was losing control over a world the princess had expected me to control for so long. I had never felt so helpless. Suddenly *The Times* newspaper's lead article about "consulting the discreet insider who knows" seemed to count for nothing. It was not in my nature to stand by and watch everything roll out of control, but I found myself in a dilemma about whom I could discuss my concerns with. None of the Spencers would understand: I wasn't family. William and Harry were too young, and the Prince of Wales was an impossible counselor to seek. I'm not sure he would have listened, let alone understood. There was only one person who *would* listen: Her Majesty the Queen. I wouldn't need to go through the pompous royal household to get an audience. I knew that.

I picked up the telephone and rang someone close to the Queen, someone discreet whom I could trust.

"Do you think the Queen would see me, and spare me five minutes?" I asked.

"Leave it with me, and I will let you know."

The following day, the answer was delivered. "The Queen would be delighted to see you at two o'clock on Thursday, December 19. I think you know your way here."

In through the side door off Buckingham Palace Road. Past the policeman, who was expecting me. Down through the tiled underground corridors. Past the stores, wine cellars, linen room, and flower room, and into the tiny two-person lift. I knew my way around Buckingham Palace, even after such a long time away from its warrens.

As the lift doors opened, I stepped out into a familiar utility area before opening a huge oak door, and walking out onto the red carpet of the Queen's corridor, timing my arrival for exactly 1:55 P.M. I approached the narrow Pages' Vestibule, halfway along the corridor, where I had waited to serve the Queen so many times. I sat and waited now until she had finished her coffee after lunch. Then, virtually at the stroke of 2 P.M., a page said: "The Queen is ready for you now . . . It's Paul, Your Majesty."

There she was in her private sitting room. The diminutive figure stood at her desk in the bay window, wearing her half-rimmed spectacles. Government papers and red boxes were strewn across it. Nine or ten corgis were littered around the room. Some, from a generation I did not know, raised their heads and growled.

The Queen walked across to me, and I bowed before she extended a hand and said: "Hello, Paul, how are you?" The smile was as warm as it had ever been, even if the lady was slightly older, slightly grayer. She was dressed in blue, wearing three rows of pearls, and a huge heart-shaped diamond brooch.

She saw I was clutching a small offering. "A bunch of flowers, Your Majesty."

"How kind of you," she said, taking them, "and they do smell good."

She was relaxed, friendly, unguarded, and she knew from the informal briefing she had been given that certain matters regarding the princess were troubling me.

"It is a very strange business," she said, starting the conversation, and handing the flowers to her page.

"I know, Your Majesty. There is absolutely no one whom I can confide in. You are my only answer, and thank you for affording me the opportunity to speak with you. It means such a great deal to me."

Her Majesty asked me how I was coping, and I said I was keeping myself busy. She asked about Maria and the boys. I provided the update. Then I got to the point: sharing with her the internal politics at KP, how I felt the Memorial Fund was being handled, the characters involved, the problems I perceived. We spoke about Anthony Julius, about Lady Sarah, about Patrick Jephson, about my future, about the huge legal costs the Fund was incurring: £170,000 alone for October. Then we spoke about Dodi al-Fayed, and the princess's fascination with him.

It seemed the Queen had been under the same impression as the rest of the country: that the relationship was the start of a long-term union rather than a summer fling.

"Your Majesty, this romance would have ended in tears. The princess was aware that he had problems: money, drugs, drink, and even prostitutes, which will, I have no doubt, come out in the end." I continued: "I always said to the princess: 'Be in charge of your own environment.' But the truth was that she was not in control on that boat. He had the air-conditioning on full; he chose the boat's destination; he chose the food; he decided to go to Paris. She wanted to come home, Your Majesty. She wanted her independence back."

The Queen listened intently and, as she did on many subjects that day, gave a frank and honest opinion. She then told me how Mrs. Frances Shand Kydd had occasionally called her since August.

"May I say, Your Majesty, that you were very brave to be in!" I joked.

With that name raised, there was no better time to express my concerns about what I had witnessed at KP: the seemingly indiscriminate shredding of documentation, letters, and memos that, I felt, could have historical importance. "Your Majesty, I cannot allow history to be erased. I intend to protect the princess's world and keep safe her secrets, and I intend to keep documents and artifacts she gave me."

Again, the Queen listened. She did not object, and I think we both understood that I felt it was my duty to do something. I didn't need to go into detail about what items would be secured and where I would take them. The absence of a frown from the Queen was enough to tell me that I would simply deal with the matter in a way I felt appropriate.

I think she could empathize with what I was experiencing. She told me: "I remember that when my grandmother died, I went across to Marlborough House to find stickers on everything. They had all descended like vultures—and that, I know, is the most awful part following a personal loss."

Then we spoke about William and Harry, including their visit to collect possessions from KP.

I had never had such a long conversation with the Queen, and it was a privilege to be in her company for what turned into a personal and intimate meeting. It lasted, to the best of my recollection, from 2 P.M. to shortly before 5 P.M. Standing throughout. We did have ten years to catch up on, and it was like a reunion with a long-lost relative. It felt that informal.

Of course, the prospect of a butler having a near three-hour audience with the Queen was "fanciful rubbish," according to the newspapers in the days following the collapse of my theft trial at the Old Bailey in 2002. Incredulous royal experts dismissed it as "unthinkable" and "highly unlikely" and "pure fiction." "The Prime Minister only gets fifteen minutes, so it is unlikely that a butler would be granted such an audience," scoffed one disbelieving former member of staff.

The *Sun* newspaper waded in with its usual amount of accuracy, trumpeting how the meeting was three minutes long, and never went beyond an hour.

Then Buckingham Palace issued a statement to clear up the truth and enlighten a few people. The Queen's personal recollection was that "The meeting lasted *at least* ninety minutes."

Whatever the version, we seemed to be standing there for an inordinate amount of time. We might as well have been feeding the corgis.

Of course, we spoke at length about the princess. In fact, I told the Queen that Prince Charles was the one man she had truly loved all her life; knowing that the princess had, herself, relayed that same message in that room in February 1996.

As we spoke about the princess, the tone of the conversation changed. I could almost sense the Queen wishing the clock to turn back. "I tried to reach out to Diana so many times. I wrote many, many letters to her, Paul," she told me.

At that moment, I could visualize us in the sitting room, reading the kind correspondence from Buckingham Palace or Windsor Castle. "I know. I saw those letters, and the princess always replied. But the trouble was, Your Majesty, that you spoke in black and white, the princess spoke in color." I was suggesting that they were from different generations, speaking different languages.

For the first time in my life, I felt like embracing the Queen but, of course, she wasn't the princess, and it was impossible. I just stood there, listening to her and thinking that if Britain could have seen how genuine and warm she was toward the princess, there would have been no controversy about her distance in the immediate days after the princess's death. I remembered the note the princess had left me about the Queen: "I long to hug my mother-in-law."

I was witnessing the genuine concern of a mother-in-law, not a distant sovereign; someone who had sincerely tried to help, and the Boss knew that. Which was why she never regarded the Queen and the Duke of Edinburgh as enemies. The Queen knew that much, but she added, "My gestures were either not welcomed or simply misunderstood." And her sad frustration was evident—"and all one was attempting to do was help."

As the meeting neared its end, the Queen said one more thing to me. Looking over her half-rimmed spectacles, she said: "Be careful, Paul. No one has been as close to a member of my family as you have. There *are* powers at work in this country about which we have no knowledge." She fixed me with a stare with eyes that underlined her words. "Do you understand?"

EVER SINCE THE END of my trial, when I first detailed that meeting with the Queen, there has been much speculation, and scoffing, over the tone and meaning of the "Be careful" message from Her Majesty. So, what did she mean? All I know is what I heard. It wasn't quantified or expanded upon, neither was it melodramatically delivered. I walked away and accepted what had been said as it had been intended: as sound advice to be vigilant. In my opinion, she was telling me to be careful of everyone because no one more than the Queen understood the position in which I found myself, and the closeness I had shared with the princess.

The reference to the "powers at work in this country about which we have no knowledge" has often played on my mind in the intervening years and, yes, I have worried about it too. The Queen might have been referring to the power base of media barons and editors who can topple

individuals from their pedestals. She might have been referring to that unknown quantity called "the Establishment," an undefined, invisible network of interlocking
social circles of the great and the good. She might have
been referring to the domestic intelligence service of MI5
because, have no doubt, though the Queen may not know
of its secret work and darker practices, she is aware of the
power it is capable of wielding. Like the royal household,
the intelligence services are given carte blanche to act in a
way that is considered to be in the best interests of state
monarchy.

All I do know is that, within four years of Her Majesty's
warning, I was arrested and sent to trial for a crime I never
committed, in a case that barely had the legs to stand up.
All the time, the undercurrents running beneath the surface of that case were about the secrets of the princess.
Who had them? Where were they?

But, in all honesty, I cannot pinpoint what the Queen
was referring to. I have beaten myself up mentally many
times over why I didn't ask her at the time what she meant.
No one is more aware than I of the knowledge locked
away inside my head. In choosing to impart certain information to me, the princess ensured I shared a historic
knowledge. I was her independent witness to history, in the
same way that I was her witness to the letters she wrote
and received, the divorce papers she handled, and the will
she made.

She also shared with me her concern that she was constantly monitored. It is naïve of anyone to think that the
princess, from the moment she married Prince Charles,
would not have had her telephone calls bugged, or that the
associations she made were not checked. It is a matter of
routine that members of government and the Royal Family are monitored. She knew that. So, in that regard, "the
powers" were discreetly at work in all my years at Highgrove and KP. She made me constantly aware of it, and the
need to be vigilant. If there was one thing about life at KP
that the princess loathed, it was the inescapable feeling of
constantly being listened to or watched. It was one of the

reasons that she shed her police protection. She didn't trust the police as tools of the state. In fact, she had a deep-seated suspicion about anything and everything to do with the state.

When both of us were away from the palace, she even suspected that listening devices had been planted in apartments 8 and 9. Once, both of us moved all the furniture to one side in her sitting room and rolled up an Aztec-style rug, the blue fitted carpet, and its underlay. Then, we prised up the floorboards with screwdrivers. She was convinced there were listening devices in the palace but we found nothing. She worried about devices being placed in plug sockets, light switches, or lamps. Some will dismiss this kind of worrying as outright paranoia. If such worries were in isolation and devoid of rational reasoning, I would tend to agree. But the critics who were far too eager to dismiss her as paranoid didn't realize that she was acting on sound information received from someone who had worked for the British intelligence services; a man whose expertise, advice, and friendship the princess came to rely on.

Even another member of the Royal Family warned the princess: "You need to be discreet—even in your own home—because 'they' are listening all the time." (Before my trial, I witnessed, with my legal team, documented evidence that even my telephone lines, during the course of the police inquiry, had been "intercepted" without my knowledge, and at least twenty telephone numbers had been monitored.)

Armed with such advice, I defy anyone in the princess's position not to go on the hunt for the devices. When she found none, she called on the help of her ex–intelligence services friend. One weekend afternoon, he visited the palace, using a pseudonym. He carried out a sweep of the apartments to detect listening devices. Every room was checked. Nothing was found.

Then, in demonstration after demonstration, the princess and I were given a sharp lesson in high-tech surveillance techniques. But what startled the princess most was to learn that "monitoring" did not necessarily require devices to be planted in a household. So high-tech were the intelligence facilities that a conversation could be listened to from a surveillance van parked outside, transmitting a signal into the building and using mirrors to bounce it back. As a result, she took down the round convex mirror that hung above the marble fireplace opposite the window in the sitting room. She was not paranoid; she was being advised.

In the final two years of her life, the princess grew increasingly concerned about the security around her. Ever since the separation in 1992, she felt she had grown in stature, and she was ready to take on the world in her humanitarian mission. But, right or wrong, she felt that the stronger she became, the more she was regarded as a modernizing nuisance who was prepared to go out on a limb and do the unconventional. She was later proved right, to some degree, when her humanitarian work in Angola in early 1997 led to suggestions that she was a "loose cannon" who was doing more harm than good. In the autumn of 1996, she had an overpowering feeling that she was "in the way." She certainly felt that "the system" didn't appreciate her work and that, for as long as she was on the scene, Prince Charles could never properly move on. "I have become strong, and they don't like it when I am able to do good and stand on my own two feet without them," she said.

In one particular period of anxiety, in October 1996, the princess called me from my pantry. I met her halfway down the stairs. A question of self-doubt led to reassurance from me, and one more question led to us sitting on the stairs and talking through her concerns. She felt there was a concerted attempt by what she referred to as the "anti-Diana brigade" to undermine her in the public's eyes. We spoke about the continuing role of Tiggy Legge-Bourke. We spoke about Camilla Parker Bowles and whether Prince Charles really loved her. Inevitably, we spoke about how the princess felt undervalued and unappreciated. But the basis of the conversation seemed to be her worries about what the future held. She said she was "constantly puzzled" by the attempts of Prince Charles's sympathizers to "destroy me." It was a "down day," and the princess needed to talk. With all sorts of jumbled thoughts racing through her mind, we went into the sitting room to write it all down and then make sense of it. Again, the pen put her thoughts into some form of therapeutic order.

As the princess sat at her desk, I sat on the sofa, watching her scribble furiously. "I'm going to date this, and I want you to keep it . . . just in case," she said. For she had another reason to write down her thoughts and present them to me that day. She was, rationally or irrationally, worried about her safety, and it was playing on her mind. She wrote down what she was thinking but didn't articulate her justification for doing so. I think she would have felt silly, or perhaps embarrassed. She just wanted to put it down. It was, in a way, her insurance for the future.

When she finished the letter, she popped it into an envelope addressed to "Paul," sealed it, and handed it to me. I read it the next day at home, and thought nothing of it. It wasn't the first time, or the last, that she would express, verbally or in writing, such concerns to me. But, with the benefit of hindsight, the content of that letter has bothered me since her death. For this is what she wrote ten months before she died in that car crash in Paris:

I am sitting here at my desk today in October, longing for someone to hug me and encourage me to keep strong and hold my head high. This particular phase in my life is the most dangerous. [The princess then identified where she felt the threat and danger would come from] is planning "an accident" in my car, brake failure and serious head injury in order to make the path clear for Charles to marry.

I have been battered, bruised and abused mentally by a system for 15 years now, but I feel no resentment, I carry no hatred. I am weary of the battles, but I will never surrender. I am strong inside and maybe that is a problem for my enemies.

Thank you Charles, for putting me through such hell and for giving me the opportunity to learn from the cruel things you have done to me. I have gone forward fast and have cried more than anyone will ever know. The anguish nearly killed me, but my inner strength has never let me down, and my guides have taken such good care of me up there. Aren't I fortunate to have had their wings to protect me . . .

That letter has been part of the burden I have carried since the princess's death. Knowing what to do with it has been a source of much soul-searching. All I can say is, Imagine if that letter had been penned to you by a loved one and then, within the next year, they died in a car crash. In trying to make sense of it, you tend to waver from considering it a wild coincidence to a more bizarre, paranoid explanation. I had hoped that the matter would be put to rest by an inquest into the princess's death—a full examination by a coroner and court in the UK of the events of August 31, 1997. But, for some inexplicable reason, there has not been an inquest. If it were anyone else, an inquest would have had to be held and yet that essential inquisitorial process has been pushed to one side.

In the late summer of 2003, it was announced that an inquest was being planned in Surrey, primarily to examine the circumstances of the death of Dodi al-Fayed. It was unclear whether the hearing's scope would include the death of the princess. Whatever the situation, the lack of the inquest, and the attempt by Scotland Yard and the CPS to destroy my reputation with my Old Bailey trial in 2002, has led me to make the contents of that note public. I agree that it may be futile in what it achieves because it can do no more than provide yet another question mark. But if that question mark leads to an inquest, and a thorough examination of the facts by the British authorities, it will have achieved something. Perhaps there is a desire to allow the matter of a British inquest to go away, but that cannot be allowed to happen.

FIFTEEN

A KNOCK AT
THE DOOR

IF THE PRINCESS WAS HAPPY to have me at the helm when she was alive, then those charged with enshrining her memory in death would have preferred to see me thrown overboard.

In what would become the story of my life between 1997 and 2002, few people grasped the nature of the privileged relationship I had shared with the Boss behind closed doors at KP, and the implications of that misunderstanding would ultimately conspire with ignorance to haunt me for years to come.

The problem with sharing such an intensely private world is that its unique qualities are not witnessed by outsiders. When something is not witnessed, especially when ordinary codes of conduct are breached, it is misunderstood. I was a butler who had done his duty, nothing more, nothing less. But, in some people's eyes, perhaps, I was a butler with delusions of grandeur, who was getting too big for his boots.

An overwhelming desire to cut me down to size, and squeeze me back into some sort of livery where I belonged, became apparent not long after February 1998, with my appointment to the Diana, Princess of Wales Memorial Fund as its salaried fund-raising and events manager. The charity was independent of the work on the government's committee, which reports to Gordon Brown.

I was catapulted from a quiet and secret area of a palace into a public arena at Millbank Tower in southwest London. I wanted to harness the new role I had been given and help steer funds in a way that would have made the princess proud. I was receiving checks galore: from $2 million from the manufacturer of Ty Beanie Babies, to £26,000 from Tower Records, to a few hundred pounds from a young farmers' group near Highgrove. I opened charity events all over Britain, including the Junior National Disabled Games in Birmingham, and went to meetings with the Memorial Committee in Downing Street. There would be no problems on the committee. The power struggle would come with the Fund.

I felt I could bring a unique perspective to the table and inject the princess's wishes into the Fund's work. I had known the princess inside out, understood how her mind worked; had been alongside her on her humanitarian missions, had dreamed with her on paper about future missions and charity work that were close to her heart.

One evening at KP, the princess and I were in the sitting room, jotting down ideas about the way forward because she felt her good intentions were being misunderstood:

> I have been given a quality, much to the horror of Charles, and it is a quality I must nurture and use in order to help those in distress. I will never let down those who believe in me, and I will always bring love wherever I go in the world, to whomever: leper, AIDS patient, King, Queen, or President. I have a path of fate to follow, and tread it I will with pride, dignity, and abundance of love and understanding for those in need and that I give with open arms . . .

I knew the humanitarian direction in which she was going. In sharing her thoughts about the way forward when she was alive, I honestly felt I was qualified to lead the way forward on her behalf, ensuring that her wishes and way of thinking informed the work of the Memorial Fund. The princess's personal assistant Jackie Allen and secretaries Jane Harris and Jo Greenstead each brought their own passionate beliefs to the table of what was right and wrong to do in the princess's name. Like me, they, too, would find themselves distanced for being too emotionally involved. I felt I was treated as the butler who was fast becoming a nuisance, with his convictions about what the princess would have wanted. But what really started putting lofty noses out of joint was when the press began identifying me as "the voice and face of the Fund." Especially when Lady Sarah McCorquodale was its president.

"Remember where you come from, Paul."

"Look, Paul, stop walking around like the walking wounded. We are *all* grieving, you know."

"I'm afraid he's an emotional cripple. Emotional people don't make the best decisions."

"Paul, wouldn't you rather find employment elsewhere, and get away from all this? There are some rather nasty rumors circulating about you."

Such comments, to my face or behind my back, were becoming commonplace in London circles. I remembered what the princess used to say about putting her head above the parapet: "You always get shot!" But she stood up for what she believed in and stubbornly dug in her heels. I could only do the same.

The princess's leatherbound green address book had been left on my desk in a locked room, separate from the main general office at Millbank Tower. Jackie Allen and I had locked that room every night. Then, one day, during the infancy of the Memorial Fund, the address book went missing. It contained the names and numbers of all the princess's friends. It was a directory of her life, the book I had read to her during the all-night vigil.

With Jackie, I reported it stolen to the then office manager, Brian Hutchinson. He, in turn, reported it to Lady Sarah McCorquodale. The police were not called. There was not even an internal inquiry. Contact with the princess's circle had been denied to me. The theory in the office was that it could have been taken by a cleaner, a night watchman, or a security guard. It was never investigated, and that alone made me suspect that something wasn't quite right.

Dr. Andrew Purkis arrived as the Fund's chief executive, and we never did see eye to eye—because the princess would never have seen eye to eye with him. He made it clear that he was the "voice of the Fund if there was going to be one." He had not even *met* the princess, so my bewilderment at hearing this stranger talking about her memory was profound. He had been the Archbishop of Canterbury's private secretary at Lambeth Palace. He was the High Church and the Establishment rolled into one: everything the princess had rebelled against. He had been given the position because he had a good brain and an excellent management pedigree. Yet I felt that he had no conception of how this precious legacy should be managed. He could never empathize with the passion or conviction that ran through the majority of her friends. A charity in memory of a special someone is starved of essential inspiration and guidance if it is incapable of harnessing or understanding the personality of the name it operates under. Surely.

Whenever I made a passionate defense of the princess's remarkable personality, I felt I was screaming from behind a thick glass wall. Dr. Purkis had known I was not going to hang out the bunting to mark his arrival. "I know you may resent me taking this post, but I will try and work alongside you the best I can. I do not want there to be any animosity," he told me.

BY THE START OF July 1998, apartments 8 and 9 had been stripped bare. No carpets. No silk wallpaper. Not even a lightbulb. It seemed as if no one had ever lived there. The Royal Collection had gathered its fine furniture and paintings. Jewelry had been returned to Buckingham

Palace. William and Harry's requests for their possessions had been carried out. The Spencers took away the rest to Althorp, including the Nelson Shanks portrait on the stairs and the wedding dress. Even the princess's BMW was sent to a secret location to be destroyed so that no one could benefit from its provenance.

The erasure of everything I knew meant that my inevitable departure from KP was imminent; I had put it to the back of my mind ever since the previous December when Maria and I were given notice that, because I was no longer employed by the Royal Household, we did not qualify for grace-and-favour accommodation at the Old Barracks. So July 24, we said goodbye to so much: the palace, our home, the boys' schools, their friends, our friends, our parish priest, the Vauxhall Astra that had come with the job, my pension plan. We lost an entire lifestyle. But, more than anything, I finally had to let go of the private world at KP to which I had clung since the princess's death. This was the physical letting go, although I knew that the mental letting go would not be possible. I'm not sure it ever will be.

When Mrs. Frances Shand Kydd learned of our eviction from royal accommodation, she offered to buy us a £120,000 apartment in London on the conditions that the deed was in her name and that we would allocate her a room so that she could stay there whenever she was in the capital. It was an incredibly kind offer, but we had our little cottage in Farndon, Cheshire, so we decided to move north and start afresh. Maria and the boys would live in that village, surrounded by family, while I spent the week working with the Memorial Fund in London and staying with a friend.

On our final day at the Old Barracks, Maria and the boys packed up the boxes and cleared out the flat. They left me to make one final visit to KP. Across the green. Up the road alongside the palace. Past the cottages on the left. Along King's Passage and into the back door of apartment 8. I wandered through the ground-floor workroom, past the empty wooden pigeonholes, and into my pantry, where the cupboards had been cleared, the telephone and the fax had been removed. My mere presence—the footsteps, the opening of doors, the creaking floorboards—seemed to leave an echo in a house that I remembered to be so full of life. I roamed around the apartment, standing in each room for ten or fifteen minutes, reflecting on what had happened in that space. I was mentally projecting images over a blank background, replaying and fast-forwarding five years of life at KP, all condensed into that hour in which I was lost in complete silence. It was a shell, but, in my mind, I was visualizing everything as it had been.

I carried those thoughts with me on the long journey up the M6, to a new life in the North.

M OVED OUT JULY 24. That August I appeared in *Majesty* magazine—a profile.

There were more frowns at the Fund.

I LIVED, breathed, and slept my role at the Memorial Fund. I was up and down the country, helping to raise money in memory of the princess: at a London Lighthouse fashion show; at a golf club in Telford, Shropshire, with former England goalkeeper Peter Shilton, to host a disabled sports day; at a charity cricket day in Retford, Nottinghamshire; at the Great North Run in Newcastle-upon-Tyne; at a bagpipe competition in Glasgow. I traveled the length and breadth of Britain, and the Fund didn't seem to care that I was working for those causes on my weekends off. I went to accept checks personally because I felt it was important for someone from the Fund to recognize the efforts of the people who had raised money for the princess.

By October, the offices had moved from Millbank Tower to County Hall at Westminster, and I had an office with stunning panoramic views of the Thames, the Houses of Parliament, and Big Ben.

My horizons were not looking so good, though, because

I wanted to run in the New York Marathon in November. Dr. Andrew Purkis wrote to me, making it clear that he was not going to allow my profile to get out of hand: "If and when you go to New York . . . you will be doing so as a private trip . . . to fulfill a personal ambition. You are not representing the Fund . . . and you will not do anything or give any interviews relating to the work of the Fund. Even any media interview, which started off purporting to be about Paul Burrell the person, would in fact, pretty soon, start highlighting the fact that you work for the Fund."

So I completed the marathon in four hours and forty minutes. In my own capacity.

Later that month, a Masquerade Ball was held at the Grosvenor House Hotel in London's Park Lane to raise money for the Diana, Princess of Wales Memorial Fund. A host of celebrities turned up in her honor, and the rock star Bryan Adams donated a signed guitar, which was auctioned to former-soccer-player-turned-actor Vinnie Jones. But after such a night of glitz and glamour, I could almost hear the sniping that I was "star-struck" and "too interested in the showbiz side of life." The writing was on the wall.

In the last week of November, I was asked to attend a one-to-one meeting with Dr. Purkis. The neatness of his brightly lit office symbolized how efficient this man was in his capacity as chief executive. Wood paneling covered the four walls; not a piece of paper was out of place on his desk. Above where he sat hung a photograph of the princess, taken by Mario Testino for a CD compilation in tribute to the Boss.

Dr. Purkis, a small, nervous-looking man, soon got to the point. He suggested I should start to look elsewhere for a career, because they were intending to close down the fund-raising and events department. "The future for you within the Fund is rather limited," he said.

All I heard was an insignificant voice, droning in the background. I didn't snap what he was saying because I was focusing on the Mario Testino portrait. This man does not have a clue about you, I thought.

I interrupted him in full flow. "Are you telling me that

you're going to eliminate my position? Because I will not be tendering my resignation. This is what I know and do best. You'll have to surgically remove me from this Fund, and then out I will go with the dirty laundry and—"

"Paul, I don't like to use analogies like that, but I do feel that it is time for you to move on."

How dare he? "It's all very well for you to sit there and say that," I said, "but you're not affected publicly in the same way that I am. If you push me out, it will affect the work of this Fund."

Dr. Purkis wasn't listening.

A few days afterward, Lady Sarah McCorquodale rang me. "Are you all right, Paul?"

"No, I'm not. Not really," I replied.

"Let's have lunch next Tuesday. I'm at Mishcon de Reya's for a meeting, so we can meet up and and talk," she said.

When I agreed, I had expected it to be a one-to-one informal lunch. So, after receiving one more check at County Hall from the organizers of a charity day, I went to the arranged rendezvous at a wine bar near Southampton Row on Tuesday, December 8. In the corner, I spotted Lady Sarah at a corner table—with solicitor Anthony Julius, onetime interim chairman of the Fund who had remained as a trustee.

"I had no idea that the big guns were coming," I said lightheartedly, in a vain attempt to break the ice. I looked at the rather serious face of Anthony Julius and, true to legal form, he was in no mood for banter. I knew a lot about him because the princess had told me more than he would ever know, but at least we had one thing in common: he and I had been the only people trusted to handle her divorce papers.

He opened the conversation by stating that both he and Lady Sarah had been instructed to explain the current situation. As he rambled on toward the inevitable regrets that people often express when kicking you in the backside, I thought how funny it was that the person doing all the talking was the one I had not arranged to meet. Lady Sarah was quiet as a mouse.

"You have two alternatives, Paul," he said. "One is to leave with acrimony, which will hurt you, your family, and the Fund, and which you would bitterly regret in a few years' time. The other is to accept the hand of friendship that is being extended to you now. We will utilize the tremendous goodwill and resources of the Fund to find you alternative employment."

A hand of friendship, he called it. All I felt across the table was the cold aristocracy of Lady Sarah and the arrogant legal might of Anthony Julius strangling me.

I pointed out that I still felt there was much more work to do.

Then Lady Sarah came to life. "But *what* do you want?" she said, clearly irritated. "Your job is redundant!"

Anthony Julius waded in again: "Remember, Paul, when the money began to arrive at Kensington Palace, Lady Sarah, myself, and Michael Gibbins decided to set up the Fund. If it hadn't been for us, you would not have had this job to go to in the first place."

I think he wanted me to be grateful. "But you can't say 'if,' because 'if' is a very big word. 'If' the princess hadn't died, you wouldn't have needed to give me a job," I pointed out.

"Oh, yes, you can, Paul," said an indignant Lady Sarah. "Oh, yes, you can say 'if.'" Then she tried another argument. "Wouldn't Maria and the boys rather you were with them than here in London?"

When in trouble, dig deep for the emotional screws. "Look," I said, "my family are, and always will be, behind me in whatever I choose to do." I had to bite my lip on what I knew about the value the Spencers placed on close families.

"Paul, all we want to do is help you make a decision," said Anthony Julius.

I asked him if the meeting was on or off the record. "It's on the record, unless you specify otherwise," he replied. "The trustees are aware that we are meeting and expect a report of this conversation."

Lady Sarah was fiddling with her salad. I hadn't even

started tackling the fish on the plate in front of me. I felt myself becoming emotional and tried to control it, but I couldn't. "I don't recognize the two people I'm sitting with, I cannot listen to this anymore." My voice cracked. "You will have to excuse me for being rude and leaving the table."

I got up, grabbed my coat from the back of the chair, and headed for the door. "So we'll see you later, Paul?" Lady Sarah's voice chased me out of the wine bar. Her sister would never have treated me so badly, and that thought sent tears rolling down my cheeks as I dashed into the open air.

I flagged down a taxi, and jumped into the back. I could not contain a roar of grief.

"Are you all right, mate?" asked the driver, looking into his rearview mirror.

"I'll be fine. I've just had some bad news. Can you take me to Kensington Palace, please?"

It was the only place I could think of going. I could no longer have access, but I could walk around Kensington Palace Gardens. There, I managed to compose myself, then headed for the Dome Café in the high street, where I met up with the *Daily Mail* reporter Richard Kay: someone else who had known the princess better than anyone on that Fund; someone who would understand the injustice of it all. Not one word appeared in the *Daily Mail*. But by Friday the *News of the World*'s royal reporter, Clive Goodman, was on to my imminent redundancy.

When I was called into the office of Dr. Purkis on the Monday after the *News of the World* had printed its story, the weekend's press coverage was spread across his desk. He told me that he had confirmed reports that I had met with the media "to discuss the Fund's business." I was beyond caring. After one more heated conversation, he told me: "Right. I will ring you later in the day to tell you of my decision." Those were his final words to me.

To quell the press furor over my impending dismissal, Dr. Purkis put the matter into context in a memo to all staff: "This episode is a piddling storm in a teacup being generated by the lower end of the tabloid press."

On December 18, the Friday before Christmas, Dr. Purkis rang me at home to explain that he had "no alternative but to give you a month's notice." I returned to work on December 21 to clear my desk and speak my mind to a chief executive who was attempting to be conciliatory. I walked into his office and said: "I have come to say goodbye."

Dr. Purkis replied: "I want to thank you for everything and for all your hard work during the past ten months."

"I did what I did for the princess. In memory of her, not for anyone else," I said.

"I know how upset you must feel."

"No, you don't. I doubt whether you have any idea. You and the trustees have totally mismanaged my role ever since I arrived here, not once realizing the potential I had to offer," I said.

Dr. Purkis mounted his defense. "That is not true, Paul. The trustees have fire in their bellies for this Fund."

"Andrew, this Fund bears no resemblance to the person whom I knew. It does not fulfill her wishes or her requests!"

"We believe that it does, and we will do everything we can to make sure that it continues, Paul," he said.

"Andrew, I leave here with a heavy heart, but I wish you all the luck for the future." I placed an unopened Christmas card on the table. "And if this card is from you, then I have to return it."

Outside, Jackie Allen gave me a hug on the steps as the press were waiting to capture my departure from the Fund. It was a sign of solidarity. In time, she, Jane Harris, and Jo Greenstead would also be leaving: three more passionate voices lost from the Fund.

"How do you feel, Paul?" yelled one reporter.

"Very sad."

"Will you continue the princess's charitable work?"

"I'll do my best." Then I scrambled into a waiting car, and I was away. Lady Sarah McCorquodale no longer had a meddlesome butler on the Fund. But it wasn't going to be my final confrontation with the princess's sister.

$\mathcal{L}$et's have a happy snap, Paul," despite Prince Charles making fun of her sense of style

"The Boss" and her
"right-hand man" on
a landmine
mission in Angola

"The Boss" with her new friend, Betty, Maria's mum

We would come face to face once more. Four years later. In courtroom number one at the Old Bailey, London's Central Criminal Court.

O N NEW YEAR'S DAY 1999. Clive Goodman, of the *News of the World,* rang me at home. "I have been told that a pair of earrings that belonged to the princess have gone missing. Would you like to comment on that?"

"Can I ask you where you got that information?"

"You know I can't tell you that, Paul, but, needless to say, it's a very good source," said Clive.

My concern was obvious. David Thomas, the Crown jeweler, Lady Sarah McCorquodale, and I had carefully dispatched all of the princess's jewelry to Althorp. I had cataloged all of the earrings and seen them leave.

I rang the Fund's press officer, Vanessa Corninghan, to inform her of the conversation that had taken place with Clive Goodman.

In a letter, dated January 2, 1999, to my friends in Kentucky, Shirley and Claude Wright, I wrote: "It has occurred to me that someone might be trying to damage my reputation, particularly that I come from the Fund with such good press, and my profile is riding high. Someone might wish to see my name tarnished, or am I getting paranoid?"

Age forty-two, I found myself adrift with no attachment to a palace or a princess. For the first time since joining the household staff at Buckingham Palace in 1976, I felt out on a limb. I decided to put to good use my years of royal training. I published a book on social etiquette and manners, entitled *Entertaining with Style* (*In the Royal Manner* in the USA), and found that I could still rely on my trade. The proceeds of that book allowed us to move from the then £110,000 Old Barn property in Farndon to a larger, Georgian house, on the market for £185,000. Based on the book, I started to give lectures on entertaining, royal style, occasionally charging £3,000 but, a lot of the time, without a fee at charity events.

It was an income, based on royalties and lectures, that would ultimately grab the attention of Scotland Yard. With regard to my bank statements, the black-and-white figures didn't add up. Two and two would equal five.

SOMEONE HAD PULLED BACK the brass knocker and rattled it against the blue front door. It was still dark outside. Maria was already up, making breakfast downstairs. I rolled over in bed, and the bedside clock told me it was shortly before 7 A.M. It was Thursday, January 18, 2001, and Scotland Yard's "Special Inquiry Team"—a unit known as SO6—had arrived.

"Paul!" Maria shouted up the stairs. "There's some people who want to talk to you."

I pulled a robe on, left our second-floor bedroom, and went down the steep, narrow, right-turning staircase. At the bottom, I saw Maria, still in her blue nightshirt. Her entire body seemed to be shaking.

I dropped off the bottom step of the stairs, went past the kitchen through the next doorway off the narrow hallway, whose peach walls are lined with group staff photographs from the royal tours I spent with the Queen or the Prince and Princess of Wales.

Two smartly dressed, stern-looking individuals greeted me: a rather buxom woman with blond hair, DCI Maxine de Brunner, and a tall, debonair man with thick black hair, DS Roger Milburn. A warrant card flashed out of a leather wallet. "I am arresting you on suspicion of the theft of a golden dhow. You do not have to say anything, but it may harm your defense if you do not mention, when questioned, something which you later rely on in court. Anything you do say may be given in evidence," said DS Milburn.

They had arrived to arrest me in connection with an inquiry, which had begun the previous year, into the theft and sale of an eighteen-inch-long jewel-encrusted Arabian dhow worth £500,000, a wedding present to the Prince and Princess of Wales from the Emir of Bahrain. It had been offered for sale at an antiques shop called Spink in London. The police "had been told" that I instructed its disposal, and that tall story had brought them to my door. It set in motion a personal nightmare for me and my family, and a process that would be recorded for its embarrassment factor in the books of British legal and political history.

Perched on the arm of the sofa, I could smell the sausages Maria had been frying in the kitchen. The boys were still asleep upstairs. Belle, our West Highland terrier, waddled in and began to sniff the strangers' shoes.

Did I have anything in the house that had been removed from Kensington Palace? Did I know the whereabouts of the dhow?

Then DS Milburn asked me two bizarre questions: "Do you have a manuscript to the memoirs you are writing?"

If there was one moment when I knew the officers were stabbing in the dark, that was it. No such manuscript existed. I was not writing my memoirs. I only began writing this book, *A Royal Duty,* in April of 2003, and this book is the *result* of that arrest, a response to the confusion and doubt Scotland Yard raked up over my true closeness to the princess. But in January 2001 I had no idea what "manuscript" they were talking about.

Then came the next query: "Lady Sarah McCorquodale has said that you had a box which belonged to Diana, Princess of Wales. She would like you to return the contents of that box."

The questions kept coming. "Did you ever remove this box from Kensington Palace?"

I knew exactly what they were referring to: the deep mahogany box that the princess had kept in the sitting room as a storage place for her most sensitive papers and documents. The box Lady Sarah and I had opened together at KP after her death. The box that, to the best of my knowledge, was with her.

My manuscript. The princess's secrets. That was what Scotland Yard had come looking for, together with "documentation relating to the sale of a golden dhow," which was something else that they would not find in my house.

Maria went into the kitchen, followed by DCI de Brunner. DS Milburn stayed with me. "If you give us what we want, we'll be out of here. If you don't, we'll have to search the house," he told me.

In the kitchen, DCI de Brunner was making the same point to Maria. "I suggest, Mrs. Burrell, that you speak to your husband and tell him to give us what we're looking for."

At my Old Bailey trial in 2002, both detectives would deny that they had ever said such a thing. "That is completely incorrect," said DS Milburn. "That is absolutely wrong," said DCI de Brunner.

Three more detectives, who had been waiting in a vehicle outside, entered the house to carry out a robust search after I had insisted I had no material relating to a golden dhow, no contents of a box, and no manuscript for a book. Every cupboard, drawer, wardrobe, cabinet, and shelf was searched. One officer was told to shadow me wherever I went: he was outside the bathroom as I showered, on guard outside the bedroom as I dressed. An officer riffled through every possession in every room: first floor, second floor, third floor, loft. Dozens of large polyethylene bags were being filled with sentimental items given to me by the princess, gifts she had bought us, dresses, shoes, hats, and handbags she had passed on to Maria, sentimental photographs, items she had entrusted to me, items she had discarded but which I couldn't bear to destroy. Precious memories and possessions were being bagged up as evidence, labeled as items that Paul Burrell had stolen from Diana, Princess of Wales, after she died.

Not for the first time, I was losing control of a world I was meant to protect. The Memorial Fund had denied me a voice, and perhaps didn't want to attach any significance to my closeness to the princess. But now Scotland Yard was questioning the very thing that was sacred to me: my *duty* to the princess. The Fund may have thought I was emotionally handicapped, but my devotion was never in question. Scotland Yard was rummaging through my home, questioning my very loyalty.

Maria had to take her mother to an urgent hospital appointment. My niece Louise Cosgrove, who was then working as my secretary, came for work as usual at 9 A.M. and walked into chaos. Maria had got the boys off to school, having told them the police were "carrying out certain checks." I cannot remember seeing them that morning. Louise got on the telephone to speak to a legal firm. Shortly before 10 A.M. a solicitor, Andrew Shaw, arrived. He was a district judge who had happened to be the duty solicitor at his firm, Walker Smith Way, in the center of Chester. His support and no-nonsense approach, then his friendship, helped me survive that day, and for the next eighteen months.

I was at my desk in my office. An officer stood over me as I stared, in a trance, at everything around me: to my left on the wall, a photo of the princess wearing her blue baseball cap; a 45 r.p.m. record of Tina Turner's single "Simply the Best" signed "Diana"—a fortieth birthday present from the princess to Maria; to my right on the desk, a Lord Snowdon portrait of her in a pink beaded gown. All I could hear was footsteps above, and the rustling of the police exhibits bags coming down the stairs. I was witnessing a burglary.

Detectives had gone upstairs to pursue a hunch on the golden dhow, and they were finding what they considered to be a royal treasure trove that no servant should have: crockery, ornaments, photo frames, clothes, photographs, paintings, CDs, handbags, hats, shoes, letters.

I heard a voice travel down the stairs: "We're going to need more bags . . . MORE BAGS!"

"We're going to need a furniture van!" shouted another.

Good God, I thought, the children have been let loose in the candy store.

In the afternoon, I was arrested a *second* time: "Mr. Burrell, I'm now arresting you on suspicion of theft of the property we are finding in this search."

Instead of receipts for the sale of a golden dhow, they were finding endless items with royal connections. Why that should have been a surprise was beyond me. Since the age of eighteen, I had only ever lived in palaces and castles where hardworking staff had received hand-me-downs, unwanted ornaments, generous gifts, discarded clothes. But Scotland Yard were oblivious. This was a royal find like never before. A servant caught red-handed, they thought. And they had only ever come in search of documentation relating to the sale of a dhow.

THE RANDOM SEARCH went on from 7 A.M. until 8 P.M. My home was turned upside down.

They found the writing bureau the princess had given to Alexander. Then they read its engraved plaque: "Presented by the City of Aberdeen to HRH the Prince of Wales and Lady Diana Spencer on the occasion of their marriage on 29th July 1981." Must be stolen, they thought.

They found an *Indiana Jones* bullwhip that the princess had given to me, knowing my love of movie memorabilia. Then they read the attached documentation: "Presented to HRH Prince of Wales at the première of *Indiana Jones and the Last Crusade* on 27th June 1989."

They found the biblical text I had read to the princess during the all-night vigil at KP, and thought it was stolen. The misunderstandings were endless, and the police were having a field day as they seized and bagged more than four hundred items.

I sat, crying over my desk, shivering with fear. I had watched my world disintegrate, and it was heartbreaking. In an instant, I knew—even if no one else did—where it was all leading.

"What are they doing? They don't know what they're doing," I cried to Louise.

Andrew Shaw came in to speak to me. He said I looked lost, and he was so concerned about my mental state that he called for the police surgeon. He duly arrived, noted my devastation, but observed that I was "fit to be detained." All I could think about was that these detectives upstairs had no idea what they were opening up. There were secrets in that house that no one should know about. The princess had filmed her own private video diaries: footage in which she would talk about her love life and her most intimate secrets; hours of tape, which, with the help of her speech-making coach, she had recorded secretly. She would sit down in front of a camera in her sitting room and talk. It was therapeutic, and gave her extra confidence for talking live into a camera. Those highly sensitive videos had been entrusted to me. They were kept in my loft, and I had never viewed them. Yet the detectives were bagging them up and taking them to Scotland Yard, where they would be gawked over by all and sundry. (How ironic that once the court case was over, these tapes would be leaked to a Sunday newspaper.) The princess's privacy was being compromised in the raid, which I was powerless to stop. Bundles of letters she hadn't wanted to be kept at KP were being scanned; sealed boxes I had taken from the palace for safekeeping in Farndon were being torn open. Strips of negatives were taken away to be developed and passed round. The police were ripping through the Boss's most personal items, and it was obscene. In my eyes, I had let her down by allowing these men through my door. I have never felt so useless. So numb. So physically sick.

If the police were blind to the consequences of their actions, then I had never seen so clearly. The princess, Princes Charles, William, Harry, the Queen. The world I had been protecting was being dragged down a road to where exposure was inevitable: because the police would make sure that my arrest, and the carloads of items they had seized, got maximum media exposure.

My devotion to the princess was not only being questioned in the course of a "discreet" inquiry. It was going to be held aloft before the nation, doubted, then analyzed. Everything I had stood for was about to be dragged into a humiliating public arena.

"DI BUTLER ARRESTED," screamed the *Daily Mirror* the following day, with a photograph of me being led into a police station in Runcorn. The humiliation was complete.

*   *   *

"You understand the charges that have been made against you, Mr. Burrell?" asked the desk sergeant in the custody suite at Runcorn police station.

In that bare room, which was not dissimilar to a basement at Buckingham Palace, I didn't understand a thing as I began to empty my suit pockets onto the counter.

"Could I also have your belt, Mr. Burrell, your shoelaces, and your tie?" the sergeant added. Nothing that could form a ligature would be left in my possession. "It is normal procedure, Mr. Burrell."

A female custody officer, with short, spiky blond hair, then took my arm. "Don't worry, I'll take care of you," she said, in a Scouse accent. She led me down a tiled corridor to the cells. Kate Murphy's face was the kindest and warmest I had seen all day, after so many hours with the brusqueness of Scotland Yard.

Andrew Shaw was behind me, and the three pairs of heels echoed down the corridor. All around us, he could hear the other occupants of the cells shouting, moaning, and banging. The fresh activity had roused them. We stopped when the officer faced a thick steel door. I could not believe what was happening as she heaved it open and I walked in. It was a soulless room, with bare, cream-painted stone walls, and one tiny square window. There was a stainless-steel toilet in the corner. "I'm afraid we cannot offer you five-star cuisine. The food is microwaved, but I recommend the curry," she said, with a reassuring smile.

When my solicitor had gone, urging me to be strong, I ate curry as my first meal of the day, out of a plastic container with plastic cutlery.

I tried to sleep, but it was difficult to get comfortable on a "bed" that was no more than a wide stone step. There was no pillow, no blanket. The "mattress" was like one of those plastic mats gymnasts use.

The next morning, DS Roger Milburn returned. On instructions from Andrew Shaw, I said nothing to his volley of questions. Again, his curiosity seemed to focus more on the contents of a box, sensitive paperwork, and a manuscript. It was almost as if the four hundred or so items taken from my house were a postscript to be addressed later. For five hours I sat, wondering what on earth was going on. Each time he asked me a question, I replied: "No comment."

Surely, this was a mistake. Surely when the Royal Family heard what had happened, this nonsense would end. When I was released on police bail, pending further inquiries, I honestly believed that somebody somewhere in the system—Scotland Yard, Buckingham Palace, Kensington Palace, St. James's Palace, the Queen, Prince Charles, Prince William, someone—would realize there had been a misunderstanding. Gifts of royal provenance were in hundreds of royal servants' homes up and down Britain: sentimental symbols of time spent working for a senior royal. Gifts were an unwritten perk of the job, going back to George V's days. Everyone in the Royal Household knew it. Everyone in the Royal Family knew it.

But the silence was deafening.

SIXTEEN

CLOAK AND DAGGER

"PAUL, THE ELDEST SON would like to meet you," said the voice at the other end of the mobile-telephone line. It was the discreet, household staff code name for Prince Charles; "the favorite son" was Prince Andrew, and "the youngest son" Prince Edward.

In the weeks and months after my arrest the need for discretion was paramount. Twenty telephone lines of my closest family and friends were bugged, as documentation later proved. It was prudent, on a monitored telephone line, to use no names and keep the conversation deliberately vague.

After months of waiting, and wondering why the Royal Family had decided to leave me hung out to dry, the call came through to my house in Farndon on August 2, 2001. The well-spoken voice, ringing from London, was that of a trusted intermediary who had been in discussion with the most senior advisers to Prince Charles at St. James's Palace. The wheels had been in motion for months. The go-between, who was acting on behalf of me and the palace, was caught between different sides, who shared a deep concern about the implications of a potentially damaging, high-profile court case.

I didn't want to enlighten Scotland Yard about private issues concerning the Royal Family. I had wanted the chance to speak, privately and confidentially, to Prince Charles. To make him understand. To let him know the madness of what was happening. To make sure that he, William, and Harry knew what a terrible mistake was being made.

One telephone call had brought me hope. At long last something was about to happen, and it was going to happen at twenty-four hours' notice. All I did was listen. "A meeting has been authorized. What you should do is drive to Gloucestershire. You will be given further instructions once you've gotten there. The meeting will not be at the country house; it will be at someone else's house. The eldest son will meet you there. He is anxious to sort this out once and for all."

After spending many months wallowing in self-pity, euphoria swept over me. Once Prince Charles had heard what I had to say, he would know my innocence. He would just *know*. For an entire spring and summer, I had been trapped in one of those nightmares when you are screaming to be heard but you emit no sound. Now the man who used to employ me, the father of the boys I had seen grow up, was going to do what no one from the House of Windsor had done since January: listen.

It had taken seven terrible months to reach such an optimistic point.

THE HOUSE OF WINDSOR had made its first tentative, indirect contact within two weeks of my arrest. The media that had been camped outside my home had dispersed, and I was at home in Farndon when the trusted intermediary made his initial telephone call after starting discussions with Prince Charles's advisers. It was at a time when I was still trying to come to terms with the enormity of what had happened. He told me: "The view that has been conveyed to me is that he believes his ex-wife's staff are being persecuted. You still hold a special place in the affections of his sons. There is deep concern within the family. It has been suggested that you write a letter to him, explaining why such property was ever in your house. This could be the first step toward sorting all this out."

It was the last week of January 2001. That date is significant because, in the posttrial inquiry held by Sir Michael Peat into the conduct of the Prince of Wales's household in relation to my trial, the clear inference was that it was I who made all the approaches to St. James's Palace. They suggested that I had made all the requests, in a cynical attempt to lay the foundations of a future defense. Indeed, in the absence of any further details, it was suggested that those approaches did not start until April 2002.

But the truth is that my telephone rang first. Not vice versa. It was my intermediary who, after one of many discussions about the case, relayed a message to me to pen a letter. That request came from the prince's deputy private secretary Mark Bolland, a shrewd aide whose loyalty to his employer was as strong as mine to the princess. Both he and the prince's private secretary, Sir Stephen Lamport, were fully up to speed with the police inquiry and were acutely aware of the potential public-relations nightmare of a high-profile court case. But the suggestion that it was me making the approaches is not true. The truth was that it was *his* idea for me to write to Prince Charles, just as it would be his idea for me to write, in a similar vein, to Prince William.

Mr. Bolland would inform Fiona Shackleton, the prince's solicitor, that he was in communication with me indirectly, but he could not divulge the identity of the intermediary who was running as a go-between on behalf of both sides. Prince Charles, it was clear in those early days, was keen to avoid a prosecution. I harbored faint hopes that, in time, he would know my innocence. But I also had a dilemma.

The constraints of the legal process—I had been bailed out by the police—had taken from me the freedom to express myself candidly in any proposed letter. A full and frank explanation would be a defense in court, so any correspondence had to be carefully written. I sat in the Chester office of solicitor Andrew Shaw, and together we penned a letter, outlining how my intentions had been honorable and my loyalty should not be questioned. I had wanted to say so much, but, instead, it became a letter couched delicately in legal language. On February 5, it was in the hands of the intermediary. In time, he personally delivered it to Mr. Bolland. My letter had arrived at St. James's Palace.

It was, I thought at the time, the most important letter I would ever write, and would rescue me from a nightmare that made no sense. Prince Charles would understand, surely, when he read it.

> *Your Royal Highness,*
>
> *I am most grateful for the opportunity to convey my thoughts to you concerning the recent situation . . . I have been bailed to return to answer further questions on 27 February.*
>
> *As you know, Maria, my sons, and I received tremendous generosity from the Royal Family during our years of service. Specifically, we were given gifts by the princess and I was entrusted with confidences, both verbal and written. The police have taken from my home many gifts and items of sentimental value given to me by members of the Royal Family. Most sensitively, some material which was entrusted to me. There are also a number of "family" items which, quite simply, I incarcerated firstly in storage, and then recently in my attic for safe-keeping . . . I have not been charged with any offence at this stage.*
>
> *It is terrible to be accused personally and publicly of dishonesty, and I cannot bear the thought of you, Prince William, and Prince Harry thinking that I have let you, or the princess, down in any way. All I ever wanted to do was "take care" of what I considered to be "my world."*
>
> *Perhaps a meeting would help to resolve any misunderstanding and stop this sad episode escalating beyond control.*
>
> *I remain Your Royal Highness' humble and obedient servant—*
> *Paul*

It was a plea that fell on deaf ears, as would all my pleas for common sense over the following months.

My intermediary telephoned with news that made my heart sink. "It doesn't tell him anything. It is not explanatory enough. I'm afraid the letter is not going to be forwarded."

Mark Bolland had wanted to be enlightened. Instead, he had got a plea of innocence. The letter was returned to me, its envelope slit open. It had reached St. James's Palace but had not, I was told, been seen by Prince Charles.

It was a missed opportunity—because when my trial ultimately collapsed, the prosecution said I had not told anyone of my intention to retain items from KP for "safekeeping."

But they could not have been more wrong. I had told the monarch in my meeting with her in 1997. I had tried to tell the heir to the throne in that letter on February 5, 2001. And in April I would send a letter to Prince William, the second in line to the throne, and that was certainly seen by royal eyes. I could not have made it clearer to a more powerful trio in the land. Yet no one listened. Indeed, no one *would* listen to me until my livelihood, health, and sanity had been taken right to the wire.

ON APRIL 3, Sir Stephen Lamport, Fiona Shackleton, and Sir Robin Janvrin, the Queen's private secretary, met at St. James's Palace with the Spencers, Scotland Yard, and the Crown Prosecution Service. One of the CPS officials made it clear that, if convicted, I would be sent to jail for five years or more. "An aggravating feature would be the serious breach of trust," the meeting was told. There was one other interesting note taken that day: because the items found at my house were not the property of Prince Charles, the final decision over the continuance of a prosecution lay with the executors of the princess's estate. The Spencers were in the driving seat of the Scotland Yard express—and there was no prospect of them applying the brakes.

It didn't seem to matter that Lady Sarah McCorquodale

and Mrs. Frances Shand Kydd were oblivious to the lifestyle and generosity of the princess. All that mattered was their blinkered view: that Paul Burrell should have nothing more in his possession than a pair of cuff links and a photo frame. He *should* be prosecuted. In having the executors on their side, the police felt they were onto a surefire conviction. The *real* family of the princess, those closer to her than her mother and sister, could have enlightened them because, unlike the Spencers, those friends knew the whole picture:

Lucia Flecha de Lima, mother figure: "The princess told me she entrusted private correspondence to Paul."

Debbie Frank, astrologer to the princess since 1989: "Diana considered Paul to be family."

Rosa Monckton, sister figure: "The princess frequently gave gifts . . . she couldn't function without Paul."

Lady Annabel Goldsmith: "Diana said Paul was her rock . . . she talked to him like a girlfriend."

Susie Kassem: "Paul was the third person she trusted the most after William and Harry."

Lana Marks: "Diana told me that she gave Maria dresses and accessories."

Even if they had asked the shoemaker Eric Cook: "Paul and Diana were more like brother and sister than employee and employer."

But Scotland Yard sat on the periphery and listened to the Spencers, who, by the time of the princess's death, were not even aware of who her closest friends were. Detectives cast aside the need to get to the heart of the matter with the princess's inner circle when the first golden rule is "know your subject." Officers from SO6 didn't have a clue about Diana, Princess of Wales, in a case that revolved around her very world.

In the first two weeks of April, Mark Bolland made another suggestion to the intermediary: that I should now write a letter to Prince William. The young prince was away on his "gap year" travels, but a letter, when it had been received at St. James's Palace, could be faxed confidentially for his attention. On April 19, I penned this letter to him:

I so wish that I could have spoken with you in confidence during the past few months. There is so much to explain. Items which have been taken from me, many of which were given to me for safe-keeping, should be returned to you. I know that you realise that I would never betray the trust and confidence which your mother placed in me, and that I remain the person you have always known—Paul.

With that letter, had I made clear my safekeeping role? It baffles me that the prosecution case at my trial in October 2002 had proceeded, in the words of its counsel William Boyce, QC, on the premise that "Mr. Burrell had never told anyone that he was holding anything for safekeeping." Yet the CPS, the very institution Mr. Boyce was representing, had seen my letter to Prince William eighteen months before the trial. One of its own lawyers, as the Sir Michael Peat inquiry made clear, "said the letter reflected Burrell . . . trying to lay the foundations for a defence . . . and this letter may need to be exhibited."

The CPS had clearly read that letter, but, come the time of my trial, they would claim not to have seen it.

The main thing for me was that I knew Prince William had read it. "The letter was delivered. It has been effective this time," my intermediary told me over the telephone. That letter would also be read by Prince Charles. As his solicitor Fiona Shackleton said in a meeting on April 30: "Mark Bolland got that letter written . . . we knew it was coming, someone told Prince Charles it was coming."

At that very meeting, which was attended by the CPS, Scotland Yard, and Lady Sarah McCorquodale, the crucial question then arose, in the light of the letter I had sent, whether Prince William would lend his support to the prosecution. When Lady Sarah pointed out that she had the final decision, Fiona Shackleton "said she did not want Prince William to move out of tandem with the executors, adding that it needs to be all or nothing."

Prince Charles had the opportunity there and then to

vouch for me and confirm my bona fide role as a safe-keeper of the princess's belongings. He chose not to do so.

In his defense, Prince Charles said that he made it clear that he would "prefer it if the prosecution did not go ahead." He seemed to think it was enough to watch his former butler being beaten up in the street while telling the muggers to back off.

As his palace's own posttrial inquiry would later make clear, if it had been one of *his* members of staff, it would have been different. DS Milburn's recollection was that "Sir Stephen Lamport indicated that the household would support a prosecution which did not involve an employee of the Prince of Wales's household; the implication being that there might be less enthusiasm if a member of that household had been intended to be prosecuted."

IF IT SEEMED that I was friendless in royal circles, then I was a pariah in professional terms. The telephone was suddenly silent—though until now, it had been ringing off the hook since publication of *Entertaining with Style.* No one wanted to hear lectures from a butler accused of the biggest betrayal. No one wanted to employ me, even the charitable organizations that had asked me to do free after-dinner speeches. Only one company remained true: Cunard. The company whose job offer my mother had thrown on the fire in 1976 was the one who stood by me, continuing to employ me on the lecture circuit on the transatlantic voyages of the *QE2.*

BUT IT DIDN'T LESSEN the impact when the real blows came, for others who had hired my services decided to wash their hands of me post-arrest. The *Daily Mail* dropped me as household-management columnist in its Weekend supplement. It no longer wanted my advice on how to be the perfect host, guest, or cook. Then the household-products giant Procter & Gamble came to view me as a PR disaster. I had signed a lucrative television-advertising deal to promote its disposable Bounty paper towels. A promotional photo shoot had taken place at a private house in London, and filming was due to begin. But its executives couldn't wait to wipe the Burrell stain from the company image. My arrest had apparently brought "disrepute" to its door, and I was sent packing with a £20,000 fraction of the money they had been going to pay me. That, combined with our savings, would be enough to see us through until the end of the year.

God knows how much money I must have wasted on knocking back bottles of merlot and Chianti at a time when we were supposed to be cutting back on luxuries. Maria had selflessly given up her treats, refusing to buy makeup. Then she got a friend to pay her by the hour to clean her house— she fell back on her Royal Household skills. And I was falling into a more morose state with each new day, lying in bed until beyond 11 A.M., then sitting at my desk, doing nothing but thinking, and then in the sitting room, knocking back three bottles of wine a night just so that I would sleep.

I would wake at 4 A.M., sit on the edge of the bed, and peer through the curtains to see if any strange vehicles were in the street. I woke up sweating and fretting more times than I care to remember. I was convinced, for nearly two years, that Scotland Yard would come back. Even to this day, if a postman knocks on the door with a package, I am sent back to January 18, 2001.

I did nothing but wallow in self-pity. So, thank God for my wife's strength. Maria's support and sacrifices had always been there: the time when she moved, against her true desires, to KP from Highgrove; the constant occasions when she "lost me" to the princess; the years when she had brought up our boys while I did my duty; or when I lived away from home to work for the Memorial Fund. I only woke up to her remarkable support when I was at my lowest. During the years when the princess had been leaning on me, I had been subconsciously falling back on Maria. Forget the fact that the princess called me her rock. The only rock, in all that time, had been mine: Maria. She pulled me out of my despair, and took those wine bottles away on so many nights.

"Look!" she would say. "Stop feeling so bloody sorry for yourself. There are two boys upstairs who need you to be strong. They don't need to see you falling to pieces. You have responsibilities here as well."

"But I can't cope with it!" I would yell.

Then Maria would pick up one of the many photographs of the princess and yell back, "You chose *this* path. Now you have to get on with it. So get on with it—like I'm having to get on with it. She had you by the balls in her lifetime, and she's still got you by the balls now!"

For so long, Maria had wanted to move on, but I was happy to remain in 1997 with the ghost of the Boss. Her photographs were everywhere, in every room, and that made me feel better. Even when she had been dead for four years, I was still putting her before my family.

In October 2001, Scotland Yard pounced again and arrested another "suspect"—my brother Graham. As before, it was a dawn raid, and the Special Inquiry Team officers searched his house high and low. He was arrested and taken away for questioning on the basis of a signed photograph of the princess, two plates bearing the royal cipher, a naval painting of HMS *Sirius,* and a framed print of a polo match. The paintings had been gifts to me from Prince Charles, which I had given to Graham when I had been living at Highgrove. We even had a photo showing that HMS *Sirius* painting on a wall at the cottage, hung there in 1994. But Graham was dragged away on suspicion of handling stolen goods in 1997.

Graham, like me, attempted in vain to educate the officers about the royal world, and the kindness of the Boss. He told them how he had chased her around Highgrove, having water balloon fights, and how she had rung him three times at home to console him over his marriage difficulties.

He might as well have told them he had just landed from Mars.

"And what would an ex-miner be doing mixing with a princess exactly?" scoffed one of the detectives.

Graham was never charged, but his ordeal of waiting, of being under suspicion, lasted ten months before the police realized they had no evidence against him. But I was condemned as a royal outcast.

IN LATE MAY, I had been out shopping in Chester when the cell phone rang. "You'll never guess what's come in the post," squealed Maria. "An invitation . . . to Windsor Castle!"

When I arrived home, it was on the kitchen worktop: a white envelope bearing the seal of the Lord Chamberlain's office in St. James's Palace. Inside, there was a gold-edged, stiff card invitation with "EiiR" embossed in gold. It read: "The Lord Chamberlain has been commanded to invite MR AND MRS PAUL BURRELL to a service of thanksgiving at St George's Chapel, followed by a reception at Windsor Castle, to celebrate the 80th birthday of HRH the Duke of Edinburgh."

Maria was so excited, and I was thrilled for her. The duke had thought to invite his former maid to the event on June 10. It was ostensibly for Maria, but the kindness had been extended to me too. It wasn't just the recognition of his consideration that brightened our day, our week, our month, our year; it was that we had been invited when we had felt that everyone was against us. No one will ever know how much that lifted our spirits at a time when I was still on police bail and not charged. Letters to Prince Charles and Prince William had passed without acknowledgment, and that had hurt. I had been clinging to a fading belief that, if there was justice, common sense would prevail and the madness would end. After all, in my mind, all I had done was take care of someone in life and in death. Was that such a crime? I didn't expect people to understand, but neither did I think that devotion was illegal. So, when that envelope arrived, it didn't just bring a rather posh invitation; it brought hope, and a hand of friendship from the Queen and the Duke of Edinburgh. Maybe it would mark the turning point.

Then the telephone rang on June 6—my forty-third birthday. A rather pompous, grand, military voice asked to "speak with either Paul or Maria Burrell." It was a Brigadier Hunt-Davis, private secretary to the Duke of Edinburgh, and our former neighbor from the Old Barracks. He got straight to the point. "After a great deal of deliberation, and after taking considerable advice, I have come to the conclusion that it would not be in your best interests, Paul, to attend His Royal Highness the Duke of Edinburgh's eightieth birthday celebrations this forthcoming Sunday."

The silence of my disbelief encouraged him to continue.

"We have had a great deal of inquiries regarding your attendance and, as the media are going to be present, it would not be fair to detract from what is essentially His Royal Highness's day. I am sure that you understand that this decision was not taken lightly, and was taken with everyone's best interests in mind."

Shock made it hard for me to say more than a few words. Or maybe the pompous voice had intimidated me. I put down the telephone after an awkward goodbye and stood in the second-floor sitting room, staring out of the window, replaying the conversation.

No, I thought, the Queen and the Duke of Edinburgh had invited me. Regardless of this aide's advice, I would go. I had nothing to be ashamed about. I picked up the telephone and dialed Buckingham Palace, and rang back Brigadier Hunt-Davis in his office. I told him: "I have thought about your advice, and am still intending to attend the birthday celebrations on Sunday with Maria, but thank you for your concern."

"Paul," he interrupted, "you don't understand. *Your* invitation has been withdrawn. You are no longer invited."

Now anger replaced shock. "And what would happen if I decided to attend, and brought along the invitation?"

"You would be refused admission," he said, "and that would be rather embarrassing for you and the Royal Family. I feel sure that you would not wish to put them in that position."

Then he offered the most breathtaking olive branch, which, I think, was intended to mollify me. "But if Maria wants to attend, she is, of course, still invited," he said.

I couldn't wait to slam down the receiver. When I told Maria, I don't know who was more angry: me or her. "Right!" she said. "If that's how they want to treat you, stuff 'em," and that was that. Another wound to add to our collection.

We knew immediately that the late decision had nothing to do with Her Majesty. It was the "gray suits" of the household, who act in what they believe to be the best interests of the Royal Family. It is a discretion that gives many of them rather odd delusions of power as they attempt to keep the wheels of the system rolling along. Eventually I discovered who was behind the withdrawn invitation: it was the Keeper of the Privy Purse, Sir Michael Peat—the man who would lead the Royal Family's inquiry into the collapse of my Old Bailey trial. He had spotted the name "Burrell" on the guest list and had queried the invitation with the brigadier.

I also know with certainty that the decision was taken without consultation with the Queen. She had privately made it clear that week that she had been looking forward to seeing both Maria and me again. In Her Majesty's eyes, someone is innocent until proven guilty, and she saw no complication in the Burrells being invited to a function, especially since I had not been charged at that point with any offense. It is another frustrating example of a system that is full of people who think they know better than the Queen; the same suits who suffocated the spontaneity of the princess.

When Prince Charles learned of what had happened to me, I heard that he had expressed his disgust. His point was that my name had been on that guest list for at least four weeks without objection, so what had changed? He was as nonplussed as his mother, but the household had ensured that my attendance was stopped.

O N JULY 24. the intermediary brought together the prince's deputy private secretary Mark Bolland and me. Again, it was Mr. Bolland who had made the contact to ask if the rendezvous could be arranged in London. Subsequently, the intermediary and I traveled by tube to Covent Garden station on the Piccadilly line, then walked to the front of the Garrick Club. Mr. Bolland was waiting near two telephone boxes in the street outside an office of Channel 5. The three of us began to walk down toward St. Martin's Lane, heading in the direction of Trafalgar Square.

As we approached the entrance of the Duke of York's Theatre, Mr. Bolland's mobile telephone shrilled in his pocket. He answered it. It was clear whom he was talking to.

"Yes, Your Royal Highness . . . Yes, he is with me right now . . . Yes, of course I will . . ."

It was Prince Charles. It was clear that he knew the meeting was taking place.

The deputy private secretary, who continued to walk and talk, was listening intently. "Yes, sir . . . and good luck with the Prime Minister, sir."

By then, our walk had taken us down the length of the street, past the London Coliseum, and to a corner where the doorway of the Corney and Barrow pub seemed to be the most inviting venue. It was shortly before 3 P.M.

"I remember when I used to have informal chats like that with the Prince of Wales," I told Mr. Bolland, and he smiled. We got some drinks in, and sat on high stools around an elevated table at the window, no doubt looking like a trio of businessmen enjoying an afternoon drink in the middle of a hectic day. It was certainly a formal, businesslike conversation.

Mr. Bolland said that both William and Harry were upset over what had happened, and that Prince Charles "was keen to resolve this situation." He added: "The Prince of Wales is very concerned about you. He feels you have been out in the cold too long. But we need to know why you were in possession of the property the police found at your house."

I told him what I had told my solicitor: that the items were either in safekeeping, were my own, or had been given to me by the princess or the prince. I added: "This is a big mistake. It shouldn't be happening. It is ruining me and my family, and I do not understand why I have been arrested. If this continues, it is going to open a real can of worms. I need to meet the Prince of Wales to explain everything."

We were in that wine bar for thirty or forty minutes. Mr. Bolland talked as much as I did. Which is why I find it strange that he later described the meeting as "Paul Burrell giving me a sob story in which he stated his life was in tatters." If it was the sob story he claimed it had been, then it was a sob story that had an effect: Mr. Bolland was accommodating, not dismissive. He shook my hand, and departed after making clear that he would recommend to the Prince of Wales that he himself should meet with me the following week.

True to his word, Mr. Bolland organized a meeting in Tetbury, near Highgrove. My intermediary called me on the mobile on August 2 with the words: "The eldest son would like to meet you." The rendezvous was set for the following day.

As the posttrial palace inquiry made clear, Prince Charles believed that "if Mr Burrell apologised and confirmed ... his earlier letter to Prince William ... and agreed to return all the property and promise not to reveal information personal to the princess, it might be unnecessary for the police to charge Mr Burrell."

It was decided to keep Fiona Shackleton and Scotland Yard in the dark about the meeting.

As backup, my brother Graham joined me on the journey south in my car. We set off at 6 A.M. on August 3, with a flask of tea and some sandwiches. It was a warm, sticky day worthy of shorts and a T-shirt, but I had to look my best in my smartest gray suit, worn with the blue *D* cuff links that the princess had given me. I had no idea of the exact location of the meeting. All I knew was that it was going to be held after Prince Charles had finished a game of polo. He had personally requested that it take place away from Highgrove to avoid the prospect of my having to pass through the permanent police security. We seemed to be traveling for an age, and had passed the county boundary for Gloucestershire on the M5 when the cell phone rang. It must have been sometime around noon.

It was the voice of the intermediary. "It's off. He's had an accident."

With a sinking heart, I pulled the car into the next petrol station. "You have got to be joking!"

Prince Charles had been playing polo when he fell off his horse and was knocked unconscious. He had been taken to the hospital and, after a near five-hour journey, I had to turn the car round and drive back to Cheshire. "Well, that's it, then. There's no stopping it now," I said to Graham. All I could think was, How very convenient that a fall from a horse has stopped him from making the meeting.

In time, my suspicions were further aroused. For on the morning of August 3, *before* the polo match, both DCI Maxine de Brunner and Commander John Yates of Scotland Yard had visited the prince and William at Highgrove to provide a briefing about the case. It was a briefing that included a gross misinterpretation of the facts—and one that had hoodwinked Prince Charles and his son into doubting my innocence.

On August 8, the police moved in to ensure that no more clandestine meetings could take place between myself and St. James's Palace. DS Milburn took a signed witness statement from Mr. Bolland that made him a prosecution witness. As such, it would make it very difficult for him to have any further contact with me.

As the posttrial inquiry by Sir Michael Peat concluded: "The police candidly told me that their obtaining of this statement . . . was Machiavellian. By this device, they

sought to inhibit or prevent further contact between Mr
Burrell and Mr Bolland."

Scotland Yard had misled Princes Charles and William
and had ensured that all lines of communication were severed. They were going to drag the case, kicking and
screaming, into court, and the blinkers that they were
wearing were going to keep them focused on the job at
hand.

ON THURSDAY, AUGUST 16, I returned for more
questioning to West End Central police station in
London. With my solicitor Andrew Shaw at my side, I took
with me a prepared statement. Over thirty-nine pages and
in twenty-six lengthy paragraphs, I detailed the closeness
of my relationship with the princess, explaining why certain items had been in my possession, enlightening them
about the trust placed in me. It was intended to be my final
plea for common sense. From behind the sober legal language, a hysterical voice was shouting back at the police to
stop, read, and understand the damage they were about to
unleash.

"This is the statement we would like to present to you,"
Andrew Shaw announced, pushing it across the table in the
interview room.

DS Milburn left the room to read it. Within one hour,
their minds were made up. "Mr. Burrell, we are going to
charge you with three counts of theft."

My stomach lurched.

Charged with stealing 315 items from the estate of the
late Diana, Princess of Wales.

Charged with stealing six items from Prince Charles.

Charged with stealing twenty-one items from Prince
William.

All accusations based on a belief that, sometime between January 1, 1997—eight months before the death of
the princess—and June 30, 1998, I had thieved a furniture
van load of royal items from Kensington Palace.

As DS Milburn charged me, it wasn't sinking in. Why is

the Royal Family letting this happen? What on earth is going on? What the hell have I done to deserve this? were among the thoughts racing around my head. Then the detective sergeant sat opposite me across the table and his words hit me like a sledgehammer: "I believe you have stolen everything, and in twenty years in the police force, this must be one of the largest breaches of trust I have ever encountered."

But it was clear that he had read the prepared statement, because I had spoken about the various personal relationships the princess had had, without naming names, as illustration of my knowledge and closeness. "So, was *your* relationship with the princess purely professional?" asked DS Milburn. It seemed that even police curiosity couldn't be satisfied.

As I was led down a corridor and into another room, I turned to Andrew Shaw, trying not to cry, and said: "I cannot believe it. I cannot believe it."

A doctor told me to open my mouth. A lollipop-like stick was scraped along the inside of my cheek to take a DNA swab. In another room, my fingers and thumbs were pressed against an ink roller for prints. Then I was told to stand against the wall to pose for the camera: right profile, left profile, full face. Three flashes that captured my despair on camera. I felt like both a freak and a criminal; the infamous star of a royal peep show that had the police rolling around and laughing at me.

One police flashbulb turned into a blinding floodlight the next day as the first act of this Scotland Yard farce was played out on the steps of Bow Street Magistrates' Court. As a bewildering scrum of media and police shuffled me into that building, I kept my head down. I didn't see the fist that connected with the right side of my head. I just felt the stinging blow it left on my ear. A member of the public had run in from the street and thrown a punch.

"Just keep walking, Paul," shouted my brother Graham, doing his best with the police to fend off the crowd around me. It dawned on me that some people had already made up their minds that I *had* looted the princess's world, and public hatred would follow. But first would come the humiliation.

You cannot help but feel like a criminal, no matter how innocent you are, when you sit in court. I couldn't wait for the formal procedure of that first hearing to be over with. There is nothing like a legal arena to ram home the enormity and reality of a situation that has, until then, seemed horribly surreal. The innocence I had been clinging to for so long was replaced by an overwhelming feeling of shame. That is what court does to you. It dresses you in shame, and prevents you looking up to see who is staring.

Just to ensure that my humiliation was complete, the police press office decided to trumpet the full scale of the case against me. Ordinarily, only a summary of the charge would be revealed: the three counts of theft as they appeared on the charge sheet. But not this time. The press was handed the full, detailed breakdown of the 342 items taken from my home: each strip of negatives, and the precise quantity; each CD title, and its artist; each piece of clothing or fashion accessory, complete with its color and design. It went from "Item 193: Black leather handbag, white metal handles, contains Boots receipt, black plastic lighter and blue lipstick" to "Item 3: one white metal pepper grinder" to "Item 240: Biblical text" (the one used on the all-night vigil) and "Item 245: notepad with details of mine victims."

On August 30, Sir Michael Peat, who had been appointed as private secretary to Prince Charles, met with Scotland Yard and questioned the strength of the case. His own post-trial inquiry concluded: "Sir Michael's principal concern was the possible adverse repercussions of this court case . . . He was also worried that this was not a strong case, and that there was a risk of acquittal. He believed the police evidence against Paul Burrell was weak."

Despite that concern, there was going to be no turning back. The Spencers wanted to see me walk the plank.

I FLEW OUT of the country the next day to find refuge with eleven members of my family on a prebooked holiday to Florida. All around Manchester airport, everyone was reading the front-page headlines about me. "DIANA'S ROCK IN THE DOCK," screamed the *Daily Mirror*. "DIANA BUTLER ON £5M THEFT CHARGES," said *The Times*. "DIANA TRIAL SENSATION: BUTLER ON THEFT CHARGES AFTER HIGH-GROVE SUMMIT," said the *Daily Mail*. When we arrived in our rented villa outside Orlando, the pent-up emotions of the previous forty-eight hours were finally released. "Wept like a baby" is how my brother Graham described it.

I could escape the spotlight in Britain, but I couldn't escape the hell. The mental pressure was indescribable. There seemed to be no room for rational thought, and I felt constantly agitated. I could hardly sit still, let alone relax, in the sunshine. I was losing my mind with worry, and the very fact I had been charged seared its mark into the personal pride that meant everything to me.

Desperate to ensure that the family enjoyed their break, I went along with them all to Disney World and the NASA Space Center, putting on a brave front.

Halfway through the holiday, I collapsed with exhaustion. A blood condition meant that all the skin on my feet peeled away, leaving them raw. I was treated in a Florida hospital. Doctors told me it was a nervous condition.

BY THE END OF 2001, our finances were in a parlous state. Both the bank manager and the accountant warned that if there was no income within the next three months, we would have to consider remortgaging the house. Maria sent back her favorite aquamarine ring, a Christmas gift from me to her, to a London jeweler in an attempt to raise some extra money. Things were becoming desperate, and we were running into arrears with our mortgage payments. If it wasn't for the generosity of friends, I don't know what we would have done: the Edwardses from Wrexham, the Wrights in Kentucky, Susie Kassem in London, and the Ginsbergs in New York. When Scotland Yard traced a substantial cash amount in our bank accounts back to the Ginsbergs, they went to interview them in their apartment on Fifth Avenue, believing that, perhaps, there was an ulterior motive.

"It's a bit excessive to give such an amount, isn't it?" they were asked.

"We are wealthy people, officer, and we were helping a friend in need. What is so hard to understand about that?" The British police were sent away with a flea in their ear.

We also plundered Alexander and Nick's life policies, which we had taken out when they were babies. Eventually we scraped together enough resources to open a florist's shop in the neighboring village of Holt. Using the floristry skills I had learned in the basement of Buckingham Palace, my "little shop on the corner" became a lifeline—not just financially: it gave me something to focus on. I am a proud man, so I appeared strong to the many customers whose support was incredible. But when that closed sign flipped over in the window at 5:30 each evening, I would sit in the back room and refuse to go home. Maria had so often wanted me to be strong for the boys. I wanted to be strong. But I wasn't. So, crying my eyes out in that room was my release, hidden from the family because they had endured enough upset. If I cried by myself, no one need know. Yet, of course, Maria knew. Some nights I wasn't coming home until 9 P.M. I lied about having to carry out essential bookkeeping and stock taking.

One night, the telephone rang. It was Maria. "Honey, when are you coming home?" I burst into tears yet again. It killed me to know that she was hearing me so weak. Some people grow strong in the face of adversity, but I seemed to be weaker by the day, and, because I am not a naturally angry person, the injustice of it left me with nothing but a soul-crushing depression. Maria sent round my brother-in-law, Peter Cosgrove, and he found me in pieces. He just put his arms around me and said: "Come on, let's get you home."

Writing this, I look back and scold myself for being so pathetic. My perspective is different now—but only because justice prevailed. At the time, I was no good to anyone, and the irony of that was not lost on me. I had looked after and taken care of the emotionally needy princess, and soaked up all her despair and tears. As she had said, I often had the right answers in her most traumatic of times. Yet in my own trauma there were none.

In such a downward spiral, thinking straight is not a possibility. I was a hopeless father. A hopeless husband. I had been an ineffective protector of the princess's world against Scotland Yard. My reputation was going to be pulled apart in public. Everything I had ever cared about was, seemingly, being destroyed. At my lowest point, nothing seemed to matter apart from the prospect of being with the princess again. I wanted it all to end. I wanted to stop crying. I wanted to die. Then I would find her again. It was calculatingly selfish, but it is what I thought. I knew exactly where to go: a turn-off from the road in Cheshire. A quiet spot in the countryside.

I told Maria that I needed to deliver some flowers, and left the shop without even thinking about goodbyes. After a ten-minute drive, I pulled into the lay-by. Mine was the only car. The sun was shining. The sky was blue, save for wisps of white cloud. In the field beside me, a horse lowered its neck to eat the grass. On the passenger seat beside me, there was a bottle of water and a little brown bottle containing sixty painkillers. I sat there, looking at that horse, thinking what a beautiful day it was, that at least Alexander and Nick had Maria, and her family, who were our neighbors, would be there for them. They all had one another. I thought about all this. About Maria having the boys. Me being with the princess. About the finality death would bring to the court proceedings. About the way it would swiftly end the ordeal, and spare me the shame of taking the stand.

I had taken a sip of water and was looking at the unopened bottle of paracetamol in my hand, wondering if sixty tablets would be enough. Then all the emotions welled up again, and disrupted the calm. Cowardice—or something—jolted me to my senses as quickly as the wind changed direction. Because I started to think about the finality of death in a different way. I would die as someone whose guilt had forced him into suicide; someone who had known Scotland Yard was right. Maria and the boys would be left with that stigma.

Besides, the princess *was* still with me. It was her legacy that I had to defend. I threw the tablets back onto the seat, started the engine, turned around, and went home to Maria. When I walked in through the door, Maria asked where the hell I had been.

Calmly, I told her the rationale behind my warped thinking.

She grabbed me by both arms. "You have to think of me!" she said, shaking me. "You have to think of me and the boys." She must have looked into my eyes and seen nothing. "Paul," she shouted. "You have to keep going. We all have to keep going. How would we cope without you?"

If ever there was a turning point in the hell that was 2001 and 2002, it was perhaps that moment. Call it a sudden realization. Call it what you will. Maria made me seek help, and help made the hell seem bearable.

The doctor put me on a course of antidepressants. Maria persuaded me to see a counselor. Every Monday morning, in a private room at the doctor's surgery, I sat and talked to a lovely lady called Jill. For the first time since 1997, I sat down with someone and confronted the loss of the princess.

Jill listened. I rambled on—I had bottled up so much. I had felt guilty, especially for Maria, that I had been unable to let go of the princess. For so many months, I had believed I was going mad, because the smallest thing set me off crying. Even as I unloaded my mixed-up thoughts to Jill, I suffered the excruciating embarrassment of crying in front of her.

But Jill was an immense source of comfort: "Your behavior is perfectly normal, Paul," she told me.

It was as near to "normal" as I was going to get for a while, and we moved into 2002, wondering what the year would bring.

*   *   *

SCOTLAND YARD had made its "Machiavellian" move to ensure that there would be no contact between me and St. James's Palace, but it was powerless to do anything about other channels of communication with the House of Windsor. By the spring, I was maintaining contact with a senior member of the Royal Family, and the discreet support of this longtime ally of the princess proved to be a huge source of strength for me. In the biggest boost to my morale, I was told in a letter: "I would shout your innocence from the rooftops if I could."

I had first written to the royal figure, expressing how "totally trapped and alone" I felt, and venting my frustration at how the "police could not comprehend the world in which the princess lived." In knowing the princess, in knowing the workings of KP, this royal knew much more than Scotland Yard ever could. In my letters I asked for nothing. I wrote: "Why have I been abandoned by the Prince of Wales and Prince William? . . . Surely someone must realize that October 14 [the trial] will unleash a media feeding frenzy, completely out of control . . . There is little I would ask of you, but to pray that there is justice."

What I received in response was a letter promising a lot more than prayer. This senior royal penned me the warmest of letters and reminded me of the duties I had performed and the innocence that others believed in. Then, in the same letter, came an overwhelmingly generous hand of friendship: an offer of a secret bolt-hole, which would provide accommodation for the duration of my trial at the Old Bailey; an address that would offer me both security and privacy. The proposal was that I should stay at a residence used by senior royals. My refuge would belong to the Crown Estate while I stood trial in a case brought by the Crown.

I was getting secret support from within the House of Windsor, and it was an enormous relief. Someone reminded me, around this time, in a telephone call, that the Queen believed that any individual is innocent until proven guilty. All of this acted as timely support when solicitor Andrew Shaw

and my defense barrister, Lord Carlile, QC—the erstwhile
Liberal Democrat MP—and his junior counsel Ray Herman were spending hours in legal conference with me,
working on the minutiae of my defense.

I remember that my first explanation to Lord Carlile
was that "My life will seem stranger than fiction." There
were many times when the jaws of solicitor and both barristers hit the paper-strewn tables as I spent hours detailing
the closeness I had shared with the princess. I was trusting
these exemplary professionals with my life, having to explain aspects of a unique role in the shadow of the princess
to clear my name.

"Your liberty is on the line, and if we don't know everything, Paul, we cannot help you," said Lord Carlile. As my
duty at KP unraveled, the legal team began to realize the
level of trust that had existed between the princess and me,
and how my work went beyond the call of duty and deep
into her personal life.

Lord Carlile said: "Your story is almost like a Shake-
spearian tragedy. It is a ticking time bomb. I think we can
be quietly optimistic about a successful result."

The correspondence with the senior royal continued to
act as a fillip. "Your Royal Highness. I do not want to cause
you any problems," I wrote. The kind, warmhearted offer
remained. Until Sir Michael Peat discovered what had
been proposed. He was informed in the late summer of
2002 about the invitation that had been extended to me.
Aghast, he made his opinion quite clear: that such an
arrangement would be wholly unacceptable in the circumstances, especially for a former servant without authoriza-
tion to stay in such a property. An ally in the Royal Family
had been forced to back down in the same way that the invitation to the Duke of Edinburgh's birthday party had
been revoked. Royal hands were tied once more by the influence of a gray suit.

On both occasions that gray suit belonged to Sir Michael
Peat. So I found it consistent that it was he, with Edward
Lawson, QC, who, at the end of my trial, was charged with
the responsibility of leading the inquiry on behalf of the

Royal Family into the circumstances surrounding the collapse of the Old Bailey court case. It was an inquiry with which I refused to cooperate. As Sir Michael Peat stated in his report: "I do not know what, if any, views on the topic are held by Mr Burrell, who declined to be interviewed by the Inquiry." And he wonders why.

Actress Amanda Barrie, who had formerly starred in *Coronation Street*, then stepped in with a kind offer to share her accommodations in London. It was an overwhelming gesture but I opted to stay with old family friends in Hampton, near Richmond.

THE BEST WITNESSES I could ever have called for my trial were the two remarkable women I had served, and who knew me best. One had died five years earlier, and the other was legally untouchable. For, in one of the many ironies of my case, the Queen is the Law. As head of state, she is the only person in the country who cannot be called to give evidence. It is, I suppose, one of the hazards of the job when you have been a personal footman to Her Majesty, and end up being accused of theft from the estate of Diana, Princess of Wales.

Not that my hand was weak. Scotland Yard had prepared its de facto case, and it had the Spencers—Lady Sarah McCorquodale, Mrs. Frances Shand Kydd, and Lady Jane Fellowes—all lined up as key prosecution witnesses. Detectives, and it seemed the CPS, were happy to rely on the word of the executors to the princess's estate.

In my defense, I would rely on the word of the princess's innermost circle of friends, who were all prepared to take the stand and defend me: Lucia Flecha de Lima, Rosa Monckton, Susie Kassem, Lady Annabel Goldsmith, Lana Marks, Richard Kay, Lord Attenborough, Dr. Mary Loveday, Simone Simmons, Debbie Frank, Jacques Azagury, Father Anthony Parsons, U.S. attorney Richard Greene, Sir Jimmy Savile, and numerous others, whom I will not list for reasons of discretion. They know who they are, and know how eternally grateful I remain to them for joining what I considered to be the most formidable list of witnesses. I also remain convinced that, had the jury heard what these people had to say, the transparency of the prosecution's case would have crumbled before the jurors ever reached the deliberation room.

But the concern at St. James's Palace was the likelihood of Prince Charles and Prince William being called by the defense as witnesses. Indeed, the CPS was so concerned about the prospect of my calling the heir to the throne and his son to the stand that its officials began to examine the possibility of hearing their evidence *in camera*. A prosecution document stated: "We have every reason to think defence lawyers will seek to explore the private lives of Diana, Princess of Wales, HRH the Prince of Wales and HRH Prince William. It may be necessary to restrict who would be in court, and [explore] whether it will be necessary for the court to sit in camera."

At one point in February 2002, as was established by the posttrial inquiry, Commander John Yates of Scotland Yard had assured the anxious St. James's Palace legal advisers "that the prosecution would avoid their being called and going as far as to say . . . that the prosecution would be stopped [before the trial] rather than doing that."

It seemed that both princes were being constantly reassured that they would not be called as witnesses because the majority of the items on the charge list were the property of the princess. But Scotland Yard and the CPS seemed to miss the point. Prince Charles knew how much time the princess had spent at my cottage at Highgrove. He knew how often I had been caught in the crossfire of their marital breakdown. He knew that she took me everywhere with her, because that used to puzzle him. What he didn't know was that the princess had used me as her independent witness to history as it unfolded—the separation, the letters from the Duke of Edinburgh, the divorce—and all of that would have had to be examined to illustrate the true closeness I shared with her.

As for William, he knew better than anyone how close I was to his mother.

For those reasons, and because of the dire circumstances that had forced my hand, St. James's Palace could have been in no doubt that, going into the trial at the Old Bailey, on October 14, Lord Carlile, QC, would have stood in courtroom number one at some point during my defense and said: "We call His Royal Highness The Prince of Wales." Not since 1891 had a member of the Royal Family been called into a courtroom to give evidence. But one hundred eleven years later, history might have repeated itself.

SEVENTEEN

✠

REGINA V. BURRELL

ONE OF THE QUESTIONS most asked about me is: "What makes that Paul Burrell tick?" Some, perhaps, see my perception of duty as an unhealthy, obsequious obsession. Others, like me, prefer to view it as a duty born out of dedication to a devoted friend, one of the most inspirational women of our times. But on going into the Old Bailey trial, I knew the focus and fascination was always going to concentrate on the intricacies of my relationship with the princess.

The paradox of my life, and I know this, is that I was selfless in my role as a butler yet selfish in my other roles as husband and father. All I can say in my defense is that we meet few people in our lives who are capable of making such an indelible mark on our souls. The princess was a truly remarkable one-off. She afforded me the privilege first of entering her world, and then of giving me her friendship. It was not a gift to be relinquished: you hung on to it, cherished it, and ran with it. The problem for some is that I'm still running with it, refusing to let go.

I have never been one for deep introspection or psychobabble. Depending on your viewpoint, my duty to the

398

princess, in both life and death, will either be healthy or unhealthy. But unswerving loyalty to others is something that can be misinterpreted as well as misunderstood by anyone who lives outside palace and castle walls. When someone becomes dependent on another to function, as many royals do, then the need to be needed and the knowledge that you are in control can become almost addictive. The closer the relationship, the more addictive it becomes. In the end, the royal and the aide need each other in equal measure.

No one is supposed to be indispensable, and the princess certainly did a lot of dispensing with her staff. But, as she told friends who would have told the court, she felt she couldn't function without me. Her words, not mine. If I'm honest, I could not have imagined life not working for her, no matter how rough the ride became. I was as dependable to her as John Brown was to Queen Victoria; as Margaret "Bobo" MacDonald was to the Queen; as valet Michael Fawcett was to Prince Charles. I have never been unique or original in that regard. But if Scotland Yard couldn't comprehend the concept of being at home with the royals, the giving of gifts to servants or the trust reposed in certain staff, would a jury? Would the behind-the-scenes account of life with Diana, Princess of Wales seem to ordinary citizens too far-fetched to be true? That was my worst fear as we prepared our case: that my defense would appear as real as an account of life from *Alice in Wonderland*.

In an attempt to get inside my mind and understand my way of thinking, my legal team sent me to lie down for five hours on a psychiatrist's couch in Beckenham, Kent. Even to this day, questions about my state of mind are asked. It seems to me that the best way of understanding me is to read the words of the expert who examined me: Dr. Andrew Johns, of the South London and Maudsley NHS Trust. It saves me the introspection and provides you with an independent voice. After a five-hour examination, he concluded:

Paul spoke several times fondly of his wife, and of her strong support for him. In relation to his relationship

with Princess Diana, he told me that he had "far more respect" for her, saying that "she trusted me more than any
other man." He argued that his relationship with his wife
Maria was "in a different compartment."

The professional relationship between Mr. Burrell and
the princess became one of considerable closeness. She
appears to have greatly relied upon him . . . He appears
to have been responsible for much of her daily care and,
also, companionship . . . The key features of their relationship were as follows: she appears to have confided in
him to a marked extent: he would console her when necessary; when she was on holiday, she would phone him
on a daily basis; she discussed with him her personal
problems, showed him her personal correspondence, and
trusted him to make occasional arrangements to see her
male friends . . . Mr. Burrell derived considerable self-
esteem from her intimacy and friendship, and appears to
have been devoted to her care, to the extent of spending
less time with his wife and sons.

In my opinion, the death of Princess Diana in August
1997 had an overwhelming impact on Mr. Burrell . . . He
saw her traumatised body a number of times . . . The impact of these events was increased when he received a bag
containing the clothes and personal effects that the
princess had been wearing when she died. Mr. Burrell developed a range of psychological symptoms and behav-
iours. His initial response was of helplessness, and he
functioned almost automatically. He slept . . . with recur-
rent nightmares . . . He cried uncontrollably, and felt low
in his mood. He meets diagnostic criteria for a prolonged
depressive reaction. It is not inappropriate to suggest that
his emotional state was such that he has "entombed" important memories and items of the princess.

In my opinion, Mr. Burrell does not . . . show signs of
material mental illness, or personality disorder. He is of
normal intelligence.

I was declared fit to stand trial in the Old Bailey on Monday, October 14, 2002.

*   *   *

"FORGET THE WEST END theatre, and take yourself to the Old Bailey to See the Greatest Show in Town," heralded one newspaper.

The royal freak show—the case of Regina v. Burrell—was about to begin in London's central criminal arena. Even the press would only get access by a ticket system, and almost fifty yellow media passes were issued. Outside, the lines stretched the full length of the building as the public lined up for entry into the public gallery, which looks down on the courtroom. The world had its eye pressed against the keyhole of Kensington Palace, a sneak viewing brought to them courtesy of Scotland Yard and the Crown Prosecution Service. From that moment on, a protected privacy would be exposed. My life, and that of the princess, would be open to close scrutiny, speculation, doubt, and ridicule.

In writing this book, the darkest, most intimate secrets remain protected. But the truth of life at KP, and the essence of my relationship with the Boss, is intended to correct the distortions and wild claims peddled by the prosecution, the police, and, at the end of the case, by poisonous newspapers, speculative royal commentators, and embittered ex-staff released from the employment of the princess. In the end, there seemed to be a stampede to turn me into an unreliable historian. From the outset, my word, my life, my account of history—and therefore of the truths the princess entrusted to my care—were going to be dragged through the mud.

On the eve of the first day in court, I stayed at a budget hotel near Euston station. A mini-army of family and friends arrived in London to support me and Maria. As we pulled up outside the Travel Inn, I noticed a huge BBC advertising billboard suspended above the pavement on the hotel wall. A giant smiling face of the princess, looking her glamorous best, stared down on us as a question asked: "Who is the Greatest Briton?" Sometimes, even when I am not looking for her, there is no escaping the Boss.

A journalist friend joined us all in the bar that night, and I needed several pints of Guinness to calm the nervous shakes that the mere prospect of appearing in the dock had brought on. Maria chain-smoked as we sat in that room, bracing ourselves for the next day's media circus.

Solicitor Andrew Shaw ensured that a smart, chauffeur-driven Mercedes would take us to the court, followed by a minibus full of equally apprehensive but faithful supporters. In the back of that car, I can't remember anyone saying a word. Maria and I just gripped each other's hands. Andrew and junior counsel Ray Herman were lost in thought in the front seats. In that silence, as we neared our destination, I began to feel unwell. My mouth was dry, and every vein seemed to be throbbing.

We traveled up Ludgate Hill, with St. Paul's Cathedral in the distance. It was the same route I had taken on a state procession with the Queen to attend the Queen Mother's eightieth birthday thanksgiving service, but this time we would never reach the cathedral. We turned left, passing the Crown Prosecution Service offices on the corner. As the car straightened up, I could see a crowd milling in the distance. Within seconds, it had become more distinct. It was the media. Dozens of them. Television crews running across the road with cameras on their shoulders. Two separate groups of photographers stacked high, all of them crouched, kneeling, sitting, or standing on small metal stepladders. There were radio reporters, newspaper reporters, hangers-on, crowd barriers to hold them back, police to keep order. Maria clenched my hand tighter. As the Mercedes pulled up to the curb, I looked to my left and noticed a makeshift platform supported by scaffolding. It was the BBC camera point opposite the court's main entrance. Maria and I began to shake, almost in unison.

"Come on, let's get this over with," I said.

"Good luck, everyone," said Andrew, and got out to open the rear passenger door for us. I took a deep breath, swallowed hard, and waited a few seconds.

"Arrivals and departures, Paul. Arrivals and departures . . ." I heard the princess say.

Then we were out and onto the pavement. The first thing that hit me was the sound of the camera shutters; a rapid chorus of fluttering as if a thousand birds had been startled from a tree. Then the flashbulbs. I stood beside Maria, and put an arm around her waist. She did not let go of my hand. Two policemen held open a door as Andrew and Ray Herman ushered us inside. It was horrible to know that Maria was enduring the ordeal, but she had insisted on being by my side. As we got inside, she turned to me: "You are my husband. I am standing beside you, no matter what."

"Paul!" boomed a voice. "How are you?" A friendly hand was thrust out to me. It was James Whitaker, the royal correspondent of the *Daily Mirror.*

"I've felt better, Mr. Whitaker, but thank you."

I always called him "Mr. Whitaker," even though the princess referred to him affectionately during tours as "the Red Tomato." Then, on a corridor, I spotted the BBC's Nicholas Witchell, another of the court correspondents' true gentlemen, "Carrottop," as the princess called him. But the first face I had looked for wasn't there. The BBC's Jennie Bond, long admired by the princess, was covering the Queen's tour in Canada. "Look out for the ankle bracelet she wears!" said the princess. She was fascinated by it.

When it came to keeping abreast of the media, the princess never missed a trick. She knew everything about them: those she loathed, those she liked, those who she knew found the royal pressure a bit too much. All of a sudden, the faces who had followed the Boss around the world were now glued to the fate of her butler.

As the building's clocks ticked toward 10 A.M., we took the lift to the second floor, and I followed the flowing black cloaks in front of me as my defense counsel Lord Carlile and his junior, Ray Herman, led the way, wigs in their hands. We walked from the more modern end of the Old Bailey, and through some double doors into the Victorian, marble-lined area outside the primary courts, where general defendants and their legal teams stood in huddles, or sat on oak benches. It reminded me of the Natural History Museum. Large murals reminded me of the Titian paintings the princess had hung in KP. Daylight poured through the glass of the huge dome above us all. I craned my neck and read the words inscribed into the curved stone: "The law of the wise is the fountain of life." Gathered around the glass-paneled door of court-room number one, reporters—from as far away as America and Australia—huddled in a tight, impatient group.

"Don't worry," said Lord Carlile, as we walked to the door. "Today is all about formality, and the jury being sworn in. It takes a while for the actual case to begin."

I took my first steps into the courtroom: with its oak and green-leather-cushioned seats, it mimicked the House of Commons. The glass-shielded box of the wide, square dock would be my working base for the next two weeks. Maria walked with my dad to a relatives' seating area on the right. I walked to the dock, the seat for murderers, rapists, and armed robbers.

A female security guard politely stopped me from taking my seat. "Mr. Burrell, you will have to come downstairs with me," she said. It was protocol, apparently: defendants should not be seen in the dock until the judge has entered the courtroom. Early in the case, Mrs. Justice Anne Rafferty dispensed with this formality.

Behind me, a small flight of steep steps led into a white-tiled cell. Once I had disappeared from view, the blue-jumpered guard stopped me. "You're okay there. Just stay here with me," she said, and we sat on the bottom steps. It was as if she had wanted to spare me the prospect of going into the cell. She saw my hands trembling. "You'll be all right, you know," she said. "I've sat in here plenty of times. I asked to do this case because it was you . . . and I've got a funny feeling about it." Her name was Michelle, and I shall never forget the sensitivity and kindness she showed me.

The chattering in the packed courtroom above was silenced by three loud knocks. Mrs. Justice Anne Rafferty had entered. Michelle nodded to me. I walked up the stairs and took my seat. Eyes pierced me from every direction. Above me to my right, the public sat forward to get their first glimpse. Behind me, obscured from the judge's view by the dock, the media sat on three stepped rows of benches. In the left corner, a huddle of other reporters squeezed into the spillover press benches. In front, Mrs. Justice Rafferty stared straight ahead. To the left, facing the counsel benches, were the empty oak benches where the twelve jurors would sit. Their eyes would take in everything: me, secrets, sensitive documents, the memories, and hundreds of photographs of the Boss, William, and Harry.

I was asked to stand as the indictment against me was read out as offenses contrary to the Theft Act of 1968. My legs went to jelly, and I tried to hold myself bolt upright. I had this feeling that, at any moment, I would topple over. I was a nervous wreck.

Count one: theft from HRH the Prince of Wales. Count two: theft from the estate of Diana, Princess of Wales. Count three: theft from HRH Prince William of Wales. In the formality of the Old Bailey, it all sounded so much worse than it ever had in the magistrates' court. To each count, I replied, "Not guilty." I looked down to the right and saw Maria suppressing tears on my dad's shoulder as the jury was sworn in.

One thing had changed in the preceding months. The 342 items I was initially charged with taking had been whittled down to 310, but it was no reason for optimism. The jury only needed to conclude that *one* item had been dishonestly in my possession to be sure of my guilt. The prosecutor William Boyce explained that such a collection of royal items was something "someone just should not keep and should not have."

I was determined to hold myself with dignity at all times. Andrew Shaw had reminded me of the don'ts of being a defendant in the spotlight—he'd sounded like Cyril Dickman on my first-ever royal duty at Windsor Castle. "When you are in there, don't stare at the jury, don't fidget, don't pass too many notes to us, and don't let them get to you."

What no one could see below the ledge of the dock was that I was constantly rolling two little quartz crystals between my fingers. I had borrowed them from Nick's collection; a reminder of the energies the princess relied on. I truly believed, throughout every day of those mentally draining proceedings, that both the princess and my mother were with me.

Beneath my shirt, my mother's engagement ring hung on a chain round my neck. In my right-hand trouser pocket, I kept my hand on Mother Teresa's miraculous medal, which the princess had given me after the trip to the mission in London with Maria's mother.

It was hard to listen to Mr. Boyce detailing the layout of my house and the contents seized from it. He went on and on: "Cool and calculating decision . . . What were these items doing in his house? . . . Mr. Burrell's varying explanations are not consistent . . . Pause to consider the potential value of one autographed CD . . ." I wanted to scream. I had far more potentially valuable items in my house than a Michael Jackson or Tina Turner album that the princess had signed—she always labeled them hers; it was a habit from her childhood. Whenever anyone visited KP and expressed a fondness for a particular record or song that the princess was playing on the stereo, she gave it to them. Besides, Mr. Boyce had missed the point. I had never, ever sold an item that had belonged to the Boss, so the potential value he was asking the jury to consider was irrelevant. Its origin, the fact that it had been hers: that was what was valuable to me.

It was more interesting to watch Mrs. Justice Rafferty. She became mesmerizing, making copious notes, filling her fountain pen from a bottle of ink. I wonder if it's blue-black Quink, I thought.

Then she would fidget with her blotting paper, wiping the nib dry.

Is she listening to any of this? Or is she bored too?

She fascinated me as she sat there in her scarlet robes and white wig. A lady who was the image of elegance. Far too glamorous to be a judge, I thought.

She walked in procession into court every morning and afternoon with an almost regal presence; and while her smile was warm, her icy stare demanded silence if the press behind me shuffled or chatted before she had adjourned.

I switched my focus on to the royal crest carved into the wood above Mrs. Justice Rafferty. I read the words I knew so well: *"Honi soit qui mal y pense."*

M ARIA WAS A WITNESS for the defense, so she wasn't allowed to stay in court. We decided she should return home to Cheshire and keep herself occupied by working in the flower shop. My refuge would be the home of our friends Kevin and Sharon Hart—the first people we ever met after returning from Highgrove to London. Their Victorian terraced house in Hampton, near Richmond, was an escape each evening from the madness of the court and the publicity. Kevin and my niece Louise's husband, Tom McMahon, were my friendly shadows on alternate days of the trial. During that fortnight, strong friendships saw me through.

The evening of that first day in court we avoided the BBC and ITN news bulletins. The television was turned off as the prosecution's assassination of my character was aired and reported. I was sitting at a table with the nicest of families, eating spaghetti Bolognese.

"Wearing his second natty tie of the week—another £65 Hermès creation," wrote James Whitaker in his column, then, ". . . and I sat opposite him in the canteen and watched him eat a healthy meal of moussaka . . . He copies Prince Charles in his dress sense . . . and his handshake is firm."

Daily Mirror reporter Steve Dennis conveyed to me the attitude in the press room: "You are smiling too much and looking way too relaxed—and it *is* being noticed. It is being said that you don't give a damn."

Relaxed! I had never felt such a nervous wreck in all my life, but it seemed not even a brave face was allowed. At least at the Harts' home, with their son, Joe, then seventeen, and daughter, Amy, nineteen, we could unwind with a bottle of merlot, and I could be myself without my moves being watched and analyzed. If Kevin ever spotted me slipping into a morose state, he would leap up and say, "Come on, then, let's go for a pint," and we walked to his local pub, the Jolly Cooper.

"This is all so not fair, Kev," I moaned.

"Paul, life never has been fair. You've just got to hang in there and be strong," he said.

That first week, I received the most heartwarming letter from the Sisters of Assumption Convent in Galway, the Republic of Ireland. Sister Teresa, who had once met the princess with Maria's mother, ensured that all the nuns prayed for me every day. "Never underestimate the power of prayer, and we are praying for you," said the letter. So many people seemed to be rooting for me. I received literally bagfuls of mail. My friends know that my feelings for that go beyond appreciation, but I have to mention Richard Madeley and Judy Finnigan. For Richard, too, had once sampled the bitter taste of injustice when he was scandalously branded a thief in a Tesco store while he was a presenter on ITV's *This Morning*.

In the months and weeks before the trial, he wrote many letters of encouragement. Even when things were hectic at work, he found time to scribble notes of support on the back of his scripts. They gave me a massive lift. His insight was crucial. He wrote: "It will seem as if you are in the eye of a storm, and everything is happening around you. I have been there. Let the legal process happen and do what we did: remain close as a family and be strong—Richard."

It was heartening to know that others were on my side, because William Boyce, in his clever articulation of the prosecution case, made everything sound so damning. I had been spotted sneaking into KP at 3:30 one morning. The Spencers had told police that I should not have any royal property in my home. I hadn't told anyone that I was taking things for safekeeping. But I had. I *had*. In a letter to Prince William in April 2001. What was wrong with these people?

I vented my anger and frustration in a little legal conference room on the first floor. This was our "safe room," where exhibits and papers could be stored, and our discussions could take place away from the ears of the police and prosecutors. "Let's go downstairs and discuss the day's events," announced Lord Carlile, at the end of each day's evidence.

I had watched my QC at work in the courtroom with growing fascination, deftly mixing eloquent charm with a sharp legal brain and eye for detail. But he came alive, and ultimately kept me sane, in that small room, surrounded by crates of files and books.

Andrew sat at the table, sharing his thoughts as the man who had done all the initial groundwork on the case. Standing behind him was Shona, the clerk, who scribbled away on a back bench in the courtroom. Then there was me, squashed into a corner, wondering what all the legalese meant, remembering what Richard Madeley had said about it "all going on around you."

I lost count of how many times Lord Carlile exclaimed, "It's absolutely ridiculous!," as we all became engrossed in the prosecution case, the way it was being handled, and the evidence we had never felt was evidence in the first place.

But no sooner had we become engrossed in a particular point than Richard's humor would change the mood. His takeoffs of the characters in the courtroom were a hoot, and I'm glad that, on occasions, we were able to be light-hearted.

If it became too much, I would leave them to it and walk the corridors, pacing up and down, looking at the names of the defendants in other courtrooms, wondering if any more innocents were being made to look guilty too.

ON DAY TWO of the proceedings, the farcical nature of the trial was summed up when someone spotted a plainclothes policeman enter the room, flash his warrant card, and sit down in the public seats. He caught the attention of a female member of the jury, and they acknowledged each other. When this rather curious connection was brought to the attention of Lord Carlile, the jury was asked to retire, Mrs. Justice Rafferty asked that inquiries be made, and we were sent home for the afternoon. The following day, courtroom number one was startled by the findings of those inquiries. Scotland Yard's crack detectives were about to strike another blow for their staggering levels of common sense.

William Boyce was forced to explain that the plainclothes officer, a detective inspector, had acknowledged his *wife* on the jury. It was their wedding anniversary and he had come into court to take her out for lunch. But it emerged that the officer had worked as a member of the Royal Protection Group between 1986 and 1989: he had been with the Royal Diplomatic Section, looking after foreign embassies. Not only that, but he had carried out his duties in the embassies neighboring Kensington Palace. *And* he had served as a police officer in Peckham, London, in the early nineties with none other than DCI Maxine de Brunner, the senior investigating officer on my case. They had also worked together on a Metropolitan Police Service inspectors' promotion study group. The male officer now worked for the Special Branch.

I was dumbstruck.

"But DCI de Brunner's recollection is that she has not spoken to him in the last five years. She could not now put a face to the man," explained William Boyce.

Lord Carlile was having none of it. "If there is a police officer's wife who has an allegiance on that jury, then there is a danger of that allegiance being translated to other members of the jury. There should not be any connection on that jury to the Metropolitan Police."

After a day of legal argument, Mrs. Justice Rafferty agreed. The jury was discharged. The trial of Regina v. Burrell had to start again with a fresh jury of five women and seven men.

EVEN AS THE princess's world was spilling out into the Old Bailey, I was desperate to do what I could to protect her secrets. Secrets I did not want to be aired in court. Secrets that have not gone into this book. When I handed over my thirty-nine-page statement to police at the time I was charged, it was only ever intended to be an explanatory document, to be seen only by the trial judge, the barristers, and the jury. There were sensitive paragraphs of the most personal nature, involving medical issues and her love life, which summed up my role and unique closeness to the Boss. I did not want them to be aired in open court before the press.

In the initial prosecution opening, William Boyce had allowed the first jury to read the contents quietly to themselves. As he pointed out: "It is the defense's wish for relevant paragraphs not to be read out, and the Crown is content to accept that course."

But the media was not. It challenged my request. Thankfully, Mrs. Justice Rafferty agreed with us and, using her "judicial discretion," she made a ruling that certain contents within the blue folders in front of the jury would remain confidential to protect Princes William and Harry. "CENSORED," screamed the *Daily Mirror* the next day. "AFFRONT TO JUSTICE."

The media and defendants use the same door to exit the court. As we shuffled out that day, one female reporter turned to me and said: "I've never known a case shrouded in such secrecy. You don't know what's going to happen next."

DS ROGER MILBURN was on the witness stand, and Lord Carlile was pressing him to shed some light on what they had initially gone in search of when they raided my home. Documentation in relation to a golden dhow, said the detective.

Then my barrister kept pressing him, curious as to the contents of a box the police had kept asking for: the mahogany box with the initial *D* on its lid; the box in which the princess kept her most sensitive documentation; the box I was supposed to have removed from KP.

"So, what did you know about the alleged contents of this box?" inquired a curious Lord Carlile.

The press seemed collectively to hold their breath, pens poised.

DS Milburn hesitated. "Great parts of this case are very sensitive," he said, before looking to the judge and asking her: "May I write it down on a piece of paper?" and Mrs. Justice Rafferty nodded.

The press exhaled a sigh of frustration; all pens dropped onto the paper.

Then the case was adjourned for the first weekend, prompting next-day headlines of "DIANA'S SECRETS" and "WHAT'S IN THE BOX?"

By the following Monday, the intrigue was over. The full picture emerged with the judge's approval. Scotland Yard was looking for a signet ring given to the princess by Major James Hewitt; a resignation letter from her private secretary Patrick Jephson; letters from Prince Philip to the princess; and a tape, which became known after the trial as "the Rape Tape." It was a recording made by the princess in 1996 when she informally interviewed former KP orderly and ex–Welsh Guardsman George Smith. He had alleged that after a night of heavy drinking he had been raped in 1989 by a male member of staff who worked for Prince Charles. It all came to a head because George, who had worked at Highgrove, St. James's Palace, and KP, had been suffering nightmares, was drinking heavily, and his marriage was falling apart. He blamed it all on an incident that he said he was bottling up.

The princess was fond of George, and when he confided in her, she was appalled. Armed with a Dictaphone, she went to visit him at a clinic where he was undergoing treatment for depression. She wanted his allegations on record. (George Smith has since waived his legal right to anonymity.) The Boss made the tape to protect the interests of someone she cared about, and she vowed to do something about it. In her eyes, he was the victim, and the perpetrator was still at large, working for her husband. She had placed the tape, without writing anything on its label, in the box where she knew its explosive contents were secure. But she was determined to make sure action was taken, so she rang Prince Charles, relayed the incident as it had been explained to her, and begged him to fire the man in question.

She made the call in the sitting room at KP. I was beside her as an independent witness, and listened to every word. She was almost trembling with exasperation at her husband's lack of urgency over a situation she felt was criminal. "Charles, are you listening to me? This man is a monster," said the princess.

I only heard one side of the conversation, but it was clear that the prince had little time for what he saw as his wife's unnecessary hysteria. He told her "not to listen to staff tittle-tattle."

"You have to let him go. You have to do something." Her pleas fell on deaf ears.

The princess knew the member of the staff in question. From that moment on, she loathed him. "I know what that evil bugger did. I know what he did to George, and I will never forgive him for that," she seethed, after her futile attempts to bring about justice.

Little action was taken. In October 1996, George Smith received a visit from royal solicitor Fiona Shackleton. The upshot was that the alleged rapist was not sacked, and George's stress and depression were blamed on Gulf War syndrome. He never returned to work, and accepted a settlement at the end of his employment of around £40,000.

The princess ensured that the tape never saw the light of day. But the mystery of its whereabouts, and the threat its contents posed, emerged during the police investigation of my case. Lady Sarah McCorquodale had asked that Scotland Yard "ascertain" the contents of the box. The princess had shown me the cassette tape, but she never gave it to me. After her death, both Lady Sarah and I noticed the blank-labeled tape in the box, but it was not removed, and it was kept under lock and key. Only Lady Sarah and I knew of the key's location. But the lock was later forced and broken, said police.

In court, DS Milburn said: "I was looking for the contents of that box."

All of a sudden, the undertones behind the raid on my home became clear.

DCI MAXINE DE BRUNNER took the stand, and everyone in courtroom number one was, in their mind, transported to Highgrove on August 3, 2001, when she and Commander John Yates briefed Princes Charles and William about their investigation of me—before I had been charged.

According to the female detective's notes, and as the posttrial Sir Michael Peat inquiry confirmed, both princes were told that police had a "strong case" because they "were in a position to show that Mr. Burrell's lifestyle and finances altered drastically after the death of Diana, Princess of Wales" and that "police are in a position to evidence that large quantities of items have been sold abroad to several dealers." The briefing also explained: "In addition, an independent source has shown police photographs of several staff members dressing up in clothing belonging to Diana, Princess of Wales at a party . : ."

None of that was true, and DCI de Brunner admitted they did not have a shred of evidence, and never had, to support the claims that painted me as a thief who sold the princess's items around the world, and dressed up in her clothing. God knows what my former employer and the boys I had watched grow up thought of me.

A briefing that was intended to paint "the full picture" had been riddled with falsehoods, because it was presumed that my financial status had improved because of the sale of royal items from KP. But my finances had improved because of my book and the lectures I had given to promote it. As an illustration of just how exhaustive and thorough the police investigation was, DCI de Brunner said she was not aware of the book I had written or the lectures I had done. She said the briefing was based on "intelligence that we had gained."

Then Mrs. Justice Rafferty, who looked as incredulous as the rest of us, stepped in and asked: "Is it right that you allowed the two princes to remain under that gross misapprehension?"

DCI de Brunner, who had not once corrected the wrong information she had imparted, replied: "Yes, it is."

Lord Carlile carried on: "You do not think that the failure to correct these falsehoods was grossly misleading and unfair to Mr. Burrell?"

DCI de Brunner: "All I can say is, I didn't inform him of the changes."

Lord Carlile: "It would not have been difficult, would it, for you to telephone the solicitor to the Prince of Wales, Mrs. Shackleton, and tell her that he had been given some mistaken information? You could have done that, couldn't you?"

"I could have done."

"And you did not?"

"No," replied DCI de Brunner.

In the posttrial inquiry of Sir Michael Peat, it was made clear: "The Prince of Wales very clearly remembers the revelation relating to there being evidence of sales by Mr. Burrell . . . strongly influencing his view."

YET MY LEGAL TEAM, because of the case papers we had seen, had tried, two months before the case began, to sound the alarm bells, bang on the palace doors, scream through loudspeakers, and light the warning beacons. Short of putting up a giant neon sign outside St. James's Palace with the words "PLEASE WILL YOU LISTEN: YOU HAVE BEEN MISLED," there was little more we could have done to grab the attention of the Royal Household.

On August 20, 2002, Lord Carlile met with Fiona Shackleton and her criminal-law specialist Robert Seabrook, QC, to warn them that "The decision as to whether the Prince of Wales should support a prosecution had been taken on the basis of unsupported, false information . . ." One month later, on September 30, 2002, Lord Carlile again met with Mr. Seabrook. As the posttrial inquiry stated, Lord Carlile said: ". . . The essence of the defence was Burrell's unique and very close relationship with the princess . . . their closeness was a ticking timebomb . . . and I suggested the case was a disaster waiting to happen for the Royal Family, and they had been deceived by the police at Highgrove."

OUTSIDE THE DOOR of courtroom number one, a piece of paper was stuck to a board, detailing the case being tried. It said "Regina v. Burrell," which seemed a warped title for the truth. It wasn't the Queen or the Royal Family who had wanted to see me on trial. The reality was that it was "Spencers v. Burrell." What had been a sound working relationship between a butler and the princess's family had broken down.

I had been told, by someone who knew the family, that the Spencers "were sick to the back teeth of hearing how much that bloody butler was a rock to Diana." In the Old Bailey, they had been offered the perfect chance by Scotland Yard to prove otherwise.

Mrs. Frances Shand Kydd shuffled unsteadily into court, one step at a time, aided by a stick. She was the picture of frailty. A gaunt old lady with white hair, her croaking, rasping voice made it sound like she was incapable of saying boo to a goose. As the jury took in that sympathetic image, I knew better. As she steadied herself into the wooden-framed witness stand, Mrs. Justice Rafferty leaned forward to ensure that she was all right. "Mrs. Shand Kydd, which is more comfortable or less comfortable, standing or sitting?"

"I am very happy to stand for a bit."

"What I suggest, stand until you want to sit, and vary it as you may wish."

"Thank you, my lady," said a grateful Mrs. Shand Kydd.

William Boyce stood to commence his examination. "I hope you do not consider us insensitive, discourteous, or disrespectful, but during the course of the case, we are referring to your late daughter as Diana, Princess of Wales . . ."

Don't worry about that, Mr. Boyce, I thought. She's called her daughter much, much worse.

As she was led through bundles of files by the prosecutor, I didn't take my eyes off her. She never once looked in my direction. I willed her to turn her head and look at me. Why are you doing this to me? I wondered. Have you forgotten all those times you spent at our home after her death? The cross and chain you gave me for protection? The kind offer to buy us a home in London? What have I done to deserve this?

But I knew the answer to that one. I had become too close to her daughter, had been regarded as family more than she was, and that pained the Spencers. In her evidence, she sometimes called me "the defendant" or "Mr. Burrell," never Paul.

Mr. Boyce's next question brought me out of thought. "How would you describe your relationship with your daughter?"

"Loving and trusting," she replied, and I began to shuffle toward the edge of my seat.

"Was it always? Or were there sometimes ups and downs?"

Mrs. Shand Kydd cleared her throat. "There were sometimes ups and downs. I would suggest to the court that was normal family behavior, and in every family there are disagreements . . . and those disagreements are irrelevant to the future."

My mind flashed back to a vivid recollection of a scene at KP, a few months before the princess's death, in the spring of 1997. I had been in my pantry when I heard sobbing upstairs.

"Paul! Come here . . . quickly," shouted the princess, over the banister.

I sprinted up the stairs and was almost behind her. The princess, in her white robe, picked up the telephone receiver, which she had left on the carpet, off the hook, in front of the gray marble fireplace. A voice was rambling at the other end of the line. I had often heard the princess cry with frustration, when she felt sorry for herself, but this was a heartbreak I was witnessing. She sat, cross-legged, on the carpet, clutching the receiver to her ear, hunched forward. She waved me closer. I knelt beside her, and tilted my head as close as possible to the receiver.

I detected the slurring voice of Mrs. Shand Kydd in full flow. The princess was sniffling and shaking her head in disbelief. She was absorbing a volley of verbal abuse from her mother, who was making it quite clear what she thought of her own daughter going on dates with and being associated with Muslim men. "You are nothing but a . . ." She used words that no mother should say to a daughter.

The princess slammed down the telephone and wept again. I sat with her and placed an arm around her.

"I am never going to speak to my mother again, Paul, never," she vowed. They never did speak again, and every time Mrs. Shand Kydd sent a letter to KP asking for forgiveness, the princess recognized the handwriting and sent it back, unopened, marked: "Return to Sender."

Back in the Old Bailey, it was Lord Carlile's turn to begin his cross-examination. He had to tread carefully. "As far as your relations with your daughter Diana are concerned, I am not going to pry in any detail at all, except to put this aspect of it to you. You and your daughter Diana last spoke to one another in the spring of 1997."

"That's correct, but it happened with all our family and she made it up with all . . ." And then, in the same breath, she switched the focus onto reducing the importance of my role in the princess's life. Mrs. Shand Kydd feared the path my barrister was about to take. ". . . I think there has been a slight misinterpretation by Mr. Burrell . . . that he was referred to as 'my rock.' This was a term she used regularly and often to many people. She called me her 'rock' and 'star.' "

"But your daughter regarded Paul Burrell as, let us put it this way, a rock?" asked my barrister.

"Yes," she replied, "but no more so than other people, which included, of the same vein, her drivers . . . her protection officers . . . her family."

So the jury heard how everyone, even those who had deserted the princess in service, was her "rock." And how

Mrs. Shand Kydd, who I knew had caused her daughter such heartbreak, was her "rock." If only that jury knew the full story as it flashed around inside my head. I so wanted Lord Carlile to let it be known, but law, as I learned, can be a precarious game when your liberty is at stake.

At that juncture, all the jury saw was a frail, white-haired old lady, whose sharp wit had made many in the court smile. In their eyes she was the mother of the princess and an attack on her at that stage would have been foolhardy. It might have turned some members of the jury against me, said my legal team. Lord Carlile had to skirt around the edges, and the truth would have to wait until *after* the court case. For that moment, Mrs. Shand Kydd would trample all over my reputation, putting distance between me and the Boss.

Then Lord Carlile asked: "You knew that Paul Burrell was the person who was there, if required by your daughter, from the time she awoke in the morning to the time she dispensed with his services at night?"

She replied: "Maybe. She didn't discuss times with me."

"Do you accept that it is likely?"

"Not really. Because many, many days she was out, away," and Mrs. Shand Kydd felt better to believe that.

I could not believe what I was hearing. But it got worse, as she demonstrated her woeful lack of knowledge of life inside KP, and its clear-outs and handouts of unwanted royal gifts. Referring to the princess, she said: "She was very, very careful with all things royal. She was also very careful with gifts from people . . . I can promise you, she gave nothing away other than gifts she usually bought for Christmas and birthdays."

But, at least, she came clean about the documents she had shredded indiscriminately; the destruction of a history that had led me to raise the handling of the princess's world and memory at my December 1997 meeting with the Queen. As my statement had made clear: "I feared at the time of the princess's death that there was a conspiracy to change the course of history, and erase certain parts of her life from it. Mrs. Frances

Shand Kydd spent two weeks shredding personal correspondence and documents."

Lord Carlile: "You spent many hours on many days shredding documents, didn't you?"

Mrs. Shand Kydd: "On many days."

"How many documents do you think you shredded?"

"Between fifty and a hundred."

"And you never told Paul Burrell what you were shredding, did you?"

"No, I don't think I did," she said.

Lord Carlile now focused on my rescue of the princess's world. "You knew that Paul Burrell was genuinely concerned about the preservation of as good a reputation as possible for your daughter Diana?"

"Yes."

"You knew that he was concerned that history should not be rewritten in a way which was in any way critical of the princess?"

"Those views were not expressed to me."

She was being defiant to the end. At the end of her evidence, as she shuffled past me one last time, Mrs. Shand Kydd still couldn't look me in the eye.

The last time I had seen Lady Sarah McCorquodale was about six months after my enforced departure from the Memorial Fund. She was walking across Westminster Bridge in London, and we exchanged a few brief curt words. But the Old Bailey was, essentially, our first proper reunion since that meal with Anthony Julius in the wine bar near Southampton Row.

In the witness stand, she came across as assertive, with the confidence of aristocracy. I never took my eyes off her, hoping my stare would somehow be noticed. Spencer number two had taken the stand to testify against me.

Lady Sarah, out of all her family, had been closest to the princess. The Boss had often said she liked her sense of fun. It was a prime reason why she took her as a lady-in-waiting on foreign tours. After the princess's death, Lady Sarah and I had been great allies, working well together. I remembered the cuff links she had placed in my hand, the

Versace dress she had given to Maria, the £50,000 variation of the will in recognition of my loyalty. Perhaps I had become too close to her sister, raved about her memory too often. But, as she spoke, all I thought was, How did our relationship come to this?

Her words to that court summed up how much she hated the fact that I felt it was my duty to be a keeper of her sister's secrets.

William Boyce asked her: "What, in your view, might Mr. Burrell have had lawfully in his possession?"

She replied: "Cuff links, photographs in frames, enamel boxes, tiepin, ties, and I think that would be all."

WHEN YOU SIT in the dock of a courtroom, you tend to note the onetime friends or colleagues who suddenly crop up to testify against you. In compiling a defense, you also notice the reticence of those people not prepared to raise their heads above their parapet to stand by you.

I had considered the comptroller at KP, Michael Gibbins, to be a friend. I was wrong. This trained accountant had arrived at the palace about a year before the princess died. Yet he took the witness stand for the prosecution, professing to know the truth about the closeness between butler and princess. Which was odd. Because he worked in an office that was completely separate from apartments 8 and 9. He had no idea of life in the princess's sitting room, dressing room, dining room. But because I had once complained to him about the long, exhausting hours, he felt he was in a position to speak about my feelings of "insecurity" within my employment.

William Boyce said Mr. Gibbins had told police that the relationship was not as strong as I believed. "There was a closeness, but it may not have been entirely as Mr. Burrell has described," said the prosecutor. He even suggested that I was thinking of moving to America. Which was correct—because the princess was too.

It was Friday, October 25, when Michael Gibbins took

the stand. That same day, around the corner at St. Paul's Cathedral, the Queen, the Duke of Edinburgh, and Prince Charles arrived for a memorial service for the victims of the Bali bombing. Her Majesty's Rolls-Royce purred up Ludgate Hill, passing the end of the street leading to the Old Bailey. A few days later, the conversation that took place in that car would have an enormous impact on "Regina v. Burrell."

On the following Monday, part-time nanny Olga Powell was another surprise face on the witness stand. She had been a firm favorite of the princess, William, and Harry. She was also the last person I expected to see up there. We had shared many aspects of our service at KP. Before the trial, we had spoken and she said she had no intention of becoming a witness for anyone. "I don't want the fuss and bother at my age," she told me.

As she stood in court, telling the jury about the habits of Prince William, I wondered why she was now turning against me. I could see what she was doing. She was defending William and Harry. But, in doing so, she was wielding the prosecution hammer that was intended to nail me to the wall.

OUT OF ALL the numerous dressers I had worked with, Helen Walsh was probably the most spiritual, a practicing Catholic like Maria. Perhaps that was why she walked into the witness box and spoke the truth. The moment she took an oath I sensed her reluctance to be part of the prosecution case. Speaking with a candor not expected by the prosecution team, she told how the princess used to dump unwanted clothes into the middle of the floor, or hand unwanted royal gifts or trinkets to staff. She, too, had been given numerous items.

A startled Mr. Boyce asked her what she had been given. "That's really none of your business," she told him, and I tried to suppress a laugh.

"Didn't know she was rowing in his boat," one of the prosecution was heard to say by my legal team.

The prosecution case was being held up to scrutiny, and was failing on its own questions. The gift-giving culture that had been so prevalent in royal households for so many years was coming to the surface.

Outside the courtroom, I saw Helen in the marbled hallway. Defendant and prosecution witness rushed up to each other and embraced. "Thank you, Helen, for being so honest," I told her.

"I just told the truth, Paul. That's all I did."

Throughout that day, Prince Charles's solicitor Fiona Shackleton had been talking to Commander John Yates of Scotland Yard. We wouldn't know that until the next day.

TUESDAY, OCTOBER 29, dawned as any other. The previous evening, my legal team had surmised that we had gained ground; that, in terms of evidential point scoring, we had come out on top. My opportunity to give my version of the truth was almost upon me. Lord Carlile had prepared me to take the witness stand the next day. The defense was due to start within twenty-four hours.

None of us had any inkling of the behind-the-scenes activity until we walked into the courtroom. The press, Lord Carlile, and the rest of the defense team were asked by the ushers to clear the court. The prosecution was locked in chambers with Mrs. Justice Rafferty. The case was adjourned for an hour.

"What's all this about? Is it bad for me?" I asked Lord Carlile. He had no idea.

When Mrs. Justice Rafferty reentered the courtroom, the news stunned everyone. Turning to the jury, she said: "Ladies and gentlemen, I am sorry, there has been a slight delay. We can't sit today and I am going to send you away now."

Just like that. She sent the jury home and adjourned the case until further notice. Lord Carlile leaped to his feet. He inquired about the reasons for the unexplained adjournment. Mrs. Justice Rafferty declined to inform him. She stood. Everyone rose. And that was the day's court proceedings. It was shortly after eleven o'clock.

"What on earth is going on? Is this normal?" I asked Andrew Shaw.

"Er, no. It's all a bit strange," he said.

I didn't know what to think. My head was spinning with speculation. The press crowded outside the courtroom, equally baffled. Mystery hung in the air above the chatter of intrigue. Something was happening, but nobody milling around that hallway knew anything.

In our safe room on the first floor, we pondered the possibilities.

"Could it be more evidence? What if they think they've got more evidence?" I panicked.

"No, Paul. If it was that, we would most certainly know about it. It has to be more serious than that," said Lord Carlile. He thought for a bit longer. "Paul," he said, "is there anything you can think of, something you haven't told us, which might have relevance to your case? *Anything?*"

We sat there—Lord Carlile, Ray Herman, Andrew Shaw, Shona, and I—and raked over old ground in a monotonous recall of the facts, a bit like one of those movie detective squads that has reached a dead end. He knew about the offer of accommodation from a senior royal—everyone knew about the meetings with Mark Bolland. Was there anything about Prince Charles? Anything about Prince William? Anything about my meeting with the Queen?

You see, I had already disclosed *that* meeting with Her Majesty. It was disclosed to the police in a pretrial statement. It was also mentioned in a sixty-four-page statement that had been intended for my legal team's eyes only: It read: "It seemed to me that everyone the princess ever knew wanted to relay their own personal grief to me. Even the Queen . . . granted me an audience which last [*sic*] almost 3 hours in her private apartment at Buckingham Palace." That was all it said because that was all I thought to write down at the time. I hadn't detailed the actual conversation.

After that sudden adjournment, all I could concentrate

on was one question: What is going on? In that safe room, we began to speculate about Prince Charles being called as a witness, and we could all live with that prospect.

But what if Prince William was to take the stand? I couldn't bear the thought of sitting in the dock as the elder son of the princess stood in front of me, testifying against me. As soon as that seed was planted in my mind, my imagination went into overdrive. In my mind, the talks behind the scenes were all about orchestrating the handling of the evidence of a royal, and that left me fretting endlessly.

Later that day, we were informed that the court would not be sitting for three days, until Friday.

I DIDN'T SLEEP a wink all night. The more the hours dragged, the more paranoid I became. The not knowing was driving me mad. It was mental torture, and it infuriated me that the legal system was toying with me in such a way.

After pacing around the Harts' home all morning, I needed to get out. After days of thinking the case was going my way, I viewed the adjournment as a blow. I had never felt so down since the first day of the trial. The need to pick up a pint of milk became my excuse to go for a long walk.

I walked and walked and walked, and found myself wandering into the open spaces of Bushey Park. It was raining hard, and the incessant downpour sent men and women scuttling along the footpaths, heads down. In the distance, I could hear the swishing of passing traffic, and the rain bounced off taut umbrellas. The only person who didn't care about getting wet was me. I looked at my watch. I had gone out for that pint of milk three hours earlier. I watched the world go by, thinking that I should be in the Old Bailey, clearing my name, not in the park fretting about what was happening. I felt like screaming. I did the next best thing. I rang a journalist friend who was covering the case, and vented my frustration. I rambled on to Steve Dennis for fifteen minutes: "I don't know how much more I can take—I'm losing my mind. How dare they toy with me like this? What have they got that is taking so long? I know this is bad news. I know it."

"Paul," said Steve, "you don't know what it could be. It could be another witness, it could be the end. I don't want to raise your hopes, but this could be anything . . . and it could be good news."

He was attempting to lift my spirits, but I didn't thank him. "It won't be, not in my wildest dreams, so don't tell me that."

The uncertainty was excruciating.

Kevin Hart had been driving around Hampton, looking for me. He found me in Bushey Park, placed his arm around me, and said, "Come on, let's go for a pint."

ON THURSDAY NIGHT, we had a legal conference in the London chambers of Lord Carlile. Once more, the team sat around, racking its brains. We went back over the letter I had sent to Prince William, then the meeting with the Queen.

"What did you talk to the Queen about?" asked Lord Carlile.

"We talked about many things," I said. "Maria and the boys, her family, the princess, William and Harry, and I told her everything that was happening at Kensington Palace. We spoke about lots of things," I said.

"Did you express your concerns about Mrs. Frances Shand Kydd shredding documents?"

"Yes."

At that point, all the other eyes in the room flashed in my direction.

"Well," said Lord Carlile, clearly at a loss, "why didn't you tell us that earlier?"

"It was a private conversation with the Queen. We spoke about a lot of things."

I'm not sure that even then in that room with my lawyer and barristers, the significance of that conversation truly dawned on us. It was useful to know, it was an important piece of information for the defense. We could incorporate it into my testimony when I took the stand.

That was our thinking at the time. Never did any of us think that we were armed with the capability to destabilize the trial.

There seems to have been a lot of bewilderment, cynicism, and conspiracy theories surrounding my meeting with the Queen and what was said. Yes, I had told Her Majesty that I had taken papers for safekeeping. But I had told her no more than I had relayed to Prince William in my letter of April 19, 2001, and the CPS had seen that letter. The CPS had seen the words "for safekeeping," and it didn't seem to matter. In light of my declaration to William, the silence from St. James's Palace and the pursuit of a conviction by Scotland Yard merely told me that none of my written pleas was important.

What, after all, is the difference between telling the Queen about retaining items for safekeeping and telling Prince William? In fact, I had also written a letter to Prince Charles on February 5, 2001, telling him exactly the same thing. It was said that the letter never reached him. But his deputy private secretary Mark Bolland saw it. For me, therefore, the significance of informing the Queen of my intentions was lost.

It is still lost on me, to this day, why it was such a surprise to the CPS, because its officials had known I had told Prince William of my safekeeping intentions. What William Boyce would go on to tell the court would sum up, in my eyes, the farcical nature of the prosecution, and the blindness it had displayed since January 2001.

THE AIR WAS THICK with anticipation on Friday, November 1, All Saints' Day. There seemed to be more press than ever before. I didn't want to think what the day would bring. Having settled into a legal routine over the previous two weeks, I was back to square one, and trembling inside.

"Something of significance is happening," Lord Carlile had said the previous evening.

As if to add to the drama, in the middle of the morning,

the fire alarms went off at the Old Bailey. Everyone was evacuated into the street. It was chaos. I stood on the pavement between Lord Carlile and Andrew Shaw. Television cameras and photographers swarmed around me. I tried to look relaxed, tried to concentrate on the conversation around me, but it was useless. I was distracted and tense.

Then clearance was given to return to court.

A few minutes later, Lord Carlile offered the first reassurance of the morning: "The police are starting to shuffle around and pack up their boxes. It's a good sign."

I waited outside courtroom number one. My cell phone rang in my pocket.

It was journalist Steve Dennis. His voice was shaking. He was standing at the other side of the double doors near the staircase. "Paul, it's gonna collapse. No one knows why, but it's coming to an end. There are press officers for the CPS and Metropolitan Police on hand."

It didn't dawn on me. "So what does that mean?"

"It means they're here to clear up the mess. Paul, we all know it's going to end. We know!"

I couldn't believe it. "No—not in my wildest dreams! Look, I've got to go." I clicked off the phone.

"Paul, it's time to go in," said Lord Carlile.

All of a sudden, I felt completely detached from myself. I walked into the dock. Michelle, the guard, smiled at me. Three knocks on the door. Mrs. Justice Rafferty strode in, and the horrible quiet of a courtroom descended.

William Boyce got to his feet. "My Lady, it has been an important part of the prosecution case that there was no evidence that Mr. Burrell informed anyone that he was holding any property belonging to the executors of the estate of Diana, Princess of Wales . . ."

I was too hooked on his next words to dwell on the inaccuracy of that claim.

"Further, prosecution witnesses have been examined in chief, and cross-examined, on the basis that the prosecution had no evidence to show that he had ever notified anyone that he was holding property of Diana, Princess of Wales . . ."

Wrong again, I thought. The letter to Prince William had been under your noses the whole time.

He continued: "On Monday of this week, the prosecution was informed by the police that, during a private meeting with the Queen in the weeks following the death of Diana, Princess of Wales Mr. Burrell mentioned . . . that he . . ." Mr. Boyce carried on, explaining the "false premise" of his case. It transpired that the Duke of Edinburgh had mentioned to Prince Charles, as they traveled to the Bali bombing memorial service the previous week, that the Queen had been told by me that I had taken documents for safekeeping. Prince Charles informed his private secretary Sir Michael Peat the next day. He then confirmed the account with the Queen. St. James's Palace then reported the topic of that conversation to Scotland Yard.

Then I heard William Boyce say: ". . . and the proper course would be to invite no further evidence against Mr. Burrell, and invite the jury to find him not guilty."

I was sitting there, heart thumping, trying to grasp the rushed legal statement he had just delivered. I threw a look at Lord Carlile. He smiled. I looked at Andrew Shaw, who had been with me from when the police had raided my home, and he was sitting back. Relief in the camp. Then she said it. The words I shall never forget. "Mr. Burrell, you are free to go." Mrs. Justice Rafferty smiled warmly.

For a second or two, I didn't move. I looked back at Lord Carlile. He nodded. "Come on," he mouthed.

I didn't know if my legs would support me as I got up and stood tall in the hush. A huge swell of emotion rose in my throat. Every noise I made—the chair going back, the shuffling, my footsteps—was heard by everyone watching me. Michelle, the guard, gave me a guiding hand. The press stared at me in silence. I left the dock, turned right, went down three steps into the well of the court, and sat down as three not guilty verdicts were entered against my name in the absence of the jury.

Mrs. Justice Rafferty stood and walked out of court. The press darted out to explain to the world the magnitude of the Queen's historic intervention. The one witness I knew

I could never call from the outset had come through for me. The Queen I had served all those years ago had spoken up for me in defense of my memory of another remarkable royal: Diana, Princess of Wales. As reporters and television producers rushed into the street, I walked over to Lord Carlile. "Is that it?"

"Yes, that's it, Paul. It's over . . . it's all over."

I couldn't stop the sob that sent me leaning into the shoulder of my defense barrister. The QC who had been brave enough to take on the Crown in a case involving the Crown, and he had done a superlative job in seeing me home. As my eyes wet the shoulder of his cloak, he patted me on the back. "I think we should all go to lunch. I know a nice little place in Covent Garden," he said.

Then Andrew Shaw passed me his mobile telephone. "It's Maria."

I took the phone, and the first thing I heard were her tears of joy.

I think all I managed to say was "Maria?" before we started crying together. "It's the Queen, It's all thanks to the Queen," I said, and I was surrounded by my legal team. The roller-coaster ride we had all been on was finally at an end.

Maria was hardly making sense in her euphoria, but she told me to listen. She held out the phone, and a mass of cheers broke out. She was in our florist's shop in Holt, and family and customers roared out their support.

Andrew Shaw and I went out into the street. I don't think my feet touched the ground as a scrum of reporters, photographers, and television crews swarmed around me, all fended off by shoulder-to-shoulder policemen. I had to steady myself on the backs of the officers in front of me.

"Paul! Paul!" the photographers screamed. "Paul! Over here." I tripped over the leg of a newsman who had toppled over. I looked up and faces were pressed against the windows of the buildings towering above me; other office workers hung out of the windows and waved. I tried to wave back, but my arms could hardly move.

Then Andrew Shaw spoke on my behalf to the media. A

railed-off pen at the top of the street was the prearranged press conference point. He thanked everyone, told of my relief, and everyone was shouting my name. I was drained and numb, but had I been able to, I would have screamed to the world: "God, it feels good to be free!"

We all went to celebrate in a restaurant in Covent Garden. It was quiet, save for four other diners sitting round a table. As I walked in, that table broke out in spontaneous applause, and each one of those kind strangers shook my hand.

Two special people joined our celebration, and added to the poignancy of the occasion: Richard Kay and Susie Kassem, friends of the princess. I don't think I've ever hugged Susie so tight. "Someone is looking down on you," she said, and that set us both off.

As we sat down, another face walked in: Fiona Bruce of the BBC. It was raining outside, and she looked soaked, but she didn't seem to care. She had come to drop off a bottle of champagne. "I just wanted to say congratulations, Paul." She kissed my cheek and left us to toast my acquittal.

That evening, I returned to Cheshire and the sanctuary of a relative's home. Ultimately, despite being denied the opportunity in court, I was able to issue my defense, as it would have been told in court, in the *Daily Mirror*. Then the rest of the newspapers—Britain and America—turned on me. Having survived the prosecution of the state, I had to survive a two-week persecution by the media. I had sold my soul. I had betrayed the princess, and, once more, the ignorance of the many blurred the knowledge of the few.

Even in doing this book, I know I have not betrayed the princess. For to grasp the definition of betrayal, you first to need to know the amount of knowledge. It is for that reason that I know I have remained true. The princess would understand that too. It goes some way to answering the question: Where do you go from here?

I walked away from the Old Bailey to begin a new future, and yet I refuse to get rid of the past. It is either a flaw or a strength. But having cleared my name in court, it re-

mains my duty to clear the name of the princess, and ensure she is remembered for the remarkable woman she
was. Memories are there to be treasured. People worry
about my being obsessed, but I am merely haunted by an
exceptionally kind ghost.

I am stronger than I have been in a long while and, despite the actions of the police, I still have faith in human
nature and the millions who believe, like I do, that the
princess's memory should remain as vibrant and as vivid as
the magical mark she left on people's lives.

Will I move on? Of course.

Will I let go? Never.

The princess gave me something special, and, in sharing
with you some of those warm memories and stories, I hope
her personality shines through. Forever and a day, I will
continue, in the face of whatever may come my way, to
stand in the princess's corner and defend her memory. It is
what she would have expected.

I know what we had. I know the depth of what we
shared. I know the future we were heading to. And the one
thing that people cannot take away from me is her final letter to me, left propped up on the desk in my pantry the
month of her death.

I read it often as a source of immense strength and comfort. It turned out to be a written farewell, and it seems a
fitting farewell to this book:

Dear Paul,

*Clearly from your third eye, this coming weekend is
an important one!*

*I know that, too, and I wanted to write on paper how
enormously touched I am that you share this excitement
with me as well. What a secret!*

*You are marvellous how you cope with my questions
day after day and it's quite annoying that you're constantly right!*

*But, on a serious note, your support, as always, has
been invaluable and kept me sane during some of the
nightmare times . . .*

Now, the tide is changing and we can all now have peace of mind and look forward to happier times and different homes!

Thank you, Paul, for being such a tower of strength.
Love from Diana

What's the secret?
Sorry. That's between the butler and the princess.

EPILOGUE

"H APPIER TIMES AND DIFFERENT HOMES" . . .
"Happier times and different homes."
Over and over again, that phrase, from the final letter the princess left me, repeated itself to me as the British
Airways flight dropped gently through the cloud cover over
New York on the descent into JFK Airport. I could imagine
her saying it: that ghostly voice in my thoughts—a ghost from
the past denied her future. It was a future that would, without
doubt, have seen the Boss making a new home of America—
the very country she had in mind when she wrote in that letter:

> And we can all now have peace of mind and look forward
> to happier times and different homes!

As the Boeing 747 scorched its tires on touching down, my
head was still aching from the British media free-for-all that coincided with the first publication of *A Royal Duty* in October
2003. It was an inevitable consequence in the UK for those like
me who would dare to have a voice against the upper classes.

At the time of her death, the princess was planning, by the
admission of her own hand, to take Maria, the boys and me
with her to America on that journey into "happier times and

different homes." It is why she had pinpointed the former home of actress Julie Andrews in California, imagining us all sharing the American dream.

As soon as I stepped off the plane and onto American soil, I felt happier to be in a land where the media and its people are not so judgmental; happier because this is where the princess was the happiest for that very same reason. America is where she felt the most free. And, like me, she simply adored the American people.

It didn't take long for me to realize why. Proof of that class-free, upbeat American spirit was provided somewhere between the arrivals gate and the luggage belt.

"Hey," said one New Yorker who had recognized me as "Lady Di's butler," "hang in there. You're doin' a great job! The princess was sure lucky to have a guy like you." And he shook me firmly by the hand. With that one greeting, at the start of a promotional book tour of the States, that ebullient American, with a grin as wide as Fifth Avenue, rid me of the cobwebs and shackles of British traditionalism that states that butlers have no right to pen books.

In America, the interviewers and people are caught up with the actual life story, and it created a "Let's give this guy a chance and see what he has to say" accepting attitude. The Americans listen, read and then judge for themselves. I cannot ask for fairer than that.

CALIFORNIA, AND ITS SUNSHINE, may have attracted the house-hunting princess in the final year of her life. But it was the intoxicating buzz of the frenetic, horn-blowing streets of Manhattan that transfused itself into her blood-stream, and put that energetic spring into her step. She loved taking chunks from the Big Apple lifestyle.

I had four days in New York, visiting television studio after studio on the media treadmill that controversies create. I remember walking to one Barnes & Noble bookstore in Manhattan for a book signing, and stopping in my tracks as I walked past the front window. Pictures of the princess adorned a huge window display, those beautiful eyes of hers staring out into the street. Inside the store, a queue snaked its way around the bookshelves. In a back room, I took a sip of water and wondered what the public reaction would be.

One moment of support at JFK Airport did not constitute a mandate of the people, but I need not have worried.

The Americans brought with them not only a reassuring word and friendly smile—they brought with them their own memories of the princess: where they were when the Boss died, what she meant to them, how she empowered them in different ways, where they had once seen her on a royal visit. Some brought photographs. Some brought royal souvenirs. And every single person who took the trouble to queue brought one special thing for me: words of assurance that I was doing the right thing.

Even Welsh singing legend Tom Jones gave me a small dose of that feel-good factor. Not that he knew it at the time! I had been sitting in the ABC radio studios, earphones seemingly glued to the sides of my head, speaking to what seemed like every radio station the length and breadth of America, back to back. One three-minute interview after another, for two hours, from radio breakfast to midmorning shows . . . Before going into such an airwaves marathon, I had known that Tom Jones had a dressing room farther down the corridor for a televised performance, and yet our schedules had kept us from meeting in the hallway. Nevertheless, I could still tell my boys back home that I was in the same studio as the Welsh crooner himself.

I think I was talking "live" to Alabama via a radio station, holding the earphones tight to my head, when from the corner of my eye I detected a slight commotion on the other side of the studio window. The Tom Jones entourage—backup singers, band, makeup and publicist—were passing. The great man himself was just behind. Tom Jones himself was ambling down the corridor, adjusting the cuffs on his sparkling black shirt in anticipation of his performance, when he looked to his left and saw me in the radio booth. He stopped in his tracks.

"Hey, Linda!" he shouted ahead to one of his team, and he began walking again. "It's the butler! It's the bloody butler! I told you he was 'ere."

How peculiar, I thought. Life on a book tour, and in the middle of a media storm, can be most surreal.

It is the kind of anecdote that would have had me gossiping like an excited child with the princess back at KP. She got giddy about meeting Oprah Winfrey. Or getting a phone call from Kevin Costner. She would have been impressed that the one and only Tom Jones had recognized *her* butler!

In my time in America, and especially in New York, I found myself momentarily imagining the princess in Manhattan in 2003. I walked into the lobby of the Carlyle Hotel for the interview with ABC and Barbara Walters and immediately thought: "The princess's favorite hotel." I stayed at the Four Seasons and thought: "The princess loved dining and meeting friends here."

With memories of the princess not far from my mind, and knowing that I was defending her memory in a country that embraced her as one of its own, I knew that the American tour—from New York to Los Angeles, San Francisco to Dallas, Atlanta to Washington, Orlando to Miami, Boston to Washington—was going to be one of those memorable experiences. I knew, from day one, I was going to "hang in there" and keep smiling. Even though a storm was raging against my family and me back home in Britain.

IN ONE FLORIDIAN HOME in Claremont, not far from Orlando, there are photographs of the princess. That home belongs to family friends Chuck Webb and Ron Ruff, who knew the princess in the latter years of her life and, together with me, encouraged the Boss to take an interest in movie memorabilia. Especially Disney memorabilia, because of William and Harry. Taking pride of place in Chuck and Ron's home is a CD soundtrack of the Disney animated film *Hercules,* signed by Diana. The princess had sent it to Chuck as a thank-you in the months before she died, and he treasures it to this day. He is one of those rare Americans who knew the magic of being touched by the kindness of the princess: the importance of a small thank-you, once again, not lost on her.

So it was fitting that it was Chuck, a master of organization, who dreamed up one of the highlights of the American tour in Winter Park, that chic area of Disney's heartland in Orlando. He had arranged an evening book signing at a Borders store, but what made this evening special was that the occasion was the annual Special Olympics (Florida) for children and adults with disabilities. That magic formula of the princess and charity combined to create the biggest and most successful book signing *A Royal Duty* had witnessed in its galloping promotion across the States.

I remember driving from Chuck's house in time for the 7 P.M. start time, wondering about the usual issues ahead of a prepublicized event. Will it be a success? How many will turn up?

And I remember thinking desperately: I just hope this is a success and not a flop for the sake of the people from the Special Olympics. As it turned out, the only real worry should have been if my wrist would drop off from writer's cramp, because I have never seen so many people nor signed so many books. As I sat down at a table at the back of the store, an official from Borders came over to me and said: "People have been lining up here to see you since 5 P.M.—we've never seen a crowd like it!"

And they kept coming. And queuing. And queuing. And queuing. Until the line of people snaked its way in tight U bends throughout the store. People clutching books lined up patiently from 5 P.M. until 11 P.M.

I dared not stand up and look at the crowds. I just kept my head down, and kept signing. All night long, people from around the Orlando area came with the books to be signed, and messages of support. Just thinking about it now makes me shake my head in disbelief. I am attached to a phenomenon. It is an association of which I am extremely proud. But to witness such an overwhelming turnout from such a genuine army of ordinary people was as staggering as it was humbling.

I remember wiping away the tears of a few ladies that evening. In remembering the princess, so many people still get emotional. It is the power of the Boss, and what she meant to people throughout the world, that she still, all these years on from her death, has the capacity to provoke strong emotions with her memory. How she would shake her head with puzzled disbelief over that. And giggle nervously.

It was a marvelous evening, and it was significant that such a breathtaking spectacle unfolded near Orlando, the place where my family and I have been planning to begin spending part of each year in the future. I am, at last, going to be living (albeit on the East and not the West Coast) that American dream with my family, the one we shared with the princess.

After the arduous and traumatic journey of the past few years, we, once again, can look forward to happier times and different homes. . . .

THERE WERE, and still are, many secrets between butler and princess. The men in gray suits and the media, who have accused me, rather too readily, of selling every ounce of my soul, would blanch if they knew every confidence the Boss entrusted to me because she had become so concerned about the manipulative system around her. Those within it cannot have believed that certain home truths had been buried with her. Neither could they have expected that her voice would fall silent with the passage of time. An icon like the princess wields a powerful influence that sears an indelible mark on society long after he or she has gone from this world.

When I sat down to write this book, I composed every page with her memory in mind: in life she had relied on my judgment so many times, as her final letter to me makes clear. My sincere hope was that my judgment was still relevant, now that her knowing smile and mischievous look had gone as a reliable barometer. In deciding what to do with the knowledge I had acquired, I made a clear distinction between the most intimate, sensitive secrets the princess would have expected me to keep and historical fact so that I would not impinge on or invade her most private world—even if the facts damaged others whose selfish interests would have been better served had I remained quiet. When the princess felt the balance of truth was tilted against her, she ensured that her version of events was heard in some form. Hence Andrew Morton's *Diana: Her True Story*. Hence *Panorama*. And on my part, *A Royal Duty*.

It was never part of a public-relations game plan for me, her butler, to defend the princess's memory, and I knew that by going down this particular route, I would be exposed to fierce repercussions: a servant should never be so presumptuous as to define what elements of royal history should or should not be known. But as thousands upon thousands of letters from the public have confirmed, this book was a tribute to the warmth and magic of both the monarch and the princess. Call me naïve, but I never expected it to be labeled "a betrayal." I still maintain that it is nothing of the sort. Besides, there are many others, and chief among them is Prince Charles, who know more about the betrayal of a princess than I ever could. But perhaps it was because of Prince Charles that the most unexpected hostile response came from the most unexpected quarter.

"HVE U SEEN THE TV? U've been upsetting Wills & Harry!" said a text message from a friend on the evening of Friday, 24 October. It was the fifth day of the *Daily Mirror* newspaper's serialization of this book ahead of its launch on Monday, 27 October, and my family and I were holed up in the Rowton Hall Hotel, under the protection of the newspaper's journalists; our home, a few miles away in Farndon, was besieged by the press. There were even reporters in the hotel lobby, so Maria, Alexander, Nick and I were confined to our rooms. After a week of headlines about the book, Maria had said only that afternoon that she couldn't wait to return home and "get back to normal."

I erased the text message, and flicked on the television. I'd upset William and Harry?

The BBC's *Six O'Clock News* told me that Prince William and Prince Harry had issued an unprecedented statement against me. Royal correspondent Nicholas Witchell was reporting that the boys "couldn't take any more" after what *Newsnight* described later that evening as "lurid headlines."

"They've had enough," said Witchell, from outside Buckingham Palace.

Five days of newspaper coverage had passed before the boys had decided, seemingly, to make a move. Why wait until now? Why create fresh headlines when the initial furor over the butler-penning-a-book shock had died away?

The penny dropped. It was forty-eight hours before the book's official launch. In my eyes, the timing could not have been more calculated. A cleverly worded statement, delivered from the mouths of the princess's sons, could distort the true intentions of this book.

The statement appeared in full on the television screen. For added impact, the statement was read aloud, in front of the television cameras, by Colleen Harris, press secretary to Prince Charles, who looked as dazzled by the enormity of this event as I felt.

In a tabloid generation, the princes were responding to a drastically curtailed serialization of my book—rather like reviewing a twelve-track album after hearing three of its loudest songs.

That afternoon, the private secretaries and press advisers to the heir to the throne had mobilized their strategy. A character assassination carried out in kid gloves can be as brutal as those in the bare-fisted world of politics. Wicked whispers from spin doctors are not the sole preserve of the Houses of Parliament. They are now part of the eye-for-an-eye public-relations maneuvering within royal palaces when its advisers feel the image of the House of Windsor is under attack. On that tumultuous night it emerged that the gray suits had launched into an "off the record" and nonattributable forty-minute-long briefing to discredit me. Or, as they would no doubt justify it, to put the depth of my so-called betrayal in its proper context.

Royal correspondents from every newspaper in Fleet Street were invited—except the *Daily Mirror*, which was excluded because of its close association with me: that man Burrell was going to be kept in the dark just as the Palace had been unaware of the production of my book. The journalists rushed to Clarence House and a meeting with Colleen Harris and Sir Michael Peat, a familiar gray suit whenever an incident involves my name. An "off the record" conference, which goes much further than any on-the-record statement can, spreads the message of the day, which on this occasion declared Paul Burrell was a traitor. The House of Windsor was swinging its cannons in my direction. Grateful reporters listened and left with plenty of quotes that were intended to increase the pressure on me. The next day, the newspapers duly carried the anti-Burrell message, all the quotes of disapproval and dismay placed in the mouths of anonymous "courtiers" and "senior aides."

I balanced the words of the princess's sons with those of two of her true friends, Susie Kassim and Lana Marks, who had both rung me during the previous forty-eight hours to offer me their full support.

Susie: "I trust you, darling, and know that what you have written is appropriate and not a betrayal."

Lana: "I have every confidence in you, and already know that the book is a fitting tribute. The princess will be smiling down on you."

Their support helped me make up my mind to make a statement to the press. My sons tried to encourage me, knowing I was anxious. I drafted a speech, pacing the carpet, and rehearsed it out loud. The phones were going mad. The statement had to be ready in time for the BBC's *Ten O'Clock News*. The urgency sent me into a spin. Adrenaline made my hands tremble.

From the room, I could hear the satellite trucks rumbling up the hotel driveway. I peeped through the curtains and saw the media waiting, cameras and spotlights poised.

"Right, Paul, are you ready?" said a voice.

I rehearsed my speech one last time.

"Go for it, Dad!" shouted Alexander and Nick, as the hotel door clicked shut behind me.

Outside, a leaf on the tarmac marked the prearranged spot where I should stand for the cameras. My stomach was in knots. Be strong, be strong, I kept telling myself. And then I began, appearing stronger than I felt:

> I am saddened at the statement issued on behalf of Prince William and Prince Harry. Saddened because I know that this book is nothing more than a tribute to their mother. I am convinced that when the princes, and everyone else, read this book in its entirety they will think differently. My only intention in writing this book was to defend the princess and stand in her corner. I have been greatly encouraged by calls of support from some of the princess's closest friends within the past forty-eight hours. . . . I have told the truth where the British public should know the truth.

I meant every single word, and I could not have spoken with more conviction.

My hopes were also shored up by letters such as this one from a woman in Georgia, USA.

> I will admit to you that I was hesitant to purchase it [the book]. As a matter of fact, I adamantly refused. I will also admit to being angry that you would write such a "tell-all" book. Then came Christmas 2003. My mother . . . purchased it for me. Finally, my curiosity overcame my sense of outrage. I found that I could not put it down. You did something for me that I have only dreamed about. You allowed me to meet the princess. Your book was tastefully done.

Regardless of the tabloid headlines, no matter what hysteria the royal pundits stir up, despite the best attempts of the press advisers to the House of Windsor, the truth and sincerity of my tribute to one woman's life, personality and work cannot be tarnished.

By that weekend, it seemed I might have the chance to offer an explanation to William at least. Well-briefed royal correspondents were reporting that he wanted a face-to-face meeting. It was portrayed as peace talks—but it was an invitation I wanted desperately to accept.

AFTER LIFE WITHIN the walls of KP, I was well used to witnessing—and weathering with the Boss—an approaching media storm, battening down the hatches to apartments No. 8 and No. 9, and lying low for a few days. Outside, the reporters and paparazzi worked themselves into giddy excitement that, after their columns had been published, would pass until the next controversy stirred around her or Prince Charles. On many occasions, the princess inflicted the headlines on herself, but she had a well-rehearsed drill in place to cope with it. At these times of perceived crisis or press hostility, she would retreat into the solitude of KP. The stereo, which sat in the white-painted bookcase in her sitting room, belted out classical music and Gregorian chants, drowning her thoughts. Loud music, which always made the pantry ceiling throb, signified a palace under siege or an emotional crisis. It was as if the princess was assuming a protective shell, taking comfort from familiar territory, until it was safe or wise to emerge. Lunch appointments at London restaurants were canceled and girlfriends were invited to the palace; friends were rallied for their support; advisers were sounded out on the telephone for their wisdom. These fusses inevitably petered out, and the princess remained fairly philosophical—if in need of reassurance—about being at the epicenter of yet another "crisis for the monarchy." As she said: "If you place your head above the parapet, you have to be prepared to get shot."

She was often more savvy than people gave her credit for: she placed her head above the parapet, but she knew when to duck and take cover. I would marvel at her ability in dealing with the fierce pressure of the media's scrutiny, even when it took its toll on her. But when she was the architect of a headline-grabbing moment, incident or revelation, she was strong and defiant. She reveled in being a rebel if it was in the cause of truth. In that regard, she taught me valuable lessons, and would not have expected me to sit back and do nothing if myths, lies and misconceptions congealed on her memory. That is why I wrote *A Royal Duty*.

There were times in recent months when I wished that I, too, could retreat into a fortress once I had said my piece in the interests of the princess and history. But for a onetime servant who had decided to go against the grain in telling the truth, then being judged for it, there could be no hiding from exposure.

The book was kept secret until that week of newspaper serialization. On the first day, October 20, certain perspectives were going to change and a disturbing question mark would be placed over the circumstances leading to the princess's death. The *Daily Mirror*'s first headline was going to be: "DIANA LETTER SENSATION: THEY'RE PLANNING 'AN ACCIDENT' IN MY CAR SO CHARLES CAN MARRY AGAIN." The world soon knew the fears the princess had harbored for her safety. Long before William and Harry had issued their statement, I knew the approaching media storm would be one of the mightiest.

On the weekend prior to that newspaper headline, and before I headed to my publishers in America, I booked into the Marriott County Hall Hotel, just off Westminster Bridge, to get my head together. It was an appropriate location: I had worked opposite the hotel's reception area, in the same building, which encircles an internal courtyard, in the offices of the Diana, Princess of Wales Memorial Fund. Same nighttime view toward the golden glow of the Houses of Parliament and Big Ben, and the darkness of the River Thames. It had often mesmerized me when I was dwelling on memories of KP rather than dealing with the frustrations and politics of the Fund. Now my tribute to the princess—and, indeed, the Queen—was about to be made public.

I took courage from my memories of the princess's resolve and her stubborn determination in pursuing a course she felt was right. In my own mind, and to this present day, I am convinced that I was right to defend the princess with a portrait no one else could paint. But at that stage there was no telling what the media and public reaction would be. I had to wait and wonder—and brace myself. By the time Britain was waking up to the news of the princess's prescient letter about the car accident, I would have left London to be in Manhattan.

AT 2 A.M. NEW YORK TIME (7 A.M. in London) the telephone at the Four Seasons Hotel, Manhattan, began to ring. "All hell is breaking loose over here!" said one London caller, and placed the receiver next to his television, which was tuned in to GMTV.

"This is a chilling premonition" . . . "It is the most devastating thing you will ever read" . . . "It is just incredible." Those were the phrases I caught from *Daily Mirror* editor Piers Morgan in an interview with Fiona Phillips. The color reproduction of the "crash letter"—as this disturbing piece of correspondence from the princess became known—was being shown on every television channel: her handwriting spoke for itself. More important, it was being beamed round the world, reviving the need for a belated inquest into the princess's death.

In those early hours, I sat on the edge of my bed in a dressing gown. It was deathly quiet in New York, and there was bedlam in London. I could imagine the people's incredulity that the princess had almost prophesied the manner in which she would die. It might not have been regarded as new evidence, but it was a crucial indicator to her state of mind in the final year of her life.

I felt tremendously sad but mightily relieved that the letter was out and part of the burden I had carried was off my shoulders. My mind raced about the consequences. I got up and started pacing. I must have done more than a dozen laps of the room that day. I imagined the panic buttons being jabbed in the Buckingham Palace press office, Prince Charles's fury, the outrage of the British public. Soon enough the latter were making their feelings known. One television poll indicated that, in the light of the letter, 91 percent of respondents felt the princess had been murdered.

By the start of America's morning, the "crash letter" was flashing up on the ABC news channel. That afternoon I discovered the most breathtaking view of Manhattan from one of the city's palatial apartment blocks. I was in the New York home of best-selling crime writer Patricia Cornwell, which was a huge thrill because I can be included in her worldwide army of fans. I am still not sure whether her home recovered from my invasion because sixteen other people were crammed into it that day, with an entire television crew. She was interviewing me for American television because, in an uncanny coincidence, she had spent months working in secrecy, too, bringing her forensic eye and investigation skills to that car crash in Paris. As her program was lined up to be screened, I had reproduced the letter of the princess. I was more than happy to cooperate with Patricia's program at a time when an inquest date had not been announced.

Before filming took place, Patricia invited me into her office for a private chat, and there, overlooking Manhattan, I remembered all the great times the princess had had in New York. "She was so lucky to have someone like you," Patricia said, as we sat down.

I joked that in Britain everyone was saying how *un*lucky the princess was to have had someone like me.

Patricia Cornwell's passion for her investigative work is as sincere and strong as mine to ensure that the princess's memory is well served. She was a tremendous source of encouragement to me that afternoon as we spoke about the letter, and whether it had been right or wrong to reveal it.

She said, "Look, Paul, you need guts to stand up for the truth and to stand up to Buckingham Palace. You should be proud of what you've done."

Proud may not be the right word. But I firmly believed I was right, and people like Patricia Cornwell have helped me continue to believe that.

"HIS ROYAL HIGHNESS the Duke of Edinburgh would like to have a copy of the book," said an official from Prince Philip's press office in Buckingham Palace.

On day two of the serialization, London had awoken to the headline: "PHILIP'S AMAZING LETTER TO DIANA: I CAN'T IMAGINE ANYONE LEAVING YOU FOR CAMILLA." I could almost see the princess smiling with satisfaction—whenever she was smiling over the newspapers at breakfast, it was a safe bet that the men in gray suits were not.

I had been walking in Union Square, New York, and was just hailing a yellow cab when my publishers rang me on my mobile. In the din of Manhattan traffic, I could hardly hear what was being said to me, until the cab door had shut.

"Prince Philip has requested a copy of the book," my caller repeated calmly.

I told her not to give it to him.

"The book is not available," the duke's press office was told.

The Palace attempted another route. "May we buy a copy of the book, then?"

"No. That is not possible either, because the books are currently embargoed from sale," they were told.

The Palace then turned the screw a little tighter. "It does seem extraordinary that we cannot obtain a copy of the book when its content, and property belonging to His Royal Highness the Duke of Edinburgh, is now in the public domain!"

Again, the publishers resisted. But, in a compromise measure, the pages that related to Prince Philip were photocopied and taken, by hand, to the Palace. By midafternoon on October 21, 2003, the royal lawyers were scanning every word. In time, they decided they could do nothing to prevent the publication of the truth. The gray suits would have to think of another way to discredit me.

When I returned from America to the UK, it was just as Prince Charles had opened the front door to Clarence House—in tribute to the late Queen Mother. He had granted access to *World of Interiors* magazine; I had spotted its October edition on the newsstands at Heathrow Airport. The glossy front cover featured an interior shot of Clarence House, showing off the Robert Kime–influenced refurbishment. The article told the world that this was how Prince Charles and Camilla Parker Bowles would be living while maintaining and respecting the memory of its former occupant, the Queen Mother.

This is the opulence and style to which Camilla will become accustomed, I thought—the woman who had been the subject of much correspondence between a princess and a duke. The princess wrote lengthy replies to the Duke of Edinburgh's letters. She was rather clever, if a little mischievous, when it came to penning them. Instead of using her own burgundy-edged stationery, she borrowed her husband's cream paper with the blue crest of the Prince of Wales's feathers surrounded by the garter and surmounted by a coronet. The princess always had a sense of irony, which would not have gone unnoticed by the duke when he opened the envelopes. The princess's letters to him focused on the "chief problems" in the marriage. Camilla was a chief problem, she told him. Camilla—who now has a room under a royal roof. That magazine cover would have infuriated the princess.

In the summer of 1992, she had taken great satisfaction from telling her father-in-law the harsh truths she had been forced to face up to with regard to Camilla. If he could vent his private feelings about Camilla, then the princess would do likewise, as she unraveled her inner torment layer by layer, phrase by phrase. She might have kept a vocabulary list propped up on her desk to help her find the right words. The Boss had a sharp turn of phrase, and used it to devastating effect when she felt the need to know the full scale of her husband's behavior.

In one reply to Prince Philip, she wrote that Charles "resumed his relationship with Camilla rather sooner than you might have imagined," and that "he was never emotionally divorced from her."

Nineteen eighty-six was the year that everyone, including the duke, widely believed that the royal marriage had "irretrievably broken down." In writing that calculated response, the princess was making it known that she believed her husband's infidelity had happened "rather sooner," and she made that assertion with force. She was telling her father-in-law that, emotionally, she had been cast adrift from the beginning. I still maintain that, for the first five years of their union, the Prince and Princess of Wales were in love. But love can mean different things to different people, and it seemed the princess was convinced that her husband's version was never a match for hers.

She was doing so because, around the same time, she suspected that Prince Philip—and perhaps others—had been a collaborating architect in the marriage's downfall; that he had given his blessing, with a nudge and a wink, for Prince Charles to renew his liaison with Camilla. A blind eye turned to marital indiscretions is part and parcel of the unofficial protocol in royal and aristocratic circles.

Of course, critics will typically accuse the Boss of paranoia in considering that Prince Charles had had any sort of blessing to return to Camilla. It is worth emphasizing now that it was not a figment of her imagination, but had been planted in her mind by Prince Charles himself, during a fierce row. She never specified when the argument took place, but in the heat of the moment, Prince Charles had told his wife that he had always had his father's blessing—from the outset of his marriage—to return to Camilla if the princess did not make him happy. The words were poison to one who had believed in the sanctity of marriage. She was made to feel that 1981–86 had been her period of grace. Of all the hurtful arrows that Prince Charles could fire at her, that was, perhaps, the most devastating. And she wanted the duke to know what his son had told her. In writing to him, she laid bare her hurt:

> *Charles told me that you said that if the marriage was not working well after five years, he could essentially return to Camilla.*

She went on to say that she'd loved Prince Charles and had been devastated to learn that she'd been "offered to your family on a sale or return basis," like an unwanted piece of merchandise.

The princess had felt like a pawn in a royal game to find a suitable wife for the prince, who could not marry Camilla, as she was already married. Perhaps now the public can better understand why the princess felt that there were always three people in the marriage, and why her sense of injustice burned deep. In her eyes, she had been sold to the royal family to produce an "heir and a spare," in the form of William and Harry, then returned to the wilderness. And yet, despite what such knowledge must have done to her, she never stopped loving Prince Charles. Her strength and decency did not allow room for loathing or hatred. Even jealousy, with all its justification, only turned into resentment, and the princess made no secret how she felt towards the other woman. The radiantly beautiful Diana, Princess of Wales—the most beautiful woman in the world—could feel jealousy towards Camilla Parker Bowles, definitely not one of the most beautiful women in the world, but Camilla was the woman the princess yearned to be: the woman Charles *needed* emotionally.

The princess was not afraid to express her jealousy to her father-in-law. In the same letter, she described what it felt like to be treated as an "irrelevant part of the menage" by Charles's circle, while Camilla was treated as the "Prince's chatelaine." "Presumably you find it suitable for my husband to have a mistress," she wrote. That led the duke into a quick riposte: he said that neither he nor the Queen approved of either party having lovers, and he strenuously denied telling Prince Charles that he could return to the arms of Camilla. The princess wrote many pages to the duke, and said many things, but it was her views on Camilla that I noted.

As I leafed through that magazine at Heathrow, I found it hard to visualize Camilla living like a wife in everything but name in the splendor of Clarence House. But the mistress who had always wanted to get her feet under the table had finally done so.

THERE WAS A DEVELOPMENT in the princess's thinking about the significance of Camilla Parker Bowles. In the eighties, "that other woman" had been the source of her private suspicions. But by the start of the following decade, she had become the reason for the marital breakdown. And by the end of 1995, the princess had exposed Camilla, in the BBC *Panorama* interview, as the villain of the piece, telling millions of viewers that her marriage had felt a little crowded. History has taught us to accept that Camilla Parker Bowles was destined to be with Prince Charles; that she, and only she, was the woman for the heir to the throne.

But by 1996 the princess had thought otherwise. She was convinced that Prince Charles had a roving eye, and that while Camilla was his principal mistress, she was not the only one. Despite the clear contradiction such a belief paints, against the backdrop of history and that Prince Charles and Camilla are now officially an "item," it demonstrates the princess's lack of trust in her ex-husband. She felt strongly that he had the capacity to cheat on Camilla, as he had cheated on her; that while he needed Camilla for love and solace, he could not help wandering in search of adventure. That much is consistent with the saga involving Tiggy Legge-Bourke. At one point, the princess felt Charles was more likely to run off with her than with Camilla.

The Boss could never accept that Camilla was the one and only "other woman." Indeed, she believed that Camilla had learned to tolerate this trait in Charles, which royal consorts have done in the past and which the princess never could.

On February 22, 2004, I was flying from Manchester to Madrid to promote the Spanish edition of this book when an article in the *Mail on Sunday,* on the private life of the prince, captured my attention.

"IS THIS THE SEXY BLUE BLOOD CHARLES BETRAYED CAMILLA FOR?" asked the headline. The report said that rumors, which have been strongly denied, had swept royal circles that Charles had been "infatuated" with an unnamed brunette aristocrat.

Is time going to prove the princess right? I wondered. It was suggested that "Camilla was party to the relationship and that she, however implausibly, apparently sanctioned it."

Implausible? Hardly, I thought. A blind eye turned again on a royal partner's indiscretion.

I read on:

The Mail on Sunday *has established that the rumours relate to a period soon after Princess Diana's death—around the time that his relationship with Camilla was intensifying.*

Had those been the words of the princess, they would have been considered the ramblings of a rejected wife. I could almost hear the antiprincess courtiers dismissing her scornfully.

But now, once again, her words do not appear so hollow. She was so convinced that she would be proved right that she wrote, in the "crash letter,"

Camilla is nothing but a decoy, so we are all being used by one man in every sense of the word.

The *Mail on Sunday* article quoted one royal commentator:

"Charles would not think it odd—to him it would seem natural."

I folded away the newspaper, sat back and looked out across the skies: startling white cloud reflected the sun, making me squint. Somewhere in the heavens the princess could allow herself a wry smile.

I seemed to spend the winter of 2003–4 in the skies and in airport departure lounges, flying back and forth to different continents on promotional work. In every country other than my own, the book has been viewed largely as supportive of the princess, and the warm response of the public—from Australia to Japan, Hungary to Spain—has been overwhelming.

BUT I SHALL NEVER FORGET that last week of October 2003 when the book was launched, and the "crash letter" from the princess had made world headlines. When I returned to Britain from New York, the reception awaiting me was anything but warm and friendly.

The mobile telephone buzzed in the inside breast pocket of my suit, interrupting a news bulletin on the car radio, in which *A Royal Duty* was dominating the headlines, as it was on every television channel and radio station. I was driving through London, being whisked between studios by the publishing team as part of a hectic two-day book-promotion schedule. It was Tuesday, October 28. I reached for my phone. A number I instantly recognized was on the caller display. It was one of the princess's closest female allies, and what she said jolted me out of my absorption in the relentless interviews.

"Paul, the eldest boy would like to meet you," she told me, and my stomach lurched.

Just like the call I had received to set up a meeting with Prince Charles following my arrest in 2001, a code name was used to avoid revealing a senior royal's identity on an insecure phone line. "The eldest boy" referred to, of course, was Prince William.

The woman, who had been contacted by an intermediary St. James's Palace had used before, was sounding me out, she said, to see how I would feel about a possible meeting with Prince William. Nothing had been agreed or arranged, but a meeting could be set up without going through official Palace channels. She went on: "He would want to see you alone. You could use my home—where it will be private—and no one will ever know."

In the Espace people carrier, surrounded by others, all I could do was listen. It was an honest attempt to bring us together, a tentative approach made to broker an understanding of the upset and distress both sides felt for different reasons.

"You have a lot to say and catch up on," said the female friend. She knew because, in many visits to KP, she had witnessed the sort of avuncular relationship I had with the two boys.

She also knew that the prospect of a meeting, after all these years, would make me apprehensive, especially under the circumstances. It should never have been like this, I told her.

"Look, if you want me to be there, I'll be there, or you can be entirely alone. But I think it's something you should consider," said the caller, and left me to think about my next move.

I had to think long and hard about the unofficial approach to meet him. I took advice from people I trust and decided, in a phone call I made that afternoon, to turn down the opportunity. Its unofficial nature unsettled and unnerved me. I was not going to involve myself in a clandestine operation—too much of that had taken place before my trial, and done me no favors. But I remain hopeful that, one day, I will be afforded the chance to meet him and explain my side of the story. And much more that only he and I will ever know.

DOING A PROMOTIONAL tour is like being superglued to a high-speed conveyor belt hurtling along nonstop seven days a week, from 5 A.M. starts for breakfast shows to 10 P.M. finishes for late-night radio. At the end of each day, it dumps you into another strange hotel bed, then whisks you off at another unearthly hour for another day of media déjà vu. From state to state, city to city, studio to studio, bookstore to bookstore, airport to airport, we traveled north, south, east and west, and the experience was exhilarating and exhausting. I don't think we came up for air from October 20 to December 21. But during most of my travels through America, the UK media's focus was on the monarchy and Prince Charles. According to some commentators, both were facing their worst crisis yet. Predictably, I was blamed for precipitating the chain of events that had led to it. The debate surrounded the tape recording that the media had labeled, in the aftermath of my trial, the "rape tape." As I have already stated, this had nothing to do with me. It is not in my possession, and the allegations contained on it revolve around my old friend George Smith. Its potential damage is not within my control, yet I was being blamed for it. The issue led to Prince Charles issuing a statement denying separate allegations about his sexuality because of other claims said to have been made on the same audio recording. Again, it is a matter that does not involve me—but I was blamed for bringing on the crisis—not helped by headlines such as "DOES BURRELL HAVE A DARKER SECRET TO TELL?"

Not unlike certain decisions of the princess, my intentions in writing this book were always going to be misrepresented and misinterpreted by the media. Sometimes, thankfully, the message can retain its true meaning when analyzed by others. Such as Mark Lawson of the *Guardian*, who wrote of this book:

> *Diana always comes out best, followed by her sons and then the Queen, while her mother, brother, Charles and Camilla are intermittent baddies. These would surely have been the priorities observed in any memoir Diana had lived to write.*

But in Buckingham Palace and Clarence House, it is a matter of principle, not content. I later learned that one prim and proper lady-in-waiting ranted her views on the book to anyone who would listen. "It is treachery! Downright treachery! After all his years in service, the man is a disgrace," said this middle-aged veteran of the Royal Household.

I reread the Mark Lawson article for extra reassurance:

> *Burrell has not betrayed the trust of the Boss. Her ghost must be raising a flute of champagne.*

No one needs to be Einstein to grasp that, within the minds of the pedants of the Royal Household, the act of defending the princess, and haunting those palace corridors with ancient home truths, is enough to be viewed as treachery. The fact that I decided to tell the world how wonderful a human being the Queen is did not seem to matter. It is not done to pull back the curtain on the Wizard of Oz. I believe that William and Harry are old enough now to handle the truth, however harsh and however much it may be sourced from the distant days at KP rather than from Highgrove, St. James's Palace and Buckingham Palace. I truly hope that they may yet escape into a quiet corner, free from interference, and read about how wonderful life was with their mother, and how she had to learn by herself to be the magnificent royal and human being she became.

The hard times and rough experiences of the past six years have allowed me to grow a thick skin. I have learned to block out the harsh words and criticisms of those who stand in the spotlight and pour forth to the millions, and take courage from the views of the people who matter: the public and, especially, the fans, in the millions, of Diana, Princess of Wales. I believe that the spirit of the princess is resting easy with the information I have imparted, the secrets I have kept safe and the names and certain circumstances I have never mentioned.

It was William who asked to meet me to "draw a line under the past," and I accepted the invitation in good faith. I also made a promise, which I keep to this day, that nothing will emerge from me about any discussions that take place. It is not a fair conclusion—although it may be a convenient one—to say that just because I have written a book for the sake of banishing certain myths I will divulge the private conversation that he wanted to have with me. I can only hope that William maintains the courage of his convictions, as a future king should.

Quietly and discreetly, though, friends still exist behind the walls of the House of Windsor. At Christmas, I got home from Japan to find an envelope addressed to me in a familiar hand. It was from someone who has always been there for me, as well as a huge inspiration. And the card was signed "With love." The knowledge of such friendship and support remains a source of comfort.

It was also my wish, in setting out to write this book, that an inquest into the princess's death should be held. Within two months of the first edition's publication, which revealed the letter that the Boss had written ten months before her death, Her Majesty's Coroner, Michael Burgess, announced a date. It was opened on January 6, 2004, and a full hearing is expected in 2005. It is a final irony in my story that I have since been notified that the coroner's officers wish to interview me, officers from Scotland Yard's SO6—the same unit who raided my house and sent me to trial, with all the gaping holes that were found in their investigation. No doubt, the unit comprises a different set of officers now. Whether it does or not, though, it will have my full cooperation as an independent witness. Because this due process is ultimately in the interests of the princess.

If the legacy of this book is that its new information provided the final push for the inquest to be held, then I have done my duty.

ABOUT THE AUTHOR

PAUL BURRELL served the Royal Family for twenty-one years after arriving at Buckingham Palace as an eighteen-year-old footman, in 1976. Within a year, he was appointed as the Queen's personal footman, and he spent ten years by Her Majesty's side at all royal residences and on the Royal Yacht *Britannia*. In 1987, he became butler to the Prince and Princess of Wales at their country residence, Highgrove, where he remained until the couple's separation, in 1992, when Diana requested that he move to Kensington Palace to serve as her butler.

Out of all the servants, staff, and protection officers who ever worked for the Princess, Paul was the only one who remained loyally by her side until her death, in 1997. Following that tragedy, he was honored by the Queen with the Royal Victorian Medal in recognition of his loyalty and service to Diana, Princess of Wales. He was also appointed as the fund-raising and events manager of the Diana, Princess of Wales Memorial Fund, spearheading the drive that raised £100 million in her memory.

Paul and his wife, Maria, live in the Cheshire area of England with their two sons, Alexander and Nicholas.